The Pleasures of Children's Literature

Second Edition

Perry Nodelman

The University of Winnipeg

Longman Publishers USA

The Pleasures of Children's Literature, Second Edition

Copyright © 1996, 1992 by Longman Publishers USA.
All rights reserved.
No part of this publication may be reproduced,
stored in a retrieval system, or transmitted
in any form or by any means, electronic, mechanical,
photocopying, recording, or otherwise,
without the prior written permission of the publisher.

Longman, 10 Bank Street, White Plains, N.Y. 10606

Associated companies:
Longman Group Ltd., London
Longman Cheshire Pty., Melbourne
Longman Paul Pty., Auckland
Copp Clark Longman Ltd., Toronto

Associate editor: Travis Lester
Assistant editor: Matt Baker
Production editor: Linda Moser/Professional Book Center
Cover design: Susan J. Moore-Stevenson
Cover illustration: Gwen Connelly
Compositor: Professional Book Center
Text and art credits appear on p. iii

Library of Congress Cataloging-in-Publication Data

Nodelman, Perry.
    The pleasures of children's literature / Perry Nodelman. — 2nd ed.
        p. cm.
    Includes bibliographical references.
    ISBN 0-8013-1576-X
    1. Children's literature—History and criticism.   2. Children—
Books and reading.   I. Title.
PN1009. A1N63   1996
809'.89282—dc20   95-23477
                                                         CIP

5 6 7 8 9 10-MA-999897

COPYRIGHT ACKNOWLEDGMENTS

Contents

v

CHAPTER 7   LITERATURE AND IDEOLOGY   117

PART III   CHILDREN'S LITERATURE AND
THE LITERARY REPERTOIRE   141

CHAPTER 8   CHILDREN'S LITERATURE AS REPERTOIRE   143

Preface

Intended for undergraduate and graduate courses in both departments of Education and English, this book asserts and elaborates on two major convictions I've developed in my two decades as a children's literature scholar. The first is that experiencing and responding to children's literature can be, and ought to be, a deeply *pleasurable* experience, for both adults and children. The second is that much of the pleasure children's literature offers children and adults comes from dialogue—from thinking about it, talking about it, and even arguing about it with others. In expressing these convictions, I describe a range of pleasures literature—and especially children's literature—offers, from the basic joy of immersion in a fictional world through a variety of interpretive strategies and contexts that provide the satisfaction of deeper thought and understanding for readers of all ages.

And that does mean readers of *all* ages. I'm convinced that children, even very young ones, can and should learn to share the interpretive strategies and contexts that allow adult readers to make more sense of their encounters with literature and take greater pleasure from them. Throughout the book, therefore, I encourage adult readers to find ways of sharing their own strategies for reading and thinking about literature with children.

In order to stimulate thoughtful dialogue, I've concentrated throughout the book on describing key issues, many of them contentious, relating both to children's literature itself and to the larger subject of adult interactions with children's reading. For example:

- Why do we or should we read literature? Why should children?
- How should we read it? How should children?
- What part does literature play, or can it play, in our understanding of ourselves and of our world?

- How much can or should children understand about themselves and their world?
- To what extent can literary theory, cognitive theory, and pedagogical theory help us to make sense of these matters?
- Who does and should select books for children? What books should they select, and why?
- How do toys, TV, and movies affect the ways in which children experience and understand literature?
- What special part might picture books, fairy tales, and poems play in the imaginative and intellectual life of children?

In considering these questions and many others, I make use of a spectrum of contemporary research and theory in a variety of relevant fields. For instance, I look at picture books in the context of theories of art and perception, at fairy tales in the context of folklore scholarship, and at TV and movies in the context of media theory. And I explore children's response in the context of current research in cognitive development and pedagogy. I've tried to describe these difficult ideas in straightforward terms that make them available to nonexperts.

In terms of ideas about literature itself, I've made use of and offered introductory descriptions to a range of current theoretical approaches, including semiotics, psychoanalytical analysis, and feminist and gender theory. But the central stance and main focus of the book represents a blend of two key theoretical approaches: reader-response theory as developed by Louise Rosenblatt and Wolfgang Iser, and the variety of approaches to ideological concerns currently gathered by scholars under the name *cultural studies*. Throughout the book, I take a *constructivist* approach: what Arthur N. Applebee identifies as "a view of knowledge as an active construction built up by the individual acting within a social context that shapes and constrains that knowledge, but that does not determine it in an absolute sense" (3). In the spirit of this comment, I consider both the individuality of response and the variety of constraints upon it. I explore ways in which not only literary texts, but also TV programs and toys, express societal values and work to encourage children's unconscious agreement with those values. Awareness of these matters should allow both adults and children more freedom of choice in determining who and what they are.

METHODOLOGY

In *Pleasures,* I advocate the positive value of thoughtful responses to literature and, indeed, to all other aspects of existence, not only by children but also by students in children's literature courses. The book has a number of features designed to encourage such responses from students and other readers:

- The book begins with a discussion of and invitation to dialogue with literature and with other people's ideas about it.

- In order to encourage interaction with the information and opinions I myself present, I've tried not to hide my own personality under a mask of false objectivity or to present my opinions as if they were facts.

- I focus throughout on asking hard questions rather than on providing easy answers. Readers must think their way towards their own answers.

- To encourage thoughtfulness, there are brief sections called *Explorations* interspersed throughout the text. These are invitations to think further about the implications of the opinions I describe or express, accompanied by specific strategies for doing so.

- To encourage readers to develop their own standards, I offer no specific recommendations of particular children's books, and the many texts I discuss represent a wide spectrum of children's literature. They are by and about people of a variety of racial and cultural groups, and include everything from word books for babies to complex novels for young adults, from classics to popular series books. While the focus is twentieth-century children's literature written in English, there are references to books written across the decades of the twentieth century, and to a few written in earlier times. This wide selection of texts underscores my conviction that children are capable of enjoying diversity and deserve access to it—in spite of or even because much of it has so little to do with their own immediate experience.

In these ways and others, *Pleasures* advocates the belief that a true sense of one's own being and a true tolerance for diversity can develop only through experiencing and being thoughtful about other ways of being and doing. It suggests ways of fostering that experience and developing that thoughtfulness in young readers. And it invites its own readers to become engaged, annoyed, delighted, infuriated—and involved enough to become thoughtful about their own reading and their own opinions.

New to This Edition

In this second edition, *Pleasures* has been reorganized to suit teachers' and students' needs better.

- Part I now offers a more complete introduction to basic techniques for reading and thinking about children's literature. In response to many requests, it now includes, as chapter 3, the discussion of teaching children literary skills and strategies that used to be the last chapter of the book. This chapter makes the point that all the ideas and practices described throughout the rest of the book can and should be shared with children. Its new position will help it to persuade readers, as they make their way through the rest of the book, to think not only about their own opinions and responses to the matters discussed, but also, about how to share knowledge of these matters with children.

- Also in response to requests, Part I now includes, in chapter 4, my description of strategies for reading and making sense of texts. Being equipped with knowledge of these strategies early on will help students make better sense of the children's literature they will be asked to read as a course progresses.

- Part II, substantially revised and expanded, now includes three chapters that outline some basic principles of ideological analysis and describe the effect of current cultural assumptions and practices on children and their reading. Chapter 5 provides an amplified discussion of censorship, and practical suggestions for dealing with it, and also, a new look at economic and cultural forces that influence publishing for children and the availability of books. Chapter 6 includes a revised section on nonfiction. Chapter 7 offers an expanded discussion of methods of "reading against a text"—exploring how literature expresses cultural or ideological assumptions that authors may not have intended to express or even been aware of including. This chapter also includes extensive new sections on multicultural texts and on the construction of subjectivity. With this more cohesive presentation of central concerns, Part II now clarifies the basic stance of the book as a whole.

In addition to this augmented discussion of issues relating to cultural concerns, *Pleasures* has been substantially expanded in a number of other areas, in order to represent the main trends in current discussions of children's literature better.

- Chapter 1 now makes a more specific statement about the theoretical stance the book takes, and offers readers guidelines for understanding current issues in literary study at all levels from elementary school through university. In order to stimulate a questioning attitude in readers, chapter 1 also now describes a change in focus in literary study in the last few decades from certainties to questions.

- To encourage dialogue, the book now features a greater diversity of opinions. A number of readers of the first edition shared their comments and disagreements, and some of these are included as new *Explorations*.

- The discussion on interpretive strategies in chapter 4 includes a new discussion of *concretization* to help readers describe their reading experiences.

- Chapter 8, on the characteristics of children's literature as a genre, has been expanded and reorganized, so that its structure now mirrors the discussion of reading strategies in chapter 4. Questions relating to fiction have been absorbed into the discussion of the characteristics of children's literature as a genre.

- Chapter 9, on children's literature in the context of literary theory, now includes fuller explanations of unfamiliar terms and concepts.

- A new appendix provides students with a guide to finding further discussion of children's literature in books and journals.
- A new glossary offers readers easy access to definitions of the terms from literary theory, cognitive psychology, psychoanalysis, and other disciplines.
- A new instructor's manual contains commentaries by a number of instructors who have used *Pleasures* in children's literature courses in universities across North America, including myself. These pieces describe our experiences with the book, comment on the dialogue we and our students have with it, and offer suggestions for classroom activities and strategies. The manual also includes a revised and updated version of the bibliographic guide to specific resources that appeared as the final chapter of the first edition of the text.

These changes and additions have been designed to make *Pleasures* better fulfill its main goal: to offer students in children's literature courses an understandable and up-to-date introduction to a number of key issues regarding literature and children's response to it, in the belief that thinking about these issues can be the basis of a rich and stimulating dialogue both with literature and with other readers of all ages.

I invite all readers of this book, instructors, students and others, to enter into the dialogue. If you have comments about the book or suggestions for improvements to it, please tell me about them. You can reach me by mail at:

Department of English
University of Winnipeg
Winnipeg MB R3B 2E9
Canada

or by E-mail at:

nodelman@io.UWinnipeg.ca

or by fax at:

(204) 453-5930

ACKNOWLEDGMENTS

This book would never have existed if my friend Jill P. May, who teaches in the Faculty of Education at Purdue University, hadn't got the idea for it in the first place. As a librarian with a strong interest in literature, Jill was conscious of the many different fields of academic study that investigate children and their literature, and the surprising lack of communication among them. Cognitive, developmental, and perceptual psychologists, sociologists, folklorists, library and media specialists, reading specialists and other educational theorists, historians of childhood and family life, specialists in literature and literary theory and in art and art theory: all were arriving at intriguingly useful conclusions. But more often than not they seemed to be paying little attention to each other's work. Jill saw a strong need for an introduction to children's literature that would make use of recent research in as many of these different disciplines as possible, in order to place children's literature in the context of children's literary education.

Jill used her considerable energy and enthusiasm to persuade me to collaborate with her on this project, in the flattering belief that our shared interest in children's literature and our different backgrounds—hers in library science and education, mine in literary studies—would make us the perfect team to produce the book she imagined. Together, she and I decided what the book should contain and mapped out a plan of how it would be presented, and together we set out on the intimidating task of trying to learn as much as two nonspecialists could about a variety of abstruse disciplines relating to the study of childhood.

If the book you have in your hands lacks the sort of balance Jill envisioned, it's only partially because of the inevitable limitations of our nonspecialist grasp of these many different disciplines. It's mainly because unavoidable scheduling conflicts prevented Jill from carrying on with her part in the project. While she and I continued to discuss the book extensively, and while she read the manuscript of the first edition in various stages and provided me with valuable comments on it, I finally ended up doing all the writing myself. I have also produced all of this second edition, although not without many more extensive conversations about it with Jill. The good intentions, then, are all Jill's; I take all the blame for the flaws in my execution of them.

Many people who offered constructive advice about the first edition have done so once more: my friend and partner in fiction Carol Matas; my University of Winnipeg colleagues Mavis Reimer, Kay Unruh-Desroches, and Neil Besner; and of course, my long-suffering wife Billie and my three children, Josh, Asa, and Alice Nodelman. I've received additional advice for this edition from Debra Schnitzer, University of Winnipeg; Michael Cadden, Illinois State University; Ray Jones, University of Alberta; Lois Kuznets, San Diego State University; Bev Clark, Wheaton College; Cornelia Hoogland, University of Western Ontario; Daphne Kutzer, SUNY Plattsburgh; Linnea Hendrickson, University of New Mexico; Alice Naylor, Appalachian State; Darwin Henderson, Purdue; Eliza Dresang, University of Wisconsin–Madison; Richard Flynn, Georgia State; Frieda Bostian, Virginia Tech; Nancy Huse, Augustana College; Caroline Hunt, College of Charleston; and Tim Wolf, Middle Tennessee State University. Susan Gannon of Pace University, Caroline Hunt of the College of Charleston, and Mary Rubio of the University of Guelph were overwhelmingly generous in providing me with ideas about articles and books to read. I also learned much of value from detailed comments and critiques offered by Mary Rubio's students at Guelph, Tim Wolf's students at Middle Tennessee, Alice Naylor's students at Appalachian State, and my own students at the University of Winnipeg. Patty Hawkins, my secretary at the University of Winnipeg, was her usual efficient and unflappable self.

I would also like to acknowledge the following reviewers:

Doris Dale, Southern Illinois University
Delores P. Dickerson, Howard University
Peter J. Fisher, National-Louis University
Richard Flynn, Georgia Southern University
Susan Gannon, Pace University
Darwin Henderson, Purdue University
Daniel Hade, Pennsylvania State University
Caroline C. Hunt, College of Charleston
Alleen Pace Nilsen, Arizona State University
Barbara F. Rahal, Edinboro University of Pennsylvania
Lucy Rollin, Clemson University
Merritt W. Stark, Henderson State University
Donna R. White, Clemson University
Rosemary Winkeljohann, Millersville University of Pennsylvania
Virginia L. Wolf, University of Wisconsin–Stout
Terrell A. Young, Washington State University

The first edition owed much to those who helped to produce it at Longman: the editor Ray O'Connell; the production editor, Kathryn Dix; and the copyeditor, Susan Joseph. For this second edition I owe thanks to Laura McKenna, the editor, for her faith in the project; to Travis Lester, for her support and advice; and to the production editor, Linda Moser; and the copyeditor, Jennifer Ballentine.

WORK CITED

Applebee, Arthur N. "The Background for Reform." *Literature Instruction: A Focus on Student Response*. Ed. Judith A. Langer. Urbana: NCTE, 1992. 1–18.

part I

Thinking About Children and Literature

The *Pleasures of Children's Literature* is about children's literature: all the many kinds of poems and stories adults produce for audiences younger than themselves, from board books for babies through picture books for toddlers and novels for adolescents. This book has two main purposes. The first is to provide adults like you with contexts and strategies of comprehension that can help you understand and, above all, enjoy reading literary texts written for children. The second is to suggest that children too can be taught—and would benefit from learning—these same contexts and strategies.

The contexts and strategies I refer to are ways of responding to and thinking about literature based in both literary and educational theory. While these practices are used in increasing numbers of literature classes at all levels from elementary school to university, they are somewhat controversial. Not only are they different from the strategies used to teach literature until fairly recently, but they are often exactly opposite to the traditional methods and assumptions about literature with which some people still feel more comfortable. For that reason, this book begins with a discussion of these methods and the implications of choosing whether or not to use them.

Since I do choose to use them myself, my most basic assumption is that you read children's stories and poems differently from the way I might, or from the way a young child might. We all read the same texts in different ways—partly because of our differing tastes and interests, partly because each of us has responded to our different experiences of life and literature by developing different *expectations* and *strategies* for determining meaning. A major focus of this book is the exploration of some specific expectations and strategies that can influence our response to children's literature.

1

Such expectations and strategies influence our reading not only of literature but also of textbooks like this one. You're likely to approach this book differently from the way somebody with different expectations of textbooks would. Unfortunately, not all the expectations we bring to our reading are equally productive. For instance, people who read expecting to be bored are more likely to be bored than those who anticipate pleasure. In my own experience as a reader, I've found that my expectations hampered my response on two occasions in particular. When I was a student reading textbooks like this one, I sometimes found myself wanting to disagree with the conclusions the authors reached. But expectations based on previous classroom experiences convinced me that I had to pretend to accept these opinions in order to get through the course. Later, as a literary specialist in another field, I was assigned to teach a children's literature course, and I suddenly found myself trying to read and make some sense, as an adult, of books that were intended for children. I believed I should be thinking about how a child might read them, and I couldn't imagine how.

I know that many other readers share the assumptions that caused me these problems. The chapters in this introductory section explore the implications of these assumptions and recommend some reading strategies I believe to be particularly useful—first for getting the most from this book and second for reading texts of children's literature.

chapter 1

How to Read This Book

STUDYING LITERATURE: SOME BASIC ASSUMPTIONS

When I was a university student some years ago, my English professors shared a set of assumptions they believed so firmly that they simply took them for granted. The same assumptions were taken for granted by most people who taught literature, even by most people who read it. As a student, I was also expected to take them for granted. I did, for the most part. Because I wanted to be part of the community that knew what to think and to say about literature, I happily accepted these universal assumptions as unquestioned truth or else just ignored any questions I had about them. I continued to do so through the graduate studies that prepared me to become a teacher of literature myself, and even through my beginning years as a professor.

But as the years went by, the world of literary studies outside my classroom began to change. People began to question all those old certainties, and I realized I couldn't take them for granted any longer. I had to consider the questions people were asking about them, and I had to acknowledge that they were good questions.

Very good questions: My asking them, and the kinds of answers that I and many other people interested in literature have been considering in the last few decades, are behind much of what I say and do in this book. In order to make sense of what I say, then, you might find it useful to know something about the old certainties that I and most other literary scholars used to take for granted, and the questions that we came to ask about them. Here's a brief list:

Old Certainties	*New Questions*
It's possible to tell the difference between good literary texts and bad ones. They are inherently and permanently good or bad.	If good texts are so different from bad ones, why do so many people, including literary experts, disagree about these matters? Might value be at least partially in the mind of the reader?
The good literary texts are worth studying. The bad ones are not.	If value is so disputable, how can we know *which* texts to study?
The good literary texts are good, and therefore worth studying, for two main reasons: They are wise, and they are beautiful.	Who decides what is wise, what beautiful? Why should we trust their judgment? Might they have some vested interest in identifying certain ideas as wise, or a certain kind of beauty as desirable?
The bad literary texts are bad because they are neither wise nor beautiful.	For that matter, what's wrong with studying something you *don't* find beautiful? Maybe we could learn more about beauty and wisdom by studying their supposed absence.
Since good works of literature are beautiful, studying them makes students conscious of beauty—develops an aesthetic sensibility and an appreciation for finer things that makes them better people.	But does reading literature automatically make us appreciate finer things? And if some students don't learn this appreciation, does that mean they are basically inadequate or lesser human beings? Could this be a form of snobbery, imposing one's own taste on others?
Since the good literary texts are wise, studying them also has the purpose of introducing students to great ideas: ways of thinking about people and the world that we all ought to know and to share.	Is literature only important for its ideas and its aesthetic values? What about the simple fun of reading a good story or laughing at something funny? Must reading always be such a high-minded pursuit?
Discussion of literature in classrooms and elsewhere should focus on the great ideas and the great beauty.	Can we not discuss what gives us immediate pleasure? Why not?
The great ideas that we find in good literature are universally true, for all people in all times and places. To know them is to share a wisdom common to all educated and enlightened human beings.	Is it possible that the vast diversity of human cultures could actually share a uniform wisdom? Do time and place have no serious effect on what people believe about themselves?

Old Certainties	*New Questions*
Because they are universally true, the ideas found in good literature are above and beyond the prejudices of individuals or people of different cultures, races, or sexes. They transcend politics of all sorts.	Is it possible that a literary text could transcend the conscious and unconscious assumptions and intentions of its author? Or for authors to transcend the assumptions of their place and time? If we look for them, might not we find in literary texts the prejudices of writers about people they perceive as being different from themselves? Might not the good books be viewed as propaganda for those with the power to declare them good and important?
The ideas of good literature are fixed—comprehensible in the same way to everyone who learns how to read them properly.	If the ideas in literature are so fixed and so shareable, why do people, even educated ones, have such different interpretations of and responses to texts?
A main purpose of studying literature is to learn how to read and understand it properly—the way in which all other educated people read and understand it.	Doesn't the idea of a "correct" interpretation ignore differences in individual response and understanding? *Should* we ignore the differences? Is there no way we can take them into account?
A second main purpose of studying literature is to learn how to appreciate what is truly and inherently beautiful, and likewise to see the deficiencies of bad literature and art—to develop an educated sensibility.	Does this actually happen? *Do* all educated people share the same taste? If they could, would that be good? Doesn't such conformity limit the potential for individual freedom and the richness of diversity?

Asking all these questions was a painful process for me, to begin with, and a humbling one; but it was also liberating—and eventually, I discovered, great fun, a pleasure in itself. While certainty is comfortable, it can also be oppressive and limiting. The more we know for sure, the less we have to think about. Since I like to think, particularly about literature, I was delighted to have the freedom to do so.

I continue to be delighted that I haven't had to give up that freedom. The old certainties haven't been replaced by new ones. The new methods that have replaced them, in my own classrooms and in those of many other literature professors and elementary and high school teachers around the world—and also, in this book—actively resist closing off thought. The focus is on questions, rather than on answers. The only thing the new methods take for granted as unquestionable is the conviction that *nothing* is unquestionable. All the questions we can ask about literature in general or about specific texts have a variety of possible answers, and while individuals will be satisfied with some of those answers, no one answer is

likely to be universally true or universally acceptable to everyone. Studying literature is a matter of having questions and asking them, of exploring the implications
of many different answers as we try to arrive at the answers that will satisfy us individually. It is also a matter of being open to the possible value of the answers that
satisfy others, both for what those answers mean to the others and for their potential to enrich our own thought.

   If you're not familiar with this sort of approach to literature, you may well find
it surprising, even distressing—as I did when I first started to ask questions. I know
that having to learn new ways of thinking is as challenging and often as painful as
it is liberating. But I can promise that it *is* liberating—and that coming to think in
the ways I encourage here has the potential to provide you with a deeply satisfying
understanding of the literature you read and your response to it, and an equally satisfying pleasure in both. So if anything in this book represents new ways of thinking for you, I encourage you to persevere past the fear and the discomfort, and into
the liberating pleasure of new understanding.

OPINION AND DIALOGUE

In this book, I raise a lot of questions; and while I often say what my own current
answers to them are, you may find that you don't like my answers and don't want
to share them. In fact, I would be surprised if you didn't disagree with at least some
of what I say: As individuals with different tastes and different ways of making
sense of things, readers inevitably disagree, not just about what we read, but often
about the significance of literary experiences in general. As I hope to show
throughout this book, that disagreement accounts for much of the pleasure our
conversations about literature offer us.

   If you do find yourself not wanting to accept any of my ideas, I encourage you
to acknowledge your resistance. Try to be conscious of the ways in which what I
say doesn't explain your own response or match your own views—the ways in
which my opinions *don't* persuade you.

   But, you might say to me, you're an expert, aren't you? I wouldn't be wasting
my time reading this book if it weren't written by someone who knew something
worth knowing about the subject. So aren't your expert opinions more likely to be
right than mine are? Wouldn't I be smart just to accept what you say and forget my
own less-expert responses and opinions?

   I'm happy to admit that I *am* something of an expert. I've spent many years
reading and learning about children's literature and developing the ideas I express
in this book. I may well know more about this subject than you do. I hope, if I
have any right to have written this book and you have a good reason for reading it,
that I at least have different thoughts about it than you do at this point. But I don't
think that means you should accept my answers as the only possible right ways of
reading and thinking about children's literature.

   For one thing, I'm not the expert I'd like to be. I know there's a huge amount
about children's literature and children's reading that I don't yet know—and will

never know completely, because there are new children's books and new ideas about literature all the time. I'm always finding out new things that force me to change my old opinions, and I expect to keep on doing so. What I say here may well turn out to be wrong, next week or next year, despite my claims to expertise.

For another thing, the mere fact that my opinions *are* those of an expert could make them suspicious. My ways of thinking and reading could be meaningless and inappropriate for someone with less expertise; I may take way too much for granted. Or my ideas may not work for you simply because they don't accurately account for your different experience.

For yet another thing, even if my opinions are based on some knowledge of the subject, they're still just my opinions; I suspect my adoption of them depends as much on the uniqueness of my character as it does on my knowledge of children's literature. Even if you shared my expertise, the uniqueness of your character might lead you to quite different conclusions.

In any case, I believe you'll get more of lasting value from this book if you acknowledge your disagreements with me rather than try to ignore them. For that reason, I've made a point of expressing my opinions strongly—strongly enough to make it glaringly obvious that, despite my knowledge of children's literature, they *are* my own personal opinions. I hope you'll respond by saying something like, "Hey, wait a minute, that's just *his* opinion, based on *his* responses, emerging from *his* character. I'm not sure I can go along with it."

This doesn't mean that you should simply dismiss my opinions altogether and just go on thinking what you've always thought. While it's true and democratic that everyone is entitled to his or her opinions, that doesn't mean that any of us are ever free from our obligation to consider the opinions of others. Not examining what other people think—especially when it differs from or directly contradicts our own ideas—represents a refusal to engage with them or to take them seriously at all. It does nothing but isolate us from each other. True respect for the opinions of others, I believe, demands that we acknowledge our disagreements with each other and explore their implications.

I hope, then, that as you read this book you'll try not just to acknowledge disagreement but also to figure out *why* you might not accept something I say: why it might or might not actually be true, how it connects with your own responses to literature and with knowledge and beliefs you already have, and what it might suggest about your future reading or your dealings with children. Reading in this way will protect you from being manipulated into accepting (or pretending to accept) ideas you don't really go along with. And that will have the wonderful advantage of making you conscious of what you yourself already know.

In other words, this book offers just one part of a conversation. I invite you to enter into a *dialogue* with it and provide the other part yourself. If you do, the task of fitting the information and the opinions in this book into your existing context of knowledge and values will inevitably change your understanding both of my ideas and of your own. What you learn from my opinions will have at least some effect on your thinking, and you're bound to adapt and change my ideas in the process of coming to terms with them. What should emerge from this process is not your agreement with me but, instead, your own thoughtful opinions about children's literature, opinions that I hope will be as strongly felt as my own and as significant for you as mine are for me.

Something About the Author

Before you can commit yourself to a dialogue, you have to know something about the person you're talking with—at least enough to make you comfortable about sharing your ideas. Furthermore, the more you know about someone else, the more you can understand about how that person's ideas and opinions emerged from and were influenced by family background and previous experiences. Understanding that should help you both to grasp the opinions better and to determine which of them you do or don't agree with, and why. In order to make the best sense of this book for yourself, then, you should know something about me—at least something about those aspects of my history that have affected my opinions.

I was born in 1942, in Toronto, Ontario, Canada. My parents were Jewish. I am male. I believe that these three facts alone account for much of what I've ended up saying in this book.

My birth date five decades ago and my being male mean that I spent the first few decades of my life happily and quite unconsciously sharing the assumptions of most of the people around me: that males were the superior gender, born to run things, while women were meant to stay home, vacuum, and agree with the men in their lives about everything. My unquestioned acceptance of these supposed truths as a child and teenager made me as assured about my right to express my opinions and get my way as most males always have been. The fact that my mother worshipped the ground I walked on didn't help to disabuse me of this view.

On the other hand, I wasn't very good at being male, as the conventions of that day understood males were supposed to be. I was always small for my age, skinny, and nearsighted; and my lack of physical coordination was about as absolute as you can get and still manage to stand upright. As a child, I hated sports and other "guy-type" things, and this made me something of an outsider.

So did being Jewish. My father was just about the only Jew in Canada who decided to stay in the army after World War II ended, so I spent my childhood living on a military base where we were the only Jewish family. Even so, my parents didn't practice Judaism, or speak Yiddish, or maintain many other ties with Jewishness. I grew up feeling as much of an outsider with the few other Jews I met as I did with the non-Jews I spent most of my time with.

I suspect that all of this being outside of things prepared me to be as likely to identify with and adopt unpopular or unusual outsiders' positions as I am aggressive in the expression of them. You should realize that many of the ideas I advocate here are not the most popular ones; but of course I'm cocky enough to believe that they're the *right* ones.

As a short, uncoordinated child, the only thing I was really good at was school. And I always loved to read a good story. So as I grew up, I kept on being a student for as long as it was possible, and what I studied was the reading of stories. I ended up with a Ph.D. from Yale University as a specialist in Victorian literature.

Meanwhile, though, the world was changing around me. A lot of people with far more convincing reasons than I had for thinking of themselves as outsiders—African Americans, Native Americans, gay men and women, women in general—were beginning to stand up for their rights. For all my male cockiness, I was still enough of an outsider to find it easy to sympathize with their situation, and to agree with their complaints about the arrogant assumptions of white men of European background like me. In other words, I had my consciousness raised. I found it a humbling and exhilarating experience. I hope the opinions I express in this book represent both the humility and the exhilaration of that experience

As I suggested at the beginning of this chapter, those new ways of thinking that transformed my views of people also had a profound effect on my profession—the study and teaching of literature. I had to reinvent myself as a scholar and a teacher. As I said before, I'm glad I did; I hope this book expresses the pleasure that comes from thinking new thoughts.

One of my reinventions of myself was a change of professional focus to children's literature; I've been reading and thinking about children's books as an adult for about two decades now. In the past few years, I've even begun to write children's literature; my first novel, a children's fantasy called *The Same Place but Different,* has been published, and so has my second, a young adult fantasy written in collaboration with my friend Carol Matas called *Of Two Minds.* Others are on the way. I hope all this means that you can trust the breadth of my knowledge of children's literature, even if you don't share the conclusions I've reached on the basis of it.

During the same two decades, meanwhile, my own three children were born and have gone through their childhoods. I read to them from their early infancy on, and then I talked to them about what they read on their own. That certainly doesn't make me an expert on childhood reading in general; in fact, I suspect that the main thing I learned from the fascinating eccentricities of my own children was how uniquely individual are the characters, and consequently, the reading experiences of all children. That conviction is behind much of what I say in this book.

As I've written this section, I've come to a much deeper sense of how the opinions I express throughout the book have been produced by the circumstances of my life. I realize that those circumstances have influenced even my most basic assumptions about what my subject consists of.

For instance, I often claim to be discussing children's literature in general. But as an English-speaking person living in the twentieth century, I've focused almost exclusively on children's books written in English in this century—not so much as a deliberate choice but simply because those happen to be the children's books I know. I have a pretty firm suspicion that my claims about the general characteristics of children's literature would be easily challenged by books written in other languages or in earlier times.

Furthermore, and despite my best efforts to represent a wide spectrum of different voices in the children's books I discuss, I find myself unconsciously drawn to discuss books written by middle-class, white people like me for middle-class, white children like my own; and I tend to read other sorts of books as variations from what I assume to be typical. Nor am I alone in doing this, I realize. As I think about what I've read about children's literature, and about the conferences on it I've attended, I have to conclude that most people who claim to be experts, at least most middle-class, white people, act just as I do and focus their attention on books by and about mainstream, middle-class children.

But I still have to conclude that do so is only logical. Most children's literature is still about such children, despite the emphasis publishers and educators have placed upon multicultural texts in recent years. If I attempted to offer absolutely equal representation to minority voices, my discussion would itself be unrepresentative of what children's literature as a whole is actually like.

It's humbling but helpful for me to realize these things, both about myself and about my subject. I have a clearer sense now of what the subject actually is and of what the limitations of my conclusions are. I urge you to remember those limitations. And as you work your way through the rest of this book, you might find it similarly helpful to do the same kind of thinking about yourself. Examining how your own opinions and your responses to mine relate to your background and history ought to help you to enter into a richer and more productive dialogue.

THINKING ABOUT WHAT YOU READ

To help you to enter into a dialogue with my ideas and opinions, I've included short sections called *Explorations* throughout the book. They look like this:

EXPLORATION: Open this book at any page and begin reading. Read until you come to an idea that strikes you as being strange. Consider why it seems so, and what in your own experience of life or literature might cause you to accept or reject the idea.

Like this one, all the explorations relate to the sections of the book that immediately precede or follow them. They contain questions for you to explore, ideas to think about that will allow you to engage more actively with what follows, or suggestions of issues to think about that emerge from the passage immediately preceding them. You don't have to do any or all of the *Explorations:* I've tried to write the book so that it's possible simply to skip them. But if you do decide to do what the *Explorations* suggest, remember that they're meant to help you think actively about the issues and ideas that the book is investigating *as* you are reading. While there's no harm in reading a chapter first and then coming back to the *Explorations* it contains, it will probably be more helpful for you to do what they suggest as you read.

I realize that some of the *Explorations* may sound like the questions that appeared in the literature textbooks in use when I was a child: "Do you think Dick is doing the right thing? Why not?" In other words, they may seem to imply that you should reach very specific conclusions about the questions they raise: the conclusions that I myself reach and tell you about. I've tried not to make them sound that way; if you think that I've not always succeeded, I urge you to defy me.

In addition to the explorations printed throughout the book, there's another—invisible—one that you might imagine appearing at the end of almost every sentence:

EXPLORATION: Is that true? Am I willing to accept it? Why or why not?

Reading the book with these questions always in mind should help make it a stimulating and productive experience.

EXPLORATION: Some of my students at the University of Winnipeg pointed out a contradiction in the section above. In it, I'm using my authority as an expert author to encourage you not to respect my authority, but to think for yourself. So if you do think for yourself, you're just agreeing to do what I asked—bowing to the will of the expert. This interests me mainly because it suggests the paradoxical position teachers often put students in, and adults in general often put children in; we invite them to enter into a dialogue with us as equals, but we retain unequal authority as the makers of rules and evaluators of performance. Consider the implications of this paradox in terms of your own interactions with this book, with your instructor, and with children.

WRITING ABOUT WHAT YOU READ

While you can simply do the thinking the explorations recommend, you may find it useful to write down what you think. In *Writing to Learn,* William Zinsser says, "Writing organizes and clarifies our thoughts. Writing is how we think our way into a subject and make it our own. Writing enables us to find out what we know—and what we don't know—about whatever we're trying to learn" (16). As we write, gaps and illogicalities in our thinking become apparent to us, and then we can think about ways of filling the gaps and clarifying the logic. You'll know you've done a useful piece of exploratory writing if you feel you know more about the subject or your thoughts about it when you finish than you did when you started writing.

Writing down your ideas—not just your responses to explorations but any thoughts that strike you as you read—has another benefit. It will provide you with a record that will help you develop insights into your patterns of reading and thinking. If you write down what you think as you think it, you'll be able to come back to it later, perhaps after reading further, and reconsider your ideas in the light of newer ones. You can explore the implications of any change, or absence of change, in your thinking. And if you're using this book in a course in which your instructor requires you to write essays, the job will be made easier by the fact that you've already written so much about the issues.

The writing you do in response to the explorations or to other aspects of the book should be different from the writing you might submit as a finished essay. Essays represent the best way of presenting ideas you've already thought your way through and understand; the writing in them should be clear, correct, and controlled—organized to guide a reader through the ideas you want to present. But when you start to write an exploration, you don't yet know what your conclusions will be. You're writing your way toward a conclusion, not trying to find the best way to describe a conclusion you already have. In other words, your job in the explorations is to describe the *process* of your thinking, not the product of finished thought.

Because we think best in our own individual ways, there's no ideal pattern or procedure for exploration. It might, however, be useful to start by establishing what you want to try to learn more about, why you want to think about that, and what method or procedure or tactic you've chosen to explore it. Then, at the end, you might try to sum up what you have or haven't learned, whether or not you think it's valuable, and why. In other words, an exploration is a sort of thought experiment and might well follow the usual plan for scientific experimentation:

- Problem (and why you think it problematic)
- Hypothesis (what you think the solution or "answer" might be)
- Method (how you plan to go about discovering or proving the solution)
- Conducting the experiment and describing what happens as you conduct it
- Conclusion in relation to the original problem and hypothesis

However you proceed, what matters most is that you get your ideas down in as much detail as you can, before you forget what they are, and that you follow them wherever they take you. Don't be too concerned about contradicting yourself or about following a potentially useful thread of ideas that takes you away from where you started. Don't worry about spelling or grammar or whether your writing is neat or your typing accurate. In order to make your explorations as useful as possible, try to describe your responses as completely as you can—not just general summaries, but detailed descriptions of what you thought in the order in which you thought it. Remember that your purpose here is *to know more when you've finished writing than you did when you began.*

As you write, you might ask yourself questions about what you've written so far:

- What do I mean by that?
- Can I explain it more clearly, or in more detail?
- Why did I say it? Why does it seem important to me? Does it reveal something about my own assumptions about literature or my strategies for making sense of it?

- Why do I think it's true? What evidence do I have to support it? Can I test it out by a deeper consideration of or more detailed look at the text I'm discussing?
- What are its implications, either for the topic or for my own reading strategies?

Think about these questions, and write your answers to them—and then ask the same questions again about the answers you've given.

If you follow this process, you may find yourself concluding with questions rather than answers: You may at this point have no definite answers for the questions you've asked yourself. If that happens, avoid pretending that you do have an answer, and leaving out information you know or ideas you have that seem to contradict a point you are trying to make. Record everything, so you can think further about it later on. In the long run, the best thing to do about not having reached a conclusion is to not be too concerned about it. There really aren't *any* definitive answers to questions about literature, only the answers we can reach based on our experience so far. Whether exploration or essay, a piece of writing that acknowledges contradictory possibilities and ends unresolved is more honest and more intellectually stimulating than one that deliberately distorts and leaves things out to arrive at a specific resolution.

Many of the explorations in this book can be done by children as well as by adults. As I suggest throughout and assert in some detail in chapter 3, I firmly believe that everything in this book can be communicated to children, and that having strategies for understanding children's literature can only deepen children's pleasure in it. As you read the book, then, I urge you to consider ways you might make use of its contents to enrich the literary experience of children.

EXPLORATION: After reading this chapter in the first edition of *Pleasures*, Dieter Neumann, a student in one of Mary Rubio's children's literature classes at the University of Guelph, wrote:

> Nodelman is possessed of a profound optimism. He seems to genuinely believe that if all points of view are given informed consideration, then fairness, goodness, and justice will prevail at the end of the day. I do not share that optimism. We live in what is at once the best-informed and most brutal epoch in history. The naive sense of hopefulness that may still be a legitimate part of middle-class society is not relevant today to many sectors of society. This is a reality that the middle-class teacher will encounter soon enough. . . . Nodelman has gone to some lengths to make the reader aware that there are usually conflicting opinions about any statement of "fact." The problem with this approach is that any reader can bring their preconceptions to the book, read through it, and walk away quite comfortable in the knowledge that his

or her opinions are just as valid as anyone else's. What my generation
needs desperately is a jarring wake-up call, and unfortunately that isn't
provided by being "well-balanced."

That's a possibility well worth considering.

WORKS CITED

Matas, Carol, and Perry Nodelman. *Of Two Minds*. Winnipeg: Blizzard, 1994, and New York: Simon & Schuster, forthcoming, 1995.

Nodelman, Perry. *The Same Place but Different*. Toronto: Groundwood, 1993, and New York: Simon & Schuster, 1995.

Zinsser, William. *Writing to Learn*. New York: Perennial Library-Harper & Row, 1989.

chapter 2

How to Read Children's Literature

SEEING BEYOND AN ADULT PERSPECTIVE

Before you can understand children's literature, you have to read some. That's not necessarily as easy as it seems.

Whether baby books or young adult novels, what all the different kinds of texts described as children's literature have in common is the gulf between their writers and their intended readers: They are written by adults for people younger than themselves. Indeed, something called "children's literature" exists only because people are convinced that children are different from adults—different enough to need their own special texts. Knowing that these texts are intended for people assumed to be unlike ourselves makes it difficult for us to respond to them. How can we develop the most useful understanding of them, in order to make judgments about them that will best serve children?

I'm going to try to answer that question by describing an experience I once had as a teacher. I asked a group of adults beginning to study children's literature to consider whether or not they'd share a certain poem with children. The poem was Edward Lear's "The Owl and the Pussy-cat":

> The Owl and the Pussy-cat went to sea
> In a beautiful pea-green boat,
> They took some honey, and plenty of money
> Wrapped up in a five-pound note.
> The Owl looked up to the stars above,
> And sang to a small guitar,
> "O lovely Pussy! O Pussy, my love,

What a beautiful Pussy you are,
    You are,
    You are!
What a beautiful Pussy you are!"

Pussy said to the Owl, "You elegant fowl!
    How charmingly sweet you sing!
Oh let us be married! too long we have tarried:
    But what shall we do for a ring?"
They sailed away, for a year and a day,
    To the land where the Bong-tree grows,
And there in a wood a Piggy-wig stood,
    With a ring at the end of his nose,
        His nose,
        His nose,
    With a ring at the end of his nose.

"Dear Pig, are you willing to sell for one shilling
    Your ring?" Said the Piggy, "I will."
So they took it away and were married next day
    By the Turkey who lives on the hill.
They dined on mince, and slices of quince,
    Which they ate with a runcible spoon;
And hand in hand, on the edge of the sand,
    They danced by the light of the moon,
        The moon,
        The moon,
    They danced by the light of the moon.

EXPLORATION: After you've read "The Owl and the Pussy-cat" (and ideally, before you consider the discussion of it that follows), decide whether
or not you think it's a good poem for children. Try to figure out the reasons that led you to your judgment.

After some discussion, my students decided they wouldn't share "The Owl and
the Pussy-cat" with children. They told me that young children wouldn't be likely to
know obscure words such as "runcible" and "bong-tree" and that their frustration at
not knowing these words would not only make them dislike the poem but possibly
lead to a general dislike of poetry.

I was surprised by this response; not only do I like the poem myself, but I
know it's considered to be a classic of children's literature and often recommended
for sharing with children. So I asked these students if they enjoyed the poem themselves. They said they did. Why then, did they assume children wouldn't?

The answer was fairly obvious. In thinking about the poem as a text for children, they had ignored their own responses, and instead, guessed about how some
hypothetical child might respond. In fact, many adults base their judgments of chil-

dren's literature upon guesses like this about how children might respond to it. But making accurate guesses is difficult, maybe even impossible. It forces us to make generalizations about children—about how they read, how they think, what they enjoy or don't, and how they absorb information. As I suggest in some detail in chapter 5, such generalizations can be dangerously misleading; if nothing else, they misrepresent the tastes and abilities of many individual children.

Worse, while we're trying to guess about how a typical child might respond, we aren't paying attention to the only thing we can know for sure: our own response—what happens to *us* as we read. My students had ignored their own pleasure as they worried about the vocabulary deficiencies they assumed children possessed.

Nor was that all they had ignored, as I tricked them into discovering after a sneaky question occurred to me. "By the way," I asked, "Just in case some of us don't actually know, can anyone tell us what 'runcible' means, and what sort of a tree a 'bong-tree' is?"

Nobody knew. Nobody could have known—that's why the question was a sneaky one. There's no such thing as a bong-tree, and "runcible" is in the dictionary only because somebody created a strange sort of fork shaped like a spoon and called it a runcible spoon *after* Lear made up the word and used it in this poem over a hundred years ago. If my students had thought more about their own pleasure in "The Owl and the Pussy-cat," they would have realized that their lack of knowledge didn't prevent them from enjoying it. And if the pleasure this poem offered *them* didn't require absolute mastery of its vocabulary, then why might it not offer at least some children a similar pleasure?

In fact, I know from experience that it does—that many children *do* enjoy "The Owl and the Pussy-cat." Even children too young to read the poem themselves can enjoy the experience of having it read to them, in spite of or even because of their unfamiliarity with its strange language.

But while I believe that texts of children's literature demand as honest a response from adults as all other literature does, I have to acknowledge that texts written for children do tend to create their own special worlds, and to evoke moods and feelings unlike those provided by other forms of literature. My students told me that the pleasure they took in "The Owl and the Pussy-cat" wasn't the same pleasure they derived from poems by Sylvia Plath or William Wordsworth. So even though we should try to respond to a text of children's literature in the same way that we would respond to any other text, we also need to be conscious of the ways in which it might differ from other texts. If we really want to understand stories or poems written for children, we need to ask ourselves not only whether they are enjoyable, or interesting, or thought provoking, but also, what is special about them *as* texts of children's literature.

Furthermore, it seems likely that the special qualities of these texts relate to the fact that they're written with an audience of children in mind. How can we, not ourselves children anymore, both respond to children's literature honestly and take into consideration the fact that it was meant to be read by an audience unlike ourselves? I believe that the answer to this question lies in an idea proposed by theorists of reader response such as Wolfgang Iser: the concept of the *implied reader*.

THE IMPLIED READER

Appreciating the uniqueness of children's literature involves, first, thinking about who its audience might be. Who *are* the "children" in the phrase "children's literature"? As I suggested earlier, we won't identify the audience by thinking about children or childhood, at least not if we're dissatisfied with inaccurate generalizations. Instead, I believe, we should look at the literature itself: What can *it* tell us about the children in its name?

All texts imply in their subject and their style the sort of reader most likely to respond positively to them. Some texts—Shakespearean tragedies, for instance—dwell on tragic characters and gloomy situations; they imply a reader with a taste for exploring the darker side of existence. Some texts, like James Joyce's *Ulysses,* are filled with complex descriptive paragraphs and strange symbols; they imply a reader who takes pleasure in such writing and has the ability to make sense of it. If we think about "The Owl and the Pussy-cat" in this way, we might decide that it implies a reader who enjoys unfamiliar words like "runcible" for their strangeness and who isn't annoyed by not knowing their meaning.

In requiring us to possess the interpretive skills they demand and to know how to enjoy the pleasures they offer in order to get the most out of them, literary texts invite us to become something like the reader they imply as we read them. Or perhaps more accurately, they invite us to *pretend* to become that reader, somewhat in the way actors take on the roles they play. As many ardent readers know, one of the main pleasures reading literature offers is its ability to take us out of ourselves and imagine we are someone else. We tend to talk as if that someone else is a character we identify with and imagine ourselves being; but most of the time, I suspect, it's actually the implied reader—the person the text allows us to imagine ourselves as being in the process of making sense of it.

As well as taking pleasure from that process, we can use it as a strategy for understanding texts. We can learn much, both about texts and about ourselves as readers, from thinking about the nature of the readers a given text implies.

EXPLORATION: Choose (or invite children to choose) a literary text. By exploring the kinds of characters and situations it dwells on, the kinds of mood and atmosphere it creates, and the kind of language it uses, develop a description of the reader the text implies to you. What are the tastes, interests, and skills of the reader you think would be best equipped to understand and enjoy this text? To what degree does the implied reader you perceive in this text match yourself? To what degree has the extent of the match influenced your pleasure in the text?

The implied readers of children's texts are, most obviously, children. Each text intended for children can be seen to imply a child reader with specific knowledge, comprehension skills, and tastes. We can compare the implied readers of the children's texts we encounter both with ourselves as readers and with the actual children to whom we might recommend the texts. Doing so has a number of benefits:

- In order to make sense of literary texts, we need a *repertoire,* a body of knowledge of literature and life that texts assume and allude to, and as part of that repertoire, a set of *strategies,* ways of thinking about texts in order to see them as meaningful. In discovering how the repertoire and the strategies of the reader implied by a text intended for children vary from our own, we can learn what is distinctive about what the text offers.
- In thinking about the repertoire and the strategies that the implied readers of various children's texts share, we can learn something about the characteristics of children's literature.
- By comparing our perception of a text's implied reader with children we know, we can determine what particular repertoire or special strategies of meaning-making might be required to understand and enjoy that particular text. We can decide whether the children we know are likely to be familiar with this repertoire and these strategies—and if they are not, how we might help them develop this knowledge.

For instance, "The Owl and the Pussy-cat" implies a reader with a sizable repertoire. This repertoire includes knowledge of life: what a pig is, what love is, why someone in love might need a ring. It also includes knowledge of literature: not just accepting that in a kind of text called "nonsense" some of the words might be inventions of the author, but also understanding how to make sense of animals who, unlike real owls and pussycats, can talk and play the guitar. As far as I know, such animals exist only in literature, but readers are meant to take them for granted— have the repertoire to understand that they shouldn't be surprised or horrified by such peculiar beings. Once we realize that young children without much literary experience might not have this repertoire, we can work to help them to obtain it. The next chapter offers some suggestions about how to go about that.

CHILDREN'S LITERATURE AND ADULT LITERATURE: DIFFERENCES AND SIMILARITIES

A consideration of implied readers makes it clear why children's texts are different from other texts and even, to some extent, *how* they are different, and how we must read them differently. There's obviously a great distance between the reader implied by a Mother Goose rhyme, who doesn't need to know much more than that words put into patterns can be fun to listen to, and the reader implied by T. S. Eliot's *The Waste Land,* who must be conscious of the history of the world and many of its mythologies.

But we can't have a satisfying experience of either of these poems unless we're willing and able to imagine ourselves into being the specific reader that each of them implies and is designed to make us become. And we can't understand either of them unless we then stand back from the experience each has offered us and explore the character of the reader it has allowed us to become. The two poems are equally "literature," and therefore similarly offer these pleasures common to all literature.

The title of this book, *The Pleasures of Children's Literature,* suggests how centrally it focuses on the question of literary pleasure. While the book concentrates on the ways in which children's literature is distinct from other kinds, it does so in the belief that the differences are less significant than the similarities, that the pleasures of children's literature are essentially the pleasures of all literature.

Many of us assume that children should read primarily in order to learn, and so our response to texts for children focuses on the messages those texts might teach. But anyone who likes to read knows that, whether we are children or adults, we do so primarily because we enjoy it, not because it's good for us. Even if we do sometimes read because it is good for us, we take pleasure in how and what our reading makes us think and feel. If we're going to recommend works of literature for children and to children, I believe we should base our recommendations on the aspects of reading that make committed readers want to and like to read.

THE PLEASURES OF LITERATURE

What *are* the pleasures of literature? The list presented here outlines some of them.

EXPLORATION: Keep (or invite children to keep) an enjoyable literary text in mind while reading through the list below or responding to any one of its components. Consider specific ways in which the text might offer the pleasures described.

- The pleasure of words themselves—the patterns their sounds can make, the interesting ways in which they combine with each other, their ability to express revealing, frightening, or beautiful pictures or ideas.
- The pleasure of having our emotions evoked: laughing at a comic situation, being made to feel the pain or joy a character experiences.
- The pleasure of making use of our repertoire of knowledge and our strategies of comprehension—of experiencing our mastery.
- The pleasure of recognizing *gaps* in our repertoire and learning the information or the strategy we need to fill them, thereby developing further mastery. (*Gaps* is another term used by theorists of reader response; I discuss it in more detail in chapter 4.)
- The pleasure of the pictures and ideas that the words of texts evoke—the ways in which they allow us to visualize people and places we've never actually seen or think about ideas we haven't considered before.
- The pleasure of story—the organized patterns of emotional involvement and detachment, the delays of suspense, the climaxes and resolutions, the intricate patterns of chance and coincidence that make up a plot.

- The pleasure of *formula*—of repeating the comfortably familiar experience of kinds of stories we've enjoyed before.
- The pleasure of *newness*—of experiencing startlingly different kinds of stories and poems.
- The pleasure of story*telling*—our consciousness of how a writer's point of view or emphasis of particular elements shapes our response.
- The pleasure of *structure*—our consciousness of how words, pictures, or events form meaningful patterns.
- The pleasure of our awareness of the ways in which all the elements of a literary work seem to fit together to form a whole.
- The pleasure of the ways in which texts sometimes undermine or even deny their own wholeness. (Reading for this kind of pleasure is the basis of the kind of literary theory called *deconstruction*. I say more about it in chapter 9.)
- The pleasure of finding mirrors for ourselves—of identifying with fictional characters.
- The pleasure of *escape*—stepping outside of ourselves at least imaginatively and experiencing the lives and thoughts of different people.
- The pleasure of understanding—of seeing how literature not only mirrors life but comments on it and makes us consider the meaning of our own existence.
- The pleasure of seeing through literature—of realizing how poems or stories attempt to manipulate our emotions and influence our understanding and our moral judgments in ways we may or may not be prepared to accept. (There is more about this process, sometimes called "reading against a text," in chapter 7.)
- The pleasure of recognizing forms and *genres*—of seeing similarities between works of literature.
- The pleasure of gaining insight into history and culture through literature.
- The pleasure of discussing with others their responses to texts we have read.
- The pleasure of developing a deeper understanding of our responses and of relating them to our responses to other texts and to our understanding of literature in general.

EXPLORATION: What are *your* pleasures in literature? Consider (or invite children to consider) the kinds of pleasure you derive from your own reading. Think of specific examples of texts that gave you any of the pleasures listed above, and describe how they did it.

The list I've just provided focuses on verbal texts; but books for children often include pictures as well as words, and these visual texts have their pleasures also. If you think about your responses to illustrations in children's books, you may discover that there is a visual pleasure equivalent to each of the verbal ones I mention above. Children's picture books are discussed in more detail in chapter 11.

These different pleasures of texts all amount to one basic pleasure: the act of entering into communicative acts with others. Responding to a story or to a picture is a meeting with a text that conveys the flavor of a different personality or experience. Talking with others about a text we've experienced is a meeting of different minds. We read literature to experience something we didn't previously know or at the very least, an unfamiliar version of a familiar idea and experience. We talk about literature in order to enter into a dialogue with others about it, because good stories, poems, and pictures have the ability always to be newly rewarding—whenever we hear new ideas about them, share new experiences of them, have newly experienced texts to compare them with. In other words, the pleasure of literature is the pleasure of conversation—of dialogues between readers and texts, and between readers and other readers about those texts.

EXPLORATION: Some people believe that literary experience is essentially private and that analyzing our responses to literature or discussing them with others destroys them. Explore whether or not dialogue with others increases or decreases your understanding and enjoyment. Arrange with a friend or classmate to read the same story or poem and then have a discussion about it. Was the discussion enjoyable or destructive?

Understood as conversation, literature exists both in and out of the actual written texts or films or TV shows that contain stories and poems. In a sense, it is the entire body of writing, and of the thoughts people have had about writing, and also all of the differing aspects of life that have ever been written about. One text reminds us of another text; our conversations with others about texts lead us to see connections with still other texts, with other conversations about texts, with aspects of our lives and our knowledge of the lives of others throughout history. In these ways, all literature and all experience of literature is tied together—a network of ideas and stories, images and emotions. Literary theorists call this *intertextuality*. Every time we read a text or discuss our response to a text with someone else, we become part of the network: we learn more about the components of the network, and, in our own response and conversation, add something to it. All readers and all people who discuss their reading are in the process of making literature—of making it mean more to themselves and to others.

This process of making literature meaningful includes children: A child's response to a poem, based on limited experience of both life and literature, may seem to be less complicated in some ways than the response of an English professor like me. But the child's response may also be more complicated in other ways. It's certainly no more and no less significant than the response of the English professor. In being different, it adds to the possibile meanings texts engender and thus enriches literature as a whole.

Nevertheless, exactly because literature is an interconnected network of texts and responses to them, both the child and the English professor can learn from, and gain pleasure from, each other's responses.

EXPLORATION: Share a story or a poem with some children, and discuss their response with them. Does it differ from your own? Can you see ways in which the discussion might enrich either their knowledge of literature or your own?

From the professor, or from other adults, the child can learn useful strategies. The ability to respond to literature with an understanding of its subtleties, and with a flexible attitude to the possibilities of meanings it might convey and emotions it might arouse—in other words, the ability to enjoy literature—is a learned skill. Those of us who enjoy reading may have developed our own skills for enjoying literature unconsciously, simply by reading a lot. But many people who have read less can be encouraged by sensitive teachers to learn the skills of literary enjoyment.

Children in particular can learn to become more perceptive readers of literature—and greatly increase their pleasure in the act of reading as a result of it. The next chapter explores ways in which we might help them to do so.

In return for offering children something of our own sophisticated skills, we adults can gain something equally important from our discussions of literature with children. We can learn to share some of the more immediate, more sensuously direct, and less guilty pleasure that many children, too inexperienced to have learned otherwise, can still take from literature, specifically children's literature. We can learn to laugh at the jokes as hard as some children do, to become as involved as some children can. We can learn that exactly because it demands and encourages this sort of guileless intensity, children's literature can be a real pleasure for adults.

All engaged readers, adults or children, read intensely, without fear of strangeness or boredom with familiar pleasures and with commitment to the experience offered. And all engaged readers, adults or children, think intensely about what they read, without fear of what exploration of their responses will tell them about texts or, more significantly, about themselves. *The Pleasures of Children's Literature* expresses the belief that both adult students of children's literature and the children they teach or raise can become this sort of engaged reader, able to take pleasure both in the experience of literature and in the understanding of that experience.

EXPLORATION: Now that you've read this chapter, reconsider your previous exploration of whether "The Owl and the Pussy-cat" is a good poem for children. Does anything said in this chapter disagree with the opinions you expressed earlier? If so, has reading the chapter changed your opinions? How and why? If not, how would you counter the arguments presented here?

WORKS CITED

Iser, Wolfgang. *The Implied Reader: Patterns of Communication in Prose Fiction from Bunyan to Beckett.* Baltimore: Johns Hopkins UP, 1974.

Lear, Edward. "The Owl and the Pussy-cat." *The Complete Nonsense of Edward Lear.* Ed. Holbrook Jackson. New York: Dover, 1951.

chapter **3**

Teaching Children Literature

FOCUSING ON LITERARY STRATEGIES

While stories and poems play a prominent role in the education of children, literature itself is rarely the subject of teaching. Young children reading *Charlotte's Web* might be asked to develop their language skills by inserting vocabulary words into webs made of twine and hung in the classroom, or to expand their creativity by exploring what it feels like to try looking radiant, or to build their knowledge by developing an interest in the habits of spiders. But they're seldom asked to consider a text *as* a text—to explore the ways in which it provides the pleasures of literature I outlined in the last chapter.

Even when texts aren't being used as the basis for vocabulary or science lessons, study of them tends to focus on nonliterary concerns. Standard guides, such as those by Charlotte Huck and by Sutherland, Monson, and Arbuthnot, define literature as a vicarious experience that offers children insight into the feelings of others, as a transmitter of cultural heritage, and as a resource for the development of cognitive and linguistic skills. These guides say much about the usefulness of literature in teaching these subjects and skills, but surprisingly little about literature itself, or of the strategies required to understand and take pleasure in it.

In fact, the educational uses of literature recommended in these guides distort the experience of literature in a way that might actually prevent children from enjoying it. Those of us who like reading stories and poems don't often do so as a means of investigating spiders or of learning how to be more tolerant or more imaginative. We do so primarily because we enjoy the experience.

We might conclude, then, that in order not to interfere with children's pleasure in literature, we should just "butt out" and leave them to their own reading and their own ways of enjoying what they read. In order to do that, though, we have to make one of two assumptions:

1. Children are naturally capable of taking pleasure in what they read.
2. What sort of pleasure they take doesn't matter, as long as they do somehow enjoy reading literature.

Both assumptions are problematic.

Unfortunately, many children *don't* take much pleasure in literature. They prefer TV or playing basketball. Left to their own devices they might well choose never to read it at all. That's a pity.

Furthermore, the pleasure some children do take comes with all sorts of cultural and intellectual baggage—not all of it desirable. For instance, many adults assume, and so teach children to assume, that pleasure is best defined as the opposite of awareness or thoughtfulness, as the pleasant numbness we experience when we don't have to think. Children (and adults) who understand pleasure in this limiting way are deprived of the vast range of other pleasurable experiences literature can offer.

I have no doubt that we can open up many of the pleasures I listed in the last chapter to them. But to do so, we need to find ways of showing them that it's immense fun to think about and to discuss the literary texts they read. We also need to show them that doing so offers them a deeply satisfying mastery—a freedom from being manipulated into unconsciously agreeing with ideas that may or may not be good for them.

Surely, then, we should at least try to give children access to the strategies that allow us as adults to make sense of and take many different pleasures from our experience of literary texts. This chapter explores ways in which we might accomplish that goal.

I have to begin the exploration by acknowledging my own lack of practical experience in these matters. As I suggested in chapter 1, my expertise is mainly in literary matters. One of the scholars who reviewed a draft of this book for the publisher made the comment that I "sound like a university professor who is very philosophical and has not been in an elementary classroom to see the realities of the use of children's literature in the curriculum—and of the real pleasure children have when interacting with literature." I don't know about my being philosophical, but I can't deny that I've spent little time in elementary school classrooms since I graduated from them some decades ago. I've never been a teacher of young children, except my own sons and daughter and the occasional nursery or first or second grade class I've come to as a visitor.

But I *do* know the methods I describe in this chapter work, and I do know they give great and very real pleasure to children. I've based what I say here on my reading of work actually done with children singly and in elementary school classes, as reported both in professional journals and in many stimulating conversations I've had with working teachers. Many of those teachers have been students in the children's literature courses I offer at the University of Winnipeg, and they report using the methods I recommend with great success. Their students learned a lot, enjoyed learning it, and read and understood more as a result of it.

One other note: Many of the texts I quote in this chapter focus on the work of classroom teachers and the place of literary study in formal education. But the suggestions I make here can be used in homes and elsewhere, by parents, grandparents, librarians—anyone interested in sharing literary texts with children. This I *have* done myself, with many different children, and can report that it gave great pleasure both to them and to me.

CAN WE TEACH PLEASURE?

EXPLORATION: Do you think we can? Before you read the following section, think about your own experiences of studying literature. Have educational experiences (such as reading this book) increased or decreased your enjoyment of specific texts? Of the process of reading and responding to literature? If so, how? If not, why not?

One of the reasons the focus of our teaching of literature is not on the enhancement of pleasure is the idea that pleasure is private—too dependent on individual tastes and feelings to be taught. There's no doubt that differences in taste play a large part in our ability to enjoy particular texts, and that's as it should be. Some of us will never enjoy reading the works of James Joyce no matter how persuasively others tell us they like them. We either experience pleasure or we don't. In the words of Peter Neumeyer, "One can't say, 'Have pleasure now, damn it,' as Miss Havisham says to Pip [in Dickens's novel *Great Expectations*], 'Play, boy' " (146).

But it's also true that many people who read James Joyce simply haven't learned the strategies necessary to enjoy his work. While many people believe that critical analysis of literature somehow destroys our pleasure in it, the reverse is true more often. "I think," Neumeyer says, "we simply must have faith that as students understand more, they enjoy more" (147). I share that faith.

Nevertheless, some people who acknowledge that understanding can increase enjoyment still insist that such understanding cannot be actively taught. In *Literature for Young Children,* Joan I. Glazer says that "literature is more *experienced* than *taught*" (51), and according to Huck, "children are developing . . . a way of thinking about books. This should be encouraged but not taught" (707). Why it shouldn't be taught Huck doesn't say—but she and many others who share this assumption seem to have based it on various psychological theories of development: that children are too egocentric to develop the objectivity needed for an analytical understanding of literature; that they are at a stage of cognitive development that prevents them from making sense of abstractions; that the imposition of adult language and adult categories interferes with their active learning.

As I show in chapter 5, cognitive and developmental psychologists have come in recent years to have serious doubts about all of these assumptions. Recent scientific research reveals that children are *not* necessarily egocentric, *not* necessarily incapable of dealing with abstractions, and *not* necessarily incapable of learning through systematic instruction.

Furthermore, assuming children will learn literary strategies by themselves merely through exposure to literature leads, generally, to ignorance of these strategies. Many people emerge from their childhood exposure to literature with simplistic interpretive strategies that prevent them from getting much pleasure from their own reading—and, often, lock them inside a narrow vision of themselves and of the world they live in.

EXPLORATION: Again think about your own experience—did you learn literary strategies that helped you to enjoy literature by yourself? How did you learn the strategies—consciously or unconsciously? Are you aware of having been taught them? When and by whom?

Meanwhile, there's mounting evidence that when we talk with children in the language we use in our adult discussions of literature, we help children develop strategies of understanding and appreciation. This in turn helps them perceive and talk about the intricacies of the texts they read, thereby enjoying literature more. Barbara Kiefer describes how young children enjoy their awareness of the subtleties of picture books, and Richard Van Dongen notes how children in fifth grade delight in their consciousness of the artistry of nonfiction. Lawrence R. Sipe reports on a project in which sixth-grade students compared traditional fairy tales with modern variants, such as Fiona French's *Snow White in New York,* and then went on to write their own variations: "In short, we wanted to enable students to read like writers and write like readers" (20). Sipe concludes, "Although the reading, modelling, and discussion were valuable in themselves, they also broadened the students' choices and sharpened their thoughts for their own writing" (22).

And there's more. In a symposium on "Teaching Literary Criticism in the Elementary Grades," the editor Jon Stott reports his success in teaching children story patterns, Anita Moss and Norma Bagnall report on successful efforts to introduce young children to various aspects of the critical analysis of literature, and Sonia Landes reports how she provided children in the early elementary grades with strategies for perceiving the structure and subtlety of a picture book. Landes sums up the children's reactions: "The close study of *The Tale of Peter Rabbit* . . . gave them a sense of accomplishment and immense pleasure" (Stott, "Teaching Literary Criticism" 161).

WHAT WE DON'T WANT TO TEACH

If we believe that education works—that children learn from the behavior of their teachers—then we have to acknowledge that much of what they learn is what we have conveyed unintentionally, simply because we haven't thought about the implications of our methods. Furthermore, the evidence of many adults' distaste for reading suggests that many conventional methods of teaching children literature are counterproductive—that they produce more despair and uninterest than pleasure. This means we have to think about the kinds of attitudes toward literature that particular exercises might produce, and above all, avoid classroom experiences that might turn children away from the pleasures of literature.

Fortunately, we have one infallible principle to guide us. Lola Brown suggests it when she says, "The fundamental disharmony between my behaviour as an independent reader and the behaviour of student-readers apparently dictated by classroom conditions is, for me, the starting point in addressing the problem of rendering imaginative literature accessible to *all* young readers" (94). In other words, if we don't want to misrepresent the pleasures of literature, we should avoid *any* practice in the classroom that differs significantly from the practices typical of people who like to read: Never ask students to do anything that people who love to read don't do.

There are several things we people who love reading literature don't usually do when we read away from classrooms, but that teachers often ask children to do:

- As long as we're enjoying what we read, we don't pay much attention to the process of decoding the words, or worry about whether or not we're reading absolutely accurately. We don't interrupt our pleasure in the development of a plot by looking up every single word we're unfamiliar with. As Patrick X. Dias says, "Reading in the expectation that one's comprehension will be tested by the teacher is unlikely to promote either enjoyment of reading or the likelihood that an individual will voluntarily read such texts in the future" (135). Instead, we people who like to read derive meaning from context *as* we read. We are often so swept up by the events of a plot that we're content *not* to know the exact meaning of particular words.

- We don't read everything with the same degree of attention; we don't always read closely and analytically; we sometimes just skim through a story or poem. Nor do we keep reading books we hate or find boring just because someone else has decided they're good for us. We feel free to stop reading books we don't like before we've finished them. And we feel equally free to read *against* a text—to think about what it's trying to get us to agree to and to resist its manipulations.

- We don't often read with a primary focus on absorbing a message as truth to live by. We don't think of the act of reading literature primarily as a form of self-administered therapy, in which we treat a story or poem as good advice about our own future behavior. Nor do we usually focus centrally on the information about geography or history that novels or poems convey. We tend to see our reading of literature as a source of questions for us to continue to think about rather than answers for us to accept.

- We don't parrot the responses or interpretations provided by other people, particularly those with authority over us, in order to prove that we understood the "right" things about a book we read. We understand what we understand, and feel free to disagree with other readers who understood other things. Indeed, we treasure the stimulating discussions made possible by these differences in understanding.

- We don't express our response to the books we read by involving ourselves in entertaining activities loosely based on them: inventing board games around their events or cooking the foods they describe or making videos in which we imagine ourselves to be reporters interviewing the characters.

When we don't treat our reading in these ways, we're asserting our central interest in literature—in words and their ability to represent and communicate—as an experience deserving of attention in and for itself. We're also asserting control over our own reading, our right to respond to books as we wish and as we actually do rather than in terms of someone else's agenda of tests or activities and values to be absorbed. If we want children to learn to share the pleasure of our reading experiences, then we have to avoid hampering their own interest and control. Sutherland, Monson, and Arbuthnot assert, "It goes without saying that any response should be treated with the utmost respect" (502).

Nevertheless, we should remember that respecting the response of others doesn't necessarily mean not admitting that we disagree with them. To create an environment in which *any* response is appropriate forces us to resign our own right to try to dissuade others of opinions we disagree with and denies children the pleasures of dialogue about differing responses. It also denies the basic thrust of our effort as teachers: to encourage richer and more subtle responses—that is, to teach our students something they don't know yet. To do anything else would be to renounce our main responsibility as teachers.

WHAT WE DO WANT TO TEACH

EXPLORATION: As you read through this section, keep in mind a specific child or group of children you know. To what extent might it be possible to accomplish these goals with this audience? How? Try to think of specific, concrete ways in which you might accomplish them.

We can encourage richer and subtler responses in a number of ways. We can give children some freedom to choose what literature they'll read and discuss in terms of their own developing tastes and interests. We can offer them ready access to libraries. We can put the children's own responses at the heart of our discussions of literature with them. We can encourage them to see the value and significance of their own responses and of the ways in which they relate texts to the rest of their experience—and not just their experience of literature, but also of TV and toys and movies. In chapter 6, I focus on the deep significance of their being able to think critically about these matters.

In other words, we can encourage the kind of exploration I try to encourage throughout this book. Above all, we can confirm what children who love literature know already: not just that everyone's experiences of it are different but also that these different responses emerge from a shared text and so can be a profitable subject of discussion and a vehicle for making individuals members of a community.

A focus on individual readers' responses suggests specific attitudes and skills we want to help children develop: We want to encourage children to focus their attention away from the products of reading—the ideas or messages they end up with after finishing and thinking about a poem or novel—and onto the process of reading. Rather than leaving them to imagine that reading literature is a matter of thoughtlessly immersing themselves in a text, we want to encourage them to be conscious of the degree to which they actively intervene in and even manufacture their own reading experiences.

Ruth Graham, an elementary school teacher and one of my former students, discovered the main value of conscious reading as she encouraged her fifth-grade class to explore the narrative content of the pictures in picture books, using some of the strategies outlined in chapter 11 of this book. Her students told Ruth they enjoyed these activities simply because they actually gave them something to think about and to do as they responded to a text. Before the exercise, they had no idea about what they might do at all and so, basically, did nothing and had nothing to enjoy. They had been little more than numb.

We also want children to become aware of the ways in which texts communicate distinctive experiences, to understand how writers' specific choices of words, phrases, events, and so on work together to create the flavor and meanings of individual texts. Developing such an awareness depends on having a way to describe it, so we should be willing to teach children the language that will allow them to formulate and develop understanding of their reading experiences: words and phrases like *image, structure, gap,* or *story pattern* that I use and try to define throughout this book. In her discussion of circular and linear journeys in "Teaching Literary Criticism in the Elementary Grades," Anita Moss reports that "the children eagerly learned the meanings of these words and quickly learned to apply them, not only to stories but also to popular culture and to their own experience" (Stott, "Teaching" 169).

The appropriate language allows us to discuss literature, and fostering an understanding of and enthusiasm for discussion should be a main goal. As I suggested earlier, the ability to enjoy and discuss literature allows children to enter into a community of readers. Furthermore, as Steve Bicknell says, "Literature must be discussed. It is only by discussing with others who have experienced a book that new meaning can be effectively constructed" (45).

To encourage the construction of new meaning, we can also introduce children to the ideas of literary critics. True, a lot of literary criticism might seem to be too difficult or esoteric for children in elementary school, but Linnea Hendrickson describes how she "decided to choose a critical article and consider how its insights might be passed on to preschoolers." She concludes her listing of the insights provided in a complex article about Beatrix Potter that might be transmitted to children by asserting, "The more deeply one delves into criticism, the more ideas one gets" (202). In his fine book *Reading Narratives: Signs of Life,* Andrew Stibbs confirms Hendrickson's point magnificently by offering a spectrum of suggestions for practical and stimulating classroom activities derived from a wide variety of aspects of literary theory.

In addition to placing their response to a text in the context of other readers' responses, children can be encouraged to see their response in the context of the rest of their experience of literature and to develop some knowledge of its recurring patterns. In *The Educated Imagination,* Northrop Frye claims that these recurring themes and patterns are the "real subject" of literary study (49), because the themes and patterns represent the ways in which the human imagination has separated itself from, imposed itself upon, and transformed nature: "Whatever value there is in studying literature, cultural or practical, comes from the total body of our reading, the castle of words we've built, and keep adding new wings to all the time" (95). Having knowledge of the conventional patterns of genre and structure that critics such as Frye speak of will give children entry into a common heritage of literary knowledge beyond their own perceptions. This in turn will allow them the pleasure of being able to discuss literature with others who share that heritage. It will also give them insight into the representative nature of all literary representations: the degree to which they distort or transform reality in their depiction of it.

In order to foster an awareness of the patterns shared even by widely different works of literature, we need to provide children with diverse experiences of literature—with the simple and the complex, the old and the new, the foreign and the domestic, the tragic and the funny—even the good and the bad as we define them for ourselves. Furthermore, we should make popular literature, TV, and movies a significant part of our discussion of literature, in the classroom and elsewhere. As Leslie Stratta and John Dixon say, "Given the fact that students spend more time watching television than they do going to class, it seems suicidal for schools to ignore the media" (175). Rather than ignoring it, we should connect the literature we teach with the rest of the children's experience of narrative. And we should help children develop analytical viewing skills that will protect them from indiscriminate acceptance of the often suspicious values commercial TV and movies promote. Jo-Anne Everingham describes a worthy goal when she says, "My first aim in teaching about television has been to develop the ability to 'read television' by developing the ability to view differently" (67)—that is, with some critical distance.

We can apply a similar aim to written texts and work to help children read with a consciousness of ideological implications: of the ways in which texts represent or misrepresent reality and work to manipulate readers. "In fact," Gillian Lazar argues in her discussion of what children should learn, "our response to the cultural aspect of literature should always be a critical one, so that the underlying cultural and ideological assumptions in the texts are not merely accepted and reinforced, but are questioned, evaluated and, if necessary, subverted" (17).

We might even make children aware of the extent to which their own responses are a product of their culture and their society, and thus allow them greater freedom of choice about accepting ideas they are exposed to. What Charles Sarland reports discovering about his own pleasures is equally true for young readers; "There are some books that give me a great deal of pleasure, but . . . what I have learned is that my pleasure sits within a particular social context" (17). The pleasure children can take in what they read depends on their place in society, their gender, their racial background, and particularly, their sense of who they are. As I suggest throughout this book, I suspect all literary pleasure is influenced by these factors. But those who become aware of the connections between pleasure and social status can at least consider the implications of the connections, and perhaps learn other pleasures—one of which might be in the mastery implied by that very awareness itself.

Ideally, providing children with a variety of literary texts can help free them from common cultural assumptions about what children can or should like and develop their willingness to seek pleasure from the new as well as from the familiar. In order to accomplish that, we need the courage to offer them unusual literary experiences—something beyond the texts that seem most immediately relevant to their circumstances. Unfortunately, as Candy Carter says, "Somehow in the last decade or so, American teachers got stuck on the idea that students had to "like" everything, not realizing that part of our job was to help them like it" (59). As an alternative philosophy, Purves, Rogers, and Soter make this interesting claim: "We haven't yet met a work of literature that is too difficult for any group of students, given a good teacher and the appropriate context" (46).

TEACHING LITERARY STRATEGIES

For the most part, assumptions about children's limitations and the dangers of analytical thinking have meant that teachers often don't try to teach children ways of reading literature beyond the most basic acts of decoding and comprehension. As a result, we don't really know that much about how we might do it. Common sense offers the most important guide: We can't teach what we don't know, so anyone who doesn't know how to enjoy reading literature, thinking about it, and entering into dialogues about it shouldn't try to teach these pleasures. On the other hand, those of us who have these abilities need do nothing more than figure out what we ourselves do in the process of enjoying literature and then devise ways of teaching children to do the same.

EXPLORATION: Record your thinking as you explore your response to a text written for children. Then stand back from what you've written and try to figure out what strategies you were using. How might you go about teaching these strategies to children?

Furthermore, teachers and educational theorists do know a lot about teaching literature to older children and young adults. Once I dismiss some of the more limiting assumptions of misunderstood and misapplied developmental theory, I see no reason why much of what they've discovered might not apply equally to younger children. In what follows, I've borrowed heavily from the ideas of a number of critics, such as Stibbs and Sarland, about how to teach adolescents.

Duplicating the Experiences of Readers

Research into the history of adults who enjoy reading and responding to literature suggests some guidelines. The main one is simply that readers tend to come from homes where reading occurs. Their childhood homes contained many books, the adults they lived with read often and enjoyed discussions of books often. The children were often read to by adults who clearly enjoyed doing so, and they had access to a variety of texts from comic books to sophisticated fiction.

If we want to create readers, we need to replicate these experiences as much as we can. We should read stories and poems to children as often as possible and with as much enthusiasm as possible. We should remind children about how these texts relate to each other and to classroom and other real-life experiences. We should fill our homes and classrooms with books of all sorts and allow children the freedom to read what they want and to choose which texts they want to discuss in class. We should make ourselves familiar with the books they are reading and the TV programs they are watching and discuss these books and programs with them. And we should do our own reading in the presence of children whenever possible: when students in a classroom are involved in small-group discussions, for instance. Indeed, Ron Jobe suggests that, "as a teacher or librarian you should be regularly sharing your own adult reading with the students. Why not read favorite passages . . . ?" (9)

Exposure to a Variety of Books

The most successful literature curriculum not only creates situations in which children read copiously but also exposes children to as many different kinds of books as possible: not just "good" literature that we approve of but texts we might consider to be *trash,* and not just texts that children can easily understand, but more unusual ones. According to Aidan Chambers,

> Wide, voracious, indiscriminate reading is the base soil from which discrimination and taste eventually grow. Indeed, if those of us who are avid and committed readers examine our reading history during our childhood and look also at what we have read over the last few months, few of us will be able to say honestly that we have always lived only on the high peaks of literature. (122)

On the other hand, as Carter says,

> No one, not even the most seriously deficient reader, should be denied the opportunity to be exposed to good works of literature. If a student can't handle the vocabulary level, the teacher can put the book on tape;

there is no shame in being read to. For a teacher to take it upon himself or herself that a student is too "slow" a reader to be given a chance to tackle a good book is a serious disservice to another human being. (58)

What Carter suggests here is another important guideline: Lack of skill in decoding a text doesn't necessarily represent an equivalent lack of intelligence. The fact that a child doesn't read well doesn't mean the child isn't capable of understanding and enjoying the contents of complex texts. Indeed, knowing that reading can unlock the door to such interesting experiences is often an impetus for children to develop better reading skills. As Linda Hart-Hewins and Jan Wells suggest, "To want to read, they must see the point of it" (10).

The need for variety of types and of levels of complexity means that no graded reader can encourage literary response. Furthermore, as Michael Apple and Linda Christian-Smith point out, all textbooks, including graded readers, "signify— through their content and form— particular constructions of reality, particular ways of selecting and organizing that vast universe of possible knowledge. They embody what Raymond Williams, a renowned cultural theorist, called the 'selective tradition'—someone's selections, someone's vision of knowledge and culture, one that in the process of enfranchising one group's cultural capital disenfranchises another's" (3–4).

EXPLORATIONS: (1) Test out that assumption by exploring (or inviting children to explore) the contents of a graded reader. What aspects of experience are selected out? What groups or values are being disenfranchised?

(2) It's blushingly obvious to me as I quote this comment in the context of this book that it applies not just to graded readers for children but also to textbooks like this one. Consider what groups are being disenfranchised by *my* selections and *my* vision of knowledge about children's literature, in this chapter and elsewhere.

Children who experience literature only in the form of graded readers become subject to the vision of the person—or more likely, the committee—that created them. Furthermore, in textbooks for elementary schools, that vision is rarely a personal or even an interesting one; Apple and Christian-Smith describe the great extent to which political circumstances and economic considerations control and seriously limit what can safely appear in such books.

In these circumstances, it's very hard for children to develop any sense of their own taste or mastery of their own reading experiences, except perhaps by defining themselves as uninterested in reading. Teachers forced to use such texts should supplement them with other materials. Some enthusiastic teachers go so far as to cut readers up into separate selections, so that each selection becomes an individual pamphlet available for an individual child's reading.

A Consciousness of Response

While exposure to a variety of literature is the best generator of literary pleasure, most classrooms can't provide the degree of exposure that might create such a response. Children who arrive at school without much familiarity with literature have considerable catching up to do, and the demands of school curricula make it impossible for teachers to spend all day reading to students. We need to develop other ways of teaching literary pleasure and the strategies that foster it.

The most basic strategy is a consciousness of our own response and the responses of others, and of the processes through which we come to understand and enjoy literary texts. Here are some ways to encourage such a consciousness:

- Foster the pleasure of having questions about texts as well as answers. Judith A. Langer says, "Teachers who support literary understanding assume that . . . responding to literature involves the raising of questions. Thus teachers continually invite students' questions, in many contexts" ("Rethinking Literature Discussion" 44). What questions are raised for you by a title? By your reading of a page? By your thinking about the actions of a character? Note that the teacher's job is to ask for questions and then to take all the answers seriously, not ask questions and await specific answers.

- Offer exercises that focus attention on how we build our responses from the information in texts in terms of engaging and revising our expectations. For instance, we can read poems or stories the children aren't familiar with a line or a sentence at a time, stopping to allow discussion of the images and ideas that emerge and then, after reading further, how the children confirm or change the expectations these ideas and images arouse.

- Offer exercises focused on the ways we apply our individual expectations to the texts we read, fill in gaps (this term is explained in the next chapter), visualize characters and settings, relate texts to others we've experienced earlier or to patterns we've become conscious of. For instance, we can encourage discussion of what children expect before they begin to read a particular text and how their expectations relate to their previous experiences of literature or life. We can ask for verbal or written descriptions of what gaps children notice and how they fill them, or of their visualizations of characters or settings and what meanings the visualizations might imply.

- Arrange group discussions in which children discuss the differences in their responses to a text.

- Have the children keep journals to record their responses and to do exploratory thinking of the sort suggested by the *Explorations* throughout this book.

Like all educational activities approached in the wrong spirit, these exercises can become onerous tasks, nothing more than duties to be done for a grade. They help to encourage a positive attitude only as long as the focus remains on the pleasure inherent in the activity itself. Children I've tried them with myself seem to enjoy them most in the spirit of puzzle-solving: becoming conscious of how literary texts provide information that is incomplete but that nevertheless allows us the pleasure of trying to make sense of them, just as jigsaws and crosswords provide us with clues and allow us the pleasure of trying to make sense out of them. As Purves, Rogers, and Soter say, "Literature is language at play" (8). We need to maintain and encourage a playful attitude toward experiencing it.

We can also stimulate consciousness of the validity of individual responses by allowing for and encouraging a spectrum of responses to the same text. In Robert Protherough's *Developing Response to Fiction,* Keith Bardgett suggests many activities that children might choose from in terms of their own interests and abilities, including character studies, book reviews, writing alternative endings, imaginary interviews with characters, and drawings, in order to fill a wall display "which would represent all aspects of their responses to the book" (78).

Nevertheless, such activities become pointless in terms of developing literary pleasure if they draw attention away from literature and the experience of reading it. As Protherough insists, "The work done should not simply start from the book, but should constantly return and refer to it" (59). We should design activities that, instead of producing substitutes for literary pleasure because we think we ought to make the study of literature fun, show that literature is *in and of itself* fun.

Focusing on the Text

We want not only to encourage response but also to find ways of helping children develop an understanding of how literary texts provoke response. This means we want to focus attention on the texts themselves. Here are some ways of doing so:

- Develop exercises encouraging awareness of the effect of specific choices of words or patterns or images. For instance, children can rewrite poems in their own words and then consider how the two ways of expressing the same idea are different and what that reveals to them about the special language and specific meaning of the poem.

- Develop exercises revealing the significance of other choices made by authors through a consideration of alternatives. How would the events of a story seem different if we heard about them in a different order, or if they were told from the point of view of a different character? How would a person from another social group or country or climate understand these events? Children can write alternative versions of texts and then compare them with the original.

- Develop exercises with picture books, as suggested by Sonia Landes, that include "two simple questions that can be asked over and over again. . . . The first is simply, 'What do you see?' and the child will look closely at the picture and point to things and see what he or she had not seen before. The second is, 'What does the picture tell that the text does not?' and vice versa. This sends the child back and forth between picture and text, responding all the while to the wholeness of the story" (54).

- Offer other activities that focus on the ways in which the illustrations in picture books change the meanings of the words, or vice versa. For instance, reading just the written text and asking children to imagine and describe pictures, and then comparing the real pictures with what they imagined; or showing just the pictures and asking children to imagine the words. Many other activities are suggested in chapter 11.

- Develop exercises encouraging development of the knowledge a text takes for granted: for instance, background on the times and places in which stories are set or study of the meanings of visual symbols in a picture book. Once more, though, the focus should be on how this knowledge illuminates understanding of a text as much as on how the text offers insight into other kinds of knowledge.

- Develop exercises focusing on re-reading: how do we respond to a text differently the second time we read it, with the advance knowledge of what is going to happen? What similar or different pleasures does it offer?

Focusing on Connections

We can help children develop knowledge of the interconnectedness of literary texts by paying careful attention to the sequence in which we introduce them to children. Protherough says, "Ideally each new learning situation should incorporate features of earlier learning, provide new ones, and carry the student to a higher level of understanding, skill or appreciation" (171). We can devise exercises that allow children to compare one poem with another similar one, or to develop an understanding of what limericks have in common with each other, or to perceive how fairy tales share basic story patterns. All these matters are discussed elsewhere in this book.

As we develop sequences of literature, however, we shouldn't let developmental assumptions prevent us from mixing complex texts with simpler ones. Stott says that "teaching novels in Grade Three, while challenging, is by no means impossible" ("Spiralled Sequence" 159). We should be willing to try it, so that we don't deprive children of the rich diversity that develops skills of literary enjoyment.

We can further develop knowledge of the interconnectedness of literature by encouraging comparisons between TV or movie versions and written texts of the same story to develop an awareness of how the story differs in the two media. We can show videotapes of TV cartoons and situation comedies and focus on the patterns they share with fairy tales. We can also devise exercises that will make children conscious of the effects on meaning of such factors as camera angles and choice of shots and also of the ideological content of programs and commercials.

Encouraging Dialogue

Since a main pleasure of literature is the dialogues it engenders, we want to encourage dialogue, both among children and between children and ourselves. We can do so by creating the sort of focused but informal atmosphere that makes real dialogue possible. In the classroom, children can explore specific questions and complete specific tasks in groups small enough to allow spontaneous discussion. We should make sure that individual responses are shared: by devising exercises that encourage students to seek out, confront, and make use of each other's responses in developing their own. For instance, children can record their own responses to a text in writing, then read each other's responses and discuss the similarities and differences and their possible implications.

We also want to be able to express our own opinions as teachers or parents without turning literary discussion into a spectator sport in which students merely listen to and learn to parrot our responses instead of developing their own. We can participate in discussion without dominating it only if we create an atmosphere in which all opinions, including our own, are taken seriously enough to be examined, and in which children develop both the strength of mind to be stimulated rather than hurt by a challenge to their ideas and the skills of logical argumentation that will allow them to defend themselves. For instance, children can seek the specific details in a text to support their general impression of it or search for parallels in other texts they already know that might support a particular interpretation.

We can also encourage a dialogue between ourselves and child readers if we put ourselves on more of an equal footing by discussing texts we aren't familiar with and haven't thought about before. As Robert Probst says, "Students have too often been presented meanings and interpretations already made, finished, complete, and they have too seldom seen the stumbling, tentative, hesitating process of making meaning out of texts" (72). Children need to experience and feel comfortable with that process in order to understand the pleasure it offers and to stop believing that the product matters more than the process.

Nevertheless, producing a finished product gives us not only the satisfaction of making something others can enjoy, but also, knowledge of the process. Children can learn a tremendous amount about how literature works by producing some; for instance, small groups might act as writing and editing committees to produce illustrated versions of their own texts.

Surefire Methods?

I realize that most of the ideas I've presented here are general suggestions rather than step-by-step methods of teaching specific texts. I've been vague on purpose. I agree with Anthony Petrosky's assertion that the models and study guides often offered to teachers in books like this one "erase possibilities rather than create them. . . . They effectively remove teachers and students from possibilities outside the model" (164–165). Because of the variation in response that makes literary discussion both necessary and enjoyable, there are no surefire methods, no ideal models. Good teaching demands constant attention to what is happening to specific children and constant resourcefulness in developing ways of responding to problems as they occur.

Nevertheless, even the most resourceful teachers or parents can use some help. For those in search of it, I suggest the following:

1. As more teachers try to teach literary pleasure to children, they're bound to discover that certain methods meet with success; and when they do, they often publish articles in order to share their ideas with others. You can learn about such discoveries by reading journals such as *Children's Literature in Education, Children's Literature Association Quarterly, Journal of Children's Literature,* and *The New Advocate.*

EXPLORATION: Find a discussion of specific methods of teaching children literature in a recent journal, and try what it suggests.

2. Good teaching depends on having knowledge of what might be taught. Remember Hendrickson's suggestion that published literary criticism can suggest ideas for teachers.

EXPLORATION: Read *any* critical article in a children's literature journal and think of what might be passed on to children, and how.

3. According to Stott, "The gap between what is done in university and school classrooms can be bridged and should be bridged more often" (" 'It's Not What You Expect' " 161). Thinking about the methods your teachers used to help you develop your understanding and enjoyment of literature may help you develop ways of using the same methods in your own classroom.

EXPLORATION: Has a teacher ever stimulated your enjoyment and understanding of literature? How? How could you adapt those methods to an elementary classroom?

4. Similarly, if you find any of the ideas or exercises in this book stimulating, children might find them stimulating too. The *Explorations* often suggest thinking that might be done by children, and other ideas in the book could also be the basis for work in elementary classrooms.

EXPLORATION: Choose something in this book that interests you and devise a means of communicating the matters it contains to children.

5. Above all else: Don't forget the main guideline I suggested earlier, that good teaching of literary pleasure replicates the practices of ardent readers and avoids anything that ardent readers don't usually do. So read literature yourself, both adult literature and children's literature. Think about your response to what you read, and discuss it with other people. As long as you keep on enjoying these activities, you'll learn more about them that you can pass on to children. And as long as you remember that the pleasure

of these activities is what you want to teach, you can devise classroom practices that teach literary pleasure by offering it themselves.

If this chapter has persuaded you that children can learn to take more pleasure in literature, then I urge you not to lose sight of that possibility as you make your way through the rest of this book. As I said earlier: I'm convinced there's nothing in the book that couldn't or shouldn't be shared with children—as long as the right teacher believes it to be possible and is ingenious enough to figure out how to do it.

WORKS CITED

Apple, Michael W., and Linda K. Christian-Smith. *The Politics of the Textbook*. New York and London: Routledge, 1991.

Bicknell, Steve. "On Not Teaching Literature and Reading." Tchudi 44–45.

Brown, Lola. "Rendering Literature Accessible." Corcoran and Evans 93–118.

Carter, Candy. "Engaging Students in Reading." Tchudi 57–60.

Chambers, Aidan. *Introducing Books to Children*. London: Heinemann, 1973.

Corcoran, Bill, and Emrys Evans, eds. *Readers, Texts, Teachers*. Upper Montclair: Boynton/ Cook, 1987.

Dias, Patrick X. "Literary Reading and Classroom Constraints." Langer, *Literature Instruction*, 131–162.

Everingham, Jo-Anne. "English and Reading in the New Media." Tchudi 67–71.

French, Fiona. *Snow White in New York*. Oxford: Oxford UP, 1986.

Frye, Northrop. *The Educated Imagination*. Bloomington: Indiana UP, 1964.

Glazer, Joan I. *Literature for Young Children*. 2nd ed. Columbus: Merrill, 1986.

Hart-Hewins, Linda, and Jan Wells. *Real Books for Reading*. Markham, Ontario: Pembroke, 1990.

Hendrickson, Linnea. "Literary Criticism as a Source of Teaching Ideas." *Children's Literature Association Quarterly* 9.4 (Winter 1984–1985): 202.

Huck, Charlotte S. *Children's Literature in the Elementary School*. 3rd ed., updated. New York: Holt, Rinehart and Winston, 1979.

Jobe, Ron. *Cultural Connections: Using Literature to Explore World Cultures with Children*. Markham, Ontario: Pembroke, 1993.

Kiefer, Barbara Z. "The Child and the Picture Book: Creating Live Circuits." *Children's Literature Association Quarterly* 11.2 (Summer 1986): 63–68.

Langer, Judith A., ed. *Literature Instruction: A Focus on Student Response*. Urbana: NCTE, 1992.

—— "Rethinking Literature Instruction." Langer, *Literature Instruction*, 35–53.

Landes, Sonia. "Picture Books as Literature." *Children's Literature Association Quarterly* 10.2 (Summer 1985): 51–54.

Lazar, Gillian. *Literature and Language Training: A Guide for Teachers and Trainers*. Cambridge: Cambridge UP, 1993.

Neumeyer, Peter. "Children's Literature in the English Department." *Children's Literature Association Quarterly* 12.3 (Fall, 1987): 146–150.

Petrosky, Anthony. "To Teach (Literature)?" Langer, *Literature Instruction*, 163–205.

Probst, Robert E. "Five Kinds of Literary Knowing." Langer, *Literature Instruction*, 54–77.

Protherough, Robert. *Developing Response to Fiction*. Milton Keynes, England and Philadelphia: Open UP, 1983.

Purves, Alan C., Theresa Rogers, and Anna A. Soter. *How Porcupines Make Love III: Readers, Texts, Cultures in the Response-Based Literature Classroom*. White Plains: Longman, 1995.

Sarland, Charles. *Young People Reading: Culture and Response*. Milton Keynes, England and Philadelphia: Open UP, 1991.

Sipe, Lawrence R. "Using Transformations of Traditional Stories: Making the Reading-Writing Connection." *The Reading Teacher* 47, 1 (September 1993): 18–26.

Stibbs, Andrew. *Reading Narrative as Literature: Signs of Life*. Milton Keynes, England and Philadelphia: Open UP, 1991.

Stott, Jon C. " 'It's Not What You Expect': Teaching Irony to Third Graders." *Children's Literature in Education* 13.4 (Winter 1982): 153–161.

——, ed. "Teaching Literary Criticism in the Elementary Grades: A Symposium." *Children and Their Literature: A Readings Book*. Ed. Jill P. May. West Lafayette: Children's Literature Association Publications, 1983. 160–172.

——. "Spiralled Sequence Story Curriculum: A Structuralist Approach to Teaching Fiction in the Elementary Grades." *Children's Literature in Education* 18.3 (Fall, 1987): 148–163.

Stratta, Leslie, and John Dixon. "Writing and Literature: Monitoring and Examining." Corcoran and Evans 174–196.

Sutherland, Zena, Dianne L. Monson, and May Hill Arbuthnot. *Children and Books*. 6th ed. Glenview: Scott, Foresman, 1981.

Tchudi, Stephen N., and others, eds. *English Teachers at Work: Ideas and Strategies from Five Countries*. Upper Montclair: Boynton/Cook Publishers, 1986.

Van Dongen, Richard. "Non-Fiction, History, and Literary Criticism in the Fifth Grade." *Children's Literature Association Quarterly* 12.4 (Winter 1987): 189–190.

Williams, Raymond. *The Long Revolution*. London: Chatto and Windus, 1961.

chapter 4

Strategies for Reading a Literary Text

SCHEMATA AND READING

According to the cognitive psychologist Ulric Neisser, "Not only reading, but also listening, feeling, and looking are skillful activities that occur over time. All of them depend upon pre-existing structures . . . called *schemata,* which direct perceptual activity and are modified as it occurs" (14). In chapter 2, I suggested that making something like the intended sense of "The Owl and the Pussy-cat" depends upon a reader having the pre-existing knowledge that made-up words and talking animals can exist in certain kinds of literature even though they don't exist elsewhere. These literary possibilities are examples of *schemata* (*schemata* is plural; one such pattern is a *schema*).

By developing schemata and then applying them to our new experiences, we perceive by means of what we have learned to expect. As Neisser says, "Because schemata are anticipations, they are the medium by which the past affects the future; information already acquired determines what will be picked up next" (22). In this chapter, I explore how our encounters with literary texts can provide us with schemata that can help us make sense of our responses to the new texts we encounter. I take what is usually identified as a *reader-response approach:* I focus on the process of reading and responding to texts, and how paying attention to that process can enrich our experience of them.

Since our understanding of any given text depends on the schemata we apply to it, reading is an interactive process. Like the instructions in a recipe, the words of a text are incomplete until somebody makes them into an experience by applying the schemata of information and skills learned earlier. A story or a poem doesn't exist until a reader makes it exist.

For knowledgeable readers, however, a text implies some of the particular skills and information needed to complete it. For such readers, for instance, the visual pattern "blue" evokes the idea of one particular color. So texts aren't as incomplete as they might seem. Just as proficient cooks know which tools and operations are implied by the words "beat egg whites into stiff peaks" in a soufflé recipe, proficient readers produce similar stories or poems from the limited information present in a printed text.

But different readers never produce the *same* stories or poems. What are stiff peaks for some cooks are not quite stiff enough for others. Because we all have different previous experiences of language and of life—different schemata—we all have different ideas about what the words we share mean. That's why each of us finds a different story in the same text.

While the existence of many versions of the same text is inevitable, however, not all of them are equally plausible—at least not to other readers. Some readings are no more plausible than the soufflé of a cook who did not in fact know what "stiff peaks" were and so hardly beat the eggs at all. While the resultant gooey dish might be interesting, it wouldn't satisfy others who were hungry for a soufflé.

In other words: As acts of communication, literary texts are communal. Authors write them in hopes that readers will share a sense of what they mean and become part of a community of mutual understanding. Learning to read is a matter of joining the community: developing the repertoire of information and strategies for meaning-making that authors assume their readers will possess.

Clearly, then, knowing how to derive meanings from a text with some confidence in their plausibility for others is a learned skill. But children's literature seems so simple from an adult point of view that we forget how many schemata are required to develop the intended understanding of it. A baby given a book for the first time doesn't know whether to taste it or tear it or toss it in the air. Only after experiencing a number of books and developing some schemata can the baby approach a new book in the anticipation that the experience it offers can be understood best by looking rather than by tasting.

And not just any kind of looking is required—it's a very specific kind, as we can discover if we try to forget our own assumptions and consider the aspects of books and reading that our schemata cause us to take for granted. We could not enjoy the stories in books before we learned to read them from front to back and to read the words on each page from left to right and from top to bottom.

EXPLORATION: Look (or invite children to look) at a book intended for babies or very young children. In addition to knowing the correct order in which to process the information, what repertoire of knowledge about both life and books does it imply? What strategies of meaning-making would a baby need in order to understand it?

As their experience of books and of life widens, children develop more subtle schemata: not only more information, but ways of connecting that information to references to it in texts that allow them to make greater sense of what they read and get deeper pleasure from it. As Shelby Anne Wolf and Shirley Brice Heath say, "It is not facts that make the enjoyment and interpretation of children's literature possible, but, instead, inferences that depend on the child's gradually acquired encyclopedic knowledge of sensations, emotional responses, and reasoned approaches" (86).

But that doesn't necessarily mean that children understand and enjoy either as much as is there to enjoy or as much as they might be capable of enjoying. Many children have a repertoire of knowledge and of literary strategies that don't match the ones demanded by the books they read.

That's a pity, because even simple children's texts can communicate rich experiences—but only to those equipped with the skills to understand them. There's nothing inherently wrong with applying oversimple meaning-making strategies to the books we read, with getting simple meanings out of rich texts. But such an approach has less potential to enlighten or to satisfy us than if we can respond with more complex strategies. It also prevents us from taking our place in the community of readers—entering fully into the dialogue with others that is one of the key pleasures offered by literature.

In the last chapter, I explored how children can be taught strategies—helped to develop schemata to make their reading as rewarding as possible. In this chapter, I survey schemata that might be taught to children, but that also might influence our own adult reading and understanding, specifically of children's literature.

GAPS IN TEXTS

As is true of recipes, most of what a written text is capable of communicating isn't actually on the page. What *is* there is the minimum amount of information needed to evoke a reader's knowledge of the ways it might be made meaningful. We make sense of the minimal information on the page by understanding that it is minimal, that it leaves *gaps,* but that our knowledge of a context—our reading strategies and our repertoire of information—can tell us how to fill those gaps.

Anyone who reads knows how to fill gaps, and most of the time we do it in a more-or-less unconscious manner. For instance, when we see the visual symbols "a" and "x" and understand without much conscious thought how to turn them into a verbal symbol, the word "ax," and then realize what object that word stands for, we are filling in gaps. A gap is *any* aspect of a text that a reader makes sense of by providing knowledge from a pre-existing repertoire.

If we possess expertise in filling gaps, we can turn a small amount of information into a surprisingly rich experience. The pages that follow explore how, by considering one highly popular children's novel, E. B. White's *Charlotte's Web,* as an example. I've chosen to concentrate on just one book in order to reveal the shifting perspectives offered by the use of different strategies. I don't recommend this sort of extremely close analysis of a text as a model of what all readers ought always to be doing as they read literature, even though I find myself that doing it can be a real pleasure, especially when I've encountered a text I admire and want to understand better. But I suspect that for most of us most often, the most enjoyable reading experiences are those we have once we've learned the gap-filling strategies like the ones I outline here, and then perform them more or less unconsciously as we make our way through texts. What follows, then, is my attempt to be aware of the operations a reader might be performing in the act of reading without particularly being aware of it.

Charlotte's Web begins this way:

> "Where's Papa going with that ax?" said Fern to her mother as they were setting the table for breakfast.

Even if we can understand the basic meaning of the words, we need a repertoire of knowledge of conventional behavior to fill in the many gaps here. Using that repertoire, we might realize the following:

- That Fern is called "her," and so must be female. (Note that we do not yet know if she is human—our repertoire for children's literature might include the possibility that she is a talking animal.)
- That "setting" the table is the act of placing dishes and cutlery on it, and that "breakfast" is a meal eaten in the morning.
- That "Papa" is probably not a person's name, but a conventional designation for a father most often used by his children; so the word tells us that Papa is most likely Fern's father. Furthermore, "Papa" is more old-fashioned than "Dad." Perhaps the story takes place some time ago.
- That the directness and tone of the question implies an easy, open relationship between Fern and her mother; there's no reticence or fear of being considered disobedient.
- That, given the context of the rest of the sentence, the one surprising element is the ax—an implement we don't expect to appear during breakfast. Its presence might make us think about its customary uses, and its oddity evokes questions about what it might be used for here.

The few words of this sentence have implied much that they haven't actually said—for those who know how to identify gaps and have the information to fill them in and knowledge of how to do so.

EXPLORATION: Consider (or invite children to consider) how another section of *Charlotte's Web* or another children's text contains gaps that require a repertoire of contextual knowledge.

As we continue reading past the opening, we can fill in more gaps. When Mother says that Papa is "out to the hoghouse," we can understand that the events are probably taking place on a farm. And when Mother answers Fern's question about the ax with the statement that a runt was born, we can fill in another sort of gap: an idea or even a picture of what Papa might do with the ax. The author doesn't need to provide a literal picture of Papa taking an ax to the runt; from the information White gives, we can make an inference and imagine the scene.

In addition to filling in gaps that relate to the setting and the situation, astute readers will make use of other strategies. One is to assume that, because this is the beginning of a novel, what happens here will be of significance for what follows. Either Fern, or her father or mother, or the ax, will continue to be important, and we will look for further information to tell us which of them it might be. If we expect children's literature to concern children, then we might use the soon-provided information that Fern is eight years old not only to fill in a gap and specify that Fern is a child, but also, to guess that the story will revolve around her.

In making predictions as we read, we're using the basic strategy we apply to all stories: the idea that they are in some way complete, that everything in them relates in some way to their overall effect. In other words, we assume that stories have *consistency* of direction and purpose, and we build our sense of what that consistency might be. So when we're suddenly told, later on the first page, "Fern pushed a chair out of the way and ran outdoors," we aren't likely to assume that she has suddenly seen her best friend through the window. Instead, we probably assume that her actions relate to what we have heard already—that she wants to stop her father from killing the runt. That turns out to be the case—not surprisingly, for the text has neither mentioned nor implied a friend in the yard, but it *has* made Papa's actions important.

But the next sentence, "The grass was wet and the earth smelled of spring-time," seems to be unrelated to what has gone before. To make sense of this new information, I find myself thinking about how the statement might fit into what I know already: Why is it suddenly important to hear about the grass and the earth? I might simply assume that the grass's moisture and the earth's fragrance are what Fern herself perceived at this moment, even though the text doesn't say so. In fact, if I'm right that she's concerned about the runt pig, then she isn't likely to notice the grass or the earth. I might guess that the author mentions the grass and the earth for other reasons. Perhaps he wants to confirm what those who know when pigs usually litter have guessed already, that the book is set in spring. Or perhaps it is going to be important that it rained recently. Or perhaps he simply wants to focus our attention on the way the world looks and smells for reasons that will become apparent later.

As it happens, we hear nothing further about rain, and so I have to dismiss the idea that rain will be a significant aspect of the events to follow. But the novel as a whole turns out to focus on sensuous impressions and express appreciation for what White eventually calls "the smell of manure, and the glory of everything" (183). One conjecture is right, the others wrong. As we read, we constantly imagine reasons for details we learn about that we either dismiss and forget or else remember and build on. And we formulate questions about what we've read so far that we assume the text itself will answer later. We consciously or unconsciously process information such as the fact that the grass was wet, in a way that builds consistency.

I've talked so much about the sentence about the grass because it surprised me. The previous conversation about breakfast and a runt didn't prepare me for a description of outdoor sights and smells. The unexpectedness of this sentence suggests one of the basic strategies demanded by works of fiction: the way in which at any given point in our reading of text we build consistency out of what we know so far, and thus create a schemata, or set of expectations, for what follows—and then are surprised by something we hadn't expected and so must build a new consistency. Each new bit of information not only adds to but changes our understanding of all the former ones, so that, in the most interesting texts, we are continually forced to reconsider everything we knew before.

This basic pattern of expectation and surprise begins long before we get to a sentence like the one in *Charlotte's Web* about the grass. As soon as we see a book's cover, our context of previous knowledge leads us to develop expectations of what we'll find inside.

EXPLORATION: Choose any children's book you haven't read before. Record (or invite children to record) the changing ideas and expectations you develop as you consider your general impression of its appearance, your response to its title and the name of its author, to the cover illustration, to the words on the back cover, and so on. Describe the expectations you've developed before you actually begin to read the text. Then explore how the text itself either confirms or contradicts those expectations.

FILLING IN THE GAPS: STRATEGIES FOR BUILDING CONSISTENCY

There are six major ways in which competent readers conventionally build consistency from the information they gather as they work their way through a literary text: concretization, character, plot, theme, structure, and focalization. While these are sometimes identified as the elements of literary texts, they are actually elements of a competent reader's repertoire of strategies for responding to texts: They are apparent only to those readers who have learned to look for them. Our knowledge of each of these strategies, individually and all together, allows us to find pleasing and meaningful patterns in the literary texts we read. What follows is an examination of each of these six strategies.

Concretization

As we make our way through a text, the words often describe how people or objects look or sound or smell. We can enrich our experience and increase our understanding by forming mental pictures: by imagining what is being described as exactly as the words of the text allow us to. This process is what theorists of reader-response call *concretization*—an ugly word, but a useful concept.

As we read *Charlotte's Web,* we can concretize it. Instead of just recording the information, "The grass was wet and the earth smelled of springtime," we can engage our own previous experience of wet grass and springtime smells, and thus allow the text to evoke specific sensory memories. Doing so has a number of benefits.

The most basic and most important of these is the pleasure offered by the act of imagining itself. This is a threefold pleasure. First, there's the pleasure of the creative act—the process of turning words into pictures and sounds, of making them come alive inside our minds. Second, there's the pleasure of the pictures we imagine: If we have paid careful attention to what the text has told us, those pictures are likely to be delightfully unlike anything we might have imagined on our own without reading the text, and just as delightfully unlike anyone else's concretization of the same text. They can offer us the same kind of pleasure we might get from looking at pictures in an art gallery—or for that matter, the illustrations in a children's picture book; in chapter 11, I consider the relationship between the pictures we concretize from words and the actual illustration in a picture book. Third, there's the pleasure of exploring what we have concretized—finding our own words to describe it and thinking about the distinct nature of our own reading strategies.

EXPLORATION: Choose (or invite children to choose) a description of a place or person from *Charlotte's Web* or another text for children. Concretize it, and then try to find the words to describe your concretization as exactly as you can. What do you imagine yourself seeing, hearing, smelling? In how much detail? Is it like watching a movie, or like experiencing real-life events? Where do you imagine yourself in relation to what you imagine seeing and hearing: in the scene, or at some distance from it and observing it? What might your concretization tell you about yourself as a reader?

In my experience, concretization is a skill often possessed by children. In fact, imagining as literally and completely as possible the world and the people a text describes is the only way that many children know of building consistency from the texts they read. It's for this reason, I think, that so many children and other inexperienced readers worry about the logic and coherence of the worlds that texts enable them to concretize—why they so often get angry when there are inconsistent details in descriptions of place and people or confusions in the sequence of events.

But as I've learned from years of teaching college-level introductory literature courses, concretization is a skill that a lot of adults have forgotten. Many of us have been taught to focus so much on using texts as sources of factual knowledge or abstract meaning that we ignore the potential they have for allowing us to imagine sights and smells and sounds—to concentrate on the specific, literal experiences they evoke. That's a pity. Not only does it deprive us of a source of pleasure, but it prevents us from understanding the subtle richness of the texts we read.

Beyond the inherent pleasure it offers, concretization can be a productive means of building a consistent understanding of the significance of a text. Speaking of descriptions of characters, Wolfgang Iser says, "Our mental images . . . illuminate the character, not as an object, but as a bearer of meaning. Even if we are given a detailed description of a character's appearance, we tend not to regard it as pure description, but try and conceive what is actually to be communicated through it" (138). Once we've concretized a specific description of a place or a person, then, we can learn much about the focus and meaning of a text by considering the nature of the concretization.

EXPLORATIONS: (1) Consider a description and your concretization of it. Which physical qualities have the words of the text invited you to emphasize, which ones have been left out altogether, and what does that suggest about the thrust and meaning of the text as a whole?

(2) An anonymous reader asked by the publisher to review an earlier draft of *Pleasures* wrote:

> The process of concretization explains why some people object to film versions of novels. Films force someone else's concretization upon us. This has both beneficial and deleterious effects: the recent film of *Little Women* helped me concretize 19th-century New England, but I hated how the casting affected my image and idea of the characters.

Watch a film of a novel you've read, and consider its concretization in relation to your own. What differing meanings are implied by each?

In *Charlotte's Web,* the sentence about the grass tells us about its wetness but not what color it is or how high it is. The focus is on how it would feel to walk through, not on how beautiful it looks—a focus confirmed when the next sentence tells us that Fern's sneakers are sopping. Throughout the book, in fact, descriptions invite readers to dwell on the sensations of sensuous experience—on what it feels like to be in certain places and smell certain smells; and that defines the mood of the book. I'll say more later in this chapter about the meanings that might emerge from that focus.

Character

Character is what we discover in literature when we look for information about the personalities of the people the text describes. We assume that the consistency (and central significance) of a text depends on the ways in which it allows us to see the consistency in (and significance of) the motivations of those people—and of human nature in general. In considering the character of Fern or Wilbur or Charlotte, for instance, we can explore not just how *Charlotte's Web* holds together but also how and why people in general behave as they do, how the threat of death creates a love of life, how friendship makes existence meaningful.

In doing this kind of reading, we assume that literature mirrors life, that it is "realistic." Consequently, the limited information that stories provide about their characters is, like the limited information we have about the people we meet, merely the tip of an iceberg of more detailed information about them. As we read about how characters look and what they do, we focus on what that information implies about the kinds of people they are. We can use our knowledge of the way people usually behave to guess further about the characters' motivations, their past, and even what they might do after the end of the story.

Using this strategy, we might explain Fern's concern for the runt pig by suggesting that her grandmother might have recently died; or later, we might try to figure out whether her relationship with Henry Fussy will last after the book is over. Reading in this way implies that fiction is a kind of gossip: It assumes that authors tell us a little bit about the characters they describe so that we can have the fun of guessing about all the aspects of character and experience they do not tell us about.

Guessing about literary characters allows us to see how their actions match what we assume to be true about human behavior. But like gossip, it has its dangers: It can misrepresent people by fitting them into categories we already possess. If we want the pleasure of perceiving something more than or something different from our everyday experience of human nature, we have to work with a different assumption: that authors carefully select what they choose to tell us, and that their choices—both what they tell and what they choose not to tell—define what they wish us to understand.

For instance, White doesn't tell us that Fern's grandmother died or how long Fern will stay with Henry. If we assume that these matters aren't important to his conception of Fern, we can build consistency out of what he *has* told us, and learn something about *his* conceptions of human behavior. And if we become conscious that he hasn't provided certain information that we expected, we can derive new understanding by thinking about *why* it isn't there.

EXPLORATION: In *Charlotte's Web,* why might the author not have told us whether Fern's relationship with Henry will last?

Theorists divide characters into two types: *flat* or *round*. The flat ones, such as, say, Fern's exuberantly violent brother Avery in *Charlotte's Web,* have only one or two readily identifiable traits, and don't ever change. The round ones are more complex and tend to *develop*—to change as a story unfolds. Characters can develop in two ways: A text can provide new information about a character that causes readers to see the character differently and in more depth, or the events of the story can actually change characters, make them more complicated. In *Charlotte's Web,* Charlotte represents the first kind of development and Fern the second; in both cases, however, the development might be a signal to readers to think about what character traits are valuable and worth trying to develop in themselves. There's more about this kind of message later in this chapter, in the section on themes.

Plot

Plot is the sequence of events that make up a story. It is what we discover in literature when we look for information about how what happens forms a meaningful pattern. In approaching a story, we assume that there will be a consistent pattern of causes and effects underlying actions, through which the central significance of the story is revealed. This in turn allows us to understand how what happens in real life also has a history that gives it meaning. In this way, plot and character are closely related: Plot is the sequence of actions that reveal character; character reveals the motivations that drive the events of a plot.

If we assume that plot forms the basic pattern of *Charlotte's Web,* then, we can see how Fern's question about the ax leads her mother to provide her with the information that causes Fern to confront her father about the runt, how her concern saves the runt, and how that action eventually leads to her involvement with the animals in the barn. We see that events have consequences and how causes create effects.

In focusing on plot, our interest is continually on what happens next, on how each event develops from and sums up what went before. We are made to wonder where Papa *is* going with that ax; and when we find out, the answer makes us wonder how Fern will react to the information; and when we find that out, we wonder what she will do about it. Because each action is incomplete, we are likely to wonder about its result; and each action both completes the previous one and raises new questions about the future. This chain is what we call *suspense.*

The questions that texts raise for us range from relatively minor ones answered almost immediately to major ones that might not be answered for many chapters. In *Charlotte's Web,* we soon find out where Papa's going with that ax. It takes a little longer for White to answer the question of what Fern might do about it, and much longer before we get the final answer to the even larger question Papa soon raises about what effect raising a pig will have on Fern's life. In my experience, the stories that most involve readers do so through a carefully orchestrated interplay of questions raised, of answers given, and of answers not given yet. This interweaving of information given and information deferred encourages readers to want answers, then gives us enough to tantalize us, and holds back enough to keep us reading.

EXPLORATION: As you read through a story or novel, try to be aware (or invite children to be aware) of the questions it causes you to ask, and when they are answered. How does the raising of questions and giving of answers help to maintain your interest?

In building suspense, a well-constructed plot captures and maintains our attention until the story comes to an end. It's hard to say exactly *why* such a patterning of events creates pleasure. We may enjoy it simply because it organizes experience into a recognizable or meaningful shape—provides the ordering of random human experience that we expect and enjoy in most works of art. Robert Scholes suggests a more specific reason for our enjoyment of plots when he considers the most basic plot pattern: This is a series of actions organized to encourage our gradually increasing involvement until the events reach a culminating point at which our interest is most intense—a *climax*—and then quickly come to an end. Scholes calls this the "*orgastic pattern* of fiction" (26, italics added) and suggests that it gives us pleasure because it mirrors a basic human pleasure: the pattern of sexual excitement and fulfillment. In a consideration of feminist approaches to literature in chapter 7, I discuss the male bias Scholes might be expressing here: Female sexuality may manifest itself in different patterns. Nevertheless, good plots do provide a two fold pleasure—first, the pleasure of incompleteness, the tension of delaying and anticipating completion; and second, the pleasure of the completion.

In *Charlotte's Web*, for instance, readers hope for a climactic moment at which Charlotte's scheme will work and Wilbur will be saved, and eventually we savor that moment. But our pleasure in the anticipation of the climax increases during the events that delay it: the efforts to get all the right animals to the fair, the discovery there of a pig much larger than Wilbur, and so on.

Some plots are pleasurably suspenseful because we can't figure out what will happen next. But some plots are pleasurable simply because we've read similar stories already and therefore *can* guess what will happen next. In the first case, we are enjoying the excitement of that which is strange to us; in the second, we have the satisfaction of recognizing the familiar. In order to experience this satisfaction, we need a repertoire of plots. Writers often expect us to bring such patterns into play as we try to make sense of their stories. As we'll see, children's fiction makes use of a number of story patterns—cumulative tales, fables, wish-fulfilment fantasies in which underdogs triumph, *home/away/home* stories. I discuss the *story patterns* most common in children's literature further in chapter 8.

Even our pleasure in the unfamiliar depends on our knowledge of the familiar. For instance, we couldn't enjoy the specific humor of a story like Robert Munsch's *Paperbag Princess,* in which a princess rescues a prince from a dragon, unless we knew the conventional pattern it diverges from. And we couldn't appreciate the ingenuity of the way in which Charlotte communicates to humans if we didn't understand the way in which it diverges from the forms of communication found in more conventional stories about talking animals.

Plots form a spectrum between total familiarity and total strangeness. At one end of the spectrum are formula mysteries and romances that offer the pleasures of familiarity with very little surprise. Plots of this sort usually please readers only until they become familiar enough with the formula to be bored by it—that is, until they can use their knowledge of the formula to unlock the pleasures of less formulaic works. At the other end of the spectrum are totally innovative plots that seem to have no relationship to our repertoire of plot patterns. Ideally, I believe, readers can have the adaptability to enjoy stories all across the spectrum.

Theme

Teachers often ask elementary school students, "What is the author's message or purpose?" University students frequently try to determine the "hidden meaning" of a text. Both are building consistency in a literary text by understanding its central idea or *theme*.

Themes are meanings, and the search for meaning is a productive strategy to apply to literature. Indeed, it may be the *only* strategy: All the ways in which we think about texts are really only different ways of understanding their meanings. Furthermore, these meanings provide readers with insights into their own lives. Charlotte Huck asserts that "the literary or artistic craft of a book is not as important as its message" (705), and many politically conscious literary critics might agree with her: Marxist and feminist critics, for instance, focus on the validity of the messages literary texts imply. As I try to show in chapter 7, a consideration of the nature of these messages and of the subtlety with which they are conveyed can enrich our response to literature.

The Dangers in Message Hunting.   Unfortunately, many readers approach texts with the idea that their themes or messages can be easily identified and stated in a few words—"the moral of the story." For instance, many readers suggest that the theme of *Charlotte's Web* is the joy of friendship. Reading in this way directs attention away from the more immediate pleasures of a text: away from language, away from the evocation of vivid pictures and the creation of pleasing patterns and structures—and therefore, away from other, deeper kinds of meaning the text might imply.

Readers may fall into this trap because trying to identify easily expressed general themes requires a strategy quite different from that used in thinking about other elements of a text. As we think about character or plot, for instance, we examine how authors evoke the people and events of the story; we are taking pleasure in the immediate experience of reading itself, in our awareness of how a text is unfolding, and in our perception of the ways in which it forces us to fill its gaps. And our awareness of that process becomes part of our effort to obtain meaning from the text, so that our perceptions of meaning are richer. But when we look for a specific theme, we must defer our attempt to understand the message until we've finished reading the text. Instead of focusing on the process of perceiving and thinking that a text offers as we experience it, we must consider only the ideas the entire story has made us think of *after* we've experienced it. That limits both our enjoyment of and our perception of a text's subtleties.

In focusing exclusively on themes as messages for ourselves, we assume that all stories are *parables* or *fables*. These are stories that are not really about the characters in them, but about ourselves: Their characters represent general human behavior in order to teach us specific truths that can govern our own future actions.

When Jesus tells the parable of the Good Samaritan or Aesop tells the fable of the fox and the grapes, the storyteller doesn't expect us to be interested in what the characters are wearing or how they feel, but to think about how their actions imply specific messages about ourselves.

Adults often assume that all children's stories are fables or should be read as fables. For instance, Huck says that "the theme of a book reveals the author's purpose in writing the story" (8). Huck reveals the extent to which she believes themes are messages for readers by adding, "The theme of a story should be worth imparting to young people and be based upon justice and integrity. Sound moral and ethical principles should prevail" (8). Because it's so prevalent in discussions of children's literature, this particular strategy of consistency building needs detailed consideration.

If we view *Charlotte's Web* as a fable or a parable, we assume that it isn't really about what happens to a pig and a spider. Instead, it's about how the experiences of the pig and the spider can teach us how to act in our own lives. Reading it this way can be stimulating, but it's likely to deprive us of pleasurable insights into pigs and spiders.

Aesop's fables usually end with an explicit statement of a moral. But these stories have been retold by many different people, and Joanne Lynn points out that "those who retell the fables always manage to find 'morals' that mirror their own values" (6). When the printer William Caxton first published the fables in English in the fifteenth century, he said that the story of the fox and the grapes showed that the fox was *wise* not to want what he couldn't have. In more recent versions the fox's behavior is neither wise nor admirable but shallowly self-deceptive; the moral is something like, "It's easy to despise what we can't have." It seems that if we assume a story is a parable or a fable, the presence of a moral is so important that almost any one will do. Because we expect a moral or a message, we're sure to find one.

In doing so, we reveal the degree to which messages or themes are separate from the texts we relate them to. In reading for theme, we tend to confirm our own preconceived ideas and values: to take ideas from outside the text and assume that they are inside it. That prevents us from becoming conscious of ideas and values different from our own.

Nevertheless, because many adults assume that children's literature has the main purpose of educating its audience, many children's books *are* fables, and the most common meaning-making strategy that we teach children is to search for morals, messages, or themes. This strategy consists of two parts: first *identification,* and then *manipulation.*

Identification is the perception that a character in a work of literature is like oneself. Many of the characters of children's literature are young, small, concerned with testing their abilities or defying their elders—enough like many of their readers to make identification possible. Identification is so basic to the strategy of reading stories as fables that some adults encourage children to use the technique even when it isn't required by a text. "Look," we say to a young child as we finish reading a story about the adventures of a bunny, "Now the bunny is tired and ready to fall asleep, *just like you.*"

After identification comes *manipulation.* If you have seen yourself as the bunny, then something in the story will happen to the bunny that will teach you a lesson about yourself. For instance, in Munro Leaf's *Noodle,* children are obviously expected to identify with Noodle, a dachshund who finds his shortness bothersome; it prevents him from digging holes easily. When a dog fairy agrees to grant Noodle's wish to be different, Noodle considers some other possibilities but finally decides to stay the way he is. Young readers are meant to see his decision as a message about themselves: The dog fairy explicitly asserts that Noodle's wish is a wise one. The logic here goes like this:

1. You are short, like the dog.
2. It's wise for the dog to accept its size.
3. Therefore, it's wise for you to accept your size.

But a mature dachshund is stuck with its size and shape and had better learn to be content with it. Children grow and change, and don't need to have such firmly entrenched attitudes of acceptance. Numerous other children's stories use the process of identification and manipulation to reach similarly illogical conclusions.

Even if it is sometimes misleading, the process of identification and manipulation can be an effective teaching device. But if assuming that all stories are fables and concentrating on finding the message in them is the *only* strategy we offer young readers for making sense of stories, then we will have seriously limited their ability to respond to literature. But if we provide them with a wider repertoire of consistency-building strategies and encourage them to be flexible in their use of them, they'll be able to distinguish between texts that are fables and those that aren't, and apply the appropriate consistency-building strategies to each.

EXPLORATION: Try (or invite children to try) to determine which ones of a random selection of children's stories and poems seem to be intended to be read as fables and which ones might not be so intended. How might or might not the strategy of looking for themes limit or distort a reader's perception of these texts?

Structure: Words, Images, Ideas

As we read, we may notice that certain words or descriptions or actions remind us of others we came across earlier in the text. In *Charlotte's Web,* for instance, we might notice how often White presents us with descriptions of places and that these descriptions consist of lists of objects. Early on, the description of Zuckerman's barn includes a list of the smells in it: "It smelled of hay and it smelled of manure. It smelled of the perspiration of tired horses and the wonderful sweet breath of patient cows" (13). A few pages later there is another list of smells, this time of Wilbur's food: "The smell was delicious—warm milk, potato skins, wheat middlings, Kellogg's Corn Flakes, and a popover left from the Zuckermans' breakfast" (22). Once we notice the similarity of these passages, we can realize how often lists occur throughout the book, and we can build consistency by probing the implications of the pattern they create. In doing so, we use the strategy of exploring structure.

Structure refers to the way that the various parts of a text relate to each other and form patterns. It depends to a great extent on repetition and variations of the same or similar elements. In chapter 10, I describe how the structure of nursery rhymes and many other poems is built on repetition and variations of similar sounds and similar-sounding words, sometimes so much so that the pattern of rhythm and rhyme is more significant than the plot or the message.

Repeated words can create repeated pictures or images for readers to concretize. The words that describe food in *Charlotte's Web* create such pictures. There are Wilbur's "skim milk, crusts, middlings, bits of doughnuts, wheat cakes with drops of maple syrup sticking to them, potato skins, leftover custard pudding with raisins, and bits of Shredded Wheat" (25). There are Charlotte's "flies, bugs, grasshoppers, choice beetles, moths, butterflies, tasty cockroaches, gnats, midges, daddy longlegs, centipedes, mosquitoes, crickets" (39). There are Templeton the rat's "popcorn fragments, frozen custard dribblings, candied apples abandoned by tired children, sugar fluff crystals, salted almonds, popsicles, partially gnawed ice cream cones, and the wooden sticks of lollypops" (123).

Once we notice how often such images appear, we can both enjoy the rhythmic pattern their recurrence produces and build consistency by seeing how they make the book meaningful. These lists all ask us to experience the sensuous pleasure provided by what we would usually think of as ugly or useless: bugs and garbage. The idea that we should accept all things, including the apparently bad things like garbage or bugs or death, as part of the glory that is the world in which we live, is central to the novel—one of its major themes.

But the lists aren't there merely to make us conscious of that message: to some degree, the message is there to create a well-organized structure. The message is neither unusual nor profound: Many writers have expressed the same idea in fewer words. It's the way White uses that message as the basis for a complex structure built around descriptive lists, a repeating and varying rhythm of images and ideas, that, for me at least, makes *Charlotte's Web* such a rewarding reading experience.

Point of View and Focalization: Speakers and Narrators

Implied Speakers.   In chapter 2 I talked about the implied reader: someone with a distinct set of interests and skills whom we are asked to become as we read a text. If there are implied readers, then it's logical to assume that there are also *implied speakers,* whose personalities are suggested by the words of texts. Indeed, it's so logical I suspect most of us take it for granted. But as Wolf and Heath say of young children, "Awareness that there exists a speaker other than the parent reader or the pictured characters in the book is by no means a trivial accomplishment, since the child must realize that the words on the page not only do not originate with either the parent or the storybook character but come from an unseen source" (66).

Furthermore, just as the readers implied by texts are rarely equivalent to the people who read those texts, the speakers implied by texts are rarely equivalent to the people who write them. In fact, authors carefully control the image their texts present of just who it is that is speaking, in the knowledge that different kinds of speakers provide different sorts of pleasure.

Versions of fairy tales offer a clear example of how texts can imply the personalities of different sorts of speakers. The person telling the story in Charles Perrault's seventeenth-century version of "Sleeping Beauty" is witty and urbane, and a little supercilious about the unsophisticated qualities of this peasant's tale. Finally, the teller totally undercuts the story by declaring that its moral is this nasty judgment upon women in general:

> It seems only logical that a woman should be willing to wait some time for a husband who's rich, gallant and kind. But not many women nowadays would be patient enough to wait for a hundred years. So even though the story shows us that waiting can be a good thing, I'm afraid most young women today yearn too strongly for the joys of marriage to pay much attention to that. (Translation mine)

The speaker of E. Nesbit's version implies a quite different relationship with the reader. This storyteller is a chatty gossip who takes us into her confidence, dwells lovingly on details of clothing and food, and turns the entire story into advice about etiquette:

> Whenever you give a christening party you must always remember to ask all the most disagreeable people you know. It is very dangerous to neglect this simple precaution. Nearly all the misfortunes which happen to princesses come from their relations having forgotten to invite some nasty old fairy or other to their christenings. This was what happened in the case of the Sleeping Beauty. (88)

Since the characters of speakers implied by texts clearly suggest attitudes to the stories they tell, we can gain pleasure and build consistency by trying to perceive who they are.

EXPLORATION: Choose (or invite children to choose) a story or novel, and try to determine what the character, attitudes, and interests of its implied speaker are. In what ways does the text imply these qualities, and how do they affect your understanding and enjoyment of the story?

First-Person and Third-Person Narrators.   The speakers implied by texts reveal attitudes not only through their tone and their choices of what is significant or noteworthy in the stories they tell, but also in terms of their relationship to the events they describe. A *first-person* narrator reports from his or her own subjective point of view events that he or she has personally experienced. For instance, the main character in Judy Blume's *Are You There God? It's Me, Margaret* speaks directly to readers as she tells her own story. On the other hand, many narratives are in the *third person;* the person who tells the story is someone separate from the events. (In the language of grammar, the first person is "I" or "we"; the third person "he," "she," "it," or "they.")

Sometimes a third-person narrator is an outside observer who reports what happens but doesn't know what the individual characters think about the events. This tends to be what happens in the Brothers Grimm versions of fairy tales, in which we can only guess about what the characters think from what we are told of their actions. Sometimes, though, third-person narrators are *omniscient.* They know the thoughts of some or all of the characters, and sometimes they may even know more about the characters' feelings than the characters themselves are willing to acknowledge.

Sometimes, also, third-person narrators are similar to first-person narrators: While they are theoretically objective in describing all the characters, in fact they know the thoughts of only one character, and present events as that character would see and understand them. Narratives of this sort combine the subjective viewpoint of the first person with the objective distance of the third person.

This last sort of narrative suggests how complex storytelling can become: The person who tells us the story, the narrator, may not be the person whose point of view we are being shown—the person who sees the events being described. Furthermore, the person from whose viewpoint we see the events of a story may change even while the same narrative voice continues.

For instance, *Charlotte's Web* has a third-person narrator. Sometimes this narrator merely reports what a careful outside observer would see. He describes how Fern first meets the pig Wilbur without saying how she feels about it: "Then she lifted the lid of the carton. There, inside, looking up at her, was the newborn pig. It was a white one" (4). Sometimes, however, this narrator describes how the characters feel; a few pages later, for instance, he reports that Fern is "thinking what a blissful world it was" (7).

To account for such possibilities, and to acknowledge the difference between who speaks and who sees, narrative theorists have invented the term *focalization:* It refers to who *sees* the events being described rather than to who *tells* about them. If we notice the changes in focalization in *Charlotte's Web*—when the narrator reports objectively and when he chooses instead to convey characters' feelings—we can take pleasure from the careful way White uses focalization both to control our understanding of and attitude toward the events described and to create moments of suspense—raise questions and offer answers by choosing whether or not to tell us what characters might be feeling or thinking.

Both the point of view from which a story is told and the way in which its events are focalized affect how we understand it. "Sleeping Beauty" would be a different story if told by the neglected fairy rather than by a third-person narrator. It would be a different story again if told by a third-person narrator but focalized through the neglected fairy. And it would be yet a different story if told by, or described as it would be seen and understood by, the Prince. Jon Sciezska takes advantage of the effect of a different point of view in *The True Story of the 3 Little Pigs by A. Wolf.*

EXPLORATION: Explore the effects of point of view and focalization by considering how a story would be different if told by a different narrator or focalized through a different character. Choose (or invite children to choose) a story, and rewrite it. Tell a first-person narration from an omniscient narrator's viewpoint, or focalize the events as viewed by various characters. How do these different perspectives make the story different?

When we see the events of a story as understood by an outside observer, we tend not to get too caught up in the specific experience of any one of the characters, but to focus on the meaning of the action rather than on the way individual characters respond to the action. On the other hand, in *Are You There God?* we see things as Margaret understands them, and for many readers, much of the pleasure of the novel derives from their being able to empathize with her responses to the situations she describes.

The basic strategy required in reading the story of *Are You There God?* as Margaret tells it is to feel sympathy with her interpretation of her story. Such sympathy is often difficult for adult readers, who tend to approach the novel with broader experience than Margaret has and readers who identify with her have had, and who tend to have more sophisticated expectations of fiction and more sophisticated strategies for reading it. For sophisticated readers, the central pleasure of first-person narratives is often an ability to see through them, to come to an understanding of the events being told that differs from the way in which the narrator perceives them; and writers of such narrations often leave clues that clearly imply the inaccuracy of the words we read. So someone who reads *Are You There God?* with knowledge of the strategies required to read more sophisticated fictions may well see Margaret as a self-pitying and self-indulgent little brat, and believe that Blume has managed to create a "self-portrait" of a typical teenager that cleverly reveals the limited vision of adolescents.

But as a writer for children, Blume probably wanted her readers to see Margaret's view of things as the correct one. Ideally, we ought to have a repertoire of strategies broad enough to cope with non-ironic first-person narratives as well as more ironic ones—such as, for instance, the text of Ellen Raskin's picture book *Nothing Ever Happens on My Block.* Here, a desperately egocentric narrator's first-person report of his boring life is cleverly undercut by pictures of interesting events taking place behind his back. What he understands and says is not the whole truth. While intended for an audience younger than that of Blume's novel, this book demands what seems to be a more sophisticated strategy.

BUILDING THE CONSISTENCY OF TEXTS AS A WHOLE

Charlotte's Web has rich descriptions, intriguing characters, a suspenseful plot, interesting themes, a complex structure, and variable focalizations. As I hope I've shown, using the strategies that allow us to explore each of them can provide the satisfaction of a sense of consistency. But we won't achieve the full pleasure the book has the potential to offer unless we put the different strategies into play at the same time. If, as we read a text, we build all six kinds of consistency at once, we can enjoy each one on its own and also as they undercut and amplify each other in a complex interweaving.

I said earlier that structure refers to the way that the parts of a text relate to one another, and I explored the structural patterns created by words and by images. But plots also have a structure, a pattern of suspense that leads to a climax; and the structure created by patterns of words and images is different from and cuts across the plot structure. As we read a book, in fact, we're likely to find our attention shifting from one to the other: from the question "what happens next" to a descriptive passage that might evoke earlier descriptions and point us backward rather than forward.

In other words, what happens next *as we read* is not necessarily the next incident in a linear sequence of events. It may be a description of a barn or a report of a character's memories. So stories tend to have two plots at once: the series of actions that make up the events the story narrates and the series of actions that make up the narration of those events.

At the beginning of *Charlotte's Web,* for instance, we learn that Fern hears about the potential death of the runt pig while setting the table for breakfast and rushes outside to plead for the pig's life. These are the events of the story. But we hear about these events by means of a conversation between Fern and her mother, a report of how Fern rushes outside, a description of the grass, and another conversation between Fern and her father. These conversations, reports, and descriptions are the actions of the telling of the story—what theorists of narrative call the *discourse.*

Discourse

The discourse—how a story is told—affects how we understand the events being described. Sometimes, as in the case of flashbacks, the actions of the discourse don't come in the same order as the actions of the story. In *Charlotte's Web,* for instance, we hear at breakfast that the pigs were born the night before, and thus less emphasis is placed on the birth than if the book began by describing it. White's discourse makes it clear that the birth is less important than Fern's response to it.

The discourse can sum up a number of events in a few words, or occupy many pages with a minute description of one specific event. Most readers would respond to *Charlotte's Web* quite differently if White had simply said, "Once upon a time a girl named Fern was setting the table for breakfast when she heard that her father was about to kill a runt pig. She rushed out to the barn and tried to stop him."

EXPLORATION: Is that statement true? Explore whether your response to this alternative beginning to *Charlotte's Web* would be different from your response to the actual beginning, and if so, how.

Furthermore, the discourse can include many things in addition to the basic events of the story: descriptions of people and places, summaries of character, detailed records of what characters are thinking. It can switch from information about characters to a focus on images, and from descriptions back to actions, in a way that demands our own flexible use of different consistency-building strategies.

Trajectory

The children's novelist Jill Paton Walsh speaks of one particular aspect of the discourse as a *trajectory:* "the route chosen by the author through his material. It is the action of a book, considered not as the movement of paraphrasable events in that book but as the movement of the author's exposition and the reader's experience of it" (187–188). Paton Walsh says that "a good trajectory is the optimum, the most emotionally loaded flight path across the subject to the projected end" (188). Inexperienced readers tend to be unconscious of the trajectory, and to read looking for what happens—the events of the story rather than the sequence of the discourse: They tend either to ignore descriptive passages or to assume they are just background information of no significance in understanding the events, too boring to pay much attention to. But the trajectory of a book has as much effect on our perception of suspense and our interest as does the plot of the story. For instance, the long description at the beginning of chapter 6 of *Charlotte's Web,* listing the different events of early summer days, comes just after a promise at the end of the previous chapter that events will prove Charlotte the spider to be a loyal friend. The passage cleverly builds suspense simply by talking about something completely different from what we have been encouraged to most want to hear about next.

As *Charlotte's Web* reveals, the shifting focus demanded by a complex trajectory can create rich reading experiences. Our perception of patterns of images can help us understand the meanings implied by the events of a plot, and those meanings can help us to appreciate the images. In *Charlotte's Web* we can see how the lists implying "the glory of everything" help explain the meaning of the saving of Wilbur's life and the death of Charlotte, and how salvation by means of an instrument of death, a spider's web, and then the unavoidable death of the savior are examples of the paradoxical relations of bad and good that we find in all the lists.

EXPLORATION: Work through (or invite children to work through) a few pages of *Charlotte's Web* or any other children's story or novel. Determine which sort of consistency-building procedure (concretization, character, plot, theme, structure, or focalization) each succeeding sentence or paragraph most clearly relates to, and then consider how the shift between different procedures might help to create the specific effect of the whole. How does a writer use shifts in focus to create suspense and build understanding?

The connections between the different consistency-building strategies aren't always so clear. In some texts they may undercut rather than support each other, so that their relationship is ironic. That's certainly the effect created by the difference between the narrator's point of view and the information in the pictures of *Nothing Ever Happens on My Block*. But even then, the effect of the whole depends on our perceptions of the way the parts fit together. In the long run, the main strategy implied by consistency building is that the different sorts of consistency are all aspects of and variations on the same central consistency.

In chapter 9, I explore postmodern literary theories, such as deconstruction, that deny the value of looking for this kind of consistency. But even those who doubt the value of consistency building acknowledge that many authors write with the assumption that we will read their texts expecting consistency. Consequently, knowledge of consistency-building strategies remains a significant part of everyone's literary repertoire.

EXPLORATION: The six consistency-building strategies outlined in this chapter are the ones most commonly identified by people who teach literature. But you may have others of your own. Try to figure out if you do. As you read a literary text, try to be conscious of the thinking you do: Does it represent a consistency-building strategy different from the ones I've discussed here? In what ways is it or is it not a useful and pleasurable strategy?

WORKS CITED

Blume, Judy. *Are You There God? It's Me, Margaret*. New York: Bradbury, 1970.

Huck, Charlotte S. *Children's Literature in the Elementary School*. 3rd ed., updated. New York: Holt, Rinehart and Winston, 1979.

Iser, Wolfgang. *The Act of Reading: A Theory of Aesthetic Response*. Baltimore: Johns Hopkins UP, 1978.

Leaf, Munro. *Noodle*. Illus. Ludwig Bemelmans. 1937. New York: Scholastic, 1968.

Lynn, Joanne "Aesop's Fables: Beyond Morals." *Touchstones: Reflections on the Best in Children's Literature*. Ed. Perry Nodelman. Vol. 2. West Lafayette: Children's Literature Association Publications, 1987.

Munsch, Robert. *The Paperbag Princess*. Toronto: Annick, 1980.

Neisser, Ulric. *Cognition and Reality: Principles and Implications of Cognitive Psychology*. San Francisco: Freeman, 1976.

Nesbit, E. "The Sleeping Beauty in the Wood." *The Old Nursery Stories*. 1908. London: Hodder and Stoughton, 1975.

Paton Walsh, Jill. "The Lords of Time." *The Openhearted Audience: Ten Writers Talk about Writing for Children*. Washington: Library of Congress, 1980. 177–198.

Raskin, Ellen. *Nothing Ever Happens on My Block*. New York: Atheneum, 1966.

Scholes, Robert. *Fabulation and Metafiction*. Urbana: U of Illinois P, 1979.

Scieszka, Jon. *The True Story of the 3 Little Pigs by A. Wolf*. Illus. by Lane Smith. New York: Viking, 1989.

White, E. B. *Charlotte's Web*. 1952. New York: Trophy-Harper & Row, 1973.

Wolf, Shelby Anne, and Shirley Brice Heath. *The Braid of Literature: Children's Worlds of Reading*. Cambridge and London: Harvard UP, 1992.

part II

Culture, Ideology, and Children's Literature

As I suggested in chapter 2, our previous experience of life, language, and literature provides us with a repertoire—a body of information, beliefs, and strategies for finding meaning—that determines our response to a text. But if readers have repertoires, then so must writers. Each literary text expresses and assumes its writer's body of information and beliefs. We can, of course, read without much knowledge of a writer's repertoire, and enjoy doing so; but doing so isn't likely to provide us with ideas or images or feelings we weren't familiar with already. If we want the pleasure of reaching beyond ourselves, of experiencing something new and different, then we need to be conscious of the contents of writers' repertoires as well as of our own.

The strategies for building consistency in literary texts that I outlined in chapter 4 represent one kind of information commonly included in the repertoires of many writers. Writers produce texts with the assumption that readers will know and use these strategies. We couldn't make anything like the sense writers might have hoped we would make out of their texts if we didn't know how to do so; and I hope I've persuaded you that using them can enrich our experience of literature.

But writers' repertoires also include a variety of other contexts for their work, from the vocabulary and the grammar of the language in which they write, through their assumptions about what literature is and about what sorts of information or pleasure it can offer, to their experiences of their own bodily sensations and their most basic beliefs and assumptions about life and the nature of reality. It's matters like these that the rest of this book deals with. I try to offer doorways into a repertoire of information and ways of thinking shared by many writers for children that might help you deepen your experience of (and pleasure in) the literature they write.

As the name we give it implies, "children's literature" represents an intersection of two kinds of information in particular: ideas about children, and ideas about literature. The two chapters in Part II explore ideas about children, while Parts III and IV explore ideas about literature.

Earlier, in chapter 2, I discussed how texts imply readers. The next three chapters investigate the characteristics both of the implied readers commonly found in children's literature and the implied viewers commonly found in movies and TV shows intended for children. I explore ideas about childhood and about the nature of children common in our culture; and I examine how those ideas influence how writers write for children, how adults select texts for children to read and view, and how those texts work to influence the ways in which children understand themselves and the world they live in.

chapter 5

Common Assumptions about Childhood

CHILDREN IN IDEOLOGY

> EXPLORATION: The cultural theorists whose ideas form the basis of this and the next chapter tend to work from positions that are critical of values and assumptions many mainstream North Americans take for granted. Does this divergence from the norm give these theorists the advantage of objectivity, or does it make them too biased to be considered seriously? Explore the logic behind your answer to this question, and find evidence to support your arguments.

The basic assumption behind this chapter is that our ideas about children are a kind of self-fulfilling prophecy. These ideas may be inaccurate or incomplete as descriptions of what children are really like or really capable of achieving, but once we believe them, we act in ways that help to make them not only true, but the whole truth. In other words, these ideas operate as part of our society's *ideology*: the body of ideas that controls (or at least, tries to control) how we as participants in the society view the world and understand our place within it.

We're not always conscious of the ideologies that affect us. Or, to put it another way, we're not always conscious that they *are* ideologies. We just assume them to be the way things obviously are. The theorist Louis Althusser calls ideological concepts *obviousnesses*. He says,

> It is indeed a peculiarity of ideology that it imposes (without appearing to do so, since these are "obviousnesses") obviousnesses as obviousnesses, which we cannot *fail to recognize* and before which we have the inevita-

67

ble and natural reaction of crying out (loud or in the "still small voice of conscience"): "That's obvious! That's right! That's true!" (245)

In other words, ideology works best by disappearing, so that we simply take our ideological *assumptions* for granted as the only, whole and unquestionable truth. As Althusser says, "Those who are in ideology believe themselves by definition outside ideology" (246).

If Althusser is right, then his theory might explain why we often accuse those we disagree with about political or moral issues of being controlled by ideology, while we see the positions we adopt ourselves are merely expressions of common sense. From this point of view, ideology is what those who disagree with us believe; what we believe ourselves is the way things actually are.

EXPLORATION: If what seems "common sense" to one person is clearly ideology to someone else, then we might need to consider the obviousness of what we ourselves take for granted. Is it possible to become aware of our own ideologies? See if you can determine the ideological dimensions of your own assumptions about yourself and the world.

What we believe to be obvious determines how we operate. For instance, if everyone simply agrees—as many of our ancestors in recent centuries did—that women are inherently incapable of succeeding in business, then there is no question about it: People act as if it's true, and that's that. Even a woman who wanted to express her talent for business would understand that her desire to do so was abnormal and unwomanly and see herself as a freak. Most women would (and in the past, did) simply accept what they were always told, and not even be able to think of aspiring to enter business: they became *embedded* in their social role as women. As a result of accepting ideology as obviousness, then, women were deprived of most opportunities to support themselves, and therefore of the power to control their own lives.

Clearly, then, ideology is always a matter of politics; that is, it relates to the ways in which people get and maintain power over each other. An ideology consists of the ideas that support and empower particular segments of society, inevitably at the expense of other segments. Since the segment of society that interests us in this book is children, my main purpose in this chapter is to explore how our most common ideas about childhood, and the literature and movies that express them, define and sustain the power we adults wish to maintain over children and control the amount of power we want children to have over themselves.

In other words, I assume throughout that the way we think about childhood has political implications, and that writing and reading are inherently and inevitably political acts. According to Barrie Thorne, "Our understanding of children tends to be filtered through adult perspectives and interests" (86). What we believe about how we must control or shelter children defines their power in relation to ourselves as adults. And whatever else literary texts are, and whatever pleasure they might afford us, they are also expressions of the values and assumptions of a culture and a significant way of embedding readers in those values and assumptions.

According to Raymond Williams, the ideology dominant in a particular society "constitutes a sense of reality . . . beyond which it is very difficult for most members of the society to move, in most areas of their lives" (110). Fortunately, however, what is difficult is not necessarily impossible. Ideologies work to control our understanding of ourselves and each other, but the simple fact that we can think about this topic at all—be conscious of how ideologies operate—suggests that they don't always or completely succeed. If we can find ways of becoming aware of the assumptions about ourselves and each other that our culture's ideology may have manipulated us into simply taking for granted, then we should be able to do some clear thinking about those assumptions. We should be able to choose whether or not it seems sensible to go on believing in their truth, and even whether or not they are obvious at all. The purpose of the rest of this chapter is twofold: first, to encourage you to develop that awareness and to make those choices; and second, to suggest that it might be useful for children to be able to make them also.

CHILDHOOD IN HISTORY

To start with an especially relevant "obviousness": For any one interested in children's literature, it is obvious that children's literature exists simply because it has to. Children need books, surely, and they need books produced with their special interests and limitations in mind. But if we accept Harvey Darton's definition of children's books as "works produced ostensibly to give children spontaneous pleasure, and not primarily to teach them" (1), then children's literature didn't in fact exist before the seventeenth century and didn't really become widespread until a century after that. Even then, writing specifically for children was mainly a European phenomenon, not common in other parts of the word until Europeans began to influence those other parts. All of this suggests that we have taken as obvious something that didn't even occur to people in other places and times. Why did the invention of children's literature come so late in history?

The answer to the question offered by some scholars is, quite simply, that there could be no special literature for children until children were considered to be special enough to need a literature of their own. In earlier times and other cultures, children were not considered to be special enough—at least not special in a way that demanded a special literature. Philippe Ariès says that in medieval Europe, for instance, "as soon as the child could live without the constant solicitude of his mother, his nanny or his cradle-rocker, he belonged to adult society" (128). As equal members of that society, children acted as everyone else did; they needed no special literature because they weren't seen as having special needs or interests.

Ariès makes the case that in the Middle Ages in Europe there was no concept of childhood as we now understand it: a stage of life with characteristics distinct enough to be noticed and seriously examined. Before the thirteenth century, he claims, European medieval art contained few depictions of children, and the children portrayed have the proportions of adults. Furthermore, children were dressed like adults of their class as soon as they stopped being babies.

Ariès's ideas are controversial, and some scholars don't accept them. For instance, Linda Pollock claims that views of childhood like Ariès's depend too much on secondary sources, such as religious tracts and books offering advice to parents. She doubts that parents actually acted on this advice and asserts, "I believe there is no reason to assume that parental care must vary according to developments and changes in society as a whole" (viii).

Personally, I find Pollock's position hard to accept. I know that in ancient times, both the Greeks and the Chinese exposed unwanted or deformed babies to the elements and left them to die, and that the Carthaginians and others practiced child sacrifice. No matter how much the parents of these children loved and cared for their children, they had quite different ways of expressing their love than we do now. So, surely, did the parents of the Middle Ages, who understood their world and themselves quite differently than we understand ours; whatever childhood was back then, it was not what we imagine it to be now. As N. Ray Hiner and Joseph M. Hawes say, while "Ariès has been justly criticized for his selective and sometimes uncritical use of evidence, no one has successfully challenged his essential point that childhood is *not* an immutable stage of life, free from the influence of historical change" (xvi).

What this means is, simply, that ideas about children and childhood are part of a society's ideology. Shulamith Shahar says, "Childraising practices and educational methods as well as parent-child relations are determined not solely by biological laws but are also culturally constructed" (1). Interestingly, Shahar disagrees with Ariès and believes that in the Middle Ages, "childhood was in fact perceived as a distinct stage in the life cycle, that there was a conception of childhood" (2). But she presents a persuasive case, not that childhood then was what it is for us now, but rather, that a *different* conception of childhood operated.

That conception required no special literature. For different societies in past times, then, it wasn't obvious that children had need of a special literature; and since we know that generation after generation of children survived that lack of a special literature quite successfully, we also know that those children really didn't need such a literature. Both the children and the adults in their lives thought of themselves in a significantly different way from the way we think of children now—and what they thought became what was true and defined how they behaved.

Early Children's Literature

The children's literature that finally did come to exist in Europe in the seventeenth century confirms the theory I've just offered simply by being so different from what we now expect children's literature to be. These early texts for children were produced in England by Puritans, a group of devout Christians who were, according to Ruth MacDonald, "the first child-centered group in history" (153). Since their faith focused on the need for each individual to find his or her own salvation, the Puri-

tans developed the conviction that children were as prone to sin and in need of salvation as adults were, and they produced books specifically aimed at directing
young children to the right path. For instance, James Janeway's *Token for Children:
Being an Exact Account of the Conversion, Holy and Exemplary Lives, and Joyful
Deaths of Several Young Children*, first published in 1672, contains the story of
Sarah Howley, who gave herself to Christ after hearing a sermon when she was
eight years old, and who then became seriously ill at the age of fourteen: "She was
full of Divine Sentences, and almost all her discourse from the first to last in the
time of her sickness, was about her Soul, Christs sweetness, and the Souls of others,
in a word, like a continued sermon" (Demers and Moyles 48). She died in the blissful knowledge of her eternal salvation.

Texts like this are likely to strike many of us now as both excessively preachy
and unnecessarily depressing. "A continued sermon" isn't what we expect of children's literature. But as Darton says, "It is true that they do not provide 'amusement,' except unintentionally. But that is exactly why, at that time, they *were* 'children's books.' They *were* meant to give pleasure: the highest pleasure, that of
studying and enjoying the Will of God" (53). Furthermore, I find it hard to believe
that children immersed in the values of the adults who loved them didn't take great
pleasure in these books.

The ideological basis of children's literature in assumptions about children becomes especially clear in the comments that readers of our time make about literature written for children in the past. For instance, Mary Wollstonecraft's *Original
Stories*, like many texts for children produced in England in the early nineteenth
century, celebrates reason and views fantasy as dangerous. Geoffrey Summerfield
says that this text "has a strong claim to be the most sinister, ugly, overbearing book
for children ever published" (229). Mitzi Myers rightly asserts that Summerfield's attitude is "a presentist one that orders the past to validate today's needs" (108). Summerfield attacks Wollstonecraft for not sharing his own twentieth-century convictions that fantasy is healthy and that appeals to reason are oppressive. He forgets
that for writers and even for children of earlier times, there might well be different
ideas about children and childhood in force, and therefore, genuine pleasure to be
found in stories about children who learn to be less imaginative and more rational.

EXPLORATION: Test the conclusions of this section by reading some children's literature from a specific period in history—the Puritan texts of the
seventeenth century, the rational novels of the early nineteenth century.
Examine the extent to which they imply child readers and ideas of childhood unlike today's.

CHILDHOOD NOW

According to the sociological theorist Pierre Bourdieu, "The essential thing about
historical realities is that one can always establish that things could have been otherwise, indeed, *are* otherwise in other places and other conditions" (15). The fact

that people once thought differently about children and children's literature forces us to realize that what we now take for granted about them is not necessarily the complete or the only truth. Our knowledge of the different ideas common in the past might stop us from being too confident in our own assumptions about children and what they should or should not read. If such assumptions were a matter of ideology in the past they must be so now.

But as ideology, our own assumptions about children tend to strike us as being so obvious as to be not worth thinking about. As David Hunt says, "When we deal with the distant and relatively alien society of seventeenth-century France, it is not hard to accept the notion that the plight of children was related to the character of the social and political order in which they lived. We lack the corresponding understanding of parenthood and society today" (196). If we wish to help children in their encounters with literature, I believe we must try to develop that understanding.

SOME COMMON ASSUMPTIONS

Over the years, as I've spoken with university students, parents, teachers, librarians, and other adults about children's literature, I've been surprised by how often they agree with each other about it. Below are a few ideas that I've heard expressed often enough to conclude that they strike many people as obvious.

EXPLORATION: As you read the following list of what I claim are common assumptions about texts for children, consider (or invite children to consider) their implications. Which of them do you believe to be true? What experiences have you had that might confirm or contradict them? Are there any you've assumed without being conscious of doing so? Were you right to make such assumptions?

- The best children's stories have simple texts, bright, colorful pictures, and happy endings. Books that are too long or too difficult frustrate children, and might even destroy their interest in literature and reading altogether.
- In choosing children's books, the most important thing to consider is the age of the children we choose them for. Children who are, say, five years old, enjoy and can understand different books than do children who are three, or seven; so we need to choose books appropriate to a child's age.
- Children respond with delight to fantasies—particularly stories about animals who act like humans.
- Children like books they can relate to: stories about typical childhood experiences. Boys like stories about boys; and girls like stories about girls. And children in general are unlikely to be interested in reading about—or even capable of understanding—certain aspects of experience that belong exclusively to adult life, such as sexuality, or the boredom of ordinary daily life in the workplace.

- Children's stories shouldn't describe unacceptable behavior, such as violence or rudeness or immorality, that the children might choose to imitate.
- Children's stories should also not contain depictions of frightening things that might scare them.
- Children's stories should contain positive role models: characters who act in acceptable ways and get rewarded for it.
- Good children's books teach valuable lessons about life, but do so unobtrusively. They make learning fun.

All of these ideas about children's books say less about literature than they do about children or, more exactly, what we imagine children are like. In fact, as I suggested in chapter 2, the notion that adults choosing books for children should be thinking primarily about the distinguishing characteristics of childhood might be the most common "obviousness" of all in our ideas about this subject—and, I believe, the most dangerous.

The danger becomes clear if we consider the implications of the ideas about literature listed above, and try to pinpoint the assumptions about children they are based on. As I understand them, they assume the following "obviousnesses":

- Children have limited understanding and short attention spans. These are inescapable aspects of childlike thinking, and inherent in human development, which proceeds throughout childhood in clear stages. At any given stage, a child is capable of understanding only a certain amount.
- Children are innocent by nature, blissfully naive and inherently good. They can't really understand what evil is or what sexuality is.
- Children are emotionally vulnerable, easily upset, and often permanently damaged by exposure to ugly or painful matters. They respond to depictions of evil or deprivation not by becoming evil but by having nightmares, or even by developing permanent neuroses.
- Children are inherently savage—born animal-like and not yet disciplined or cajoled into understanding the need for law, order, and self-control that keeps us all safe and sane in our dealings with each other. Exposing children to evil or violence in books merely encourages their most basic, most unfortunate, and most uncontrollable tendencies.
- While neither inherently innocent nor inherently savage, children are nevertheless not yet fully formed. They are pliable, and therefore, highly suggestible, and they are prone to dangerous experimentation. They respond to depictions of violence by becoming violent themselves. Conversely, thank goodness, they also respond to depictions of good by becoming good. Children will become whatever they read about.
- Any or all of the above happen because children are egocentric. They assume that whatever they read is somehow actually about themselves—about who they are or who they ought to be. And they aren't interested in matters outside their own immediate experience. They dislike stories about people unlike themselves living in places unlike their own.

- On the other hand, though, children are highly imaginative. The adults in their lives have not yet persuaded them that there's only one version of truth—the one adults call reality. There's a direct connection between childlike thinking, imagination, fantasy, and creativity.
- Or maybe there isn't. Children have an inherent, basic dislike for thinking and learning, for experiencing anything different from what they know and like already. In order to teach them anything, we have to make learning fun. Without spoonfuls of sugar, the medicine will be rejected.

EXPLORATION: My list of common assumptions may well be inaccurate; and I doubt very much that it's complete. Explore current newspapers, magazines, TV shows, and so on, and see if you can find any of the above assumptions or identify *other* assumptions being made about children.

The danger in the assumptions I've listed is twofold. First, they imply that individual children are more like each other in being children than unlike each other in being individuals. Second, they define childhood almost exclusively in terms of its limitations: What most characterizes children is that they are less knowledgeable, less resilient, less resistant to influence than adults are. If these ideas are true, then children's ability to respond to literature with any degree of individuality or understanding is seriously limited. Since I'd prefer not to believe this, I'd like to consider these assumptions further.

ASSUMPTIONS AS IDEOLOGY

The strangest quality of the assumptions I've listed is that, considered as a group, they are impossibly self-contradictory. A child cannot at the same time be innocently angelic *and* cruelly savage, limited in understanding *and* quick to learn evil. Perhaps that means merely that some of the assumptions are right, and some wrong. But in my experience, people who express ideas like these tend to believe equally even ones that contradict each other, without any apparent consciousness of the contradictions. That clearly marks these ideas as ideological: One of the important effects of ideology is to make us unaware of the contradictions in how we see and understand ourselves and others. Terry Eagleton offers the example of someone who believes that democracy represents both the equivalent power of everyone *and* the freedom of everyone to gain more power than others: "The fact that I employ a team of six hard-pressed servants around the clock does not prevent me from believing in some suitably nebulous way that all men and women are equal" (41).

Why, then, do we assume our assumptions about children are true? The answer to that question can be found in history. I've described how the Puritans of seventeenth-century England produced books for children because of their conviction that all human beings are born into sin; and this idea seems to underlie our own assumption nowadays that children in their innocence need protection from their own worst instincts, their immature inability to avoid violence or immorality. In the nineteenth century, however, a quite different view of the meaning of human experience led to a quite different idea of childhood, one based on the idea that children are born untainted by the sins of a corrupt world. This idea seems to be behind our modern assumptions that children in their innocence need protection from the wickedness of the world, that childhood ignorance is bliss, and that children will find out about evil soon enough. So childhood is a time of either delightful innocence or dangerous ignorance. Children are either more angelic than adults or more savage. Even though these ideas contradict each other, they still have enough power in our culture that many adults tend to act at different times as if each of them were true.

Furthermore, both of these contradictory ideas relate at least as significantly to adult needs as they do to those of children. Thinking of children as savages requires us to see them as a threat to adult society, and to work to protect ourselves from the threat by changing dangerous children into safe adults like us. Thinking of them as innocent encourages us to worry about them as victims of adults, and to work to teach them ways of being more like us and therefore less likely to be victimized. In both case, as Thorne observes, "the experiences of children are filtered through adult concerns" (89). And doing that ignores how children themselves understand their experiences.

That sounds dangerous, or at least, arrogant. So the next obvious question is: *Are* these generalized definitions true? My answer to that question is also contradictory: first, they might be; second, they can't be; and third, nevertheless, they often are.

WHY THE ASSUMPTIONS MIGHT BE TRUE

The assumptions might not be merely assumptions: They might be scientific fact. The theories and conclusions of many experts on childhood behavior and childlike thinking certainly suggest that they are.

For instance, the theories of the Swiss psychologist Jean Piaget suggest that children pass through a number of identifiable *developmental stages* as they develop and mature. These stages always occur in the same order, and each child tends to enter them at approximately the same point in his or her life. Children from age two to six or seven are understood to be in the *preoperational* stage: They are beginning to use symbols, but lack the ability to think about what they're doing, and they are egocentric, that is, unable to understand any point of view but their own. Children from age six to eleven are seen to be in the *concrete operational* stage: They are beginning to understand some of the basic concepts that underlie our ability to think about the world, but only in terms of concrete examples. Finally, children from age twelve to fifteen enter the *formal operational* stage, and can begin to handle abstract concepts.

Piaget's idea of discrete stages has influenced many other theories of development, including Erik Erikson's theory of psychological development and Lawrence

Kohlberg's theory of moral development. These theories underlie and reinforce the popular assumption, listed above, that children cannot act in ways uncharacteristic of their current stage.

Not surprisingly, then, these theories are the basis of much of what publishers and specialists recommend about children's literature. A faith in the existence of stages leads to the labeling of books as being appropriate for children of certain ages or accessible only to children of certain ages, and the conviction that each book is appropriate for only one specific level of development. According to Alan Purves and Dianne Monson, for instance,

> the reader must possess a certain lack of egocentricity in order to be able to relate to the characteristics, problems, etc., of a story character living, let us say, in the Middle Ages. According to Jean Piaget's work on children's development, that egocentricity does dissipate during the period of formal operations, reached by most children at about age eleven. . . . Therefore, it may be that children in the intermediate grades and junior high are better suited for understanding and relating to historical fiction than are younger children. (77)

And Nicholas Tucker describes the principles of his book-length discussion of selecting books for children this way: "Following Piaget, I shall chiefly describe the more typical ways in which children seem to approach and make sense of their stories at various ages, leaving particular details—of how individuals or whole cultures can then sometimes react to such stories quite differently—to one side" (5–6).

WHY THE ASSUMPTIONS CAN'T BE THE WHOLE TRUTH

It's revealing that, in order to work with descriptions of typical children of specific ages, Tucker has to characterize individual and cultural differences as "details" to be left out of consideration. These are pretty huge details; and that suggests the main problem of working with common assumptions or general theories of childhood. They *are* generalizations, and generalizations rarely apply in all cases. In a less interesting world, it might be safe to say something like, "This is a book that six-year-olds will enjoy." But as our real experience of the real and more interesting world tells us as soon as we move past ideological assumptions, some six-year-olds like a particular book, and many others hate it. In the real world, children have as few generally true group characteristics as do, say, all lawyers, or all university students. In this world, each child is his or her own person, an individual being whose values and abilities are influenced both by heredity and environment. When we make assumptions about the similarity of all six-year-olds, we lose sight of the immense significance of individual differences in the process of literary response.

Furthermore, some of the differences in children's responses have nothing to do with differences in character or potential. When we speak of the innocence of childhood, we forget about the 40 million children in the world who live on the streets, without homes or parents or enough food. Most of our generalizations about the kind of literature children can "relate" to imply the degree to which we assume that all children live the comfortable, protected lives of white, middle-class North Americans. And while we know that isn't true, we manage to forget it when we talk about choosing books; we confuse what we'd like to be true with what actually is true. This is another one of the contradictions that define these ideas about childhood as ideological in nature.

We also often manage to forget—or, perhaps, try to hide from ourselves—the extent to which the innocent bliss of even fairly well-off children is a fiction. Nancy Weiss suggests that Dr. Spock's *Baby and Child Care,* still the most popular guide for parents, is such a fiction: "This world of rearing the young . . . is free of dissonance or conflict, or the recognition of poverty or cultural difference. Such a world has invented a motherhood that excludes the experience of many mothers" (303). It also excludes the experience of the many children who are sexually or physically abused, and of the even more numerous ones who go through the ordinary but nevertheless painful traumas of growth and of adjustment to human existence.

Developmental Theory and Scientific Evidence

Why, then, are experts like Piaget, Erikson, and Kohlberg so certain about their generalized descriptions of childhood? The answer, presumably, is that they've reached their conclusions by doing research and applying scientific method to the experiments they conduct and the evidence they discover. We might have to conclude, then, that despite individual and cultural differences, there is a core of truth in their ideas. As they develop, children might in fact pass through something like the stages described by Piaget, Erikson, Kohlberg, and other experts, albeit, perhaps, in somewhat different ways.

But a closer investigation of research on development throws significant doubt on that conclusion: It might not be so scientific after all. According to Charles Brainerd,

> Until the mid-1970s, Piaget's ideas dominated the landscape the way Freudian thinking once ruled abnormal psychology. Since then, however, the picture has changed dramatically. Empirical and conceptual objections to the theory have become so numerous that it can no longer be regarded as a positive force in mainstream cognitive-developmental research, though its influence remains profound in cognate fields such as education and sociology. (*Recent Advances* vii)

Some of the objections to Piaget's theories relate to his methodology and his logic. For instance, one of Piaget's justifications for his theory that children are egocentric was an experiment requiring them to imagine how a display might look from another point of view. In assuming that the inability to imagine something from a different physical point of view indicated an emotional inability to empathize, he made an illogical connection between the physical and the emotional. Not surprisingly, experiments asking children questions about how others might feel establish that they can understand and empathize with the point of view of others as early as one-and-a-half years of age (Borke 35, 38). This would suggest that we underestimate children when we assume, as Purves and Monson do, that their egocentricity prevents them from enjoying books about people different from themselves.

In fact, slightly redesigned versions of Piaget's experiments often have surprisingly different results. They show that children can accomplish theoretically impossible kinds of thinking at surprisingly early stages. What was thought to be theoretically impossible has proven to be possible in the right circumstances—particularly when adults make the task relevant, and phrase it in language or in circumstances that children can understand.

Other objections to Piaget take us right back to the question of ideology. They suggest ways in which Piaget may have been misled by his own unconscious assumptions, about childhood and in general.

For one thing, he often seriously underestimated children, and almost always assumed that their actual performance accurately represented the extent of their potential. According to Susan Sugarman, "Piaget invariably claims that when children *are not* doing something . . . they *cannot* do it" (112). In other words, his faith in the limitations of childhood—something he simply appears to have taken for granted as obvious—distorted his conclusions.

It continues to distort the conclusions of others. The confusion of performance with potential is common in discussions of children's books based on Piagetian ideas. We assume that because children *don't* like a certain kind of book they *cannot* like it until they reach a new stage; or, as Arthur Applebee suggests in his analysis of how children discuss stories, that because the descriptions of six-year-olds "seem to take the simplest possible form" (105), it is impossible for them to achieve more complex responses. Because they are in what Piaget calls the preoperational stage, it seems, their descriptions will inevitably and immutably display characteristics like egocentricity—at least until they reach the next stage. Opinions like this neglect the fact Robert Protherough points out: "Less fluent children may seem to react inadequately, not because of a limited response but because of inability to express it" (37).

Some of the most powerful criticisms of theorists like Piaget and Kohlberg go far beyond attacks on the design of experiments or the logic of conclusions: They condemn the basic assumptions upon which the theory of stages is based. In particular, they criticize the conviction that someone like Piaget or Kohlberg represents the height of human accomplishment, and that moral views and intellectual operations like their own are the final result of an evolutionary process. As Carol Gilligan suggests, this sort of bias "leads Piaget to equate male development with child development" (10). Gilligan suggests that the assumption that male behavior is in fact the norm leads Piagetian psychologists, themselves mostly male, to see as a deviation from the norm behavior that is in our society characteristically female. In the process, furthermore, they usually assume that characteristically female behavior is inferior to characteristically male behavior, rather than merely different from it. They prize autonomy and independence over relating to and caring for others: to develop fully is to become self-centered and unconnected.

Women are not the only group misrepresented in developmental theories. For instance, Piaget's cultural bias led him to assume that the ability to handle certain concepts represents intellectual accomplishment. But, as Brainerd reports, "There is now reason to believe that familiar concrete-operational concepts such as conservation [understanding that, for instance, the mass of an object remains the same even if its shape changes] are not culturally universal. It seems that mother nature has been shamefully neglecting the spontaneous development of primitive peoples" ("Learning Research" 83). Mother Nature also seems to have been shamefully neglecting the moral development of people of other cultures. The theories of moral development postulated by Piaget and Kohlberg define stages that advance to the ultimate goal of belief in something like the Christian golden rule of acting toward others as you would have them act toward you. Many non-Christian cultures do not accept adherence to that sort of rule as the most sophisticated form of moral behavior; for instance, many eastern religions would put a higher value on the acceptance of what fate dictates for both oneself and others.

The ideological bias of developmental theories is intellectual as well as cultural; they assume that the ability to think scientifically represents the pinnacle of mental achievement. "Looking at Piaget's protocols that report actual experiments," says Jean-Claude Brief, "one is struck by his selection of logical factors at the expense of those that are affective, sensorial, sociocultural, and linguistic. As a result, many possible interpretations are eliminated from the start" (185).

This sort of bias leads developmental theorists to make the assumption that thought develops in an evolutionary process in which what comes later is superior to what comes earlier. As a result, Piaget and Kohlberg see the stages through which childhood thinking pass as imperfect approximations of an ideal adult standard of mental functioning, and assume that the worlds children invent at earlier stages of development are false and deficient versions of an objective truth only available to mature adults. The danger in this sort of thinking is clear. As Brief says, "The child is in charge of a particular reality which is appropriate to his body and to his thinking. Hence, to privilege the adult's reality under the pretext that it represents the true world does seem presumptuous . . . " (31).

The philosopher Gareth Matthews, who angrily calls Piaget's descriptions of children's thinking "dismissive, even contemptuous" (*Philosophy* 31), suggests what such dismissiveness may prevent us from understanding as he wonders why adults fail to recognize the degree to which children are capable of philosophical reflection:

> Perhaps it is because so much emphasis has been placed on the development of children's abilities, especially their cognitive abilities, that we automatically assume their thinking is primitive and in need of development toward an adult norm. What we take to be primitive, however, may

actually be more openly reflective than the adult norm we set as the goal of education. (*Dialogues* 53)

It may also be more open to the pleasure of literary response and analysis, which require a focus on specifics rather than abstractions, and on individual differences rather than on generalized observations—in other words, the sort of thinking we usually define as childlike.

BUT THEY'RE SOMETIMES TRUE ANYWAY

Like all aspects of ideology, assumptions about childhood affect the way we respond to actual experience. As John Stephens says, "all developmental paths are ideologically constructed, involving conformity to social norms" (3–4). Children become what we believe they are; assumptions about childhood have the potential to become self-fulfilling prophecies. The more we believe that children are limited in various ways, the more we deprive them of experiences that might make them less limited. If we believe that children have short attention spans, we won't expose them to long books. If we believe they cannot understand complicated language, we will give them only books with limited vocabularies. If we believe they are susceptible, we will keep them away from interesting books that may contain potentially dangerous ideas or attitudes. And if we believe they like only certain kinds of books, we will not give them access to other kinds. Deprived of the experience of anything more than the little we believe them capable of, children often do learn to be inflexible, intolerant of the complex and the unconventional.

Furthermore, we do commonly deprive children in exactly that way. Assumptions based in developmental theory control our educational ideas. As Joseph T. Lawton and Frank H. Hooper say, "Piaget's views have been rather glibly accepted as demonstrating prima facie validity and relevance for educational application" (170). As a result, what is assumed to be obvious becomes in fact true.

For instance, the perception that development is a series of periodic, predictable changes from one distinct state to another may simply have resulted from the preconceptions that developmental psychologists once brought to their experiments. Recent research, ignoring that assumption, suggests that learning occurs gradually in a continuous series of small steps, as long as there are new experiences for children (and adults) to learn from. And while research does still confirm that distinct stages do seem to exist, studies suggest they may be culturally imposed, and relate to matters such as typical school entrance ages and our expectations of the sorts of experiences children can process. "Thus, what appears to be maturationally 'normal' in cognition and performance reflects, upon closer examination, a culturally imposed system of 'prods and brakes'" (Zimmerman 14).

Similarly, developmental assumptions have a profound effect on children's literature and reading. Because we adults believe in developmental stages in childhood, we demand, and publishers produce, texts intended for readers in specific stages, with short attention spans and a love of bright colors and animals. In other words: The generalized children of our ideological assumptions are often the implied readers of texts written for children. If it's true, as I believe it is, that response to literature is a learned skill, then children who read nothing but books of this sort will most likely be able to understand and enjoy only books of this sort. We do indeed make what strikes us as obvious come true: Far too many children learn to be exactly as limited as we expect them to be.

THE ASSUMPTIONS AND POWER:
WHY DO WE HAVE THEM?

If commonly held assumptions about childhood have such limiting effects, we might well wonder about their usefulness. Who do these assumptions benefit and how?

The answer might be found in the fact that the assumptions operate on the principle not just that children are *different* from adults, but *opposite* to us. If we always interpret what children do in terms of how it differs from what we as adults do, then, says Thorne, we "project onto infants and young children a nature opposite to the qualities prized in adults. Valuing independence, we define children as dependent; the task of socialization is to encourage independence. . . . Adults use children to define themselves, in an ideological process of domination and self-definition analogous to the way in which men have defined women and colonialists have defined those they colonized, as 'the other' " (93). Bronwyn Davies agrees: "Children are defined as *other* to adults in much the same way that women are other to men" (4).

The literary theorist Jacques Derrida points out the significance of that when he says, "Man *calls himself* man only by drawing limits excluding his other . . . : the purity of nature, of animality, primitivism, childhood, madness, divinity" (244). In other words, our idea that we are different from something that came before us and that we have evolved away from is what allows us to understand who we are: We are that which is not natural, not bestial, not mad, not divine—and most important, not childish. "If the child is not distinguished from the adult," James Kincaid asserts, "we imagine that we are seriously threatened, threatened in such a way as to put at risk our very being, what it means to be an adult in the first place" (7).

At first glance, all the "other" qualities Derrida lists are different from humanity in being superior to it: Nature is more natural, divinity more spiritual. Derrida suggests that this privileging of the prior and more primitive is a dangerous act of self-abuse on the part of those who see themselves as coming after and, thus, degenerated from, a state of innocence. We often view childhood as this sort of self-abusing "other." Our clichés about the ways in which children are closer to nature or to God, about how their ignorance is really a saving innocence, disguise a profound distrust of the realities of life as we must view it as adults—and, perhaps more significant, a nostalgia for that which in fact never was.

A surprising proportion of adult commentaries on children's literature view it in terms of this kind of celebration of childlike otherness, and focus on the appeal of "childlike" qualities like joy and wonder. Jacqueline Rose suggests that children's literature as a whole, just by existing, also represents this sort of nostalgia. She believes that the actual nature of childhood—particularly childhood sexuality—frightens adults. Because we have come to accept one form of thinking and being as normal, we see all others as chaotic and threatening, particularly those of a childhood we once shared and believe ourselves to have grown beyond. We protect ourselves from knowledge of this chaos by constructing images of childhood that leave out everything threatening; indeed, Kincaid asserts, we see being childlike as "a kind of purity, an absence and an incapacity, an inability to do. . . . Unencumbered by any necessary traits, the emptiness called a child can be constructed any way we like" (70–71). We then present the images we have constructed to children in their literature, in order to persuade them that their lives actually are as we imagine them to be. "If children's fiction builds an image of the child inside the book," says Rose, "it does so in order to secure the child who is outside the book, the one who does not come so easily within its grasp" (2).

Children's literature then represents a massive effort by adults to *colonize* children: to make them believe that they ought to be the way adults would like them to be, and to make them feel guilty about or downplay the significance of all the aspects of their selves that inevitably don't fit the adult model.

EXPLORATION: Do you think Rose's view is correct? Consider (or invite children to consider) the degree to which children's literature works to encourage children to believe in an untrue representation of childhood, by exploring the implications of a small group of children's texts.

Logic suggests that, to some degree the colonization of children is unavoidable. As Williams says, "Any process of socialization of course includes things that all human beings have to learn, but any specific process ties this necessary learning to a selected range of meanings, values, and practices. . . . Education transmits necessary knowledge and skills, but always by a particular selection from the whole available range, and with intrinsic attitudes, both to learning and social relations, which are in practice virtually inextricable" (117–18). As I hope to show in the next chapter, children's literature partakes in this sort of selective education simply because authors always take for granted, and thus work to persuade young readers, that one particular view of childhood represents normalcy.

But while misrepresentation is inevitable, I believe there is particular danger in any view of childhood that insists on its otherness. For one thing, there might be some truth in Kincaid's controversial assertion that making children representatives of all we most desire actually eroticizes them, makes them secret objects of an inevitably sexual desire: "If the child is desirable, then to desire it can hardly be freakish" (4). If we prefer a view of childhood in which such desire *is* freakish—and I do—then my next question is particularly important: Is any other view of childhood possible?

BEYOND THE CHILD AS OTHER

I think there is. If the idea that children are limited or even empty is ideological, then it need not be the only possible truth, or the truth we choose to accept. We can think about children in other, more positive ways, and in so doing create a different and, I believe, better truth. Most specifically, we can focus on the ways in which children are more significantly *like* us rather than opposite to us.

Consider, for instance, what happens when someone like Gareth Matthews imagines that young children are capable of the abstract, philosophical thinking he likes to do himself. Matthews's descriptions of his discussions of philosophy with children reveal that the sort of imaginative suppositions Piaget dismisses as primitive actually represent accurate versions of philosophical positions taken by sophisticated adults. Similarly, Robert Coles, reporting his experiences with children involved in traumatic situations of poverty and racial strife, points out the degree to which the intensity and maturity of their moral attitudes "contrasts, alas, with the categorical assurances of some theorists who have moral development all figured out, as if life were a matter of neatly arranged academic hurdles, with grades given along the way" (28).

Interestingly, Piaget's description of the mechanisms through which learning occurs might actually support a less limiting view of the capabilities of children than the one he himself usually adopted, or the one adopted by his followers when they assume stage theory means that children cannot deal with unfamiliar ideas or experiences. In fact, Piaget makes it clear that children *need* such ideas and experiences in order to move to a new stage. He speaks of *assimilation*, the process by which we integrate new information into our previously established systems of meaning, and of *accommodation*, the reverse process by which we adapt our systems of meaning-making in the light of new information. Both processes require new information in order to take place. Consequently, our perception that a book is somewhat more subtle or more difficult than we believe a child's current understanding can accommodate should be grounds not for dismissing the book but for encouraging the child to experience it. The more we successfully manage to keep children's environments free of complexities beyond their current abilities, the more we prevent them from learning and growing.

In my own experience, children treated as responsible individuals capable of understanding what I understand and able to make their own choices about what to read and what to think turn out to be responsible individuals, capable of rich understanding and able to make wise choices. In other words, this too is ideology, and therefore, a self-fulfilling prophecy. But this is one that seems to me to be much more positive for both adults and children—much more likely than the usual assumptions to allow adults to help children learn ways of reading and of thinking about what they read that might give them deeper and more satisfying pleasure and understanding.

EXPLORATION: It might be argued that teachers and parents don't always have the time or the knowledge to pay detailed attention to the individual tastes and abilities of individual children, and that Piagetian and other developmental stage theories provide useful guidelines in book selection and other dealings with children. Is that a relevant consideration, or a dangerous one?

BUT ARE CHILDREN DIFFERENT AFTER ALL?

Carried to a logical conclusion, the philosophy I've just outlined might seem to altogether eliminate any need to think about children as different from adults. If we are all, most significantly, individuals, then surely there's nothing special to be said about children—and therefore, nothing special to be said about children and their reading. Talk with children about books should be no different from talk with adults about books. For that matter, there may be no real positive need for such a thing as children's literature: Once we've moved past our limiting schemata for children, we might discover that there's no need to provide any special kind of texts for young people.

And yet I'm sure there is—and not simply because our assumptions about childhood do end up making children different. For all the arguments I've presented above, and for all the variations among different children, children considered as a group *are,* incontrovertibly, different from adults considered as a group. And, despite changes in ideology, I believe they always will be, for just one key reason: They have not lived as long, and therefore—and this is what really matters—they've had less opportunity to encounter the sorts of experiences that might lead them to develop knowledge and understanding.

EXPLORATION: If I were more cynical than I actually am, I might say that the opinion I've just expressed sounds like an appeal to common sense— an obviousness that must therefore be part of an ideology I'm unaware of. Am I not being cynical enough? Is the mere existence of children's literature a way adults disempower and entrap children, and nothing else? Would we benefit children more by *not* producing special books, movies, and TV shows for them?

I'm not, I hasten to add, suggesting that all children have less understanding than all adults, or even fewer experiences that might lead to understanding. That would be patently untrue. But it is, nevertheless, true that the main reason we isolate children as a group is that we are conscious of their relative lack of experience, and feel two specific obligations to them as a result of it: We feel the obligation to protect them from experiences they may not yet understand well enough to cope with. Above all, we feel the obligation to educate them into the sort of understanding that will enable them to look after themselves.

As I suggested earlier, it's these obligations that led to the development of children's literature in the first place—a literature for readers inexperienced both with language and with living. Good children's literature, I believe, assumes the inexperience of its readers but *not* their inability to develop greater understanding through experience—including the experience of reading literature. The best texts written for children can be understood in simple terms, therefore, but they're not as simplistic as far too many children's books are. Instead, they allow for more complex understanding by readers able to respond in more complex ways, and they're often constructed in ways that encourage readers to develop more complex responses in the very process of reading them. In chapter 8, I discuss these characteristic aspects of texts for children in more detail.

Nevertheless, the children who experience such texts may miss their complexities simply because they don't yet possess ways of thinking about what they read that might allow them to notice or comprehend complexity. In this way, our ideological assumptions do their political work: They keep children without knowledge and therefore in our control. If we find ourselves willing to give up some of that control, then there's only one difference between adults and children that we need to pay attention to: the ways in which children lack the experience they need in order to develop the kind of understanding we ourselves are capable of. If we focus on this difference, we can, as I suggested in chapter 3, consider ways in which we might provide children with experiences that will help them to develop such understanding.

CHILDHOOD READING AND CENSORSHIP

The most significant effect that common assumptions about childhood have on children's reading is to deprive children of access to books. Many adults are far more interested in determining what children should *not* read than what and how they should. From the viewpoint of the ideas I discussed above, a good book tends merely to be one that does *not* contain oversubtle ideas, potentially bad messages, descriptions of unacceptable behavior, or scenes fearful enough that they might cause nightmares.

Sometimes, we call the process by which we deprive children of such matters by a harmless-sounding name: "book selection." For instance, Catherine Studier-Chang says that *Hiroshima No Pika,* Toshi Maruki's picture book about a child experiencing an atom bomb falling on her city, "has no business in the hands of anyone under the age of twelve" (158). And in an interview with Geraldine DeLuca and Roni Natov, the science writer Seymour Simon reports, "I did a book called *Life and Death* which was certainly the poorest selling book I've ever written. It seems that librarians are simply not interested in buying things with death in the title" (22).

It is, of course, unavoidable that adults play an important part in choosing what books children will have access to. School and library budgets could never be large enough to purchase absolutely everything published. Even if they were, teachers, librarians, and parents possess a repertoire of knowledge about literature that might well be useful in choosing appropriate books for particular children. Nevertheless, we need to be careful that the principles behind our selections don't simply amount to a form of censorship. And I think we always need to be wary of actual censorship.

In *Storm in the Mountains*, his disturbing book about the attempt in West Virginia to ban the language arts text series he had edited, James Moffett suggests that censorship emerges from what he calls *agnosis*: "not-wanting-to-know" (187). In terms of texts for children, censorship, and censorious principles of book selection, amount to agnosis at one remove: *adults* not wanting *children* to know.

As I suggested above, the wish not to have children know emerges from a genuine concern for their welfare: We want to protect them from what we see as harmful. For instance, Charlotte Huck reports that, when Maurice Sendak's *In the Night Kitchen* first came out, librarians in Caldwell Parish, Louisiana, sought to protect young children from what they saw as a harmful knowledge of human anatomy by painting diapers on the book's naked hero. Similarly, many people want to prevent children from reading books containing what they consider to be sexist portrayals of characters.

In doing so, however, we may well be doing more harm than good. The discussion of ideology above suggests that ignorance is always likely to do more harm than knowledge can: The more we are aware of, the less likely are we to operate in terms of "obviousnesses" that might be harming or disempowering ourselves and others. For instance, those familiar with feminist objections to sexist stereotypes aren't as likely to accept the stereotypes thoughtlessly as are people who aren't familiar with these objections.

If that's true for adults, then I believe it is particularly true for children, who are in the process of learning about a world they are only beginning to experience. They have special need of knowledge as a resource in order to make sense of new things. Surely, then, those who are deprived of knowledge of certain attitudes or forms of behavior, and therefore, prevented from thinking about why they might be harmful, are the ones most likely to take such attitudes or commit such acts. To deprive children of the opportunity to read about confusing or painful matters like those they might actually be experiencing will either make literature irrelevant to them or else leave them feeling they are alone in their thoughts or experiences. Similarly, to deprive them of knowledge of painful or confusing matters they haven't yet experienced deprives them of the opportunity to prepare themselves to deal with those things in a conscious and careful manner when they do inevitably occur.

It also deprives us adults of the opportunity to discuss these matters with children, and to share our own attitudes with them. Without such discussions, we might actually diminish our control over children rather than increase it. Children with a quite natural interest in the functioning of their own bodies but whose parents refuse to let them look at books containing pictures of naked human bodies have no choice but to turn to the playground for information about and discussions of human sexuality. My own memories of such discussions make me suspect they are likely to communicate ideas at odds with the values of censorious parents.

Furthermore, we might want to remember the theories postulated by Rose and Kincaid that I outlined above, and consider whether our motives in keeping children from knowledge might not be more self-interested than we sometimes like to imagine. Lack of knowledge leads to lack of power—and some adults do prefer children to lack power. In February, 1992, for instance, many Canadian newspapers reported that a logger's union in British Columbia was demanding that Dian Leger-Haskell's picture book *Maxine's Tree* be removed from school libraries, calling the book "an insult to loggers": The book promotes environmental awareness and opposes certain logging practices. It seems that the six-year-old daughter of one of the union members had read the book at school and then come home and announced, "What you do for a living is bad, Daddy" (*Toronto Globe and Mail*, February, 1992). This father clearly wanted to protect himself from having to justify his occupation to his daughter. He might better have had a discussion with her in which he expressed and tried to justify his own opinion about the virtues of logging.

EXPLORATIONS: (1) To what degree do you believe it's important to expose children, through literature, to many kinds of experiences and ideas, however unpleasant? Should children's reading or the contents of children's books be censored in any way? Why or why not?

(2) Read (or ideally, invite children to read) a children's or young adult book that is often the subject of censorship, such as Maurice Sendak's *In the Night Kitchen*, Toshi Maruki's *Hiroshima No Pika*, John Neufeld's *Freddy's Book*, Judy Blume's *Are You There God? It's Me, Margaret* or *Forever*, or Robert Cormier's *Chocolate War*. Should children be given access to the book you've chosen? In what way might it harm them or help them?

Fighting Censorship

For liberal-minded people who believe in freedom of speech, being against censorship seems only logical: Such people find it hard to imagine how anyone would ever want to censor a children's book. If you individually disapprove of it, liberal-minded people say, why not just prevent your own child from reading it? Why insist on having it removed entirely from a classroom or a library? And yet, censorious people demand just that every day, often successfully: They want to deprive *all* children of access to certain kinds of information; they want all children to be as pure and as devoid of knowledge as they believe children are supposed to be. Furthermore, children are deprived of many books simply because librarians or teachers are afraid of the *possibility* of censorship. Better just not use a potentially controversial book at all, they tell themselves, than endanger their livelihood.

All of this suggests that simply being against censorship, or against the censorious selection of children's books, isn't enough. Giving children continued access to a wide variety of books requires positive and continuous action. If you believe as I do that children need and deserve that access, then I recommend the following:

- Be wary of your own censoriousness. Trust the children in your care to handle difficult or disturbing materials, and trust your own ability to help in that process. And try to avoid taking easy ways out: Choose stimulating books even though you suspect they might be controversial.

- Be prepared for would-be censors. Know the arguments they might use, and develop solid, logical answers to those arguments. It's not enough just to ask the rhetorical question, "What's wrong with a child reading this book anyway? I mean, aren't children wise enough to figure things out for themselves?" A censor will have an answer to that question quite different from your own, and you need to have thought about what that answer might be and what arguments you will need to make against it.

- In order to argue successfully, you'll need some knowledge of expert opinion about literature, literary strategies, and child development that supports your position. Know what you're talking about.

- If you're a teacher or librarian, have a procedure in place to deal with complaints. Insist that people who object to books read the entire book, not just one or two offensive passages, before their complaint is heard. Require written commentary from those who complain, specifying the basis of their objection, and have a structure by which complaints are investigated and decisions made. Many state and national library and reading organizations have developed sample policies for dealing with objections to books on which you can base your own. For instance, the National Council of Teachers of English offers a pamphlet called *The Student's Right to Read*.

- Be as energetic in your defense of freedom of speech as censors are in their attempts to censor. Speak out. Make sure other adults know your opinions on these matters and your reasons for having them, even before censorship attempts occur. Make it clear that those who wish to censor are entitled to their opinions but not to their acts of censorship. And be vocal in your support for others who are trying to fend off censorship attempts.

EXPLORATION: in response to an earlier draft of this section, Sue Gannon of Pace University made a comment that confirmed my own experience:

> I have found that many people are all too ready to sound off about how awful censorship is, and make all the expected noises without really thinking too much about the issues involved. It is almost as if they can dismiss the problem by distancing themselves from it: They would never do a thing like that, or even be tempted to. But if I ask them to focus on something they personally disapprove of very strongly, they often say they would not want to see it in books for children. Dealing with real problems and their own divided feelings makes a big difference.

Think of a specific topic about which you personally have strong feelings. How do you feel about the topic being presented in books for children? How would you deal with a children's book that took a position on this topic that you profoundly disagreed with? Try to find and read such a book, and explore your feelings and responses to it.

WORKS CITED

Althusser, Louis. "Ideology and Ideological State Apparatuses." Trans. Ben Brewster. *Critical Theory Since 1965*. Ed. Hazard Adams and Leroy Searle. Tallahassee: University Presses of Florida and Florida State UP, 1986. 239–250.

Applebee, Arthur N. *The Child's Concept of Story: Age Two to Seventeen*. Chicago: U of Chicago P, 1978.

Ariès, Philippe. *Centuries of Childhood: A Social History of Family Life*. Trans. Robert Baldick. New York: Vintage-Random House, 1962.

Blume, Judy. *Are You There, God? It's Me, Margaret*. New York: Bradbury, 1970.

——. *Forever*. New York: Bradbury, 1975.

Borke, Helen. "Piaget's View of Social Interaction and the Theoretical Construct of Empathy." Siegel and Brainerd 29–42.

Bourdieu, Pierre. *In Other Words: Essays Towards a Reflexive Sociology*. Stanford: Stanford UP, 1990.

Brainerd, Charles J. "Learning Research and Piagetian Theory." Siegel and Brainerd 69–109.

——. "Preface." Brainerd, *Recent Advances*.

——, ed. *Recent Advances in Cognitive Developmental Research*. New York: Springer-Verlag, 1983.

Brief, Jean-Claude. *Beyond Piaget: A Philosophical Psychology*. New York: Teachers College, 1983.

Coles, Robert. *The Moral Life of Children*. Boston: Houghton Mifflin, 1986.

Cormier, Robert. *The Chocolate War*. New York: Pantheon, 1974.

Darton, F. J. Harvey. *Children's Books in England: Five Centuries of Social Life*. 1932. 3rd ed. Rev. Brian Alderson. Cambridge: Cambridge UP, 1982.

Davies, Bronwyn. *Frogs and Snails and Feminist Tales: Preschool Children and Gender*. Sydney: Allen and Unwin, 1989.

Demers, Patricia, and Gordon Moyles. *From Instruction to Delight: An Anthology of Children's Literature to 1850*. Toronto: Oxford UP, 1982.

DeLuca, Geraldine, and Roni Natov. "Who's Afraid of Science Books? An Interview with Seymour Simon." *Lion and the Unicorn* 6 (1982): 10–27.

Derrida, Jacques. *Of Grammatology*. Ed. Gayatri Chakravorty Spivak. Baltimore: Johns Hopkins UP, 1976.

Eagleton, Terry. *Ideology: An Introduction*. London and New York: Verso, 1991.

Erikson, Erik. *Childhood and Society*. New York: Norton, 1950.

Gilligan, Carol. *In a Different Voice: Psychological Theories and Women's Development*. Cambridge: Harvard UP, 1982.

Hiner, N. Ray, and Joseph M. Hawes, eds. *Growing Up in America: Children in Historical Perspective*. Urbana: U of Illinois P, 1985.

Huck, Charlotte S. *Children's Literature in the Elementary School*. 3rd ed., updated. New York: Holt, Rinehart and Winston, 1979.

Hunt, David. *Parents and Children in History: The Psychology of Family Life in Early Modern France*. New York: Basic, 1970.

Janeway, James. "From *A Token for Children*." Demers and Moyle 45–53.

Kincaid, James. *Child-Loving: The Erotic Child and Victorian Culture*. Routledge: New York and London, 1992.

Kohlberg, Lawrence. *The Philosophy of Moral Development*. San Francisco: Harper & Row, 1981.

Lawton, Joseph T., and Frank H. Hooper. "Piagetian Theory and Early Childhood Education: A Critical Analysis." Siegel and Brainerd 169–199.

Leger-Haskell, Dian. *Maxine's Tree*. Orca, 1990.

MacDonald, Ruth. *Literature for Children in England and America from 1646 to 1774*. Troy: Whitston, 1982.

Matthews, Gareth. *Dialogues with Children*. Cambridge: Harvard UP, 1984.

———. *Philosophy and the Young Child*. Cambridge: Harvard UP, 1980.

Moffett, James. *Storm in the Mountains: A Case Study of Censorship*. Carbondale: Southern Illinois UP, 1988.

Myers, Mitzi. "Wise Child, Wise Peasant, Wise Guy: Geoffrey Summerfield's Case Against the Eighteenth Century." *Children's Literature Association Quarterly* 12.2 (Summer 1987): 107–110.

National Council of Teachers of English. *The Student's Right to Read*. Urbana: NCTE, 1980.

Neufeld, Jon. *Freddy's Book*. New York: Random House, 1973.

Piaget, Jean. *The Language and Thought of the Child*. Trans. Marjories and Ruth Gabain. London: Routledge and Kegan Paul, 1959.

Pollock, Linda A. *Forgotten Children: Parent-Child Relations from 1500 to 1900*. Cambridge: Cambridge UP, 1983.

Protherough, Robert. *Developing Response to Fiction*. Milton Keynes, England: Open UP, 1983.

Purves, Alan C., and Dianne L. Monson. *Experiencing Children's Literature*. Glenview: Scott, Foresman, 1984.

Rose, Jacqueline. *The Case of Peter Pan: or The Impossibility of Children's Fiction*. London: Macmillan, 1984.

Shahar, Shulamith. *Childhood in the Middle Ages*. London and New York: Routledge, 1990.

Siegel, Linda S., and Charles J. Brainerd, eds. *Alternatives to Piaget: Critical Essays on the Theory*. New York: Academic, 1978.

Spock, Dr. Benjamin. *Baby and Child Care*. Rev. ed. New York: Pocket Books, 1968.

Stephens, John. *Language and Ideology in Children's Fiction*. London and New York: Longman, 1992.

Studier-Chang, Catherine. "Point of View: *Hiroshima No Pika*—For Mature Audiences." *Advocate* 3,3 (Spring 1984): 158, 166–169.

Sugarman, Susan. *Piaget's Construction of the Child's Reality*. Cambridge: Cambridge UP, 1987.

Summerfield, Geoffrey. *Fantasy and Reason: Children's Literature in the Eighteenth Century*. Athens: U of Georgia P, 1984.

Thorne, Barrie. "Re-Visioning Women and Social Change: Where Are the Children?" *Gender and Society* 1,1 (March 1987): 85–109.

Tucker, Nicholas. *The Child and the Book: A Psychological and Literary Exploration*. Cambridge: Cambridge UP, 1981.

Weiss, Nancy Pottishman. "Mother, the Invention of Necessity: Dr. Benjamin Spock's *Baby and Child Care*." Hiner and Hawes 283–303.

Williams, Raymond. *Marxism and Literature*. Oxford: Oxford UP, 1977.

Wollstonecraft, Mary. "From *Original Stories from Real Life*." Demers and Moyles 138–145.

Zimmerman, Barry J. "Social Learning Theory: A Contextualist Account of Cognitive Functioning." Brainerd, *Recent Advances*, 1–50.

chapter 6

Children in Ideology

The previous chapter described ways in which the ideology of our culture influences the ideas adults have about childhood, and how those ideas might influence adult dealings with children. This chapter deals with children themselves. It focuses on the ways in which current ideology, as expressed particularly in literary texts, toys and games, movies and TV shows, might influence the ideas children develop about themselves and about the world they live in.

According to Peter Hunt, "It is arguably impossible for a children's book (especially one being read by a child) not to be educational or influential in some way; it cannot help but reflect an ideology. . . . All books must teach something" (3). Furthermore, the teaching can come in a variety of ways, some less obvious than others. John Stephens says,

> On the one hand, the significance deduced from a text—its theme, moral, insight into behaviour, and so on—is never without an ideological dimension or connotation. On the other hand, and less overtly, ideology is implicit in the way the story an audience derives from a text exists as an isomorph [or representation] of events in the actual world: even if the story's events are wholly or partly impossible in actuality, narrative sequences and character interrelationships will be shaped according to recognizable forms, and the shaping can in itself express ideology in so far as it implies assumptions about the forms of human existence. (2)

In other words, literary texts offer children representations of the world and of their own place as children within that world. If the representation is persuasive, it will *become* the world that those child readers believe they live in.

If that's true of books, it's at least as true of games and toys, movies and TV shows. Speaking of the importance of stories as ways in which we come to understand the world, Marcia Kinder says, "Ever since television became pervasive in the American home, this mass medium has played a crucial role in the child's entry into narrative" (93). If that's true—and I believe it must be—then exploring the ideological content of the narratives we offer children, both in books and other media, is a matter of great significance. What stories do we most often ask children to believe are true representation of both themselves and others?

CHILDREN'S CHOICES: THE FREEDOM TO BE UNIQUE?

The major thing we'd like children to believe about themselves is the major thing that most of us, as adults in a democratic society, would like to believe about ourselves: Each of us is a unique individual with unique tastes and interests, entitled to the freedom to make choices. I firmly believe what I suspect most parents and educators would agree with, at least in theory: Children, inevitably involved in the process of learning who they are, need the freedom to choose at least as much as adults do, and need to learn and believe in the importance of that freedom, both for themselves and for others. Not surprisingly, countless children's book and movies reinforce the message that we need to respect and to treasure the ways in which we are different from each other.

In terms of the subject of this book, the uniqueness of individual taste and the freedom to choose relate most significantly to matters such as what books we read, TV shows we watch, or toys we purchase. As the discussion of censorship in the last chapter reveals, our theoretical faith in the right of children to make choices about these matters doesn't always match our actual behavior. Indeed, our theories and actions about these matters display the contradictions that identify ideology at work. Some adults will insist on leaving potentially frightening or dangerous books out of a library collection exactly *because* they want children to have the freedom to make their own choices from the collection. You are free to choose, their actions imply, but only so long as you choose from the safe, limited menu we approve of.

Selection practices aren't the only means by which we limit the choices of children. Even if a library included every children's book published, its selections would be limited to the ones editors and publishers deemed suitable for an audience of children. It becomes important to consider how editors and publishers make such choices. What factors influence their decisions? How likely is it that books for children—indeed, books in general—do represent the widest possible spectrum of choices for the widest possible range of individual tastes, interests, and values?

Parents as Purchasers

In the mid-1980s, the sales of children's books in North America skyrocketed. The most obvious reason was that the children of the so-called baby-boomers (those people born between 1945 and 1965 who form the largest segment of the population) were beginning to read. Furthermore, the baby-boomers seemed more willing, or able, than their parents had been to buy children's books. Because many of them had put off having children until much later in their lives than had been typical, many had already established careers. Even those less well off were often in two-career marriages. There was more money to spend on relatively nonessential things like children's books.

Meanwhile, the political climate meant that government at all levels had less money to spend on libraries. According to Adam Hochschild, "fifteen or twenty years ago, some 85% of children's books were sold to school or public libraries. This figure has plummeted" (28). By 1993, a *Publishers Weekly* survey reported that almost 40 percent of all children's books sold in bookstores were bought by mothers; teachers bought only about 15 percent.

The dramatic increase in the proportion of books purchased by parents and other relatives transformed the children's book business. The teachers or librarians who used to buy most children's books were professional experts with a claim to some knowledge of children's literature. Now, the people who buy the most books aren't experts, and they have no way of choosing books other than to try to figure out what the children they know might like. This means, primarily, things they or their children are already familiar with.

Bookstores and publishers quickly acted to fill this need, by concentrating on books in three major categories:

1. Reprintings and new editions of favorite books from the baby-boomers' youth: books by Dr. Seuss, book versions of classic Disney cartoons.
2. Other movie and TV tie-ins: books about characters the baby-boomers' children were already familiar with from other media.
3. Books about new characters, but ones that came in series, so that once children became familiar with these characters they could read new books about them again and again.

None of these forms of publishing was new in the 1980s, of course. But they quickly became the major focus of the children's book business. While other, more interesting books continued to be published, they became less central. The one notable exception was in the publication of picture books, many of which continued (and still continue) to be imaginative and innovative—perhaps because these books, while unfamiliar, were short enough for parents to read, enjoy, and choose to buy while still in the bookstore.

EXPLORATION: Survey the collections of books owned by children you know. What proportion consists of books of the sorts I've just described? What other books do these children have access to? How diverse is their reading?

Books of these sorts are still the best-selling children's books, by far. In the calendar year 1992, for instance, the two top-selling new children's books in hard-

cover were both tie-ins to the Disney movie *Aladdin:* one sold over a million copies, the other about 800,000 (*Publishers Weekly,* March 1, 1993); and the top-selling
book in paperback was a tie-in to the Disney movie *Beauty and the Beast,* which
sold about 550,000 copies. The top-selling backlist books—those published in previous years—were *Beauty and the Beast* tie-ins in hardcover (430,000 copies) and
in paperback (790,000 copies).

These tie-ins were quickly followed on the 1992 best-selling lists by series
books. Three horror stories by Christopher Pike were the second, third, and fourth
best-selling paperbacks (over 400,000 copies each), and three of the best-selling fifteen were books in the *Babysitter's Club* series—a significant drop-off from 1991,
when ten of the fifteen best-selling books were *Babysitters.* Indeed, by the middle
of 1993, there were more than 69 million *Babysitter* books in print. Meanwhile, the
1992 backlists were dominated by old favorites from the baby-boomers' own childhoods: Dr. Seuss's *Green Eggs and Ham* (380,000 copies) and *Cat in the Hat*
(312,000 copies), and White's *Charlotte's Web* (490,000 copies).

Nothing much had changed by 1994. *Charlotte's Web* and books by Dr. Seuss
still appeared high up in a "Children's Best Sellers" list published in the *New York
Times Book Review* (May 22, 1994); and the *Times* reported that sales for books in
the wildly successful *Goosebumps* series of horror novels by R. L. Stine equaled
sales for all the other fifteen best-selling series *combined.*

These massive sales figures for popular books should be considered in relation
to the average print run (number of copies printed at any one time) in the United
States for a new non-series children's novel by a writer without a best-selling reputation: between 5,000 and 10,000 copies. For many of these books, the first printing
will be the only printing, and represents the maximum number of copies of those
titles that will ever be sold. And while those titles that make it into paperback sell
more, there's still a vast gulf between sales figures for the kinds of books experts
tend to admire and purchase for school and public libraries and sales figures for the
best-selling books.

Hunt offers an interesting interpretation of the gulf between what experts admire and what actually sells well: "The terrifying and unmanageable idea is that the
books that are positively bad from the adult point of view may be the good children's books" (187). But while large sales and a wide readership suggest that children do enjoy certain kinds of books, it doesn't necessarily mean they are the only
books children are able to enjoy. They may be reading and, therefore, learning to
like such books merely because they are the kind of book most children are most
likely to have access to.

CHILDREN'S LITERATURE IN THE ECONOMY

Books of these sorts are increasingly becoming almost the *only* kind of book most
children have ready access to. A number of business developments and economic
factors have meant that in recent years publishers tend to concentrate their efforts
on trying to produce best-selling books, and fewer innovative or unusual books for
children are being published.

In the early 1980s, in order to encourage aggressive sales, the U.S. government raised the taxes charged on goods left in warehouses at the end of each year. As applied to books, this meant that publishers could no longer afford to keep large numbers of titles on their backlists: Books that had been in print for decades suddenly became unavailable. Now, only those titles that still sell widely remain in print for very long.

In recent decades, meanwhile, many publishing companies that were once independent enterprises have been purchased by larger conglomerates. For instance: Some decades ago, Scribner's, Macmillan, and Simon & Schuster were all separate companies, each with its unique focus and philosophy. A few years ago, Scribner's and a number of other companies became part of the Macmillan group of companies. In 1993, after the international conglomerate that controlled Macmillan got into financial difficulty, the Macmillan companies were all purchased by Simon & Schuster. In turn, Simon & Schuster is now part of the Paramount Group, which also makes movies and owns various amusement parks and the MTV cable network, as well as some other publishing companies: Prentice Hall, Silver Burdett-Ginn, and Pocket Books. In 1993, the Paramount Group was purchased by the cable company Viacom.

Viacom/Paramount/Simon & Schuster has closed down the Scribner's and the Macmillan lines of children's books. While some of the other lines in this and other large groups still maintain separate editorial departments, decisions about what gets published are increasingly in the hands of fewer people.

They are also different people. While the old independent publishers were businessmen, their biographies suggest that they tended to view their work not just as a way of making money but as a humane contribution to the quality of life and literature. Famous editors like Charlotte Zolotow of Harper & Row often published books that might not sell widely but that seemed interesting, innovative, or important. The executives of the multinational corporations that now control publishing (Zolotow's firm is now part of the international conglomerate HarperCollins) tend to focus more exclusively on the bottom line. There is increasing pressure on editors of children's books to produce little beyond the kinds of books that are most likely to achieve wide sales.

Meanwhile, as I suggested earlier, an increasingly popular anti-big-government philosophy, and the depressed economy of the late 1980s and early 1990s, had a particularly powerful effect on the funding of schools and libraries. The acquisition budgets of those most likely to buy more interesting or unusual books are substantially lower than they once were.

At the same time as bookstores were starting to sell a larger proportion of children's books, the bookselling business was going through a number of important changes. Prior to the late 1970s, bookselling in North America was dominated by independent bookstores, each making its own selections of what to stock from the offerings of publishers. In the 1980s, a few chains like Waldenbooks, B. Dalton, and Crown took over a sizable portion of the business.

These chains consist of relatively small stores in malls. With little space, they tend to concentrate on books with the potential to sell strongly. Rather than a few copies of a lot of different titles, their stock tends to consist of multiple copies of fewer titles. In terms of children's books, this means a concentration on old favorites, tie-ins, and books in series in what are often the only bookstores in many towns and smaller cities.

Chains like these tend to have centralized buying: A small group of buyers at the corporate headquarters select all the titles for all the stores. The result is that all stores have the same books. This means that only books of national, mainstream interest are likely to be available. Furthermore, the books in each category—science fiction, cookbooks, children's books—are often selected by just one person in each chain. That gives a few individuals great power: If the buyers for one or two major chains decide not to stock a particular book, perhaps just for reasons of personal taste, it becomes difficult for a publisher to justify publishing it at all.

In the 1990s, the chains have been replacing their small mall stores with "superstores": large, freestanding bookstores that stock 75,000 to 125,0000 titles, sometimes even more. The development of superstores certainly represents an improvement in the potential availability of a diversity of books, but it does have dangerous side-effects. Superstores have such a huge selection that they tend to kill the market for independent booksellers even in large cities. More stores continue to be in the control of fewer people, and an increasing proportion of bookstores is owned by just two large corporations: Barnes and Noble, which also uses the names B. Dalton and Doubleday; and Borders, itself owned by K-Mart, which also uses the names Waldenbooks and Bassett. In a *Publishers Weekly* interview, Neal Sofman, owner of an independent bookstore in San Francisco, calls this "a concentration of power that threatens the diversity of what gets published" (January 4, 1993).

Superstores are large enough, and have large enough sales, particularly of best-selling books, that they can demand from publishers large discounts off the suggested retail price of the books—as high as 65 to 70 percent. Independent booksellers can rarely command better than 40 percent discounts. Publishers respond to the chains' demand for higher discounts by being cautious about producing books that might not sell widely enough to return a profit on a smaller margin. Also, some publishers have responded to the demand for higher discounts by increasing the suggested retail price of books. This means they can maintain their profits on more deeply discounted books; but it also puts higher prices on the more unusual books not likely to be so deeply discounted; and that, of course, makes book buyers increasingly unwilling to take chances on the unusual books.

All of these factors come together to make fewer books, and fewer kinds of books, available to children. The books that remain tend to be the ones that are likely to sell widely to people with mainstream tastes and values. Children still do have the freedom to choose—but the scope of what they get to choose from is much smaller than it once was, which tends to encourage conformity to the most popular ideas about what it means to be human.

EXPLORATIONS: (1) Survey (or invite children to survey) what kinds of books are available in local bookstores. How much diversity is represented in their selections? Interview booksellers about their stock and how and why it is selected, and about what books customers tend to purchase.

(2) As market trends change, the conclusions I reach in this section might cease to represent the actual situation. I based what I've said here primarily on information I found in *Publishers Weekly,* a journal read by those who produce and market books; read more current editions of this journal, and consider if the same trends continue, and what might be the implications of newer trends.

THE WORLD IN CHILDREN'S BOOKS: NONFICTION?

A sizable proportion of the books available for children is what we call *nonfiction:* informational texts about the way things are. Unlike fiction, these books claim to be true; their authors' main purpose is to communicate knowledge accurately. But in the process of doing so, they must select which facts to provide and which ones to leave out; and they must interpret those facts in order to make them meaningful for young readers. Not surprisingly, furthermore, different writers will interpret the same information differently—tell a different story about the same information; as Hayden White points out in discussing texts about history, "the same event can serve as a different kind of element of many different historical stories. . . . The death of the king may be a beginning, an ending, or simply a transitional event in three different stories" (7).

As a result, nonfiction shares many of the qualities of fictional narrative. Histories and biographies have plots similar to those of novels, with meanings emerging from the causal connections that the plots create between events; and since plots emerge from the actions of characters, histories and biographies inevitably imply interpretations of the motivations of those involved, just as fictional stories do. Even texts about science and nature have plots or are shaped around focalized points of view and structural patterns of words and images.

EXPLORATION: Read (or invite children to read) a nonfictional text, and identify the elements of fiction in it by approaching it in terms of the interpretive strategies outlined in chapter 4: how events are organized to make a plot, what themes events or objects are made to express, and so on. Does it seem that facts are being distorted in order to build these kinds of consistency?

Finally, then, the representations of reality in nonfiction have almost the same status as the ones we find in fiction: Both are always slanted or partial versions of the truth. But since nonfictional texts do claim to be nonfictional, they have an especially strong potential to *become* the truth for readers who accept their view of things and insert themselves into the narratives these texts offer. In the process of conveying factual information about science or history, then, nonfictional texts can and do easily reinforce ideological assumptions about individuals and society.

Furthermore, in a vast number of nonfictional texts for children, that world is described in surprisingly consistent ways. For this reason, they offer particularly revealing insights into the nature of the world we work to persuade children they live in.

The World Is a Simple Place

To some degree, the phrase "children's nonfiction" is contradictory. "Nonfiction" implies factual accuracy; but because of the assumptions outlined in the last chapter, "children's" implies a version of the facts specifically tailored to the needs and interests of inexperienced readers. Texts of children's nonfiction tend to eliminate or downplay complications in the belief that simple information is all that children can understand. Patricia Lauber expresses a common selfcontradictory attitude when she insists that science books for children must be accurate but then adds, "Taking dead aim at some of the concepts and theories of modern science is seldom possible. They are too hard and unfamiliar" (8). The world of most children's nonfiction is easy to understand and comfortingly (or boringly) like what many children are apt to know already.

The World Is a Happy Place

Board books intended for babies always show the world as nothing but bright and clean and new. The apples are shiny and perfect, without flaws or marks or worm holes; the high chairs are clean and freshly painted, without food stains or tooth marks. The uniform cheerfulness of this environment continues in nonfictional depictions of the world intended for older children. Aliki's *How a Book Is Made* describes the entire process of the writing, editing, and publishing of a book without reporting a single disagreement. Apparently, young readers aren't to know that adults in the publishing industry do sometimes have arguments.

The World Is a Homogeneous Place

As in *How a Book Is Made,* the world of most children's fiction is one in which adults agree so completely on acceptable behavior that they all behave in the same way without comment. In this utopian world, the behavior many adults consider to be desirable is merely normal—and not just normal, but the whole and only truth; less conventional behavior doesn't even exist.

Speaking of her biographical novel about Leonardo da Vinci, E. L. Konigsburg celebrates that fact. She says that the young man whom da Vinci supported for years was probably involved in a homosexual relationship with the great artist, "but

. . . I am glad that I write for children. For that explanation of his use of a young boy will never do. It is simply not enough; it is not deep enough" (258). Konigsburg claims that her own interpretation—that da Vinci admired a vitality in the young man that he himself lacked—is more deeply revealing of human nature than the supposedly superficial fact of homosexuality.

Personally, I doubt that homosexuality would seem like such a superficial or unimportant facet of existence to the considerable number of children who have gay or Lesbian parents, or to those who might themselves be trying to understand their own homosexual feelings. Deprived of the opportunity to read books describing situations like their own—and as Virginia L. Wolf reports, few such books exist—these children have no choice but to conclude that they are freaks. Wolf says, "The lack of information available to young people about the gay family is an injustice" (52), especially to the 6 million children of gay parents in the United States. But that injustice may be exactly the point of that lack of information: Showing only some aspects of reality normalizes them, and inevitably implies the freakish unacceptability of others in the world children's nonfiction most often asks children to believe in.

In confirmation of this unacceptability, it's interesting to note that, in a news release of February 1995, the American Library Association announced that the "most challenged" book of 1994—the one most often the target of censorship attempts—was Michael Willhoite's *Daddy's Roommate,* a picture book designed to help children understand a nontraditional family that includes a gay father and his partner.

The World Has Always Been Homogeneous

Like Konigsburg's book about da Vinci, the vast majority of books about history for children are in fact not nonfiction at all, but "historical fiction" that describes real events through the experiences of imaginary characters. The reason that happens is nicely summed up by a comment in Zena Sutherland and Myra Cohn Livingston's *Scott, Foresman Anthology of Children's Literature:* "the best historical fiction presents characters and events with an apparent spontaneity that brings them to life so vividly that readers feel no sense of distance" (688). To assume "no sense of distance" is to suggest that people are uninfluenced enough by their times or their societies to be basically the same. Much historical fiction for children works to persuade readers that we are now as humans what we have always been. That theme clearly identifies an ideological bias in the world we want children to believe in; Terry Eagleton speaks of "the *dehistoricizing* thrust of ideology, its tacit denial that ideas and beliefs are specific to a particular time, place, and social group" (59).

EXPLORATION: Read (or invite children read) works of historical fiction intended for children, and consider if the characters' values are different from your own or not.

The World and Its People Are Wonderfully Diverse

In what seems to be a contradiction to the idea that the world is homogeneous, many nonfictional texts about the lives of people in other countries insist on their differences. In Peter Spier's *People,* for instance, a page showing people dressed in the traditional costumes of different nations says, "People around the world wear different clothes—or none at all." There's no mention of the fact that few people anywhere in the world still wear these kinds of traditional costumes on a daily basis.

A few years ago, my son's elementary school teacher provided me with an explanation for this sort of misrepresentation, when she told me why the Japan he was reading and learning about was a country of samurai warriors and tea houses, a country without industrialization and with no history of nuclear destruction—a Japan that hasn't existed for a century. She said she was trying to teach her students tolerance for people different from themselves, and it would be harder to make that point about people like the residents of contemporary Japan who dress and eat much like we do. Ideology mattered more than truth.

Nevertheless, the diversity of the world we most often present to children is superficial. Books like Spier's and like the ones about Japan my son's teacher used almost always insist that despite their different clothes and foods, people everywhere are really basically the same. Indeed, these books insist, that's exactly why we can and should be so tolerant of their differences: Once we acknowledge the superficial differences, we can see past them into the shared humanity and understand that our values are theirs too, and therefore, universally and incontrovertibly true. This is dangerously chauvinistic.

The World Is a Rational Place

In *The Medieval World,* Mitsumasa Anno makes fun of the ignorance of people who were so "clouded with superstition" that they were unable to discover obvious facts such as the existence of bacteria. Miriam Youngerman Miller asks, "What is to be gained by criticizing the medieval world for failure to apply the scientific method, when the development of that method still lay centuries in the future?" (169). The answer to her question is fairly clear: It persuades young readers that the world can truly be understood only in the terms science insists on. Billie Nodelman says, "Scientists are often true believers in much the same way that fundamental Christians are. They believe they know the Truth and are furious when someone calls that faith into question" (182). Seymour Simon unwittingly offers an example of that point in his interview with Geraldine DeLuca and Roni Natov, when he dismisses the claims of creationists: "I can't believe that saying something as straightforward as 'dinosaurs are several hundred million years old' can become controversial, but among some people, evidently, it is. This is not something that is controversial as far as science is concerned. And if I'm going to do a book about dinosaurs, I'm going to do it from a scientific point of view" (23). That view controls most discussion of natural phenomena in the world of children's books; while I more or less accept that view myself, I'm conscious of the many other possible interpretations it simply ignores and refuses to let children know about.

The World Is Full of Clear and Obvious Messages about Values

Despite a frequent insistence on scientific objectivity, the people, places, and things described in most children's nonfiction represent more than just scientific facts; they stand for moral and ethical values. In countless books about nature, trees and animals represent environmental concerns; and human lives as described for children almost always contain implicit messages about character.

"Biographies for children," says Leonard Marcus, "have a secret subject in addition to the one they are obviously 'about.' That secret subject is the reader. The author, retelling someone else's life, is also to some extent thinking of the reader's own future, of how the reader will be influenced by what the author says" (28). In order to accomplish this goal, many children's biographies turn the lives of their subjects into fables: stories with a clear and obvious message about values and behavior. Charlotte S. Huck makes the ideological bias of such books clear when she says, "Biography fulfills children's needs for identification with someone 'bigger' than they are. In this day of mass conformity, it may give them new models of greatness to emulate or suggest new horizons of endeavor" (550).

The World Is a Hopeful Place

Describing books about the holocaust and nuclear disaster, Barbara Harrison says, "Although there is now greater candor in literature for the young than ever before, the one characteristic which adults are reluctant to see diminished in any way is hope, traditionally the animating force in children's books" (69). Even Toshi Maruki's *Hiroshima No Pika* expresses hope in spite of the horror of the nuclear bombing it so honestly depicts: It ends with its central character, now a deformed adult, insisting that people can learn from their mistakes and hoping therefore that such a catastrophe won't happen again. I'd like to believe that; on the other hand, I know that other, less optimistic ideas about human nature can be drawn from the story of Hiroshima, and that children are rarely given those other ideas. This means children are less free to choose an optimistic interpretation of the world than I am: Are we as adults convinced that children will be hopeful only so long as they don't encounter other possibilities?

The World Is Getting Better All the Time

Hope emerges from the confidence that things do improve over time. In *The Medieval World,* Anno encourages that confidence by presenting medieval Christianity as a dangerously ignorant set of superstitions that created a dirty and evil-filled world we have, fortunately, grown beyond. He says nothing of the virtues of that less-pol-

luted and more-stable society that we have lost. Furthermore, Anno views the intolerance of witch hunts and the destructiveness of plagues as evils that no longer exist, a view that ignores aspects of our own world like racial prejudice and AIDS.

EXPLORATION: How true are my descriptions of the world depicted in
children's nonfiction? Explore (or invite children to explore) the degree to
which a random selection of nonfictional texts express these characteristics.

Representation as Reality

The characteristics I've described work together to encourage children to be all the
things we claim to believe they already are. In other words: If children were not already the limited, egocentric, innocent, optimistic beings we like to view them as,
then most children's nonfiction would easily encourage them to learn to be those
things, merely by always insisting that the world is simple, happy, homogeneous,
easily understood, and much like the utopia adults like to imagine, and by never
giving any information that would suggest anything else.

THE WORLD OF CHILDREN'S TOYS AND GAMES

The world children come to understand through nonfictional texts might well be
one they are familiar with already: As I try to show in the chapter 8, it is the world
as described in many texts of children's fiction. Furthermore, it is the world implied
by a vast range of other materials adults provide for children, from the images on
wallpaper, bed linens, and T-shirts to the activities and characters represented in
toys and video games. As products of the same culture, all of these texts and objects tend to express the same values and assumptions and help to make obviousnesses obvious.

Toys are particularly potent bearers of ideology simply because they so often
represent adult activities (war, cooking, and so on) and have the purpose of helping children to fantasize about aspects of adult life and imitate adult behavior. In
doing so, they transmit ways of thinking about the world.

EXPLORATION: Because of the constant changes in the toy industry, the
examples discussed in the section that follows may have gone out of fashion by the time you read this book. Visit a toy store, and consider the values and assumptions implied by the toys you see there.

Toys and Gender

Many of the toys available for young children assume (and therefore teach) traditional ways of distinguishing gender. In advertising on TV and in flyers, the colors
of the toys girls play with are almost always delicate pastel pinks and mauves,

while the ones we see boys play with are strong reds and blacks. In this way, toys and the commercials for them reinforce the importance both of making strong distinctions between males and females and of knowing what one's own *gender* is and how to express it to others.

Kinder reports that her son enjoyed playing with the toys called "My Little Ponies" until he saw TV commercials in which only girls played with them: "in this way young viewers learn that television and its advertising discourse are powerful agents of the gendering process and that during the vulnerable period when their own gender identification is being established, the most effective way for them to play an active role is by choosing their own clothes and toys" (50). If choosing toys is a way of defining one's gender, then gender becomes a form of masquerade or performance: a kind of costume or image one adopts or performs as a signal for other people rather than something one automatically feels physiologically from within. As Judith Butler suggests, "Gender is the repeated stylization of the body, a set of repeated acts within a highly rigid regulatory frame that congeal over time to produce the appearance of substance, of a natural sort of being" (33). One learns to look and act like a boy or girl rather than doing it naturally—and then assumes it to be natural.

Surprisingly, furthermore, the red and black toys still tend to be weapons and superheroes, the pastel ones ponies and baking ovens. The more adults in our culture defy gender stereotypes, the more toys seem to insist on them. Baking remains an inherently female activity even for those children who often see their fathers use the oven.

One reason for that may be a quality the world of toys shares with the world of nonfiction. Both tend to confuse what a culture assumes to be ideal with normalcy, what we would like to believe with what we claim actually exists. Ideally for our culture, presumably, all girls would be what we call "feminine" and all boys what we call "masculine." Then there would be no confusion about these matters, and no need to develop subtle, complicated thoughts about them, or a spectrum of responses to a variety of different kinds of people with different ways of being male or female. Life would be simpler—better, we tell ourselves. We also tell it to our children. In toys and toy advertising, it *is* simple and better: This supposed ideal is the complete and only truth represented.

Barbie dolls are a good example of the results of this notion. They represent a supposedly ideal teenager as if she were merely an ideally ordinary one. Barbie's decidedly unusual appearance—incredibly long legs and neck, exceedingly narrow waist—is presented as both perfect female teenaged beauty and also as what all female teenagers would be if they were perfectly normal. The Barbie image is so central to our culture's ideal of female beauty that it's constantly being reinforced; in TV commercials and in fashion magazines, the vast majority of images of teenaged girls look like Barbie (or as much like Barbie as a real human can). So the younger girls who play with Barbie are learning to accept as both desirable and normal the appearance society expects them to match up to in their later lives as teenagers and adult women. Those young girls who accept the intertwined normalcy and ideality of that image but whose own appearance differs from it must then feel not only not ideal, but also, disconcertingly, not normal: freakish. Many young girls not only think that, but work hard to make themselves less freakish, sometimes to the point of serious physical illness.

When she was first invented in 1959, Stephen Kline says, "Barbie was carefully and consciously designed not as just another plaything, but as a personality. . . . Barbie was provided with a 'back-story'—a narrative that established her personality profile within an imaginary but familiar universe" (170). The original and still-central *back-story* confirms the peculiar intertwining of the ideal and the ordinary implied by her appearance. As a successful fashion model, Barbie is of course obsessed with the way she looks and highly responsive to new fashions. While she has her boyfriend, Ken, she seems to be less interested in interacting with him than in the main task of her job: attracting attention, not just from Ken but from other males and females. But Barbie's ideally successful life and career—her position as a unique star—seem to depend on her ability to stand for an ideally typical teenaged girl: typical teenaged girls, Barbie's story suggests, are *all* obsessed with their appearance, with new clothes, with attracting attention from men and other women.

These qualities are the ones traditionally associated in our culture with femininity: In John Berger's description of traditional values, *"men act and women appear.* Men look at women. Women watch themselves being looked at. This determines not only most relations between men and women but also the relation of women to themselves" (250). The Barbie back-story embeds this gender stereotype into the minds and lives of children.

Over the decades, an ever-increasing variety of Barbie dolls have come equipped with an ever-expanding repertoire of back-stories, in which Barbie is everything from a cosmetician to an astronaut to president of the United States. But in all these manifestations, she retains the same ideally typical appearance and the same ideally typical concern with appearance and clothing. All possible careers become absorbed in the same theoretically desirable image: The feminist desire to expand the aspirations of girls becomes enmeshed in the same old, restrictive image of femininity.

EXPLORATION: In this section, I've focused on popular toys that communicate assumptions about femininity to girls. What assumptions about masculinity might be being conveyed in toys currently popular with boys?

Toys and Consumption

As well as representing cultural attitudes, toys are commodities: objects to be sold and owned. Simply because children want to own them, they are a powerful means by which children learn to be consumers. As Kline says, "In the age of marketing, toys . . . are the templates through which children are being introduced into the attitudes and social relations of consumerism" (349).

Marketing influences this process in a number of ways. Toys often come in collectible sets, and much of the pleasure they offer is in the satisfaction of completing the set—in the sheer possession of them. The desire to have them is encouraged by

TV advertising, which shows other children happily playing with them. Since the main significance of these toys is owning them, they often end up in closets and aren't much played with. Manufacturers encourage children to become bored and dissatisfied with the toys they already own by dropping advertisements for one set of toys just about when many children will have completed their sets, and starting to push a new set.

In addition, the toy market is increasingly dominated by *character toys:* plastic representations of fantasy figures or superheroes who come accompanied by increasingly detailed back-stories. In 1984, the Federal Communication Commission eliminated its ban on product-based programs. Since then, an increasing number of children's TV programs involve characters also available as toys. According to Kline, "by the late 1980s close to sixty different product-tied animation programmes had been showcased on kids-time TV" (139). Much children's programming is merely detailed back-stories for toys children can own.

Kline believes that much of this marketing is successful simply because it plays into the tastes and interests of children: "the merchants and marketers of children's goods have always paid more diligent attention than educationists to children's active imaginations and incidental cultural interests" (18). He does, however, add that, "given the enormous promotional apparatus directed at influencing parents and children's preferences in the market, I also find it difficult to maintain that contemporary children's culture expresses children's autonomous choices and preserves their innocence" (19). Kinder agrees: "As long as children's television is embedded in the larger intertextual structures of commercial television, it will reproduce consumerist subjects" (46).

Clearly, then, it is ideology that produces children who take intense pleasure in ownership; who believe that their most significant relationships are, like the ones shown as desirable in TV commercials, the relationships they have with other children rather than the ones they have with adults; who are convinced that owning the right toys will allow them these relationships; who use play as a way of accommodating themselves to gender roles and other assumptions about the world; and who require adult aid in engendering the fantasy world of their imaginative play.

Toys and Flexibility

Almost half a century ago, the French theorist Roland Barthes reached this conclusion: "Faced with this world of faithful [that is, faithfully imitative of adult realities] and complicated objects, the child can only identify himself as owner, as user, never as creator; he does not invent the world, he uses it: there are, prepared for him, actions without adventure, without wonder, without joy" (54). But many toys of recent years seem to celebrate the value of change, and offer children opportunities to experience the power of making choices or the freedom to imagine different possibilities. Many character toys represent people changed into something other (and less ordinary) than human, such as Teenage Mutant Ninja Turtles or Mighty Morphin Power Rangers. Some toys actually can change, and do offer children opportunities to make choices. Barbie dolls and others have wide selections of clothing and attachments, and other character toys follow the principles of Transformers, carlike machines that can convert to humanlike machines.

But perhaps Barthes is still right after all. Rangers always "morph" and Transformers always transform in the same way. Furthermore, their back-stories always seem to be variations of the same basic tale about apparently weak people who have the inner potential to defeat powerful enemies once they find and express an aggressiveness hidden inside them. And whatever Barbie wears, it merely reinforces her central focus on fashion and the consumption of new goods. In all these toys, the idea of change is attached to the need for having different costumes or appearances, and the power that comes from having them. The transforming costumes or appearance are masks that allow the same unchanged entity to masquerade as something or someone different and more powerful. As Susan Willis points out in her discussion of Transformers, "Everything transforms but nothing changes. . . . The fascination with transforming toys may well reside in the utopian yearning for change which the toys themselves, then, manage, and control" (415–416). In other words, these toys convert any desire children might have for a better world or for control over choosing their destinies into a need to always own new goods that supports the mainstream ideology of our culture, rather than leading to real changes in the culture or any real freedom from its influence.

Something similar operates in video games. They offer players control of a fantasy world: the act of wielding a joystick offers the power to make choices and change the events on screen as one likes. Marketing supports the significance of that power: Players can purchase Power Gloves and Power Pads, and watch TV commercials for games that assert, "Now, you're playing with power!" Furthermore, the games themselves represent back-stories that focus on power struggles and put players in the position of theoretically weak characters trying to win power over strong enemies. Kinder quotes the comment of her eight-year-old son that people "wanted control. So they invented video games" (1).

Once in control, however, players of video games can find success only by learning the one correct set of choices that will lead to victory. According to Gillian Skirrow, "The fascination of video games . . . is to be looked for in the opportunities provided for repetition of a set of actions, performed with an almost neurotic compulsion" (129). Once more, the thrill of change and control is absorbed into activities demanding changelessness and submission. The more power players are persuaded they have, the more power these games have over them; in Barthes's terms, the more players can be made to believe they invent the world of their play, the more it invents them.

THE WORLD OF CHILDREN'S TV

TV is a much more obvious case of the manipulation of children than nonfiction or toys: We're all convinced of its power to influence children. Adults and governments worry particularly about the effect of TV violence on children. It might well be harmful, simply because widespread concern has led to regulations that enforce distorted depictions of violent acts. Guns are fired and people are punched, but we never see blood shed or flesh fly in the process: The results happen off-screen. Without the unsettlingly horrific effects of real-life violence, TV violence does seem clean and safe and therefore a good way to deal with problems and have fun.

Even so research in this area is confusing and seems to depend on proving what one wishes to be true. The evidence collected in different experiments suggests that TV makes people both more violent and, paradoxically, less violent. One of its effects is to emotionally numb viewers, to disengage them from involvement with others or even from thoughtfulness about themselves. "Couch potatoes" are too lethargic to do much harm—or for that matter, much good, except for the people who want to sell them things.

The ability of TV to promote numbness in viewers makes it an especially effective ideological tool. In closing down our awareness, it leaves us submissive and accepting. And because the most popular TV programming would lose its audience if it did not express mainstream tastes and interests, what it asks us to accept is mainstream values: the dominant ideology of our culture.

John Fiske and John Hartley see the function of TV as "bardic." Like the bards who recited stories of epic heroes in the oral culture of the past, TV works to "*articulate* the main lines of the established cultural consensus about the nature of reality*" (88) in a way that causes viewers to feel they are part of that consensus. It does so in the same way toys do: by constantly showing us images that represent our culture's norms or ideals of appearance and behavior—for instance, what female beauty is, or what acceptable feminine behavior is—as if they were the whole and only truth, and consequently the only truth about ourselves.

Fiske and Hartley also believe that TV works to explain away the threatening quality of individuals and events apparently alien to the culture's central values, by a process they call *claw back:* "for example, nature programmes will often stress the 'like-us-ness' of the animals filmed, finding in their behaviour metaphoric equivalences with our own culture's way of organizing its affairs" (87). Similarly, and like the nonfictional texts about past times or other cultures I discussed above, many TV shows work to prove that despite their apparent differences, people with handicaps or of different races are really "just like us." This apparently positive idea may cause us to lose consciousness of and tolerance for the validity of the "otherness" of these other ways of being human.

EXPLORATION: Can you find evidence of the articulation of "cultural consensus" or of "claw back" in TV programming for children? Watch (or invite children to watch) cartoons or programs like *Sesame Street* and think about the ways in which they might be confirming a specific view of reality and/or dissipating the threat of apparently alien ideas or behavior.

Because its central focus is the expression of mainstream ideology, TV storytelling tends to be symbolic rather than natural—to provide something more like myths than like realistic fiction. For instance, Fiske and Hartley claim that the significance of violence in TV fiction is that "it externalizes people's motives and status, makes visible their unstated relationships" (34). In other words, the violent encounters of specific individuals on TV actually represent something less specific. TV "personalizes impersonal social conflicts between, for example, dominant and subordinate groups, law and anarchy, youth and age. It is never a mere imitation of real behavior" (34–35).

In a survey of prime-time TV shows in the late 1970s, Ben Stein discovered that almost all the murderers were upper-middle-class whites, and that educated people were always criminals: "On television . . . only villains have a library" (127). In children's programming, villains often still have libraries, or scientific laboratories. Such patterns seriously distort reality, for statistics reveal that, for obvious economic reasons, much real violence is committed by uneducated members of deprived minority groups. Nevertheless, the distortions of TV do accurately express a mythic version of the world that our society finds preferable to reality—a mythic world in which the powerful are always corrupt and always vulnerable and the weak are always pure and always able to triumph. By repeating these inaccurate representations of violence and its perpetrators, TV works to deflect our consciousness of the part played by racial and economic inequality in societal conflict and the difficulty individuals have in managing to change the way things are.

While many observers agree that TV performs these culture-sustaining functions, they take different attitudes toward it. Roger Silverstone is positive. Saying that "television, above all, is a machine for the reduction of the ambiguous and uncertain" (180), he concludes that "television translates history, political and social change, into manageable terms" (182). But others worry about the deception that accompanies that manageability. Laura Kipnis is concerned that what we see on TV "disguises what it really is—relationships among people and classes—into an appearance of the objective and the natural . . . it subjugates people to its monopoly of appearance, and proclaims: 'That which appears is good, that which is good appears' " (20–21).

EXPLORATION: Which of these opposing views, Silverstone's or Kipnis's, do you share? Why?

The ideological influence of TV isn't limited to its content: the world we see depicted in programs and commercials. The structure of TV programming also influences how children think about themselves and their world.

In North America, TV continues forever. Each program is succeeded by another in an endless *flow* of pictures, words, stories—a flow that is made to seem even more amorphous because the stories themselves are interrupted and *fragmented*. Most programs are series in which any single episode is merely part of an ongoing, longer story—a story filled with events but with a decidedly shapeless plot. While individual programs often have recognizable narrative plots, they are constantly interrupted with commercials, newsbreaks, and promotions for other programs. In contemporary TV style, furthermore, few shots or sequences last for long, and within one 30-second commercial we may see more than twenty images, moving quickly from a face to a glass to a beach scene, and back to a face again. In their constant movement from one short sequence to another, distinctly different one, *Sesame Street* and many Saturday morning shows duplicate this pattern.

EXPLORATION: Test the prevalence of this pattern by recording (or inviting children to record) the shots and sequences of a particular television program. How might the awareness of these patterns affect your response to the program?

Given an endless flow of fragmented stories, we have no choice but to pay close attention only to that which specifically interests us. Rick Altman observes that "there is a growing body of data suggesting that intermittent attention is in fact the dominant mode of television" (42). Someone like me, born in a time before TV and used to the connected meanings I can derive from my experiences of individual written stories or movies, might be uncomfortable with the intermittent attentiveness TV demands and allows. But contemporary children, born into a world where TV sets come with remote controls that allow individual viewers to increase the fragmentation of programming even further by flipping from channel to channel whenever they wish, might well prefer TV to movies.

Paradoxically, then, the interactive, fragmented structure of TV may free such viewers from the ideological manipulation of the story lines of specific programs. Or, perhaps, the remote control is merely another version of the video game joystick: It offers the illusion of power and choice, but what one has the power to choose from is homogenized and unitary and constantly reinforces the same values.

It also reinforces one's right to *be* inattentive, a process that might well prevent real change or growth or learning. Someone unused to paying consistent attention to one idea or image is not likely to learn new or different ideas. The thinking and character of such a person is likely merely to replicate the disorganized fragmentation and flow of the TV experience.

THE WORLD OF CHILDREN'S MOVIES

Movies, even ones made long ago, are an important part of the seamless world of children's entertainment. Movies made decades back are shown on TV or are readily available on video; new movies generate character toys, video games, and tie-in books, and their characters turn up on TV cartoon shows.

Not surprisingly, new movies tend to express the same values as contemporary TV and toys—values so close to us that we are often unaware of their presence or their implications. Older movies tend to express older values—ones we may no longer share; and when they're still available they tend to attract criticism. For instance, contemporary children often watch the many movies produced by the Walt Disney studio since its first success with a filmed version of the fairy tale "Snow White" in 1937: the Disney studio keeps most of these films in constant circulation, and adults familiar with them from their own childhoods happily share them with children.

But many people worry that these films contain traditional, and hopefully out-moded, gender stereotypes and reinforce the limiting idea that marriage between attractive people with large incomes is the ultimate and only acceptable form of happiness. Other stereotypes occur also: Jill May points out that Disney "used black voices for monkeys and apes (*The Jungle Book*)" and "depicted Italians as aggres-sive, mindless people who spoke in broken English and were strongly influenced by their emotions (*The Lady and the Tramp* and *Pinocchio*)" (464).

In defense of Disney, Lucy Rollin insists that "Disney was no more and no less than a product of this time [the mid-twentieth century], and if therein lies the weak-ness of his work, there must be its strengths as well" (92). In other words, Disney's genius was merely that he was able to capture mainstream ideological values. If we condemn older Disney films, we are actually condemning the society that produced them and enjoyed them.

If, however, we still find them enjoyable enough to share with children, then logic would suggest that, consciously or not, we still share their values, at least enough not to be very aware of or bothered by them. Interestingly, recent Disney films offer only slight variations on the same old assumptions. The theoretically se-rious-minded and independent heroine of *Beauty and the Beast* still finds happiness in the arms of a handsome and wealthy man. So does the central character in *The Little Mermaid*—an incredible distortion of Hans Christian Andersen's original story, in which the prince ended up with another woman and the mermaid achieved hap-piness by dying and going to heaven. Meanwhile, in the original theatrical version of the film *Aladdin,* a song identified Arabs as barbarians; while this was changed, in response to complaints, for the videotape version, the film continues to stereo-type gender by depicting a theoretically Arab princess whose figure is much like Barbie's and not much like common Arab body-types, and who wears a costume the immodesty of which would offend many Muslim women and men. The conti-nuity of values in Disney films over half a century may suggest a continuity in the values of North American society.

EXPLORATION: Is that statement true? Watch a Disney film such as *Snow White* or *The Lion King*. What ideological assumptions are represented? Are they those of mainstream audiences, or are the films manipulative? Should we or should we not condemn them?

TOYS, TV, MOVIES: A REPERTOIRE FOR LIFE AND LITERATURE

The Hidden Curriculum

Values presented so widely and so consistently are bound to have an effect on chil-dren; they amount to a *hidden curriculum,* a view of the world many children ab-sorb without even realizing they are doing so. That obligates us to consider whether we approve of these values, and whether we believe them harmful to or beneficial for children. I suspect I've made it fairly clear that I personally believe them to be harmful. They represent the interests of manufacturers more than the interests of children. They work to turn children into good consumers. In doing so, I believe, they perpetuate traditional concepts of masculinity and femininity and of the pleasure of owning things and of having domination over others that have caused much suffering in the past and that need to be, at least, challenged. But I encourage you to arrive at your own conclusions about these matters.

Meanwhile, however, there can be little doubt that the hidden curriculum has a profound effect on children's ability to absorb the official ones. In classrooms and in the texts educators approve of, the focus tends to be on ideals of inner beauty, equality, sharing and self-sacrifice—the exact opposite of the obsession with appearance, severe gender differentiation, self-seeking and self-indulgence encouraged by toys and TV shows. Yet Kline speaks, accurately, I think, of the "reluctance of educators and academic commentators to recognize that commercial media and the toy industries are vital agencies of socialization" (19). Once we recognize that, we can begin to do something about it. "What is needed," Kinder suggests, "is an educational program in elementary schools on how to read media images interactively, a program that enables children to understand how meaning is constructed and encourages them to question and negotiate those readings that are privileged by the text and its corporate sponsors" (46).

EXPLORATION: Think of a way to do what Kinder suggests, and try it with some children. What happens when you attempt to make children aware of the values implicit in toys and TV shows?

Literature in the World of Children's Culture

For most contemporary children, literature isn't their first or only introduction to narrative. They come to literary texts already immersed in the world as represented by toys, TV shows, and movies; and that has a profound effect on their ability to understand and enjoy literature. Popular toys and TV provide a repertoire of information about life and of strategies for making sense of narrative quite different from that required to enjoy written literature.

Toys. Barbie supports interests and values that might well prepare young girls to enjoy reading teen romances, but which would make much other children's literature seem childish or beside the point. The fascination with change implied by Barbie's ever-renewing wardrobe and the bodies of Transformers might prepare children to feel empowered by the randomized plots of Choose-Your-Own Adventures or the interactive versions of children's stories now available on CD-ROM, but to feel constrained and bored by more conventional novels.

Similarly, the stories implied by video games use narrative conventions in ways different from conventional written texts. Many of these games have clear relationships with traditional folktales: a hero, identified with the player, embarks on a quest and struggles with villains for a prize. But unlike written folk tales, what happens in these games has no relation to moral choices. Victory or defeat depends purely upon manual dexterity, and the stories the games imply tend to indiscriminately reward or punish both moral and immoral behavior. As a result, individual events don't build into a consistent or meaningful plot. Without a cohesive pattern, there's no suspense, and so the ending isn't climactic: It interrupts what has become the main pleasure, the continuing process of the game itself. While these games relate to traditional stories, then, children who play them will develop knowledge of a set of narrative conventions that might well hinder their understanding and appreciation of more conventional stories.

TV.   Unlike books, TV simultaneously uses a variety of media, and those accustomed to receiving information from music and pictures as well as from words might have problems decoding books. Furthermore, as I suggested earlier, TV flows ever onwards in disconnected fragments, and therefore, discourages consistent attentiveness; written texts, which have not only endings but beginnings and middles, have been shaped in ways that invite and reward consistent attention. If we want children to enjoy reading fiction, then, we cannot assume that the strategy of paying the necessary attention to it comes naturally. We might well have the responsibility of teaching it to them. If we do, we will have helped them enjoy two different but equally pleasurable means of telling stories—the kind we watch on TV and the kind we read in books.

EXPLORATION: Devise a means of showing children the difference between the cohesiveness of written stories and the fragmentation and flow of TV. Explore the effect of their awareness of these differences on their response to both forms of storytelling.

But while the absorption of children in TV does complicate the process of their responding to literature, it might also actively help them develop literary understanding and enjoyment. Children who watch a lot of TV may respond more perceptively to the stories in books simply because they already have familiarity with stories. The average young TV viewer experiences far more stories, in the form of cartoons and adventures and situation comedies, than children in any previous generation even had access to.

Furthermore, the main feature of these TV and movie stories is their adherence to formula. Saturday morning cartoons often involve lovable small creatures who fight with and defeat less lovable larger creatures. Situation comedies often involve inflexible characters who learn each week to be less rigid and then start out next week's program just as stubborn as they always were. By telling similar stories again and again, TV equips children with a repertoire of basic story patterns that allows them to recognize and make sense of the new stories they experience—not just on TV but also in books, for the story patterns of popular movies and TV shows are also those of many children's books.

EXPLORATION: Test the adherence of TV programming to formula by watching (or inviting children to watch) a number of shows of the same type: superhero cartoons, police adventures, or situation comedies. Is a story pattern apparent? If so, what is it, and how might this particular story pattern relate to children's stories in written form?

Consider how much the following stories have in common:

- The ordinary clothing of a mild-mannered reporter hides a fancy costume. When the costume is exposed, he uses his secret powers to defeat powerful opponents.
- The ordinary clothing of a group of ordinary teenagers hides their ability to metamorphose into beings with fancy costumes and weapons who can defeat powerful opponents.
- The wretched clothing of a powerless young girl hides her great beauty. Once her beauty is exposed through the secret powers of a magical assistant, she triumphs over powerful opponents.
- The ordinary clothing of a boy hides a rabbit's fur. When the clothes come off, he is able to escape a powerful enemy.
- A small, apparently powerless child dons a fancy costume and uses his secret power of staring to defeat powerful opponents.
- A small, apparently insignificant spider uses her secret power of web spinning to defeat powerful opponents.
- An apparently plain young girl with red hair uses the secret power of her charm to win over powerful opponents.

These are, in order, the basic plots of the comic books and Saturday morning cartoons about Superman, the toys and TV show Might Morphin Power Rangers, the fairy tale "Cinderella," the picture books *The Tale of Peter Rabbit* by Beatrix Potter and *Where the Wild Things Are* by Maurice Sendak, and the novels *Charlotte's Web* by E. B. White and *Anne of Green Gables* by L. M. Montgomery. Whether TV cartoons or treasured classics, these stories all follow the same pattern—the triumph of the underdog—and it's the experience of many different versions of this underdog story that allows children to develop a sense of the pattern itself.

Jon Stott suggests that the similarity in the narrative patterns of comic books and serious literature can have educational value: "Not that the teacher should teach comic books, but, knowing students' familiarity with the comics, he can show how certain elements reappear in great literature, how they are used to give symbolic significance to that literature, and how, unlike the comic books, the great works help to provide pattern and meaning to human lives" (11). It might well be argued that comic books—and TV shows and movies—do provide pattern and meaning, and that teachers *should* teach them, both in order to make children aware of the inadequacy of at least some of that meaning and in order to bring children to a consciousness of the repetitive nature of formulas that will allow them a richer perception and enjoyment of less-formulaic texts.

EXPLORATION: Nevertheless, some people believe that it's dangerous to encourage children to read comic books or watch TV cartoons in any context: Whatever your good intentions, you're actually suggesting approval of what is basically trash. Look (or invite children to look) at some currently available comic books or cartoons. Should they be part of what children study in literature? Why or why not?

FREEING CHILDREN FROM CULTURE

The aspects of contemporary culture I've discussed in this chapter should give adults interested in the welfare of children much to worry about. I personally have little doubt that children suffer greatly from being caught up in the values expressed by popular TV, toys, and tie-in books, both by unconsciously accepting dangerous ideas about gender and power, and by losing their freedom to make other choices they know nothing about.

But we don't have to reach the depressing conclusion that children have no choice but to be caught up in those values. Instead, I believe, what I've described here merely reinforces the importance of offering children insight into a wider range of opinions and finding ways of empowering them to think critically and carefully about all of their experiences. Only "innocent" children learn to believe that Barbie represents the best way of being female or that beating up others the way the Power Rangers always do is both good and fun.

For this reason, children's literature can be a powerful, positive force in the lives of children. It can make them less innocent. It can make them conscious that there is more than one way of being normal. It can offer them the opportunity to experience and learn to enjoy a vast range of different kinds of stories, and so make it clear that the one story they so often hear from toys and TV is not the only possible or only desirable version of the truth. And if we adults are wise, we can find ways of using children's experiences of those many different stories to help them learn how to think about the implications of the one story they usually hear. We can give children the power not to be disempowered by the dangerous pleasures of so many toys, TV programs, and literary texts.

WORKS CITED

Aliki. *How a Book Is Made*. New York: Harper & Row, 1986.

Altman, Rick. "Television Sound." *Studies in Entertainment: Critical Approaches to Mass Culture*. Ed. Tania Modleski. Bloomington: Indiana UP, 1986. 39–54.

Anno, Mitsumasa. *Anno's Medieval World*. London: Bodley Head, 1980.

Barthes, Roland. *Mythologies*. St. Albans, England: Paladin, 1972.

Berger, John. *Ways of Seeing*. Harmondsworth, Middlesex: Penguin, 1972.

Butler, Judith. *Gender Trouble: Feminism and the Subversion of Identity*. New York and London: Routledge, 1990.

DeLuca, Geraldine, and Roni Natov. "Who's Afraid of Science Books? An Interview with Seymour Simon." *Lion and the Unicorn* 6 (1982): 10–27.

Eagleton, Terry. *Ideology*. London and New York: Verso, 1991.

Fiske, John, and John Hartley. *Reading Television*. London: Methuen, 1978.

Harrison, Barbara. "Howl Like the Wolves." *Children's Literature* 15 (1987): 67–90.

Hochschild, Adam. "That Paragon of Porkers: Remembering Freddy the Pig." *New York Times Book Review,* May 22, 1994: 24, 236.

Huck, Charlotte S. *Children's Literature in the Elementary School*. 3rd ed., updated. New York: Holt, Rinehart and Winston, 1979.

Hunt, Peter. *An Introduction to Children's Literature*. Oxford and New York: Opus-Oxford University Press, 1994.

Kinder, Marcia. *Playing with Power in Movies, Television, and Video Games*. Berkeley, Los Angeles and Oxford: U of California P, 1991.

Kipnis, Laura. "'Refunctioning' Reconsidered: Towards a Left Popular Culture." MacCabe 11–36.

Kline, Stephen. *Out of the Garden: Toys and Children's Culture in the Age of TV Marketing*. Toronto, Garamond P, 1993.

Konigsburg, E. L. "Sprezzatura: A Kind of Excellence." *Horn Book* 52 (June 1976): 253–261.

Lauber, Patricia. "What Makes an Appealing and Readable Science Book." *Lion and the Unicorn* 6 (1982): 5–9.

MacCabe, Colin, ed. *High Theory/Low Culture: Analysing Popular Television and Film*. New York: St. Martin's Press, 1986.

Marcus, Leonard S. "Life Drawings: Some Notes on Children's Picture Books." *Lion and the Unicorn* 4.1 (1980): 15–31.

Maruki, Toshi. *Hiroshima No Pika*. New York: Lothrop, Lee and Shepherd, 1980.

May, Jill P. "Walt Disney's Interpretation of Children's Literature." *Jump Over the Moon: Selected Professional Readings*. Ed. Pamela Petrick Barron and Jennifer Q. Burley. New York: Holt, Rinehart and Winston, 1984. 461–472.

Miller, Miriam Youngerman. "In Days of Old: The Middle Ages in Children's Non-fiction." *Children's Literature Association Quarterly* 12.4 (Winter 1987): 167–172.

Nodelman, Billie. "Science Books, Science Education, and the Religion of Science." *Children's Literature Association Quarterly* 12.4 (Winter 1987): 180–183.

Rollin, Lucy. "Fear of Faerie: Disney and the Elitist Critics." *Children's Literature Association Quarterly* 12.2 (Summer 1987): 90–93.

Silverstone, Roger. *The Message of Television: Myth and Narrative in Contemporary Culture*. London: Heinemann, 1981.

Skirrow, Gillian. "Hellivision: An Analysis of Video Games." MacCabe 115–142.

Spier, Peter. *People*. New York: Doubleday, 1980.

Stein, Ben. *The View from Sunset Boulevard: America as Brought to You by the People Who Make Television*. New York: Basic, 1979.

Stephens, John. *Language and Ideology in Children's Fiction*. London and New York: Longman, 1992.

Stott, Jon C. "Pseudo-sublimity and Inarticulate Mumblings in Violent Juxtaposition: The World of Comic Books." *Children's Literature Association Quarterly* 7.1 (Spring 1982): 10–12.

Sutherland, Zena, and Myra Cohn Livingston. *The Scott, Foresman Anthology of Children's Literature*. Glenview: Scott, Foresman, 1984.

White, Hayden. *Metahistory: The Historical Imagination in Nineteenth Century Europe*. Baltimore: Johns Hopkins UP, 1973.

Willhoite, Michael. *Daddy's Roommate*. London: Alyson, 1992.

Willis, Susan. "Gender as Commodity." *South Atlantic Quarterly* 86, 4 (Fall 1987): 403–421.

Wolf, Virginia L. "The Gay Family in Literature for Young People." *Children's Literature in Education* 20.1 (March 1989): 51–58.

chapter **7**

Literature and Ideology

HISTORY AND CULTURE

Because their authors shared an ideological context, texts written in the same period of history tend to have much in common with one another. So do those written in the same country. If we know something about historical events or about the
traits of a specific culture, we can see, and take pleasure in seeing, how texts relate
to the time and place in which they were written—and, also, how these circumstances can throw light on the texts. In other words, the relationship works both
ways. We can develop a better understanding of literature by learning something
about the culture or period of history that produced it. We can also develop a better
understanding of a culture or period of history by reading the literature it produced.
And obviously, that applies to our own contemporary culture as well as those of
past times.

Class and Gender

Beatrix Potter's picture books are a good example of how texts both reveal and are
illuminated by the values of their time. Even though her characters are animals,
their society resembles the turn-of-the-century England that Potter herself knew. In
that society, class distinctions were important, and those who considered themselves gentlemen were people of privilege. In *The Tale of Jeremy Fisher,* the main
character is such a gentleman—he's called *Mr.;* he's friends with an alderman, Mr.
Ptolemy Tortoise, and even with a member of the aristocracy, *Sir* Isaac Newton;
and he wears the clothes of a man of high social standing: a cutaway coat and an
embroidered pink vest. If we can see the extent of Jeremy's social pretensions, then
the joke of his being merely a frog under his fancy waistcoat, and having to suffer

indignities from creatures as insignificant as a water beetle and a stickleback, becomes even funnier.

Jeremy ends his day having dinner with his two male friends. Kenneth Grahame's *The Wind in the Willows,* published in 1908, two years after *The Tale of Mr. Jeremy Fisher,* is also about a group of exclusively male, distinctly British animals who spend their time socializing with each other. From the viewpoint of our own time, the absence of females from the group might suggest something about the sexual preferences of the male characters. Had these two books been written in the 1990s, we might assume they were designed to give children a healthy attitude toward a gay lifestyle.

But for those who know something about the social and cultural history of Potter's and Grahame's time, it's clear that their animals are merely living as many conventional young gentlemen did. As Elaine Showalter says, "Many Victorian men married late or never, lived a bachelor life, and spent their adult lives with only male friendships" (25). For audiences of their own time, then, the behavior of these animals would not necessarily have implied anything about their sexual preferences.

Or would it? These books were written at a period in English history Showalter characterizes as "decades of 'sexual anarchy,' when all the laws that governed sexual identity and behavior seemed to be breaking down" (3). Showalter argues that many adult fictional texts about groups of male friends that were written at this time—H. Rider Haggard's *She,* Robert Louis Stevenson's *Dr. Jekyll and Mr. Hyde,* Bram Stoker's *Dracula*—actually do represent a coded, secret discussion of homosexuality, particularly of men's fears of their own homosexual desire, and would have been recognized as such at the time.

Many texts for children of this time bear similarities to these adult texts—not just *Jeremy Fisher* and *Wind in the Willows,* but also J. M. Barrie's *Peter Pan* (as a play, 1904), Rudyard Kipling's *Stalky and Co.* (1899), Stevenson's *Treasure Island* (1883), and many adventure novels by G. A. Henty and others. Can we conclude that these texts are similarly coded? Perhaps they represent a hidden form of education in sexual attitudes for children of the time. Showalter suggests that many books for boys of this time "represent a yearning for escape from a confining society, rigidly structured in terms of gender, class, and race" (81) and might "mask the desire to evade heterosexuality altogether" (81, 82). Whether or not they do, it's clear that knowledge of history and culture can enrich our perceptions of literary texts and help us understand which of our possible interpretations are the ones most likely to represent the intentions of the author.

EXPLORATION: Choose (or invite children to choose) any other text written for children in an earlier time. In what ways do its assumptions about behavior vary from ones that are currently popular? After doing some historical research, determine to what extent the variations might be accounted for by the circumstances of the time in which the text was written.

Attitudes toward gender are a significant aspect of historical and cultural differ-ences. In Potter's *The Tale of Peter Rabbit,* Peter's sisters act according to then-con-ventional assumptions about femininity and passively obey their mother's instruc-tions to pick berries, while Peter fulfills traditional stereotypes of male behavior by defying his mother, striking out on his own, and seeking adventure. Other books written at about the same time display similar attitudes. In L. M. Montgomery's *Anne of Green Gables,* published seven years after *Peter Rabbit,* Anne's adventures are relatively minor, domestic ones; nothing like the exciting and life-threatening escapades that boys experience in novels like Stevenson's *Treasure Island* or Kipling's *The Jungle Book* (1894).

On the other hand, Anne is more active than Peter Rabbit's sisters, and the mil-lions of female readers who have adored Anne have tended to claim that they ad-mire her for her tomboyish independence more than for the security of her life. Similarly, the millions of girls who have enjoyed reading Louisa May Alcott's *Little Women* (1868) have generally singled out the tomboyish Jo as the March sister they most identify with—not the sweet Meg or the saintly Beth, both of whom represent more traditionally desirable feminine traits. Both Anne and Jo represent a blending of traditional ideas of masculinity and femininity; despite their supposed inde-pendence of mind, both seem willing to accept the restrictions imposed on them by their culture's view of femininity. From the viewpoint of our own time, Anne and Jo seem to engage in a form of rebellion that, in the end, doesn't seriously threaten conventional values: They give up, and give in, and we are asked to admire them for it.

Indeed, many modern readers do. In recent years, scholars have produced an extensive and fascinating body of criticism that suggests various positive and nega-tive ways to account for the ambivalence of these books. Among many articles on *Little Women* are provocative ones by Beverly Lyon Clark, Angela Estes and Kath-leen Lant, Judith Fetterly, and Elizabeth Keyser; Mavis Reimer has collected a range of articles on *Anne* in her book *Such a Simple Little Tale.* As these critics reveal, these texts play complex games with conventional notions of gender and with the desire of readers to both accept and transcend such notions. Once we know some-thing about those conventional ideas, we can enjoy our perceptions of the games.

Nationality

The characters in many American children's novels take it for granted that anyone, no matter how humble, can improve his or her lot in life and achieve a dream. That basic, unquestioned assumption defines them as Americans. It is not shared so un-questioningly, however, by the British animals in *Wind in the Willows,* who tend to be content with the ways things are, and who get in trouble when they try to live out their dreams.

I'm not suggesting that American novels like *Charlotte's Web* deny the idea that people should accept their limitations, or that the characters in *Wind in the Willows* have no aspirations. But in American texts, acceptance of limitations often actually allows the characters to keep on aspiring, but now toward realistic goals. When

Wilbur the pig learns that he can't spin webs like Charlotte the spider, he realizes how much he likes who he is and aspires to stay alive—a goal he can and does reach. On the other hand, the characters in *Wind in the Willows* who aspire to change their lives are merely silly. Rat's wish to travel to foreign lands is seen as a momentary aberration, a lapse from sanity, and Toad's lust for motor cars is shown to be both ridiculous and dangerous. The differences between these books reveal significant differences in national character, ones that can be explored interestingly in many other books.

EXPLORATIONS: (1) Read (or invite children to read) a number of books from one country, such as Canada or Australia. Consider whether they share qualities that might be accounted for by national characteristics.

(2) A suggestion from the copyeditor of the *Pleasures* manuscript: Based on the shared qualities of characters in a number of books from a country you know little about, try to guess what the country's supposed national characteristics might be. Then, explore whether nonfictional accounts of the country and its people confirm or challenge the suppositions you've arrived at from your reading of fiction. What might account for either similarities or differences between the guesses you made based on fiction and the views presented in nonfiction?

(3) Or is it dangerous to think that nationalities *have* characteristics? Does it encourage stereotyping and lead to bigotry and prejudice?

READING AGAINST A TEXT

We can focus on the ways in which books express the values of specific historical periods and cultures only if we remain at some distance from them and allow ourselves to think about how the views they present differ from our own. In other words, we must become conscious of what are sometimes called a text's *absences:* the ideas or assumptions it takes for granted and therefore does not explicitly assert. As Pierre Machery says, "A work is tied to ideology not so much by what it says as by what it does not say" (34). An awareness of what a text does not say allows both children and adults to enjoy stories written in different times without assuming that sexist or racist or just plain old-fashioned values in the stories are ones that we should share.

In order to *surface* absences—that is, bring them to our consciousness—we must first understand that they are in fact merely assumptions. As I suggested in chapter 5, human beings usually take it for granted that their own specific values or ideologies are absolutely and universally true: what Louis Althusser calls "obviousnesses." In *The Tale of Mr. Jeremy Fisher,* for instance, Potter never asserts that there is a social scale that places water beetles lower than frogs. She just takes it for granted that there is such a social scale and that everyone knows it: It's obvious. Because writers assume that their own ideology is universal truth, texts always act as a subtle kind of propaganda, and tend to manipulate unwary readers into an unconscious acceptance of their values. The representation always threatens to become a reader's reality.

But if we notice the absences in a text and think about the ideology they imply, we can protect ourselves from unconscious persuasion. Rather than allowing ourselves to become immersed in a text to the point of accepting its description of reality as the only true one, we can define its values and so arrive at a better understanding of our own. In other words, instead of going along with the values a text implies, we can read *against* it.

The closer the values of a text come to our own ideologies, the harder it is to read against it and find its absences. In some cases, it may be impossible. But even then the attempt to do so is worthwhile—and pleasurable, too, for doing so gives us some control over what happens to us as we read. We can ask ourselves *why* it is that certain books strike us as being so convincingly realistic, and we can help children understand themselves better by encouraging them to do so also.

SURFACING POLITICAL ASSUMPTIONS

The most obvious way of reading against a text is to approach it from a point of view that questions its political and social assumptions. For instance: If we choose not to just ignore Grahame's assumptions about social hierarchy, it's not hard for us to see how his *Wind in the Willows* asks readers to take that hierarchy for granted. The book never questions the assumption of the gentlemanly riverbank animals that the creatures who live in the wild woods are their social and moral inferiors. It would be revealing to think about the events the book describes from the point of view of the citizens of the wild woods.

In fact, Jan Needle has done just that in his novel *Wild Wood,* which describes how the poverty of the woodland creatures, caused in part by the thoughtlessness of the wealthy Mr. Toad, drives them to rebellion against their supposed superiors; they are not so much thieves and rascals as they are oppressed and deprived. Needle's novel cleverly fills in the absences of Grahame's.

As *Wild Wood* suggests, political ideologies almost always work to distribute power unequally among people in a society, and to justify the unequal distribution. Stories in which children question their parents' authority usually end with the children finally accepting the need for that authority: In chapter 8, I discuss this characteristic ending as a feature of the home/away/home story so central to children's literature. A little less obviously, the satisfaction offered by most triumph-of-the-underdog stories resides in an unquestioning acceptance of three questionable ideas: (1) that in every situation there always has to be a winner and a loser, so that a happy ending requires not just someone's triumph but also someone else's defeat; (2) that the best way to win is to have the individual power to take control and win by one's own actions; and (3), that a truly happy ending occurs only when a person who was oppressed achieves a position in which it's possible to oppress others. Maurice Sendak's *Where the Wild Things Are* is an excellent representation of these political assumptions. Surprisingly few texts for children celebrate the value of groups of people working together as equals as opposed to the power of individuals controlling groups.

EXPLORATION: Is that true? Survey a number of children's stories, and determine how many celebrate communal action and how many represent the triumph of an individual acting alone. What are the implications of the proportions you discover?

SURFACING ASSUMPTIONS ABOUT GENDER

Another way of reading against a text is to notice its assumptions about gender—as I did above in considering the ways in which books by writers like Montgomery and Alcott portray their female characters. As has often been pointed out, gender bias has been so deeply rooted in our culture that words like "he" and "him" traditionally referred to both males and females, while words like "she" and "her" referred only to females. In other words, while a "he" was supposed to be a genderless human being, a "she" was specifically female, set apart by gender from the typical state of being human.

Traditionally, writers have assumed that their audience consists of "he"s: that is, of either males or females who, while they read, are conscious only of that aspect of their being which is not specifically female—of their basic, supposedly genderless, humanity. But, of course, the "he"s implied as the audience of literature are no more genderless than the "he"s of traditional grammar. In equating the male with the typically human, both literature and grammar suggest that women are less than human, and that femininity is a sign of inferiority from the more totally human condition of being a "he."

The extent to which implications of male superiority color literature becomes apparent to anybody who stops reading as a "typical" human being, without consciousness of gender—as a traditional "he"—and tries to read with a consciousness of gender—as a traditional "she." A girl or a woman can read *as a woman* without ignoring her femaleness, as many *feminist* literary critics read. A boy or a man can read without ignoring the extent to which his responses are governed by the specific limitations of his maleness.

To read in this way is to become conscious of the absences of literary texts that relate specifically to gender. We can see how Anne Shirley's rebellion and ambition in *Anne of Green Gables* are controlled by the need for her to remain acceptably feminine—a good mother and homemaker. Or we can realize how much *Charlotte's Web* asks us to admire the undemanding, selfless, maternal love that Charlotte offers Wilbur: Charlotte devotes herself to Wilbur at the expense of her own needs in a way many people would find less admirable, or natural, if she were a male and he a female.

Once we've realized that, there are a different ways to understand it. We might assume that it's dangerously sexist to imagine that women are inherently maternal and selfless—that doing so effectively deprives women of any right to be independent or to have aspirations for worldly success or power. On the other hand, the assumption that traditionally female qualities such as selflessness and nurturing are dangerous and to be avoided might represent another form of sexism. There might be something anti-female in the frame of mind that sees these qualities as signs of inferiority and powerlessness, and that approves traditionally male values such as aggressiveness and independence.

Feminist literary critics might approach texts from either of these perspectives, and from a whole range of others. As Robyn Warhol and Diane Price Herndl say,

> From the outside, "feminism" may appear monolithic, unified, or singularly definable. The more intimately one becomes acquainted with feminist criticism, however, the more one sees the multiplicity of approaches and assumptions inside the movement. While this variety can lead to conflict and competition, it can also be the source of movement, vitality, and genuine learning. Such diversity—if fostered, as it has been in some feminist thought—can be a model for cultural heterogeneity. (x)

A willingness to allow a diversity of opinions is directly antithetical to the world of power struggles we find not only exemplified in much literary criticism by adults, but also, taken for granted in much children's literature about underdogs winning and villains losing. As a feminist position, it reveals the masculinist assumptions at the heart of the most common forms of both literary criticism and children's literature.

EXPLORATIONS: (1) Try (or invite children to try) reading any children's text "as a woman"—that is, with consciousness of the text's assumptions about gender.

(2) Explore the variety of "feminisms" as represented in a collection of essays like the one edited by Warhol and Herndl. Then choose one specific feminist position and think about a text of children's literature in terms of the viewpoint of that position.

Women's Writing

If it's possible to read like a woman, then it should be equally possible to write like one. Some feminist literary critics explore texts by women to see if they differ significantly from texts by men. Some pursue these investigations from the conviction that women are essentially and inherently different from men—that biological differences create differences in attitude. Others believe that the possibility of differences in attitudes means only that the different experiences society offers women and men have led them to think differently of themselves and of others.

In either case, critics have discovered that women tend not only to write about different aspects of experience—as an obvious example, domestic events rather than adventures in the big world away from home—but also to do so in different ways. For instance, it seems that the way we usually describe the plot of a story or a novel—as a single, unified action that rises toward a climax and then quickly comes to an end—accurately describes the action of many texts written by men (and also, of course, of many written by women who have accepted the conventional ideal). But that definition of plot would suggest that the more episodic events of texts like *Anne of Green Gables* are amateurish and unexciting; *Anne* has many less-intense climaxes rather than one central one, and there's not—or at least, apparently not—much unity in its action. Nevertheless, *Anne of Green Gables* is a highly pleasurable text, even though the pleasure is different from that offered by suspenseful books like Stevenson's *Treasure Island*. Furthermore, many other enjoyable texts for both children and adults are similarly episodic—and a large proportion of them are written by women. Apparently some women prefer a different kind of pattern of events from the one conventionally assumed to be desirable.

As I suggested in chapter 4, Robert Scholes has likened the pleasure in narrative to that of sexuality. He suggests that the "archetype of all fiction is the sexual act . . . the fundamental orgastic rhythm of tumescence and detumescence, of tension and resolution, of intensification to the point of climax and consummation" (26). But physiological studies suggest that what Scholes is describing here is typical of *male* sexuality—and that female sexuality might just as typically express itself in rhythmic patterns like those of *Anne of Green Gables*. As Beatrice Faust says, "Female sexuality can include both intense arousal, which seeks release in orgasm, and a pleasant drift on the plateau level of arousal, which may continue indefinitely" (59).

Furthermore, the fact that the care and education of children have traditionally been the domain of women has meant that a large proportion of the writers and editors of texts for children have been (and continue to be) women. Women have largely been responsible for the development of children's literature; so if this literature has distinct traits, they might well be those that can be identified in women's writing in general. If so, then even male writers who try to satisfy the generic characteristics of children's literature would be writing "as women."

In fact, many children's books by males do have an episodic series of minor climaxes rather than one major one. And many of the genre characteristics explored in chapter 8 might be identified as traditionally feminine.

EXPLORATIONS: (1) Consider (or have children consider) the degree to which characteristics such as repetition or the striking of a balance between the desires of the individual and the needs of the social group might be considered feminine. How might these relate to your own assumptions about female characteristics?

(2) Ellen Nelson, a student in Tim Wolf's children's literature course at Middle Tennessee State University, points out that in this book, despite my comment that women have written most of the children's literature in existence, I "scarcely use examples of texts written by females." It might be interesting to see if she is right. "Furthermore," Nelson goes on to say, "in reading books in my current class, I have been instructed to read only one

text, out of twelve assigned, that was written by a woman. If women have made this large contribution, and I feel they have, then they should be allowed the recognition they deserve for their contribution to children's literature." Explore the implications of Nelson's comment. Are my choices of examples throughout *Pleasures* influenced by my gender?

Perhaps children's literature as a whole is a sort of women's literature. That may explain why such a large proportion of the children who are ardent readers are females (although cultural ideas about masculinity and femininity in relation to reading certainly have a large effect on children's choices about these matters).

But even if we assume that one sort of plot is inherently male and the other inherently female, we shouldn't conclude that only men and boys can enjoy the climactic plots, and only women and girls the episodic ones—or that if children's literature is a form of women's writing, only girls should enjoy it. For centuries, women have learned to take pleasure in the kinds of plots that seem to be inherently male. There's no reason why men can't learn to take pleasure in the kinds of plots that seem to be inherently female—and, thus, if these *are* female plots, to develop some insight into the nature of femininity. A world in which both boys and girls had escaped conventional gender assumptions enough to enjoy, equally, *Anne of Green Gables* and *Treasure Island*—to be at different times or at all times both "masculine" and "feminine" (and a number of other possibilities added on and in between)—would surely be a healthy one.

Literature and Masculinity

If it's possible to write like a woman, then it's clearly just as possible to write like a man and express inherently masculine values and viewpoints. Indeed, as feminist theory teaches us, men (and some women) have been doing it for centuries. But in recent years, literary specialists have begun to pay attention to the ways in which texts by both men and women provide assumptions about masculinity that are often as rigid and constraining for male readers, and as dangerous for males and females, as the assumptions about femininity are for female readers.

In her study *Between Men,* the theorist Eve Kosofsky Sedgwick claims that the major force driving heterosexual men has traditionally been their desire for approbation from or mastery over other males. Therefore, men's dealings with women have most significance as the medium by which men develop their bonds and establish their hierarchies of power with each other. According to Sedgwick, this is what the anthropologist Claude Lévi-Strauss calls "the male traffic in women"—in Sedgwick's words, "the use of women by men as exchangeable objects, as counters of value, for the primary purpose of cementing relationships with other men" (123). Sedgwick describes many novels for adults that express these assumptions, and show men driven by what she calls "male homosocial desire." They find the relationships with men that most matter to them, first, through exchanging women with

other men, and second, by making clear that their desire is *homosocial* and not homosexual: for homosociality traditionally requires homophobia as a condition for its
acceptability.

Texts written for children mirror these concerns. Sendak's *Where the Wild
Things Are* and Potter's *Peter Rabbit* both describe males who defy the power of female authority and discover their own true worth in their dealings with others who
are or appear to be male.

Meanwhile, the most important relationships in Stevenson's *Treasure Island,*
Grahame's *The Wind in the Willows,* Ursula Le Guin's *Earthsea* trilogy, Arnold
Lobel's *Frog and Toad* series, and Robert Cormier's *Chocolate War* are between
males whose interest in each other is understood to be anything but sexual. The
subject of possible sexual interest is never mentioned or implied: There's a notable
(and to my mind, strange) absence of body consciousness on the part of all these
characters. In simply ignoring these matters, these texts confirm how important it is
to ignore them, to say nothing about them, to keep them hidden in the closet. They
thus help to teach the homophobia that allows homosociality. Nevertheless, as I try
to show in my article about Le Guin, "Re-inventing the Past," such texts can be read
as containing veiled allusions to a possible sexual component in their male characters' desire for each other—a component the texts work to move past or deny.

MULTICULTURALISM: SURFACING ASSUMPTIONS
ABOUT RACE AND ETHNICITY

Just as the texts of a male-dominated society inevitably express a male view as if it
were a universal one, and thus ask women readers to think like men, the texts of a
white-dominated society inevitably express a white view as if it were a universal
one—and, thus, ask African American or Native American readers to think like
whites. Consequently, another way of reading against a text is to surface its assumptions about race and ethnicity. To what degree does the behavior of the characters represent racial or ethnic stereotypes?

As with traditional statements of praise for the nobility of a woman's sacrifice
of her own goals in the service of others, racial stereotypes sometimes mask their
disdain under apparent praise. Many texts by writers of European backgrounds depict nobly innocent Native Americans or blissfully ingenuous African Americans
whose lack of sophistication prevents them from taking part in white corruption.
The apparent nobility turns out to be just a polite way of asserting a belittling deviation from white normalcy. Like children, people of color are assumed to be closer
to nature, theoretically better because they are less civilized, indeed, less human.

Furthermore, a sense of racial otherness is sometimes so unconscious that it
expresses itself in highly subtle ways. A possible example is Paula Fox's award-winning *The Slave Dancer,* a beautifully written book about life on a slave ship, which
I used to greatly admire. In a children's literature class, however, I was surprised
and then convinced by a student's claim that this book expresses a subtle racism.

The white author tells the story of the suffering of captured black slaves from the point of view of a white adolescent who has himself been shanghaied onto the ship. There seems to be an assumption that young readers of the book would probably identify with such a point of view—not with the Africans who are being so cruelly mistreated, but instead with a white outsider who learns to feel sympathy for their plight. Presumably, then, the audience is white—and perhaps, also, those African Americans willing to think about the history of their people from the point of view of a white person.

It's certainly true that the point of view makes the white protagonist's emotional upset at having to observe suffering seem more important than the physical pain he observes. And if I think about the novel in this way, I realize that the Africans in the book are left without a voice, and with no way to speak of their own suffering or tell their own story. The text tells of only three words spoken by an African—and one of these is mispronounced.

EXPLORATION: I'm confused about my response to *The Slave Dancer*. I have no doubt that it's a finely constructed work of art, one that I still find deeply affecting. But I wonder if my saying that means I'm somehow accepting these racist implications. You might read the book (or invite children to read it) and see if you can reach a conclusion about these matters. Can it be considered a work of art despite its possible racism? Are there assumptions about artistic merit that would allow us to ignore the racism in making an evaluation of the book?

Because racism sometimes expresses itself in subtle ways, it's not always easy to identify. Here are some matters to consider in surfacing assumptions about race in literary texts, particularly those by writers who are not themselves members of the racial or ethnic group of their characters:

- Most obviously, are the characters stereotypes? Are the black characters all musical or athletic? The Jews all smart? The Asians all industrious?
- What symbolic meanings are attached to blackness and whiteness? Is evil understood to be black, white good?
- The African American writer Toni Morrison suggests that white writers of American fiction often make black characters into symbols of the writers' own "dread of nature, powerlessness, Nature without limits, natal loneliness, internal aggressions, evil, sin, greed" (38). As symbols rather than people, their significance is what they represent about whites, not what they are as blacks. In texts for children, is being black, or blackness in general, represented most significantly as something forbidden to and/or desired by whites? Does an apparent admiration for symbolic blacks or blackness imply a dehumanizing of people of African descent?
- Alternatively, do characters who are members of minority groups achieve success only by giving up the distinctive values and lifestyles of their

group and adopting those of mainstream white society? Or do they find ways to succeed without losing sight of their heritage?

- Similarly, does it take people from the mainstream to solve the problems of people from minority groups? Who takes the leadership and makes the decisions?

- Current educational practice focuses on multicultural values and is much interested in promoting tolerance. The result is, sometimes, texts such as Bernard Ashley's *Cleversticks* or Patricia Baehr's *School Isn't Fair!* Both these picture-book stories about going to school contain highly unrealistic depictions of groups of children of different backgrounds existing in harmony without any consciousness that their differences might led to disagreement or prejudice or strife. But pretending that racism doesn't exist isn't likely to make it go away, or to make children very thoughtful about questions of prejudice. Consider whether texts might be presenting this kind of utopian wish-fulfillment as if it were reality.

Multicultural Texts

The previous discussion has centered on texts describing members of minority groups written primarily by whites of European descent. Not surprisingly, perhaps, most mainstream children's literature in North America *has* been written by whites of European descent, and assumes that being white and of European descent is a norm from which other kinds of people diverge. Caroline Hunt points out that Newbery medal-winning novels throughout the 1930s were almost all set outside of the American northeast, and seem to postulate implied readers living in the American northeast who need to learn about other people and places. She suggests that "nearly all the award-winning books might be said to represent an effort by an adult insider to explain a region that would be outside the child reader's everyday world" (88).

In children's literature classes, I've discovered that many white students of European descent still share such assumptions. They tell me that African American children will have no difficulty identifying with white characters, who are, after all, merely typical, but that only African American children can identify with the African American characters in books by African American writers. These children are clearly "different," atypical by virtue of their racial identity and the racial assumptions of their authors.

My students aren't alone in expressing attitudes that take this sort of more-or-less unconscious racism for granted as the way things are. According to children's literature specialist Donna Norton, "Learning about other cultures allows children to understand that people who belong to racial or ethnic groups other than theirs are real people, with feelings, emotions, and needs similar to their own—individual human beings, not stereotypes" (561). While I agree with what Norton says here, I'm interested in the assumption she seems to make that young children already think of members of other groups in stereotypical terms that they need to be educated out of. That raises the question of when and how such stereotypes are learned, particularly when we adults invest so much energy in challenging them. Despite all our efforts to the contrary, is intolerance still so prevalent in North American culture that even young children absorb it early on and then need to be taught past it? I suspect, sadly, that they do: consider the depressing degree to which the children whom Bronwyn Davies investigated and reported on in her article, "Lived and Imaginary Narratives," were firmly committed to gender stereotypes.

One way or the other, it's undeniably important that children of all races and colors read stories about children of all races and colors written by authors of all races and colors. In a world in which race and color still play such an important part in defining the experiences of individuals, books by and about people of different backgrounds are bound to offer access to a vast spectrum of ways of being human. Experiencing that spectrum is one of the key pleasures of literature. It may even encourage tolerance. In recent years, fortunately, more and more African American and Native American and Asian American writers have managed to gain access to mainstream publishers. Many texts about children of a variety of backgrounds have appeared, and an increasingly popular educational focus on multicultural diversity has introduced more and more children to them.

But for all its virtues, *multiculturalism* has its dangers also. In what follows, I outline some important ones.

Essentializing. Trying to choose texts for children that represent a spectrum of different racial or ethnic groups may foster the dangerous idea that members of an ethnic or cultural group are inherently alike simply because of their membership in the group. If a book about an African American child is included in a booklist or discussed in a class primarily because it "represents" the black experience, child readers who aren't themselves African American (and perhaps even some who are) might well conclude that the experience of the one child described in the book stands for and encompasses the whole experience of being black.

Cultural critics call this *essentializing*—that is, assuming that there's something identifiable as, say, a black soul or a Jewish character shared by all members of those groups—and strenuously object to it. The theorist Edward Said describes how in earlier centuries, Europeans justified their colonization of countries in other parts of the world by assuming their own, inherent racial superiority over those they conquered. They thus created "the supremely stubborn thesis that everyone is principally and irreducibly a member of some race or category, and that race or category cannot ever be assimilated to or accepted by others—except as itself. Thus came into being such invented essences as the Oriental or Englishness, as Frenchness, Africanness, or American exceptionalism, as if each of those had a Platonic idea behind it that guaranteed it as pure and unchanging from the beginning to the end of time" (196).

As Said points out, insisting on the positive value of Jewishness or Africanness was once a useful stance for Jews and blacks to take against the infuriating assumption that their difference from white Europeans marked them as inferior; and it still seems like a positive move to encourage people of all colors and backgrounds to perceive the beauty in a spectrum of skin colors and body types that diverge from the mainstream white norm.

In the long run, however, positive essentializing isn't all that much different from negative stereotyping. Both deny the possibility of individual growth or change, or of different but equally valid ways of being black or Jewish or Asian or Native American. Both create serious problems for people like my own children, whose parents belong to different ethnic groups and who therefore must be perceived by essentialists as somehow incomplete or fragmented rather than as the whole individual beings they are. And both deny the history that gives birth to ethnic and racial identity, and therefore the possibility of new events changing that identity and making the members of the same group different in different times and places.

In terms of introducing children to multicultural texts, these theoretical considerations have some very practical applications. To simply assert that children should be exposed to books about people of many groups in order to develop tolerance for the difference between themselves and others is to insist on and to essentialize those differences. Some of my students recently responded to Ashley's *Cleversticks,* in which each of the children in the multiracial nursery class turns out to have a unique talent, by trying to relate the talents to the presumed characteristics of the children's races: An Indian girl can write her name well due to the supposed superior verbal intelligence characteristic of Indians, and so on. My students told me that the book thus positively celebrated the talents of all races, and were shocked when I suggested their comments might be viewed as racist.

But I think they are racist. A positive stereotype is just as dangerous as a negative one. Think for instance, of the pain my student's assumptions might cause to a nonverbal child from India. We need to watch out for such essentialized stereotypes in children's books by both mainstream and minority writers.

Essentializing clearly raises problems when it comes to evaluating and selecting multicultural texts for children. There seem to be a variety of principles we might act on:

1. We could, in the name of tolerance, insist that all people are basically the same despite their apparent differences—and so, we should ignore those differences. In selecting books, then, we might aspire to be color-blind. We might act as if the author's or character's race or ethnicity is insignificant, as long as the characters seem convincingly interesting and human enough to make for a worthwhile reading experience.

Unfortunately, however, most people who select books at publishing houses and in libraries are not members of minorities, and their proceeding in this way usually leads to their underrepresenting or even eliminating books by and about members of minority groups in their publishing plans or book-buying. From this point of view, such books seem too "special" and untypical to represent the goal of inherent human sameness.

2. Alternatively, we might carefully choose books so that they represent a variety of different racial and ethnic authors and characters, but ensure that those characters are shown not to be so different after all. Tolerance

would emerge because children would learn how superficial the apparent differences are. As Ron Jobe says, "A major part of any approach to literature or indeed multiculturalism should be to place greater emphasis on the commonalities and similarities among peoples rather than the differences" (33).

But doing that tends to misrepresent the actual situation in our real world, in which color and ethnicity have had and continue to have a strong effect on people's lives. For better or worse, our membership in specific groups is part of what does indeed make us different from each other.

3. We might, then, assume that people are inherently different because of the race or culture they were born into, and therefore work to represent all these differences in our selections of books for children. That would teach minority children to have pride in their group, and teach all children the need to be tolerant of these real differences.

But as I suggested above, proceeding in this way can easily turn into essentializing, if not actual stereotyping.

4. We can avoid essentializing by selecting books that accurately represent real racial and ethnic differences, but also make it clear that these difference are more significantly cultural than basically genetic, and that they are historically constructed—group characteristics that have emerged because of the group's history and the history of its interactions with other groups.

Such texts would tend to reveal an ongoing process of what cultural theorists call *hybridization:* the process by which the values and attitudes of members of minority groups are influenced and changed by their dealings with a dominant, mainstream culture. They would also make it clear that their characters' relationships to categories of race and ethnicity are uneasy ones: that any given individual is rarely if ever certain about what it means to be black or Hispanic or Jewish. For these reasons, I prefer the fourth alternative.

Who Wrote It?   Since it's hard to perceive interior subtleties like these from the outside, it seems more likely that writers who share the race or ethnicity of their characters are likely to be able to describe them convincingly. For that reason, comparisons of texts by members of minority groups with texts about minority children written by white Europeans are revealing. Even in novels about African or Asian Americans by white writers that move past negative stereotypes, the minority characters tend to occupy two extreme ends of the spectrum. They tend to be either strangely abnormal—mysteriously exotic, as in *The Slave Dancer*—or else strangely normal, so devoid of distinguishing characteristics or concerns about race or color as to seem inhuman.

Consider, for instance, the nursery class in Ashley's *Cleversticks,* in which children whose features and names suggest a variety of different ethnic backgrounds all dress similarly, play the same games, feel the same inadequacies and the same competitiveness about them, and laugh at the same jokes. While the main character

Ling Sung's ability to use the chopsticks characteristic of his heritage does distinguish him from the rest, its true significance is that the others can then envy his ability and make him feel good about himself. He too can be a winner in the game of life, in true mainstream, middle-class fashion. In this book, ethnicity is just a superficial mask for children who are mainstream members of the dominant culture under their different-colored skins.

But when the African American writer Virginia Hamilton describes black characters like M. C. Higgins in *M. C. Higgins, The Great* or Talley Barbour in *A White Romance,* she gives them a rich individuality that nevertheless emerges from their consciousness of their special position in society as African Americans. Far from being stereotypes, M. C. and Talley are richly unique individuals partly because they are black and thoughtful about what it means to be black.

Furthermore, they're quite unlike each other—in part simply because of basic differences in their characters (and, of course, their gender), but also, in part, because of differences in their cultural situations. M. C. lives in the country in the 1970s; Talley in the city in the 1980s. In these differing times and places, the world offers different opportunities and imposes different barriers for people of color. Being black inevitably means something different for M. C. than it does for Talley, because it means something different in the world each of them lives in.

Indeed, the different situations of people from minority groups in different generations is a frequent subject of fiction by and about American members of those groups, as their relationship to the dominant culture changes, and as each generation does or does not accommodate itself to mainstream culture in varying degrees. In Angela Johnson's *Toning the Sweep,* a grandmother, mother, and daughter must work out quite different attitudes to their blackness and family history—attitudes that emerge from the degree of immediacy of their participation in the history of desegregation.

EXPLORATION: Compare (or invite children to compare) texts about minority children by minority and non-minority writers. Do they focus on the symbolic exoticism of minority members, on a basic shared humanity, or on differences created by societal assumptions? Which depictions strike you as most constructive? To what extent has your own cultural background influenced your thinking about these matters?

Authenticity.   Because tolerance is such an admirable goal, educators often choose to share books with children simply because the stories are about members of minority groups. But the tolerance is unlikely to be genuine if the books that try to foster it don't tell the truth about experience of members of minorities. It is therefore particularly important that such texts represent the people they describe with some degree of authenticity. Unfortunately, as *Cleversticks* and *The Slave Dancer* suggest, they don't always do so.

Positive Portrayals?   Rudine Sims Bishop offers as main criteria for choosing multicultural texts the following: "(1) that the book should contribute in a positive way to an understanding and appreciation of persons of color and their cultures, or (2) that the book should offer a positive vision of a diverse society and a multicultural world" (xv). The trouble with these criteria is simply that the experience of being a person of color or of living in a multicultural society isn't always a positive one—nor are members of minorities incapable of actions that might be viewed in a negative light. To insist on only positive portrayals is to insist on misrepresentations.

For example, in the spring of 1994, a school trustee in Vaughan, Ontario requested that *Sworn Enemies,* a children's novel about life in a Jewish village in Russia in the nineteenth century by my friend Carol Matas, shouldn't be added to a list of recommended reading for students. The trustee, herself Jewish, had read a synopsis that suggested the story was about a Jewish boy who worked as a *khapper,* kidnapping other Jewish boys to fill the Czar's army quotas. The trustee didn't like the idea that a Jew was being depicted in negative light: It might create prejudice. Apparently, the goal of tolerance was more important than the obvious truth that Jews—and blacks and Asians—are just as capable of self-seeking and malice as the rest of humanity is. Luckily, not all Jews are blind to that humbling truth, or the significance of children knowing it; in the same week in which Carol heard of the trustee's complaint, *Sworn Enemies* was awarded the Sydney Taylor Award by the Association of Jewish Libraries as the most distinguished children's novel of the year.

EXPLORATION: When I asked Caroline Hunt, who teaches at the College of Charleston, for a response to an earlier draft of this section of *Pleasures,* she offered the following provocative comments about the "dark side" of multiculturalism:

> Two fundamental goals of multiculturalism are knowledge and toleration. Generally, we want to know more, and want our children and students to know more, about other cultures, other races, other religions, and we would like to think that such knowledge leads to greater toleration of those unlike ourselves. But what happpens when the goals of knowledge and toleration come into conflict with other goals? For instance, attitudes toward animals, children, and helpless human beings differ markedly from place to place. Our North American idea of a book about bullfighting is Munro Leaf's *Ferdinand,* a charming fable in which the pacifist bull is rewarded by a pleasant retirement. How would we deal with a more realistic book about bullfighting in Spain? About cockfighting in Latin America? About dogfighting in Afghanistan? About infanticide in China or enforced suttee in India?
>
> In examining a number of books from Sierra Leone for a recent article, I found that several of the "finalists" for the recommended list discussed, in a perfectly casual way, the customs of arranged polygamous marriage and female circumcision (known elsewhere as "female genital mutilation"), I had to choose between respecting others' customs and

tolerating something that I personally find unacceptable—between my humanitarian ideals and multicultural toleration. I couldn't have it both ways.

In all of these instances, the same double-bind appears. Do we simply accept without comment practices such as animal sacrifice and female circumcision, thus implying that it doesn't matter how we treat animals, or girl children? Or do we reject texts that describe practices, like these, that are unacceptable to us? If so, we are not practicing any real tolerance of that which is culturally different from ourselves.

In my opinion, the dark side of multiculturalism isn't the existence of practices we don't like; it's the hypocrisy with which we select the bits and pieces that we like from other cultures, while studiously ignoring the parts that make us uncomfortable. Perhaps confronting this dilemma, to which I can't imagine any wholly satisfactory answer, will at least force us to think more clearly.

Appropriation.   Earlier, I described some common inadequacies of stories about members of minority groups by non-minority authors. Many people believe this means that writers shouldn't try to imagine the experience of people belonging to groups different from their own. Reporting on a roundtable attended by educators interested in multiculturalism, Norton says, "Many of the participants felt strongly that only members of an ethnic group should have ownership of the literature and be encouraged to write the literature and critique the literature written by others. . . . Others argued the viewpoint that anyone who writes with sensitivity and does the required research into the subject and the culture should be able to write about the culture" (605). Those who object to writers trying to describe the experience of groups other than their own see it as an act of theft, and call it *cultural appropriation* or *voice appropriation:* the act of claiming or appropriating the right to give voice to what it means or feels like to belong to a particular group.

There are several assumptions being made here. The first is that the ways in which stories represent people are always distorted by the conscious and unconscious attitudes of their authors. The second is that membership in a racial or ethnic group inevitably plays a part in creating any writer's conscious and unconscious attitudes. The third is that, since readers come to accept fictional representations as the truth, stories by writers of racial or cultural backgrounds different from their characters' will always be dangerously misleading.

I suspect there's a great deal of truth in each of these assumptions. Lenore Keeshig-Tobias, a Canadian Ojibway writer, says, "The issue is culture theft, the theft of voice. It's about power. . . . How would it be if Germans were to write Jewish history? And white Americans writing black history?" (64).

Nowadays, if Germans did write Jewish history or white Americans black history, I suspect the problem would be, not negative stereotypes, but positive ones.

Guilt over past actions might lead to the dangerous sort of focus on the positive I discussed earlier.

A particularly interesting example is *Brother Eagle, Sister Sky,* a picture-book version for children of what purports to be a speech given at the signing of a peace treaty in the 1850s by Sealth or Seattle, chief of the Suquamish and Duwamish people of the American northwest. The speech includes noble statements such as, "The Earth does not belong to man; man belongs to the Earth." It has become popular as a source of inspiration for environmentalists.

But Seattle never said these words. They were made up in the early 1970s by Ted Perry, a film writer, in the course of working on an environmental TV program. According to reporter Stephen Strauss,

> Upon hearing a modern version of what were purported to be Chief Seattle's historical words, Mr. Perry decided to appropriate the Indian leader and his aura. "It had some environmental leanings, so I said . . . I would like to make up another text which pushed the environmental idea a lot further, so I did," he told me.

What Perry based his text on was a report from the 1880s, which was itself reconstructed from notes made of what Seattle may or may not have said three decades earlier. Perry's appropriation of Seattle's voice made him and the values of his people sound nobler and more in accord with contemporary environmentalism than was actually the case: Seattle himself said that land is sacred for his people mainly because it is "hallowed by some found memory or some sad experience" (Strauss).

Perry has been trying to inform people that he wrote the words they so admire ever since he made them up, but to little avail. The publishers of *Brother Eagle, Sister Sky* credit them to Seattle despite attempts to inform them otherwise; they even added grandmothers to the speech's reference to grandfathers, thus implying an ahistorical lack of sexism in Northwest Native Americans of the nineteenth century. This idealistic misrepresentation of the values of Native Americans in the past both dehumanizes them and creates impossible (and unauthentic) standards for contemporary Native Americans to live up to.

To compound the matter, Susan Jeffers's illustrations for *Brother Eagle, Sister Sky* seem equally distorting. In a review of the book, Patricia Dooley complained that the natives depicted "appear to have come from Sioux Central Casting, complete with plains ponies and tipis (and one incongruous birchbark canoe lifted from the Algonquians)" (Jobe 138). In response, Jeffers claimed that her desire was to portray "peoples and artifacts from a wide array of nations: Cheyenne, Nez Perce, Lakota, Black Foot as well as Northern Algonquian" (Jobe 138). Dooley correctly responds that " 'The wide array of nations' Ms. Jeffers lists . . . are all either Great Plains or Great Lakes people" (Jobe 139). More important, however: these pictures imply that Seattle's words represent the values and philosophies of all Native American groups, not just those of his own Northwest group. This is a grossly essentializing generalization, implying that members of a variety of different groups are all alike. It's a blatant example of the distortions that mar acts of cultural appropriation.

EXPLORATION: Carried to its logical extreme, the concept of appropriation might suggest that men can't write authentic fiction about women, that heterosexuals can't write authentic fiction about homosexuals—or for that matter, that adults can't write authentic fiction about children. Indeed, Jo-Ann Wallace asks, "What does it mean to speak for the child, through the voice or the child, as the child?" (171). Explore ways of answering that question. (You might consider the ideas about colonization presented in chapter 5.)

SURFACING ASSUMPTIONS ABOUT INDIVIDUALITY

According to Althusser, ideologies persuade us of their obviousnesses by convincing us that we are the people who believe the things the ideologies want us to believe—that we are, in fact, certain kinds of individuals. In other words, the most significant effect of ideology is that it provides us with our sense of who and what we are. It does so by a process Althusser calls *interpellation,* or *hailing,*

> which can be imagined along the lines of the most commonplace everyday police (or other) hailing: "Hey, you there!" Assuming that the theoretical scene I have imagined takes place in the street, the hailed individual will turn around. By this mere one-hundred-and-eighty-degree conversion, he becomes a *subject.* Why? Because he has recognized that the hail was "really" addressed to him, and that "it was really him who was hailed" (and not someone else). (245–46)

TV commercials for children are clear examples of this sort of hailing: They say, in effect, "Hey, you there, child who wants to own lots of the right kinds of toys and therefore be accepted by the right kinds of friends—yes, I mean you!" A child who responds to this hailing by saying, "Yes! That's me you're talking to! I *am* that person! Tell me what I need to own to keep on being it!" has been successfully interpellated.

In the passage I quote above, Althusser calls a person hailed by ideology a "subject" rather than a self or an individual. He does so because of the ambiguous nature of the word. To be a *subject* is to be subjective—that is, capable of individual, personal thought, of being a self. But it is also to be subjected—to be dominated as a monarch dominates his subjects. In other words, to be a subject is to imagine oneself a separate, free individual in terms that put one under the control of ideology. "Thus," says Jeremy Hawthorne, "*subject* represents the individual's self-consciousness and consciousness of self after having been 'body-snatched' by ideology" (180).

One becomes a subject at the moment one learns to speak. "In order to speak," says Catherine Belsey, "the child is compelled to differentiate; to speak of itself it has to distinguish 'I' from 'you.' In order to formulate its needs, the child learns to identify with the first person singular pronoun, and this identification constitutes the basis of subjectivity" (60–61). To become a subject, then, is to be placed within a network of meanings—to learn a language, and to learn to see oneself in terms of that language.

In the process of interpellating children into language, the world offers us a variety of *subject positions:* conventional ways of being human the adoption of which can make us understandable to ourselves and others. In chapter 6, I described how toys and TV shows define femininity; they offer young female viewers subject positions, ways of looking and behaving that will define them as acceptably girl-like. Bronwyn Davies calls subject positions *lived narratives:* "the storylines that make up one's life" (318). In adopting a subject position, we enter its language, and live out the story line it implies.

Davies adds, "Lived narratives take the form they do because we can imagine ourselves being a certain kind of person who utters certain kinds of words which lead to certain kinds of outcomes. Without that imagined storyline into which our lives fit it is hard to know how we could make choices as we proceed through the everyday world" (328). Clearly, then, there's some truth in the common assumptions I described in chapter 5: Children do in this sense become what they read about. The story lines of the subject positions they know and choose do have a profound effect on them. As Marcia Kinder says,

> Narrative maps the world and its inhabitants, including one's own position within that grid. In acquiring the ability to understand stories, the child is situated as a perceiving, thinking, feeling, acting, speaking subject within a series of narrative fields—as a person in a family saga, as a spectator who tunes in to individual tales and identifies with their characters, and as a performer who repeats cultural myths and sometimes generates new transformations. (2)

If that's true, then the narratives we see on TV or read in books play an important part in making us who we believe ourselves to be. In offering subject positions, fictional texts for children work to construct their readers' subjectivity.

They do so primarily by encouraging real readers to become implied readers, to identify both with specific characters and with the point of view through which a text is focalized. For instance, Sendak's *Where the Wild Things Are* offers a subject position both by inviting child readers to think of themselves in terms of the boy Max and by offering a narrative point of view that tells them *how* to think about Max: to admire his fearlessness.

In chapter 2, I suggest that real readers can obtain much pleasure from pretending to be implied ones, and from trying to understand events from the point of view through which a text is focalized. But there's a danger that the pretending can become reality. As John Stephens says, "total identification with the focalizer is a strategy for reading which is widely encouraged in schools, and few people have questioned its appropriateness as a strategy" (68). Meanwhile, and in contradiction to that, many adults stress a theory of reader response with claims to allow children the variety of their individual responses. Stephens asserts,

> In my view, the present habit of stressing reader-focused approaches to text in combination with advocacy of identification with focalizers, inconsistent as this may be, is a dangerous ideological tool and pedagogically irresponsible. It fosters an illusion that readers are in control of texts whereas they are highly susceptible to the ideologies of the text, especially the unarticulated or implicit ideologies. (68)

In the discussion of themes in chapter 4, I suggested that identification leads to manipulation—that child readers who accept their similarity to a character are then asked to reach certain clearly asserted conclusions about right and wrong behavior. But before the intended manipulation can occur, a reader must first accept the identification—that is, agree to occupy the subject position the character represents. That subject position represents unarticulated and implicit ideologies—ideas about what children inherently are. In the long run, seeing oneself as little and animal-like may do more to define one's subjectivity than does agreeing that one shouldn't run away from home.

Knowing how to read against a text by identifying and thinking about the subject positions it offers, then, becomes a highly significant skill for children as well as adults. Stephens concludes that "adults who wish for children to develop unrestricted reading strategies and to be able to identify and resist restrictive texts will need to teach children to recognize how point of view is constructed in discourse" (27). Children who can do that, and who know all the other strategies for distancing themselves from the manipulations of texts that I describe throughout this book, are free to *negotiate* their subjectivity. They can understand and choose from the wide variety of subject position offered by both lived narratives and fictional texts, rather than just have one particular subject position imposed upon them. They may lose the pleasure of immersion in the world a text creates; they will gain the greater pleasure of being empowered to construct themselves.

EXPLORATION: Explore (or invite children to explore) the subject positions offered by a specific text, and how readers are invited to occupy them. To what degree do these subject positions represent desirable ways for children to think about themselves? If they are desirable, does it matter that the texts are manipulating children into accepting them?

The ability to recognize and consider the implications of subject positions in a text is especially important, I think, because our personalities are never so coherent or so unified as the subject positions the world around us invites us to identify ourselves with. The more we try to be coherent, furthermore, the more unhappy we become with the inevitable inconsistencies in ourselves that we might, instead, learn to accept and even celebrate. As Davies says,

> By focusing on the multiple subject positions that a person takes up and the often contradictory nature of those positionings, we are able to see individuals, not as the unitary beings that humanist theory would have them be, but as the complex, changing, contradictory creatures we each experience ourselves to be, despite our best efforts to produce a unified, coherent, and relatively static self. (322)

WORKS CITED

Alcott, Louisa May. *Little Women*. 1868. Harmondsworth, Middlesex: Puffin-Penguin, 1953.

Althusser, Louis. "Ideology and Ideological State Apparatuses." Trans. Ben Brewster. *Critical Theory Since 1965*. Ed. Hazard Adams and Leroy Searle. Tallahassee: UP of Florida and Florida State UP, 1986. 239–250.

Ashley, Bernard. *Cleversticks*. Illus. Derek Brazell. London: HarperCollins, 1992.

Baehr, Patricia. *School Isn't Fair!* Illus. R. W. Alley. New York: Macmillan, 1989.

Barrie, J. M. *Peter Pan: The Complete Play*. Montreal: Tundra, 1988.

Belsey, Catharine. *Critical Practice*. London and New York: Routledge, 1980.

Bishop, Rudine Sims, ed. *Kaleidoscope: A Multicultural Booklist for Grades K-8*. Urbana: NCTE, 1994.

Brother Eagle, Sister Sky. Illus. Susan Jeffers. New York: Dial, 1991.

Clark, Beverly Lyon. "A Portrait of the Artist as a Little Woman." *Children's Literature* 17 (1989): 81–97.

Cormier, Robert. *The Chocolate War*. New York: Pantheon, 1974.

Davies, Bronwyn. "Lived and Imaginary Narratives and their Place in Taking Oneself Up as a Gendered Being." *Australian Psychologist* 25,3 (November 1990): 318–332.

Estes, Angela M., and Kathleen Margaret Lant. "Dismembering the Text: The Horror of Louisa May Alcott's *Little Women*." *Children's Literature* 17 (1989): 123.

Faust, Beatrice. *Women, Sex, and Pornography*. Harmondsworth, Middlesex: Penguin, 1981.

Fetterly, Judith. "*Little Women*: Alcott's Civil War." *Feminist Studies* 5 (1979): 369–383.

Fox, Paula. *The Slave Dancer*. New York: Bradbury, 1973.

Grahame, Kenneth. *The Wind in the Willows*. 1908. New York: Charles Scribner's Sons, 1933.

Haggard, H. Rider. *She*. 1887. Oxford and New York: Oxford UP, 1991.

Hamilton, Virginia. *M. C. Higgins, The Great*. New York: Macmillan, 1974.

———. *A White Romance*. New York: Philomel, 1987.

Hawthorne, Jeremy. *A Concise Glossary of Contemporary Literary Theory*. London: Edward Arnold, 1992.

Henty, G. A. *St. George for England: A Tale of Cressy and Poitiers*. London: Blackie, 1890.

Hunt, Caroline. "Dick and Jane, The Newbery Medal, and the Politics of Geography." *Journal of Children's Literature* 20.2 (Fall 1994): 85–92.

Jobe, Ron. *Cultural Connections: Using Literature to Explore World Cultures with Children*. Markham: Pembroke, 1993.

Johnson, Angela. *Toning the Sweep*. New York: Orchard, 1993.

Keeshig-Tobias, Lenore. "Not Just Entertainment." *Whole Earth Review* (Summer 1991): 64–66.

Keyser, Elizabeth. "Alcott's Portraits of the Artist as Little Woman." *International Journal of Women's Studies* 5 (1982): 445–459.

Kinder, Marcia. *Playing with Power in Movies, Television, and Video Games*. Berkeley, Los Angeles and Oxford: U of California P, 1991.

Kipling, Rudyard. *The Jungle Book*. 1894. Oxford: Oxford UP, 1987.

——. *Stalky and Co*. 1899. London: Macmillan, 1899 and New York: Scribner's, 1900.

Le Guin, Ursula K. *The Wizard of Earthsea*. New York: Parnassus, 1968.

Lobel, Arnold. *Frog and Toad Are Friends*. New York: Harper, 1970.

Machery, Pierre. *A Theory of Literary Production*. Trans. Geoffrey Wall. London: Routledge and Kegan Paul, 1966.

Matas, Carol. *Sworn Enemies*. Toronto and New York: HarperCollins, 1993.

Montgomery, L. M. *Anne of Green Gables*. 1908. Toronto: Seal-McClelland and Stewart/Bantam, 1981.

Morrison, Toni. *Playing in the Dark: Whiteness and the Literary Imagination*. New York: Vintage, 1993.

Needle, Jan. *Wild Wood*. London: André Deutsch, 1981.

Nodelman, Perry. "Re-inventing the Past: Gender in Ursula K. Le Guin's *Tehanu* and the *Earthsea* 'Trilogy.' " *Children's Literature* 23 (1995): 179–201.

Norton, Donna E., with Sandra E. Norton. *Through the Eyes of a Child: An Introduction to Children's Literature*. 4th ed. Englewood Cliffs and Columbus: Merrill-Prentice Hall, 1995.

Potter, Beatrix. *The Tale of Mr. Jeremy Fisher*. London: Frederick Warne, 1906.

——. *The Tale of Peter Rabbit*. London: Frederick Warne, 1902.

Reimer, Mavis, ed. *Such a Simple Little Tale: Critical Responses to L. M. Montgomery's Anne of Green Gables*. Metuchen, NJ and London: Children's Literature Association and Scarecrow Press, 1992.

Said, Edward. "The Politics of Knowledge." *Falling into Theory: Conflicting Views on Reading Literature*. Ed. David H. Richter. Boston: Bedford Books of St. Martin's Press, 1994. 193–203.

Scheidlinger, Lucy Prince. *The Little Bus Who Liked Home Best*. New York: Fernand & Spertus, 1955.

Scholes, Robert. *Fabulation and Metafiction*. Urbana: U of Illinois P, 1979.

Sedgwick, Eve Kosofsky. *Between Men: English Literature and Male Homosocial Desire*. New York: Columbia UP, 1985.

Sendak, Maurice. *In the Night Kitchen*. New York: Harper & Row, 1970.

——. *Where the Wild Things Are*. New York: Harper & Row, 1963.

Showalter, Elaine. *Sexual Anarchy: Gender and Culture at the Fin de Siècle*. New York: Viking, 1990.

Stephens, John. *Language and Ideology in Children's Fiction*. London and New York: Longman, 1992.

Stevenson, Robert Louis. *Dr. Jekyll and Mr. Hyde*. 1886. New York: Bantam, 1981.

——. *Treasure Island*. 1883. London: Collins, 1953.

Stoker, Bram. *Dracula*. 1897. New York: Signet, 1992.

Strauss, Stephen. "Mind and Matter." *Toronto Globe and Mail*. February 8, 1992, D8.

Wallace, Jo-Ann. "De-Scribing The Water-Babies: 'The Child' in Post-colonial Theory." *De-Scribing Empire*. Ed. Chris Tiffin and Alan Lawson. London and New York: Routledge, 1994. 171–184.

Warhol, Robyn R., and Diane Price Herndl. *Feminisms: An Anthology of Literary Theory and Criticism*. New Brunswick, NJ: Rutgers UP, 1991.

White, E. B. *Charlotte's Web*. 1952. New York: Trophy-Harper & Row, 1973.

part **III**

Children's Literature and the Literary Repertoire

For a young child without any prior experience of literature or TV, hearing the story like "Cinderella" for the first time must be a strange experience, perhaps even a confusing one. Making sense of the story requires knowledge of a repertoire that is exclusively literary: Fairy godmothers and magic wands exist only within the world of literature. Never having heard a story about a mistreated girl magically transformed into a princess, the child new to "Cinderella" would have no schema to apply, no way of seeing these events as anything but strange, maybe even incomprehensible.

Later, however, hearing "Snow White," the child might make a connection, and realize that this story also tells of a mistreated girl magically transformed into a princess. The child will have begun to develop a schema for such stories. And by the time the child hears "Sleeping Beauty" for the first time, the schema might be implanted firmly enough so that the child can begin to make sense of this new story in terms of its similarities to and differences from the old ones.

As the experience of this imaginary but not unusual child suggests, the schemata we develop from our previous experience of literature have a profound effect on our responses to literary texts. They control both what we're able to comprehend in texts, and what sense or use we make out of what we have comprehended. The two chapters in this part explore how. Chapter 8 focuses on literary texts themselves, particularly those intended for child readers, and considers ways in which knowledge of some texts influences understanding of others. Chapter 9 discusses a variety of schemata for making sense of these texts from the viewpoint of a number of different theories about literature in general.

chapter 8

Children's Literature as Repertoire

INTERTEXTUALITY

Readers often assume that each worthwhile story or poem is separate and unique, something that either emerges exclusively from one person's individual creativity or else has been inspired by forces beyond mere human knowledge—a "muse," perhaps. And certainly, every interesting literary text does express the unique imagination of its writer; but we shouldn't forget that writers have repertoires, and work from their knowledge of previous texts just as much as readers do. The idea of a story about a detective figuring out which suspect committed a crime doesn't occur independently to each person who writes a mystery novel. Most mystery writers have read many such texts before deciding to create their own.

What's true of mystery novels is true of tragedies, novels about talking animals, and the whole range of literary texts. Any given text always has many other texts in its background, and shares many characteristics with them: not just obvious allusions, but also ideas, images, and basic story patterns. Finally, all texts—indeed, the many words by which humans communicate their experience in speech, newspapers, and letters, on TV and radio, as well as in books—are connected with each other: Like the words in a dictionary, they all make most sense in terms of their relationship to other words that define and explain them.

Thus, each book expresses what literary critics call *intertextuality:* the interconnectedness of human language, its patterns, images, and meanings. To focus on a text's intertextuality is to focus on the ways it depends on the reader's knowledge of its connections with other writing.

This chapter is about the intertextuality of children's literature, and ways in which knowledge of it can offer insight and pleasure to both child and adult readers. I begin with an exploration of how readers can use their knowledge of one text as a schema for making sense of other texts.

TEXTS AS CONTEXTS FOR EACH OTHER

Thinking about literary texts as schemata for each other has two uses. Most obviously, it allows us to become aware of the qualities they share. But it also allows us to become aware of the qualities they don't share.

For instance, a child who knew some fairy tales and therefore possessed a schema for stories about unlikely girls magically transformed into princesses wouldn't be surprised by Hans Christian Andersen's "The Princess and the Pea." In this story as in "Cinderella," a prince seeks a bride, and the woman he ends up marrying is an unlikely choice—in this case a stranger who knocks on the palace gate during a rainstorm. Despite her bedraggled appearance, she turns out to be a "real" princess, a fact proven when a pea placed under twenty mattresses and twenty quilts gives her a sleepless night. As in "Cinderella," apparently, true worth triumphs despite appearances, and events lead a prince to a *real* princess even when she's sooty, wet, or otherwise unprincesslike.

But as I suggested, schemata allow us to perceive differences as well as similarities. A little further thinking about "The Princess and the Pea" and "Cinderella" reveals that there are important ways in which they aren't alike. In most versions of the story, Cinderella's true worth is her moral goodness; the worth of Andersen's princess is a sensitivity resulting from noble blood. The implication of Andersen's story is that members of the upper classes are inherently more refined than ordinary mortals. As it happens, the story annoys many readers I've discussed it with because they see it as snobbish and undemocratic.

But is it? The princess's ability to feel a single pea through all those mattresses is extreme, and it seems odd that Andersen doesn't comment on its outlandishness. Thinking about the extreme nature of the princess's sensitivity, I'm personally reminded of another text from my own repertoire: Hilaire Belloc's poem "Sarah Byng, Who Could Not Read and Was Tossed into a Thorny Hedge by a Bull," in which Sarah's problem develops from her inability to decipher a warning sign. As a result, Sarah learns "to keep away/ From signs, whatever they may say," and is

> Confirmed in her instinctive guess
> That literature breeds distress.

Belloc states this unlikely conclusion with the same calm acceptance with which Andersen tells of the princess's discomfort with the pea. As I understand the poem, the discrepancy between the accepting tone and the outrageous idea is meant to be funny—and I think it *is* funny. I find myself asking if Andersen also intends me to laugh at his story; perhaps he's making fun of the supposed superiority of "real" princesses by telling this exaggerated story about one of them, and the story actually means the opposite of what it seems to be saying.

If I reach that conclusion and then think again about "Cinderella," I begin to see *it* differently also. As a member of a society that values kindness, I've assumed that Cinderella becomes a princess because of her kind heart. But now, thinking about the story in the light of "The Princess and the Pea," I begin to wonder if Cinderella can be transformed into a princess because she's something like a princess in the first place—the daughter of a nobleman. Perhaps her stepmother's crime is not so much a lack of appreciation for Cinderella's virtue as it is a denial of her rights as the eldest daughter of a rich gentleman. Perhaps Cinderella deserved a prince because of her noble blood, no matter how sweet or kind she may have been. Thinking about other texts has given me new insights into this one.

Other Texts by the Same Author

Many readers, both children and adults, seek out further texts by authors they have enjoyed because they expect a common thread, a consistency of subject and style, in all the texts an author produces. Writers for children often produce books in *series:* connected texts about the same characters in similar situations. But because of the consistencies of human personality, texts by the same author usually have a lot in common even when their author didn't necessarily intend them to.

Consequently, knowing that Belloc is being ironic in "Sarah Byng," I suspect he is being equally ironic in a poem called "The Tiger," in which he suggests that tigers make good pets:

> And mothers of large families (who claim to common sense)
> Will find a Tiger well repays the trouble and expense.

And knowing Beatrix Potter's *The Tale of Peter Rabbit,* a story about a small animal who loses his clothing in an exciting escape from a farmer's garden, prepares me to focus on the subtleties of Potter's *The Tale of Mr. Jeremy Fisher,* in which a frog puts on a mackintosh and a pair of shiny galoshes so that he can go fishing on a rainy day.

But once again, the similarity points my attention toward a difference. Peter Rabbit's clothes hinder him, and he can run fast enough to escape from Mr. McGregor only after he gets rid of his shoes. But Jeremy Fisher's clothing saves his life. A trout swallows him, but "was so displeased with the taste of the mackintosh, that in less than half a minute it spat him out again." As I suggest later in this chapter, many children's books deal with animals and their clothing as metaphors for the condition of being a child: these two books may be offering two different sorts of insights into that condition. A perception of similarities can suggest intriguing differences even in two apparently similar texts by the same author.

EXPLORATION: Choose (or invite children to choose) two texts by the same author that strike you as being significantly similar. Does your perception of the similarities also point you toward some interesting differences?

CHILDREN'S LITERATURE AS A GENRE

We can describe certain texts as being mystery novels or romances simply because we see them as similar to other texts we have previously labeled as being mystery novels or romances. Once we are aware that a number of texts have a lot in common, we can place them in a category defined by their shared characteristics. Literary specialists call such categories *genres*.

Genres exist primarily in the eyes of their beholders. There was no genre of mystery before writers produced a number of novels that readers compared, found connections between, and identified as mysteries. Once readers have identified genres and their defining characteristics, writers often create texts that fit the categories. But they have no obligation to do so; it would be foolish to judge a text as being without value simply because it doesn't follow what we perceive to be "rules" of a genre we've invented ourselves. In fact, as Alastair Fowler suggests, "the character of genres is that they change. Only variations or modifications of convention have literary significance" (18). Consequently, the main virtue of thinking about genre is *not* to provide us with easy rules to follow in understanding or making judgments about texts; it is that it allows us to perceive the variations and modifications and to think about their significance. Once more, seeing what texts have in common allows us to focus on the far more interesting question of their differences.

Texts written for children often belong to genres that might already be familiar to people who know something about literature written for adults: adventure stories, fantasies, historical novels, romances, ballads, or limericks. But even while texts of these sorts written for children share qualities with similar texts written for adults, they also have much in common with each other *as* texts for children—and that includes everything from short picture books and fairy tales to comparatively long novels. For all the ways in which Maurice Sendak's simple picture book *Where the Wild Things Are* is unlike Alan Garner's complex novel *Red Shift,* they have enough in common to be identified as children's fiction—as do even those texts for older children about apparently unchildlike matters that are often labeled as literature for young adults, such as Francesca Lia Block's *Weetzie Bat.* Children's literature can, then, usefully be considered a genre of literature in its own right.

EXPLORATION: My assertion that as forms of children's literature, sophisticated novels like *Red Shift* and *Weetzie Bat* have a lot in common with simple picture books is an idea that many people would argue with. Test it out: read one of these books or another complex novel for young adults, and think about the degree to which it expresses the characterisics of children's literature I discuss in the rest of this chapter.

What, then, defines the genre? As its name, *children's* literature, suggests, it must be qualities that relate to our ideas about children, about what they can understand and what they might enjoy. In chapter 5, I outlined assumptions adults often make about these matters. It seems logical that these assumptions would lead to the creation of a literature designed to suit that audience. I believe that's the case; the generic characteristics of children's literature emerge from these common assumptions. In fact, the implied reader of most children's literature is the child defined by those assumptions: the child whose major quality is limited knowledge and ability, and whose major needs are to be protected and to be educated.

In chapter 5, I outlined the danger of these assumptions; and I suggested that they led to the writing of limited and limited children's literature—to texts that offer children views of themselves and their world likely to do nothing but inhibit their development. But I also suggested that another kind of children's literature is possible—a kind that displays the characteristics of the genre in a way that does allow for growth. In what follows, I consider some central characteristics of the genre of children's literature in terms of how they might be expressed in both limited texts and less-limiting ones. My main purpose is to point out how knowledge of the generic characteristics of children's literature and of their relationship to common ideas about childhood can help us to distinguish between the two kinds of texts: to determine which texts work to reinforce the conservative, dull-witted children of common assumptions and which texts imply readers capable of growth and in the process of becoming less limited.

A No-Name Story: The Basic Pattern

The following are descriptions of some children's stories that, from my previous experience of reading children's literature, strike me as typical:

- In Lucy Prince Scheidlinger's *The Little Bus Who Liked Home Best,* a municipal bus becomes envious of the "great silver buses" on the superhighway. After joining them, he becomes confused by the traffic, and when he finally finds his way back, he concludes, as the title suggests, that home is best.

- In Leo Lionni's *Fish Is Fish,* a fish is left behind in the pond when his childhood friend becomes a frog and goes off to see the world. When the frog returns with stories of glamorous sights, the fish resolves to leave the pond. After the frog saves the fish's life by flipping the fish back into the water, the fish concludes that it's better to stay at home.

- In Marjorie Flack and Kurt Wiese's *The Story About Ping,* a duck avoids punishment for being the last to return to its home on a boat by staying out on the river. Caught by a boy, the duck is threatened with death. After escaping, he happily returns home despite the inevitable punishment.

While the details change, there's clearly a basic pattern underlying these stories: A young creature, an animal or object with human characteristics, enjoys the security of a comfortable home until something happens to make it unhappy. The small creature leaves home and has exciting adventures; but they turn out to be as dangerous or as discomforting as they are thrilling. Having learned the truth about the big world, the creature finally returns to the security it at first found burdensome, concluding that, despite its constraints, home is best.

EXPLORATION: Browse (or invite children to browse) through children's books in a library or bookstore to see if you can find examples of this story pattern or of stories similar to it. How many stories can you find that are completely different from it?

I believe this story is generic, like the "no-name" canned goods sold in supermarkets. While not identical to it, many other children's stories and poems relate significantly to it. In Munro Leaf's *Noodle,* for instance, a dachshund is concerned with the limitations not of its home, but of its body, and after considering the advantages of the more exotic shapes of animals at the zoo, decides that its original size and shape are ideal. One's own body, like one's own home, is best.

Many interesting and admired children's books follow the same pattern. Beatrix Potter's Peter Rabbit ignores his mother's instructions, has a dangerous adventure away from home, and returns to safety afterward. In Arthur Yorinks' and Richard Egielski's *Hey, Al,* a janitor and his dog escape from their boring life by accepting a giant bird's invitation to a paradisal island in the sky. When they start turning into birds themselves, the janitor decides that mopping floors is preferable, and they return to the comforts of home. In a somewhat convoluted move away from home and then back again, the title character in Virginia Lee Burton's *The Little House* longs for the excitement of the city until the city grows up around her and brings her nothing but noise and neglect. Delighted to be moved back to the country, she vows that she will never again wonder about the city.

Similarly, Maurice Sendak's *Where the Wild Things Are* takes Max from his imposed stay in his own room into a possibly imaginary voyage into wildness, which ends when he decides he wants to return to the comfort of his room. Many other books also describe voyages away from children's homes or bedrooms that may or may not be imaginary: to name a few fairly recent ones, Phyllis Root's *Moon Tiger,* William Joyce's *George Shrinks,* Tim Wynne-Jones's *Architect of the Moon,* Liz Rosenberg's *Adelaide and the Night Train,* Alan Say's *A River Dream,* Mary Pope Osborne's *Moonhorse,* Tibo's *Paper Nights.* All end with home restored. Meanwhile, many other books describe a child's bedroom or home invaded by something that clearly belongs elsewhere, as does the forest in *Wild Things:* for instance, another forest in Ann Mazer's *The Salamander Room,* the title character in Rob Shepperson's *The Sandman,* the title character in Dr. Seuss's *The Cat in the Hat.* In most of these stories, too, the child is happy to have the calm of home restored at the end.

Nor are stories of this sort restricted to picture books. They can be found in both classic children's novels and ones written more recently. In Robert Louis Stevenson's *Treasure Island,* published over a hundred years ago, Jim Hawkins expresses boredom with the quietness of his home. After his exciting but dangerous experiences with pirates, he returns home convinced that nothing could make him wish for adventure again. E. L. Konigsburg's *From the Mixed-up Files of Mrs. Basil E. Frankweiler* (1967) describes how a brother and sister seek adventure by running away from home to the safe pleasures of the Metropolitan Museum and then return home again. And in Gary Paulsen's *Hatchet* (1987) Brian learns to survive the breakup of his parent's marriage and his feeling of being isolated, after he leaves home in a plane that crashes in the bush and leaves him literally isolated. Having experienced physically what he at first felt emotionally, he returns home with knowledge of his inner strength.

Of course, not all children's literature follows this pattern; many stories and poems written for children bear no apparent relationship to it at all. But the fact that the pattern occurs so often is suggestive: Its characteristics must satisfy our ideas about what children's literature is or should be.

Furthermore, once we've observed the pattern and are able to use it as a schema, we can read texts that seem different from it as interesting variations on it. For instance, the plot of L. M. Montgomery's *Anne of Green Gables* represents an inversion of the pattern: A child whose life has been filled with troubling adventures arrives at a safe home at the *beginning* of the story. Meanwhile, many children's books follow the pattern of fairy tales like "Cinderella," and describe how children journey away from homes whose security or happiness have been disrupted and finally find a new home representing the old security elsewhere. This pattern can be found in, for instance, Lois Lowry's *The Giver,* Katherine Paterson's *Lyddie,* and in a number of novels by Carol Matas: *Lisa's War, Sworn Enemies,* and *The Burning Time.* In all cases though, these stories start in a peaceful place and end in a similar one.

EXPLORATIONS: (1) Consider (or invite children to consider) the significance of the generic "no-name" story. What are its characteristics? Why do so many texts share these characteristics? What are the implications of these similarities?

(2) Consider how you can use our knowledge of genre to help you to understand a text. Choose (or invite children to choose) a children's poem or story, and keep it in mind as you think about the characteristics outlined in the next section. Is the text illuminated by these ideas?

CHARACTERISTICS OF THE GENRE

The generic pattern can help us understand the traits that are typical of children's literature as a genre. This section explores typical characters, plots, themes, style and structure, and focalization of texts written for children, and considers some of their implications.

Characters

Children's literature, intended for an audience of children, is meant to relate to the interests of children. Not surprisingly, then, its central characters are children—or at least, childlike creatures. While many of the versions of the generic story I outlined above are about humanized objects or animals, their main characters are often described as being young and, in that way, equivalent to the children who read about them.

Furthermore these children or childlike characters confirm adult assumptions about children: They are limited. The generic story often informs children that they are too limited to cope with the world on their own.

Alternatively, however, many fairy tales concern ingenuously passive girls (such as Cinderella) or the youngest (and theoretically dumbest) of three brothers whose ignorance of the ways of the world, lack of self-reliance, and trusting passivity allow him to succeed when his older and supposedly wiser brothers fail. As in these tales, texts for children often praise ignorance, which they describe as a wise innocence; for instance, the title character in A. A. Milne's *Winnie-the-Pooh* confirms the virtues of ignorance by doing things that are wrong and therefore funny and adorable, charmingly innocent.

So childhood inexperience tends to be a dangerous ignorance in some texts and a charming innocence in others. In Stevenson's *Treasure Island,* something a little more complex occurs. The older and theoretically wiser Jim Hawkins who tells us about what happened when he was younger and more ignorant keeps pointing out the folly of his actions on the island. But those who enjoy this book as the adventure it is admire the exuberant young Jim who performs these exploits more than the repressive older Jim who disapproves of them. Furthermore, *Treasure Island* lets us know that Jim's ignorant thoughtlessness—for instance, his desertion of his friends that leads him to the marooned Ben Gunn—was actually what won the treasure. Many of the more interesting texts express exactly this ambivalence.

But even when children's stories praise innocence or express ambivalence about it, their climax often occurs when the main character realizes that innocence has led to danger or despair. In "Hansel and Gretel," the gingerbread house turns out to be a witch's dwelling. In *Treasure Island,* Jim learns he shouldn't have trusted Long John Silver. Both Johnny in Esther Forbes's *Johnny Tremain* and Ged in Ursula Le Guin's *A Wizard of Earthsea* pay for their egocentric trust in themselves with physical disfigurement; and Harriet in Louise Fitzhugh's *Harriet the Spy* pays for hers with emotional suffering. From the viewpoint of more experienced adults, it seems, innocence must end; and so the literature of innocence often turns out to be about the necessary and inevitable loss of innocence. While Peter in J. M. Barrie's *Peter Pan* and Winnie-the-Pooh in Milne's *The House at Pooh Corner* remain innocent, both are deserted by their peers; Wendy and Christopher Robin realize that despite the attractions of the idyllic worlds of Peter and Pooh, they themselves must grow up.

But that Peter and Winnie-the-Pooh do remain young forever, and that we are expected to love them for doing so, reinforces the ambivalence I mentioned above: a balancing of opposite values. Much children's fiction deals with attempts to grow up without actually growing up; to mature without losing the joy, optimism, and simplicity of youth; to be neither Peter nor Wendy but some combination of the two. While that sounds impossible, the adult Anne of Green Gables explicitly claims to have done it: "I'm not a bit changed—not really. I'm only just pruned down and branched out. The real *me*—back here—is just the same" (276). Characters like Wilbur the pig in *Charlotte's Web* and Harriet the Spy seem to manage to do it also, and so, despite her complicated and apparently highly *un*-innocent life, does Weetzie Bat; and many characters in children's novels who flee from broken or disrupted homes encounter bitter experience but still manage to avoid cynicism by finding new homes where they can preserve their innocence and optimism.

EXPLORATION: Consider (or invite have children to consider) the endings of some children's novels of your choice. Do their main characters stay innocent, mature, or "grow up without growing up"?

Animals.   Parents often call good children "little lambs" or gluttonous ones "little pigs," and the common name for children in our society is "kids." Apparently, we tend to think of "kids" as basically animal-like savages who must be taught how to act like civilized humans. Not surprisingly, then, many characters in children's literature are animals—animals who represent the animal-like condition of children.

Like human children, Peter Rabbit is torn between the opposing forces of his natural instincts and the societal conventions represented by his mother's wishes—and despite his relative maturity, Mr. Jeremy Fisher is equally torn between nature and societal convention. Furthermore, both Peter and Jeremy have enemies who think of them as animals, and therefore believe they have a natural right to attack them: Rabbits who steal vegetables from gardens and frogs who get close to trout are asking for trouble. But both Peter and Jeremy behave like human beings, so that their situation is ambiguous in ways that allow these characters to express common adults ideas about the nature of childhood.

For these half-animal, half-human creatures, clothing is of great significance. It marks them off from the purely animal, from the completely savage creatures who don't wear clothing, but it's often a source of discomfort, something that prevents them from behaving like their natural selves. Both Peter and Jeremy almost die because they act like humans: Peter's shoes and jacket buttons nearly lead to his death, and Jeremy dressed and acting like a human fisherman forgets his frog instincts about avoiding trout. But then both Peter and Jeremy escape disaster because they act like humans—Peter by remembering human words about the dangers of cats spoken by his cousin Benjamin, and Jeremy because his mackintosh tastes so unfroglike.

The focus on animals and their nature might explain another common feature of children's texts, especially those intended for younger readers: Their characters are often centrally concerned with questions about food. In well-known fairy tales, Little Red Riding Hood brings food to her grandmother, but is threatened with becoming the meal herself; and Hansel and Gretel become possible meals after they nibble parts of the witch's house. Meanwhile, Peter Rabbit has his dangerous adventure because he can't resist Mr. McGregor's vegetables even though his father was made into a pie by Mrs. McGregor. And in *Where the Wild Things Are,* Max is sent to his room because he threatens to devour his mother, discovers that the Wild Things want to eat him up because they love him, and is drawn back home by the smell of good things to eat.

While eating is less central in longer works of fiction, it's still an important subject. For instance, *Charlotte's Web* focuses attention on descriptions of Wilbur's slop,

Charlotte's methods of killing her food, and Templeton the rat's pleasure in the feast available at the fair.

In these and many other texts, the fact that we eat creatures that once lived but were too weak to protect themselves suggests that we—particularly those of us who are weak children—might therefore also be eaten. All of thus suggests some ambiguity about the degree to which one is a human eater, like one's parents, or an animal-like food, like the "little lambs" and "little pigs" we so often tell children they are. The focus on eating raises the question of children's animality in an especially intense way.

Machines.   Even choosing to write a children's story about a machine implies an assumption about childhood. When the youthful engine in Gertrude Crampton's *Tootle* makes the mistake of giving in to impulse and jumps the track, we know he's acting in a manner unreasonable for a train. The fact that he's also a child implies that children who read about him are or should also in some way be like trains, and learn as Tootle does to remain on the rails; that is, to act as they've been told to. Children need discipline: They should be machine-like.

Fortunately, not all machines are so depressingly representative of the virtues of machine-like behavior. Some, like the toaster in Tom Disch's *The Brave Little Toaster,* triumph in the opposite way: by managing to find flexible ways of getting around the limitations imposed upon them by their mechanical nature.

Toys, Dolls, and Other Small Things.   Reducing the size of their characters, or bringing miniature objects to life, is another technique children's writers use to explore the nature of childhood. In Hans Christian Andersen's "Thumbelina," for instance, a girl as small as a thumb has to cope with a world made for much bigger people. In Lynn Reid Banks's *The Indian in the Cupboard,* a plastic toy comes to life and interacts with a human child. In Mary Norton's *The Borrowers,* tiny human beings who live within the walls of a normal-size house survive by "borrowing" objects and adapting them to their own use.

These miniature human beings and living dolls and toys can all be read as metaphoric representations of children. Like dogs or pigs or rabbits, the miniature beings are much smaller than the creatures who control them. But unlike animals, toys and miniature humans have no instinctual defenses, no innate ability to cope with the dangers of life in the wild. Thumbelina can be controlled by whatever larger creature comes along, as can the mechanical father and son who are the main characters in Russell Hoban's *The Mouse and His Child.* As Lois Kuznets suggests, then, characters like these "suggest the relatively powerless relationship of human beings to known or unseen forces: their dreadful vulnerability" (2). When these small beings prevail over insurmountable odds, as they almost always do, they represent a potent version of the typical underdog story discussed in chapter 6: the very small can triumph over the dangerously large, the very powerless over the exceedingly powerful.

Books about miniatures tend to focus on the physical difficulties that their characters face and their ingenious solutions to them. In *Stuart Little,* E. B. White describes his small protagonist's troubles with ordinary toothpaste tubes and drain-holes; and in *The Borrowers,* Norton shows how the Clock family adapts postage stamps to wall paintings, spools to chairs, and children's blocks to tables. Much of the pleasure such books offer depends on our delight in objects that are just like other objects but on a smaller scale.

Claude Lévi-Strauss suggests the source of that pleasure when he says that the central significance of *all* works of art is that they are miniatures—small-scale versions of larger objects. The objects in paintings are often actually smaller and the ones in literature have fewer attributes than the real objects they represent; and, "being smaller, the object as a whole seems less formidable. By being quantitatively diminished, it seems to us qualitatively simplified. . . . A child's doll is no longer an enemy, a rival, or even an interlocutor. In it and through it a person is made into a subject" (23). The simplification allows us mastery and self-understanding.

If we ask children to identify with such miniatures, however, ambivalences emerge: They must see themselves as the creatures over whom others have mastery. Kuznets suggests that toy characters "embody human anxiety about what it means to be 'real'—an independent subject or self rather than an object or other submitting to the gaze of more powerfully real and potentially rejecting live being" (2).

For that reason, perhaps, in many books about toys and other small creatures, the simplification of the miniature is itself a central concern. The small creatures of children's fiction tend to express both the virtues and vices of smallness and limitation. They are exquisitely delicate but also vulnerable, and often quite small-minded.

The Borrowers are fearful. There's even a suggestion that their ancestors were ordinary-size human beings who produced smaller offspring because of their timidity and lack of emotional magnitude: Their outsides diminished to match their state of mind. Many toy characters are egocentric or conservative—"small-minded" in that they have responded to their physical condition by becoming unadventurous and inflexible. Books about animals tend to focus on the ways in which children, in their likeness to animals, are more savage, less controlled and more in need of control than adults. But books about miniature creatures tend to focus on the ways in which children, in their likeness to toys, are inherently weaker, more prone to give in to their weakness, more in need of resolve and energy than adults. The dispute tends to be not between civility and nature but between possibility and limitation.

Even the triumphs of miniatures tend to be *little* ones: The Borrowers' epic adventure is a trip out of the house and into the adjoining field. Our consciousness of the relative insignificance of these creatures and their triumphs tends to give an edge of irony to these books: Readers seem to be expected to both identify with them and separate themselves from them, in both cases because of their smallness.

For that reason, perhaps, books about miniatures often give them adult personalities and include normal-size human children for their miniature protagonists to interact with. For instance, Banks's Indian is a miniature adult whose existence depends on a human child. Alternatively, some stories center on a miniature child with an exuberant spirit at odds with its fragile state—like Arietty, the youngest of the Borrowers, or the child in Hoban's *The Mouse and His Child*. The presence of such children provides a contrast between the timidity or egocentricity characteristic of the little creatures and the greater wisdom of the child. The normal-size child acts with more energy and thoughtlessness than the miniatures, but because of his or her greater size, is also thrust into the role of an adult. For instance, the human boy in *The Borrowers* must take on the parental responsibility of helping the Clock family escape once their presence has been discovered, in part through his childish carelessness. The rebellious miniature child tends to share that mixture of childlike innocence and adult responsibility; the mouse child remains optimistic and so can guide his father beyond his theoretically mature state of despair.

Orphans.   It's interesting to note how many of the characters I've mentioned so far in this chapter are permanently or temporarily separated from their parents: Max, Wilbur and Charlotte, Peter Rabbit, Stuart Little, Weetzie Bat. The main characters in many children's stories and novels are orphans: Anne of Green Gables and a host of other heroines of girls' series books; the central character in Paterson's *Lyddie;* and characters as diverse as Taran of Lloyd Alexander's Prydain series, Dorothy in Baum's *The Wonderful Wizard of Oz,* Mowgli of Kipling's *Jungle Book,* and the homeless Jolly of Virginia Euwer Wolff's *Make Lemonade.* Many other characters are partially or temporarily orphaned; Jo and her sisters in Louisa May Alcott's *Little Women,* Jim Hawkins of *Treasure Island,* the human boy in *The Borrowers,* Tom of Philippa Pearce's *Tom's Midnight Garden,* and Brian in Paulsen's *Hatchet* have been separated from parents either by chance or by choice. The generic children's story I described earlier is about a creature who chooses to "orphan" itself and then realizes its error.

The prevalence of orphans in children's fiction seems to relate to a central concern adults have with the question of children's independence and security. Orphans are of necessity independent, free to have adventures without the constraints of protective adults; at the same time, they are automatically faced with the danger and discomfort of lack of parental love. Because we define childhood as that time of life when one needs parental love and control, I suspect we believe that the possibility of being orphaned—of having the independence one wants and yet having to do without the love one needs—is an exciting and disturbing idea for children who are not in fact orphans, and a matter of immediate interest for those who are. In depicting orphans, writers can focus on children's desire for independence, or on their fear of loss of security. In some cases, they offer interesting combinations of the two, as in *Make Lemonade:* one young girl teaches another independence by offering comfort and security. In doing so, she must herself learn, first, to compromise her own desire for independence and then, eventually, to give up the comfort of the relationship and become independent again.

Plots

Adult fiction that deals with young people who leave home usually ends with them choosing to stay away. As the adult novelist Thomas Wolfe suggested in the title of one of his books, "You can't go home again." But as in the generic story outlined above, and as happens to Jim in *Treasure Island,* Max in *Where the Wild Things Are,* and Dorothy in *Wizard of Oz,* characters in children's stories tend to learn the value of home by losing it and then finding it again. This *home/away/home* pattern is the most common plot of children's literature. As Christopher Clausen says, "When home is a privileged place, exempt from the most serious problems of life and civilization—when home is where we ought, on the whole, to stay—we are probably dealing with a story for children. When home is the chief place from which we must escape, either to grow up or . . . to remain innocent, then we are involved in a story for adolescents or adults" (143). I might further distinguish between Clausen's two categories: Stories in which escape from home leads to growing up are usually for adults, and those where escape allows the preservation of some form of innocence tend to be for adolescents. The discovery of a secure home in which one is free to be childlike is often the culmination of novels for young people: books like *Anne of Green Gables* or Matas's novels, in which characters journey from a broken or disrupted home to a new one.

Themes

Children's literature wouldn't exist at all if we didn't see children as inexperienced and in need of knowledge. Obviously, then, children's literature is almost always *didactic:* its purpose is to instruct.

I've already suggested the nature of the instruction as I've talked about character and plot: It tends to focus on some central themes that relate to adult concerns about what children are and about how they should think of themselves: as animals or as humans, as innocent or ignorant, as independent or in need of care. All these themes can be seen in the generic home/away/home story.

In fact, the various values commonly associated in children's texts with being home on the one hand and being away on the other define some of the most central thematic concerns of a surprising amount of children's literature. The list that follows represents ideas I've found being explored again and again in my reading of children's picture books, poems, and novels. I believe they are the most predominant themes to be found in texts written for children and young adults. I've listed them in terms of how they relate either to home (the left column) or away (the right column).

Home	*Away*
Human	Animal
Adult	Child
Maturity	Childishness
Civilization	Nature
Restraint	Wildness
Clothing	Nakedness
Obedience	Disobedience
Imprisonment	Freedom

Home	*Away*
Boredom	Adventure
Safety	Danger
Calm	Excitement
Acceptance	Defiance
Repression	Expression
Charity	Egotism
Martyrdom	Self-respect
Communal concern	Self-concern
Citizenship	Exile
Companionship	Solitude
Constriction	Liberation
Common sense	Imagination
Sense	Nonsense
Cynicism	Wise innocence
Wisdom	Ignorance
Old ideas	New ideas
Past practice	Future potential
Custom	Anarchy
Conservatism	Innovation
Fable	Fairy tale
Reality	Fantasy
False vision	Reality
Good	Evil
Evil	Good

As well as being connected either to home or away, the ideas on these lists also have other relationships to each other, to be discovered if you read the lists horizontally as well as vertically. Each horizontal line represents values that are usually found in texts together and in opposition to each other—just as are home and away or the human and the animal. In texts that express any of these values, characters find themselves in situations in which they must think about how the value on the left differs from or represents different consequences than the value on the right—how restraint is different from wildness, or charity different from egotism. The characters must either choose between them or find some sort of compromise between them. These values are what structural theorists call *binary opposites:* opposing ideas that conflict with and relate to each other in various ways in order to create the structure of cultures, artifacts—and literary texts. There's more about structuralism in chapter 9.

The oddest features of my lists are that both positive and negative terms appear in each column, and that words like "good" and "evil" and "reality" appear in both columns. I've made that happen because, while many if not most texts written for children deal with these concerns, they obviously don't all take the same point of view about them. As I've already suggested, what is innocent and good from one point of view is ignorance and evil from another. These different points of view lead to three main kinds of texts for children.

The main thrust of children's literature is the didactic effort to educate children into sharing an adult view of the world—and also, of what it means to be a child. As a result, many versions of the generic story try to persuade young readers that despite its boredom, home, representative of adult values, is a better place to be than the dangerous world outside. And they tend to do it in an obvious fashion: We can tell even from the title of a book called *The Little Bus Who Liked Home Best* what message it conveys—goodness consists of the adult values represented by home.

On the other hand, some texts are less concerned with telling children what they should be than with giving them what adults assume they already want and like to hear. On TV and in written texts, consequently, much popular storytelling has little to say about the safety of home, and much to say about the delightful freedom of being away from home. Goodness consists of the presumably childlike values represented by being away from home.

But as we've seen, still other texts express *ambivalence* or uncertainty about these matters. *Wild Things* purges wildness through a joyous expression of it which makes it seem as much fun as it is antisocial—and indeed, the basis for the creation of a new society based paradoxically on uncivilized wildness: The wildest of all becomes center of the social order. Similarly ambivalent, *Peter Rabbit* can be seen as being either about how a bad bunny gets into trouble for disobeying his mother or about how a heroic rabbit gets out of trouble by following his instincts. And I've already suggested that books as different as *Treasure Island, Anne of Green Gables,* and *Lyddie* express ambivalence about the relative desirability of growing up and not growing up—of leaving home and having a home.

The main difference in these three kind of texts depends on the emphasis they give to the ideas previously listed. Texts that focus on adult concerns and messages take readers from the perception that home is boring to the realization that it is safe—and forget about the original boredom. Texts that offer child readers what some adults think they want to hear focus on the excitement of being away, disregard its danger, and see home merely as boring. But the more ambivalent texts refuse to deny either the excitement of being away or the boredom of being at home. We can understand their effect by following the arrows in Figure 8.1 (page 158).

A child or childlike creature, bored by home, wants the excitement of adventure; but since the excitement is dangerous, the child wants the safety of home—which is boring, and so the child wants the excitement of danger—and so on. The arrows propel us through an unending and unendingly ambivalent circle; and all the other pairs of ideas listed above have similarly ambivalent relationships to each other.

This ambivalence defines childhood as it is depicted in the most interesting children's literature: a complex interweaving of adult and childlike concerns. As Pe-

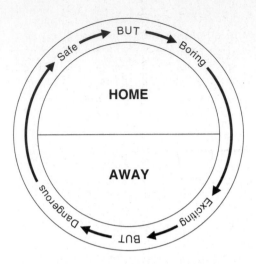

FIGURE 8.1 The home/away/home pattern

ter Hollindale suggests, it is "a noticeable feature of some major 'classic' children's books that they test and undermine some of the values which they superficially appear to be celebrating" (20). Such books offer readers room to speculate, space to grow in.

Before leaving this subject, I need to add a word of caution. The idea that much of children's literature focuses on issues relating to being home and being away, growing up and not growing up, is a theory I've developed as I've read texts written for children. It's possible that my knowledge of the split in the history of children's literature between texts designed to teach children and texts designed to offer them pleasure has given me a schemata for approaching children's literature that amounts to a self-fulfilling prophecy. I may see these oppositions in texts simply because I look for them and expect to find them.

Indeed, some feminist theorists believe that dividing up experience into this sort of opposition is a habit of male thinking that helps to repress women. Once we've created these categories and opposed them to each other, we tend to see one as superior to the other—to asume that all experience consists of opposing qualities in conflict, one of which is clearly preferable. Therefore, good is better than evil; male better than female.

But there's no reason why we need to reach this sort of conclusion: just because things seem different from or even opposite to each other doesn't necessarily mean that we must choose one over the other. Indeed, the ability to resist thinking in this hierarchical way, and working instead to include all the apparent opposites as equal parts of a balanced conclusion, represents a greater wisdom. That's certainly the case in children's literature, where the less interesting books are often the didactic fables that come down firmly in favor of the values expressed on my lefthand list or the mindless adventures that merely pay lip service to the lefthand values as they revel in righthand values. The better books work to include both lefthand and righthand values in their conclusions.

Despite the possible dangers, then, I believe that thinking in terms of balanced opposites can be a productive and enjoyable strategy. Assuming that a concern with these matters is characteristic of children's literature allows a productive exploration of texts in terms of how they express and, often in the most interesting texts, balance these oppositions.

EXPLORATIONS: (1) Choose (or invite children to choose) any text intended for children, and explore its characters, actions, and images in terms of the values listed above. Can the text be considered to be supporting "home" values, "away" values, or a balancing of the two? How does (or does not) thinking about opposites help you understand the specific pleasures offered by this text?

(2) Despite my reassurances above, the idea that exploring binary opposites is a productive strategy is the one thing that readers of the first edition of *Pleasures* most objected to. An anonymous reader asked to review the book by the publisher summed up many comments by saying, "Trained by white patriarchal academe, I too, without thought, see literary texts in terms of these oppositions. I know very well how I can use them to make meaning. I wish for a new emphasis on wholeness, interdependence, and relationship." In a letter to me, my friend Virginia Wolf, who teaches children's literature at the University of Wisconsin-Stout, suggested ways of finding that new emphasis:

> I do think more often these days than in the past of other strategies as being preferable and look for ways to explode our reductive tendency to rely on stark opposites. I want to be aware as often as possible of the continuum—of the many places one may be between these two opposing poles, rather than focus on the poles. For instance, in *Winnie the Pooh* or *Little House in the Big Woods,* if I look at all the characters at once, rather than exploring the two most sharply contrasting ones, I see not the poles, but the continuum.

Consider (or invite children to consider) a novel in terms of this suggestion of thinking about all the characters at once. How does that change your sense of what (or how) it means?

Style and Structure

C. S. Lewis, author of the "Narnia" series, once said he was attracted to writing children's books because "this form permits, or compels, one to leave out things I wanted to leave out. It compels one to throw all the force of the book into what was done and said" (236). While children's stories contain descriptions of setting and character, they concentrate on action—on what happens next. Their main focus is always on the events of the plot.

Much adult literature also focuses on action: spy novels, horror stories, romances. All of these are popular genres meant primarily to entertain readers. Motivation and meaning are deliberately kept simple so that the pleasure of the chase or the kill isn't diluted by readers' being forced to consider moral or emotional implications. But while all children's literature is action oriented, we've already seen that it's rarely without moral or emotional commentary; as I've suggested, its primary impulse is didactic. In exciting adventures or in generic stories about little creatures who learn to like home best, children's writers almost always want both their characters and their readers to focus on the moral or emotional implications of exciting actions.

In order to do so, they must find ways of expressing the deeper implications in their apparently straightforward plots. Sometimes, as in versions of the generic story discussed earlier, the process is obvious: Characters merely state what they have learned from their adventures. But in books like *Peter Rabbit* or *Where the Wild Things Are,* the complex ideas beneath the surface simplicity aren't explicitly stated. Instead, they are implied—shown rather than told. By choosing a series of actions that relate to each other in superficially straightforward but actually complicated ways, Potter and Sendak can both focus on action and imply complex emotional situations.

In part, they accomplish that task by expressing subtle emotions in the pictures that accompany their texts. In *Where the Wild Things Are,* for instance, the text itself never explicitly states that Max's visit to the Wild Things might be a complex psychological voyage, in which the Wild Things represent Max's attempt to come to terms with his anger at his mother and his own wildness, but the pictures constantly imply the possibility of that interpretation. For instance, as the book begins, Sendak reveals the constraint Max feels by depicting him in a small picture surrounded by a wide white border, his arms and legs and the ears of his costume an explosion of energetic points that seems to move outward toward that restricting border.

Many longer children's novels offer similarly straightforward narrations of actions that imply subtle psychological events: the maturing of Jim in *Treasure Island,* Wilbur's gradual acceptance of life and death in *Charlotte's Web,* Emily's similar acceptance in Angela Johnson's quite different but equally understated novel *Toning the Sweep.* While they don't explicitly tell what their characters are thinking and learning, they show actions in ways that can both excite less experienced readers and allow careful readers deep insights.

Style and Language.   A focus on action requires that much be implied by a few words. But that doesn't mean that children's literature does or should consist *only* of simple words. Potter's *The Tale of Peter Rabbit* is basic enough so that most of its language is understandable to children born almost a century after it was published; but it also says, for instance, that the sparrows "implored Peter to exert himself." In *Dr. De Soto,* William Steig rejoices in words that are not only odd but also pretentious—intentionally so, for much of the comedy of the book depends on our awareness of the pomposity of sentences like "The secret formula must first permeate the dentine." Inexperienced readers can understand and enjoy these difficult words because they appear in a context of simpler verbal and pictorial information. In *Charlotte's Web,* White provides a more obvious use of fiction as a source of vocabulary enrichment: The spider often provides definitions of the hard words she enjoys using.

The simple language of many children's texts is choppy and graceless; the passages are divided up into short sentences such as "Perry looked. He looked out the window. The window was open." The assumption is that such sentences are easy to read, despite their dissimilarity from the patterns of normal speech. Not surprisingly, many children seem to find them harder to decipher than more conventional sentences.

Language like this might suggest that the characteristic style of children's texts is lack of style. But poems like those by David McCord or Dennis Lee and stories like *Peter Rabbit* or *Charlotte's Web* are not without style. They organize their usually simple words into rhythmic patterns that are pleasing in themselves and add layers of meanings to the words they shape. When Potter tells us that Mr. McGregor had a sieve "which he intended to pop upon the top of Peter," the rhyme of "pop" and "top" and the alliterative p's and t's are musical in themselves and express the abruptness of the action they describe. And when White describes Wilbur eating his slops, the sounds communicate the sensuousness of the experience: "Wilbur grunted. He gulped and sucked, and sucked and gulped, making swishing and swooshing noises, anxious to get everything at once" (75).

Repetition.   A basic assumption about education is that repeating a task helps us to learn it—and because of the didactic impulse behind children's literature, its structures are often repetitive. I've already suggested that many children's stories involve the same narrative patterns and explored how that repetition allows young readers to develop schemata for making sense of the stories they hear. Individual works of children's literature also contain repetitions.

One common story pattern is the cumulative tale, in which all previous events are repeated after the introduction of each new event, as in the familiar Mother Goose rhyme:

> This is the house that Jack built.
> This is the malt
> That lay in the house that Jack built.
> This is the rat
> That ate the malt
> That lay in the house that Jack built.

And so on. Like this story, many nursery rhymes and children's poems contain repetitions of words, phrases, and situations. In *The Little House,* for instance, the word "watched" and the phrase "pretty soon" appear again and again.

Variation.   As the text of *The Little House* describes, in the same basic verbal pattern, how the seasons pass in the same sequence year after year, the city grows; and thus the almost static situation described at the beginning gradually changes totally. In the pictures, meanwhile, the house is always in the same place, and so are the spiral lines of the surrounding landscape; but the city expands until those spiral patterns finally disappear from view. In both words and pictures then, the repetitions are accompanied by *variations:* different forms of the same basic pattern.

Different forms of the same basic pattern: That sounds a lot like the relationship of new experiences to old schemata in our efforts to make sense of the world. Given the basic didactic impulse of children's literature, it's not surprising that variation is a characteristic structure of texts written for children. Variations occur within one text, within series, and even in non-series books by the same author.

Variations within One Text.   *Charlotte's Web* is an interesting example of how children's fiction operates in terms of theme and variations. It contains two separate but similar plots, the first about how Fern rescues Wilbur from death and the second about how Charlotte rescues Wilbur from death. The first, a realistic story about a little girl and her pet, lasts only for the first few chapters of the novel; the second is a fantasy about talking animals that lasts for the rest of the book. As I suggest in my article "Text as Teacher," the similarities between the two stories make them variations on each other, and allow readers to use the simple and shorter one as a schema to make sense of the complexities of the longer one—which is the same story but also quite surprisingly different. Using the language of the "chaos" theory of physics, Lissa Paul puts this same-but-different aspect of variation another way: "repetitions of self-similar structures produce unexpectedly varied ways of seeing the world" (55).

Many other children's books tell what is basically the same story twice, first in a fairly straightforward manner and then with added subtleties.

In *Treasure Island,* there is a short, exciting, but unsettling encounter between Jim Hawkins and the old pirate who stays at his inn, before Jim has the longer, more exciting, and more unsettling encounter with Long John Silver that makes up the bulk of the novel. The first of these encounters, a less-complicated version of the story that follows, foreshadows each of its major events.

Similarly, Grahame's *The Wind in the Willows* begins with the story of how Mole, unable to resist the temptations of the spring air, leaves his home and the duties of spring cleaning to find a more glamorous life of leisure on the riverbank. After that, the book tells story after story of animals tempted to leave home. Those who go suffer for it, and those who stay are praised; so that Mole's story exists as a kind of counterpoint to what happens in the rest of the book—as a one-sided version of the story of leaving home that acts as a schema for the more complex dilemmas of Rat and Toad.

Anne of Green Gables is like many episodic novels in that each of its chapters tells a similar story: Through her childlike exuberance and energy, Anne either charms a repressed adult into the ability to enjoy life for the first time in years or else lands herself in relatively harmless trouble that delights readers. Each chapter is a variation on all the others.

Variations within a Series.   Because the episodes described in each chapter of *Anne of Green Gables* are more-or-less separate, it seems that any one of them could be eliminated, or more added, without seriously changing the effect of the novel. In fact, Montgomery kept adding to the story of Anne until she ended up with six novels. All of the episodes in all of them can be read as variations of each other. One of the most obvious traits of children's fiction is the proneness of its authors to create variations on their work by writing about the same characters in different but similar situations. The diagram of the basic home/away/home pattern in Figure 8.1 helps to explain why: home is safe but boring, so one seeks adventure, which is exciting but dangerous: so one seeks home, which is safe but then turns out once more to be boring, thus demanding another adventure, another episode, another sequel.

Even those books that are not merely additions to the series but allow different developments to a continuing plot often read like variations of each other. In almost all of the books in Alexander's Prydain series, Taran goes on a quest that makes him realize his previous innocence and teaches him important truths about life. While the books as a whole describe how Taran gradually becomes aware of who he is, the individual books are similar enough to one another to be variations not just on that overall theme but on the other books in the series. It's the repetitiveness of Taran's various quests, the way in which he begins each book in a similar state of mind and then learns variations of the same values, that most clearly defines this series as children's fiction.

Variations in Non-Series Texts.   The repetitive nature of children's fiction may be the characteristic of the genre that most draws writers to it. Even when they're not producing series or writing about the same characters, children's writers tend to rework similar themes and ideas. Commenting on his own work, Maurice Sendak has said, "It's not that I have original ideas, but that I'm good at doing variations on the same idea over and over again. . . . That's all an artist needs—one power-driven fantasy or obsession. And to be clever enough to do variations, like a series of variations by Mozart. They're so good that you forget they're based on a single theme" (Lanes 248). Sendak claims that three of his picture books—*Where the Wild Things Are, In the Night Kitchen,* and *Outside Over There*—form a trilogy. In fact, they can be seen to operate as interesting variations on each other. All of them deal in one way or another with ideas and images of windows and walls, eating and being eaten, flying and falling, clothing and nakedness, seeing and speaking, silence and music, lassitude and energy, inside and outside, gender and sexuality, birth and death, seeing and being seen, control and abandon, freedom and responsibility, oneness and multiplicity.

Louise Fitzhugh creates another sort of variation simply because she seems to have been fascinated by children who have wealthy and exceedingly self-centered mothers. The mothers of both Sport in *Sport* and Beth Ellen in *The Long Secret* might almost be the same horrid character, and both operate as variations on Harriet's mother in *Harriet the Spy*. Furthermore, *The Long Secret* describes how Beth Ellen expresses her secret feelings about people in a series of anonymous notes—a variation on the notebook in which Harriet records her impressions in *Harriet the Spy;* the stories of the two girls then operate as interesting counterpoints to each other.

EXPLORATIONS: (1) Consider (or invite children to consider) the similarities and differences in Sendak's trilogy as discussed in this section. How might they be seen to parallel or counterpoint each other?

(2) Consider (or invite children to consider) one text, a series, a group of unrelated books by the same author, or an entire subgenre of children's fiction such as school stories or texts about talking mice as a series of variations. How significant is variation as an operative factor in children's fiction?

Focalization

The children's novelist Philippa Pearce says, "Writing about and for children, one should have a view almost from the inside, to re-create—not what childhood looks like now—but what it felt like then" (Horn Book 51). Children's books tend to present the world as we imagine (or would like to imagine) children see it, and therefore, to be focalized through children or childlike characters.

Although children's books create the effect of being inside a child's mind, Pearce's "almost" is revealing. In an important article, Charles Sarland explores why the work of British children's novelist William Mayne appeals to so few children even though Mayne writes from a small boy's point of view, "recreating for the adult reader that forgotten time when the immediate physical environment was a continual source of interest and even wonder" (218). The trouble is, Mayne does that so successfully that "the reader must forget the action and concentrate instead on the sensations of the moment" (219)—and, as I've already suggested, a focus on action is an equally important characteristic of children's literature. Rather than actually describing how children think, then, the most characteristic children's books express a childlike point of view *through* what is done and said.

Optimism: Texts for Children as Idylls.   Because we tend to assume that children are ignorant of pain and suffering and thus see the world without consciousness of the cruelty or suffering within it, we also assume that children's literature expresses that innocent and optimistic way of looking at things. Most people, asked to name the defining characteristics of children's books, would focus on the fact that they have happy endings. The critic Sarah Smedman says, "Hope is a vital dimension of a children's book, for it recognizes, at least implicitly, that readers are at the beginning of life, in crucial areas still uncommitted, even to their own personalities, and that for such readers growth and change are still to come. In a fictional world which purports to appropriate the world as we know it, the resolution must leave scope for such growth and change" (91–92).

The fact that children's stories express hope, and therefore typically have happy endings, raises a question about their accuracy and honesty. If we suspect that reality is not always so happy, then we might see the optimism of children's literature as evidence of its lack of realism. Children's books are about rabbits who talk; spiders who write; weak children who successfully defeat brawny pirates, toughminded Nazis, or poverty and homelessness. Even *Anne of Green Gables,* in which nothing particularly improbable happens, is unrealistic: Anne enters the novel as an orphan who is happy and trusting despite the fact that she has been mistreated. While it would be nice to believe that a child could survive such an ugly past in this way, evidence from the real world suggests it would be highly unlikely. Just as unlikely is the optimism that Weetzie Bat retains throughout her complex adventures in a contemporary urban environment, or that the unwed mother Jolly learns to express in the course of *Make Lemonade.*

Yet we would like to believe it could happen. As Anne's and Weetzie's situations reveal, the details that define texts as children's literature often imply a symbolic defiance of our knowledge of the constrictions of reality. In fact, the fantastic or utopian realities that children's books depict may purport to represent a *truer* reading of reality than our usual one. Elliott Gose asserts that in children's literature, "The reader is invited to share a world of imagination with the implicit offer that he or she may thereby come in contact with a potential that lies below the surface nature of each of us" (15).

Many commentators see the optimistic view typical of children's books as having the same relationship to reality as does the idealized world described in one of the traditional genres of literature—the *pastoral idyll,* a form of poem that celebrates the joys of the unsophisticated rural life, close to nature and in the company of friends. Anita Moss suggests that William Steig's children's novel *Dominic* represents "the pastoral values of childhood" (138); and according to Geraldine Poss, *The Wind in the Willows* is like many texts for children in making potentially disturbing events seem safe by placing them "within an innocent pastoral milieu" (84). There are the gardens of Frances Hodgson Burnett's *The Secret Garden* and *Tom's Midnight Garden,* the rural backwater of *Anne of Green Gables,* the safe and richly communal desert community of *Toning the Sweep,* the forest of *Where the Wild Things Are,* the peaceful river of *A River Dream.* Even books that don't describe idyllic natural environments allow children to find them in the midst of urban blight: in treehouses or backyard hideaways, or contact with the seeds that grow into a plant expressive of idyllic hope in *Make Lemonade.*

The Idyllic and the Real.   The pastoral idyll is a nostalgic form of literature. The traditional audience of pastoral idylls among ancient Greeks or Renaissance Europeans was sophisticated urban aristocrats, who enjoyed the idylls exactly because they evoked a way of life purer and simpler than their own—a way of life that surely never existed in fact. Many texts for children express exactly that kind of nostalgia for a better world that never actually existed; they describe a childhood more sweet and innocent than most if not all children ever experience.

According to Sarah Gilead, in fact, even the most idyllic of children's books imply a more painful adult knowledge, simply by being so determined to leave it out: "However successfully evoked, the projected child's experiences, mentality or feelings reflect an adult's need for escape from necessity, conflict, or compromise. Determined cheerfulness or confident morality [masks] a gentle poignancy. An ostensibly unambiguous realm, the idyll is filtered by adult intellectuality, by an awareness of irony, sexuality, conflicts, and social power arrangements" (146). In chapter 5, I discussed the ideas of theorists like Jacqueline Rose and James Kincaid about how a vision of childhood as simple and pure might be an attempt by adults to colonize children, and persuade them they are more innocent than we secretly believe they actually are—as innocent as we need to imagine they are. If we accept such theories, then we have to conclude that the focalization of many texts for children is less through an accurately childlike vision than it is through a form of childlikeness invented by adults for adult purposes.

Not surprisingly, then, the form of innocence described in many texts is one that suits adult needs. For instance, the small creatures in many generic stories leave home to achieve freedom, and then learn the wisdom of not doing so. While they claim to be happy about their discovery that they are not capable of fending for themselves, I wonder if that joyful acceptance of constraint isn't wish-fulfillment on the part of adult writers who would prefer that children didn't in fact wish for more independence.

But then, unlike the little bus who liked home best, Peter Rabbit never denies the pleasures of the world away from home or promises never to leave again. The happy ending of *Anne of Green Gables* is tinged with irony as Anne faces deep tragedy and retains her idyllic life at home only by giving up her plans for a career, and the happy ending of *Charlotte's Web* requires that Wilbur's continuing idyll involve his acceptance of Charlotte's death. At the end of *Treasure Island,* Jim's claim that the treasure he has won has cost him great pain qualifies his bliss. And in *Make Lemonade,* one girl triumphantly achieves enough self-mastery to no longer need the concern of the other girl who has invested so much in helping her, and who feels as if she has been deserted. While these endings are happy enough to imply optimism about the idyllic nature of reality, the optimism is muted by the possibility of other interpretations.

We might say, then, that while children's literature is written from the viewpoint of what adults imagine to be innocence, it does not necessarily postulate an innocent or uncomplicated world. In less interesting children's books, writers create idylls by deliberately leaving things out—as Lewis implies. But in more interesting books, the ironies are internal and deliberate, and the result is an ambivalence about the relative values of innocence and experience, the idyllic and the mundane.

While it seems likely that in such books an insistence on the knowledge of experience would undercut the claims of innocence, I've already suggested that the reverse also occurs. While the ugly truth of reality undercuts the innocent assumptions of characters like Peter Rabbit or Jim Hawkins, their innocence reveals the deficiencies of a cynical acceptance of things as they are. In these richly ambivalent books, the visions and merits of innocence and of experience can be true at the same time. Anita Moss's description of Steig's *Dominic* captures the essence of this ambivalence: "It expresses the wish that human beings may someday attain the fullness of experience and yet retain the innocent sense of newness which assures them that they are at the beginning of a new adventure" (140).

The desire to have both the comfort of home and the danger of adventure, to be both innocent and experienced, to grow up but not grow up, occurs in some form in most children's literature. It explains the double appeal of the generic story, in which the excitement of adventure is balanced by the security of a return home—and vice versa, for these texts can be read as merely pretending to accept parental authority as a means of allowing young readers the pleasure of the theoretically dangerous. In fact, such books might be offering children a different message from the one that allows pedagogically minded adults to feel it's acceptable for children to read them.

EXPLORATION: Consider the possibility expressed in the passage above. Explore (or invite children to explore) a book such as H. A. Rey's *Curious George,* which claims to convey the dangers of curiosity by showing the trouble a monkey gets into, but which makes the trouble look like a lot of fun.

GENRE AND FORMULA

As this chapter suggests, children's books tend to have a lot in common with each other. In fact, the main pleasure offered by the most popular children's books is that they are *not* unique, but similar enough to other books to fulfill young readers' previously developed expectations. Superhero comics and Choose-Your-Own-Adventure novels, books about young animals who learn that home is best, young adult novels about teenagers with physical or emotional handicaps who learn to have more positive self-images—such books offer readers slight variations of a basic *formula,* without major surprises.

For instance, each of the books in R. L. Stine's best-selling Goosebumps series describes how one, or more usually two, twelve-year-old children, often with a penchant for practical jokes that involve scaring others, confront a truly horrific monster or object: a town full of living corpses, a camera that takes pictures of the future, a librarian who turns into a froglike monster and eats flies. The children spend much of each book being terrorized and terrified, both by the monster and by imaginary monsters that emerge from their fearfulness. At the end, usually, the monstrous object or creature is defeated, often by the children's turning the tables on it. In a number of cases, in fact, it turns out that the children are even more monstrous than the monster. If the monster in one of these books finally triumphed and killed the child protagonist, or if it took the police and the army to defeat it, then readers would be rightly disappointed; the whole point of such books is their confirmation of expectations.

Adults tend to look down on books of this sort. Many people call them "trash" and believe that they hinder children from learning to enjoy good literature—that is, literature that less obviously fulfills a reader's expectations.

EXPLORATION: Should children read "trash"? Is there any point to reading many similar books by the same author in the same series?

As it happens, however, I've been told by many people who have become ardent readers of serious literature as adults that they spent part of their childhood absorbing every book in a popular series. Young readers of formula books may be learning the basic patterns that less-formulaic books diverge from. I wonder if we all need to read formula fiction (or watch it on TV) to start with, in order to learn the basic story patterns and formulas that underlie all fiction. Perhaps we can't appreciate the divergences of more unusual books until we first learn these underlying patterns.

In any case, it's certainly no accident that even the most highly acclaimed children's books often have sequels and appear in series: extended plots that develop over a number of novels (as in Alexander's Prydain series), or groups of novels that describe different characters in similar situations (like Lucy Boston's Green Knowe books). It's also no accident that even highly acclaimed children's novels that stand alone tend to fit into easily identifiable patterns: fantasies about contemporary children who travel into the past or stories about parentless children who manage to survive their loneliness and find happiness. As Margaret Higgonet suggests, "By virtue of its intensely repetitive forms, children's literature creates clear expectations about how narratives will proceed and particularly about how they will conclude" (37).

But the fact that even the best children's books are not all that unique doesn't make them uninteresting. Not only do their repetitions of familiar patterns offer pleasure in themselves, but they often contain striking divergences from these patterns. Despite their shared expression of the characteristics I've been describing, many of the texts I mentioned above are startlingly different from each other. As complicated variations on a simple schema, they represent a stage beyond the comforting similarities of Nancy Drew or Goosebump books.

Furthermore, as Higgonet points out, a number of works of children's fiction— from *Charlotte's Web* to Choose-Your-Own-Adventure books to Jon Scieszka's *The Stinky Cheese Man and Other Fairly Stupid Tales*—disrupt the unified narrative patterns we expect, and in doing so, "open up the space of the child's mental activity. . . . Rupture in the narrative line may be recognizable as soon as a child recognizes narrative itself—a stage of awareness that will vary from child to child. Furthermore, the break that at first shocks seems ultimately to produce pleasure, through the processes of rereading, speculation or discussion, and eventual mastery" (51). If we wish to encourage such mastery, then our discussions of fiction with children should center on both expected patterns and disruptions of them.

WORKS CITED

In this list I've provided the name of only the first volume of each of the many series I've referred to in the chapter. Titles of the other volumes can be found in the catalog of any good children's library.

Alcott, Louisa May. *Little Women.* 1868. Harmondsworth, Middlesex: Puffin-Penguin, 1953.

Alexander, Lloyd. *The Book of Three.* New York: Holt, Rinehart and Winston, 1964.

Andersen, Hans Christian. "The Princess and the Pea" and "Thumbelina." *Hans Andersen's Fairy Tales: A Selection.* Trans. L. W. Kingsland. Oxford: Oxford UP, 1984.

Banks, Lynn Reid. *The Indian in the Cupboard.* New York: Doubleday, 1981.

Barrie, J. M. *Peter Pan and Wendy.* New York: Scribner's, 1911.

Baum, L. Frank. *The Wonderful Wizard of Oz.* Chicago: Hill, 1900.

Belloc, Hilaire. "Sarah Byng" and "The Tiger." *Selected Cautionary Verses.* Harmondsworth, Middlesex: Penguin-Puffin, 1964.

Block, Francesca Lia. *Weetzie Bat.* New York: HarperCollins, 1989.

Boston, Lucy. *The Children of Green Knowe.* London: Faber & Faber, 1954.

Burnett, Frances Hodgson. *The Secret Garden.* 1911. New York: Dell Yearling, 1973.

Burton, Virginia Lee. *The Little House.* Boston: Houghton Mifflin, 1942.

Clausen, Christopher. "Home and Away in Children's Fiction." *Children's Literature* 10 (1982): 141–152.

Crampton, Gertrude. *Tootle.* Racine: Golden, 1945.

Disch, Tom. *The Brave Little Toaster.* New York: Doubleday, 1986.

Fitzhugh, Louise. *Harriet the Spy.* New York: Harper & Row, 1964.

——. *The Long Secret.* New York: Harper & Row, 1965.

——. *Sport.* New York: Delacorte, 1979.

Flack, Marjorie. *The Story About Ping.* Illus. Kurt Wiese. New York: Viking, 1933.

Forbes, Esther. *Johnny Tremain.* Boston: Houghton Mifflin, 1943.

Fowler, Alastair. *Kinds of Literature: An Introduction to the Theory of Genres and Modes.* Cambridge: Harvard UP, 1982.

Garner, Alan. *Red Shift.* London: Collins, 1975.

Gilead, Sarah. "The Undoing of Idyll in *The Wind in the Willows.*" *Children's Literature* 16 (1988): 145–158.

Gose, Elliott. *Mere Creatures: A Study of Modern Fantasy Tales for Children.* Toronto: U of Toronto P, 1988.

Grahame, Kenneth. *The Wind in the Willows.* New York: Scribner's, 1933.

Higgonet, Margaret. "Narrative Fractures and Fragments." *Children's Literature* 15 (1987): 37–54.

Hoban, Russell. *The Mouse and His Child.* New York: Harper & Row, 1967.

Hollindale, Peter. "Ideology and the Children's Book." *Signal* 55 (January 1988): 3–32.

Johnson, Angela. *Toning the Sweep.* New York: Orchard, 1993.

Joyce, William. *George Shrinks.* New York: Harper & Row, 1985.

Kipling, Rudyard. *The Jungle Book.* 1894. Oxford: Oxford UP, 1987.

Konigsburg, E. L. *From the Mixed-up Files of Mrs. Basil E. Frankweiler.* New York: Atheneum, 1967.

Kuznets, Lois. *When Toys Come Alive: Narratives of Animation, Metamorphosis, and Development.* New Haven and London: Yale UP, 1994.

Lanes, Selma. *The Art of Maurice Sendak.* New York: Abradale-Abrams, 1984.

Leaf, Munro. *Noodle.* Illus. Ludwig Bemelmans, 1937. New York: Scholastic, 1968.

Lee, Dennis. *Alligator Pie*. Toronto: Macmillan, 1974.

Le Guin, Ursula K. *A Wizard of Earthsea*. New York: Parnassus, 1968.

Lévi-Strauss, Claude. *The Savage Mind*. Chicago: U of Chicago P, 1966.

Lewis, C. S. *The Lion, the Witch, and the Wardrobe*. London: Geoffrey Bles, 1950.

———. "On Three Ways of Writing for Children." *Children's Literature: Views and Reviews*. Ed. Virginia Haviland. Glenview: Scott, Foresman, 1973. 231–240.

Lionni, Leo. *Fish Is Fish*. New York: Pantheon, 1970.

Lowry, Lois. *The Giver*. New York: Houghton Mifflin, 1993.

Matas, Carol. *Lisa's War*. New York: Scribner's, 1989.

———. *Sworn Enemies*. New York: Bantam, 1993.

———. *The Burning Time*. New York: Doubleday, 1994.

Mazer, Anne. *The Salamander Room*. Illus. Steve Johnson. New York: Knopf, 1991.

McCord, David. *One at a Time*. Boston: Little Brown, 1974.

Milne, A. A. *The House at Pooh Corner*. London: Methuen, 1928.

———. *Winnie-the-Pooh*. London: Methuen, 1926.

Montgomery, L. M. *Anne of Green Gables*. 1908. Toronto: Seal-McClelland and Stewart/Bantam, 1981.

Moss, Anita. "The Spear and the Piccolo: Heroic and Pastoral Dimensions of William Steig's *Dominic* and *Abel's Island*." *Children's Literature* 10 (1982): 124–140.

Nodelman, Perry. "Text as Teacher: The Beginning of *Charlotte's Web*." *Children's Literature* 13 (1985): 109–127.

Norton, Mary. *The Borrowers*. London: Dent, 1952.

Osborne, Mary Pope. *Moonhorse*. Illus. S. M. Saelig. New York: Knopf, 1991.

Paterson, Katherine. *Lyddie*. New York: Lodestar-Dutton, 1991.

Paul, Lissa. "The New 3Rs: Repetition, Recollection, and Recognition." *ChLA Quarterly* 15,2 (Summer 1990): 55–57.

Paulsen, Gary. *Hatchet*. New York: Bradbury P, 1987.

Pearce, Philippa. *Tom's Midnight Garden*. London: Oxford UP, 1958.

———. "The Writer's View of Childhood." *Horn Book Reflections*. Ed. Elinor Whitney Field. Boston: Horn Book, 1969. 49–53.

Poss, Geraldine D. "An Epic in Arcadia: The Pastoral World of *The Wind in the Willows*." *Children's Literature* 4 (1975): 80–90.

Potter, Beatrix. *The Tale of Mr. Jeremy Fisher*. London: Frederick Warne, 1906.

———. *The Tale of Peter Rabbit*. London: Frederick Warne, 1902.

Rey, H. A. *Curious George*. Boston: Houghton Mifflin, 1941.

Root, Phyllis. *Moon Tiger*. Illus. Ed Young. New York: Holt, 1985.

Rosenberg, Liz. *Adelaide and the Night Train*. Illus. Liz Desimini. New York: Harper & Row, 1989.

Sarland, Charles. "Chorister Quartet." *The Signal Approach to Children's Books*. Ed. Nancy Chambers. Metuchen: Scarecrow, 1980. 217–224.

Say, Alan. *A River Dream*. Boston: Houghton Mifflin, 1988.

Scheidlinger, Lucy Prince. *The Little Bus Who Liked Home Best*. New York: Fernand & Spertus, 1955.

Scieszka, Jon. *The Stinky Cheese Man and Other Fairly Stupid Tales*. Illus. Lane Smith. New York: Viking, 1992.

Sendak, Maurice. *Where the Wild Things Are*. New York: Harper & Row, 1963.

Seuss, Dr. *The Cat in the Hat*. New York: Random House, 1957.

Shepperson, Rob. *The Sandman*. New York: Farrar, Straus & Giroux, 1989.

Smedman, Sarah M. "Springs of Hope: Recovery of Primordial Time in 'Mythic' Novels for Young Readers." *Children's Literature* 16 (1988): 91–107.

Steig, William. *Dominic*. New York: Farrar, Straus & Giroux, 1972.

———. *Dr. De Soto*. New York: Farrar, Straus & Giroux, 1982.

Stevenson, Robert Louis. *Treasure Island*. 1883. London: Collins, 1953.

Stine, R. L. *Welcome to Dead House*. New York: Scholastic, 1992.

Tibo. *Paper Nights*. Toronto: Annick, 1992.

White, E. B. *Charlotte's Web*. 1952. New York: Trophy-Harper & Row, 1973.

———. *Stuart Little*. New York: Harper & Row, 1945.

Wilder, Laura Ingalls. *Little House in the Big Woods*. 1932. New York: Trophy-Harper & Row, 1971.

Wolff, Virginia Euwer. *Make Lemonade*. New York: Holt, 1993.

Wynne-Jones, Tim. *Architect of the Moon*. Illus. Ian Wallace. Toronto: Groundwood, 1988.

Yorinks, Arthur. *Hey, Al*. Illus. Richard Egielski. New York: Farrar, Straus & Giroux, 1986.

chapter **9**

The Repertoire of Theory

READING IN THE CONTEXT OF THEORY

So far, I've examined how we can enrich our enjoyment and understanding of a literary text by considering it in relation to other texts it seems similar to: written in the same time or place, or by the same author, or in the same genre. This chapter explores some ways in which literary theory allows us to think about individual texts in the context of literature as a whole. Theorists have made use of the discoveries of psychoanalysts, linguists, and others to uncover a fascinating variety of different patterns—symbols, myths, archetypes, motifs, codes, functions—that recur in text after text, and that underlie and give shape and meaning to them. Knowing something about these patterns enables us to identify the place of any specific book in relation to all the books we know.

The sections that follow are nothing more than brief introductions to theories that might be useful in considering children's literature. The theories are complicated, and I know that my simple descriptions don't do them justice. But I've included this material as a kind of menu of possibilities—an overview of some of the kinds of thinking that can be done about literary texts. You'll have learned something important even if you do no more than realize that this variety of possibilities exists. On the other hand, somewhere in this menu of possibilities you might find a way of thinking about literature that satisfies you, personally. If you find your interest sparked by my brief descriptions of any of these theories, I encourage you to pursue your interest in them by reading complete texts by the theorists; the ones included in the list of "Works Cited" at the end of this chapter are a good place to start.

PSYCHOANALYTICAL PERSPECTIVES

The theories of Sigmund Freud suggest that the motivations for human behavior are often unconscious; that is, buried in parts of our mind about which we have no conscious knowledge. According to Freud, the unconscious develops in early childhood, as children experience feelings and desires they understand to be unacceptable and then repress them. Many of these feelings, relating to sexual desire for the parent of the opposite sex and a consequent hatred for the parent of the same sex, are associated with what Freud called the *Oedipus complex.*

Freud believed that the material we have buried in our unconscious expresses itself through the images and narrative events of both dreams and literature. Equipped with some knowledge of Freudian ideas, we can develop complex and interesting interpretations of even very simple texts. As an example, I'll examine Bruno Bettelheim's Freudian interpretations of fairy tales. I'll also explore how fairy tales might be viewed in terms of the ideas of the post-Freudian analyst Jacques Lacan, which have greatly interested literary theorists.

Bruno Bettelheim

The American child psychologist Bruno Bettelheim, a classical Freudian, reads "Cinderella" as a story of sibling rivalry and Oedipal jealousy. Children typically believe that their parents prefer their siblings, just as Cinderella's stepmother prefers Cinderella's stepsisters; and the fact that this parent figure is not actually Cinderella's mother represents the Oedipal desire of children to eliminate the parent of their own sex and thus pave the way for the relationship they unconsciously desire with the parent of the other sex. According to Bettelheim, Cinderella's situation at the beginning of the story represents the self-disgust a child feels about his or her desire to be loved by the parent of the opposite sex; "Since the child has such 'dirty' wishes," the child identifies with Cinderella, "who is relegated to sit among the cinders . . . that is where he also belongs, and where he would also end up if his parents knew of his desires" (243).

Bettelheim explains the events of the story as a working out of these psychological problems. The slipper lost near the end of the story represents "castration anxiety": "According to Freudian theory the girl's castration complex centers on her imagining that originally all children had penises and that girls somehow lost theirs" (266), just as Cinderella loses her slipper. But the lost slipper also represents the vagina; the prince "symbolically offers her femininity in the form of the golden slipper-vagina: male acceptance of the vagina and love for the woman is the ultimate male validation of the desirability of her femininity" (271).

Jacques Lacan

In the middle of the century, Freud's ideas were reworked by the French psychoanalyst Jacques Lacan in terms of the theories of *structural linguistics*. In a famous sentence, Lacan asserts "The unconscious is structured like a language" (*Four Fun-*

damental Concepts 20). The structure of a language, its grammar, is a set of unspoken rules—ones we may even be unconscious of, for many people who have never formally learned grammar nevertheless speak grammatically. These rules of grammar allow us to make meaningful statements to each other. According to Lacan, then, the unconscious consists of something like those grammatical rules. It is a set of codes or conditions hidden from us that allow us to speak as and perceive ourselves as individuals.

An individual sentence depends on possibly unconscious knowledge of unspoken grammatical structures in order to be meaningful; likewise, a person, what Lacan calls a "speaking subject," depends on and fits into the unconscious structures he or she is unaware of. For Lacan, then, our "selves" are actually like the grammatical subjects of sentences. We see ourselves as being in control ("*I* speak" means, I am the one who chooses what to say); but our meaning is circumscribed by other components of the entity we are part of (I can be understood to be speaking only through my relationship with, and subjection to, the meaning of the verb "speak"). Because we can only speak through a shared language, the "I" who speaks must always express a communal vision rather than a unique private one. As we saw in chapter 7, some theorists believe that to have a sense of oneself is to adopt a narrative, to be subjected to language; the ideological theories suggesting that conclusion are based on the work of Lacan.

In Lacan's version of Freudian thought, the castration complex that Freud and Bettelheim see girls as suffering from remains; but penis envy is replaced by phallus envy, experienced by both boys and girls—indeed, by everybody. The *phallus* is a symbolic representation of the power of the father, an important part of the language of the unconscious: "the phallus is a signifier" (*Ecrits* 285). Its main significance is its ability to signify—to define meaning. It stands for power and authority, that which the father (or anyone male or female perceived as filling the role of the father) possesses and the child does not. As such, it represents what each of us wants and perceives ourselves as lacking: "if the desire of the mother is the phallus, the child wishes to be the phallus in order to satisfy that desire" (*Ecrits* 289).

As I've probably made all too clear in these sentences, Lacan's writing is complex and often deliberately arcane. Jane Gallop suggests that Lacan's *Ecrits* are "designed to force the reader into a perpetual struggle of his own with the text" (45). As a result, Lacan's ideas have been applied to literature in a variety of ways; one small example based on just one thread of a complex weaving of ideas can suggest the possibilities.

As I've said, Lacan believes that the subjects we consciously see ourselves as being are as fictional as the stories of written fiction—limited images like those we see in mirrors when we first become conscious of our separateness. Thus, fiction can be read in terms of the way it echoes our basic human activity of inventing ourselves and then becoming conscious of the limitations of our inventions. All that we usually call reality is in fact fiction, and it is always less complete than the actual "real," the unknowable world outside our consciousness.

A Lacanian reading of a text like "Cinderella" might then turn out to invert its apparent meaning. The "happy" ending transforms Cinderella from a multifaceted being in intimate and intuitive contact with the basic elements of existence, fire and ash and household dirt, into a fixed and limited creature comfortably placed within the fixed and limited scheme of things. She has become a subject in the double sense of the word, not just provided with a specific subjectivity or individuality, but also subject to or dominated by a specific and therefore repressive version of reality. In achieving power as a princess, she relinquishes her personal power to a social structure that requires obedience to a monarch—acceptance of the authority of he who has the phallus.

As Cinderella accepts her godmother's transformation of a variety of objects into things of immediate practical use to herself—things that will transform her into the conventional image of an acceptable woman—she becomes for herself what she imagines she should be for others. In terms of Lacan's concept of the *mirror stage,* she has imagined her whole self to be as limited as the part of herself that she sees in her mirror and that she imagines others see also. In doing so, she loses touch with the world and with people beyond her own limited imagining. For Lacan, that sort of loss is inevitable. The story of Cinderella shows how human beings develop a sense of something lacking and so inevitably lose wholeness in the process of becoming themselves.

Convincing Interpretations?

Theories like Bettelheim's and Lacan's don't convince everyone. Many people are repelled by the idea that human minds are so obsessed with sexual concerns, or frightened by the idea that so much that happens to us is beyond our conscious knowledge and control. In fact, the very concept of a Freudian "unconscious" or a Lacanian "real" that exists beyond our ability to think of it make such interpretations impossible to prove. Because they describe what happens in an area of the mind beyond rational contact, they are like the beliefs of religious faith, which also transcend rational contact, albeit in a different direction—the demands of the soul rather than of the body: We can't prove or disprove them, we can merely accept or not accept them.

Nevertheless, many of us accept them without knowing it. Even those who feel uncomfortable about the sexual content of Freudian ideas often still believe that we have unconscious thoughts, that we repress memories we can't face, or that dreams reveal something about our state of mind. And in our time, almost everyone accepts at least one of Freud's key ideas: the conviction that we can talk our way through emotional problems with the help of a therapist—that, just by talking, we can learn to see ourselves in terms of a "lived narrative" different from and healthier than one we find counterproductive. Freudian thinking so permeates the thought of our culture that even declared anti-Freudians share Freudian ideas.

Even so, and for all his claims that psychoanalysis is a science, Freud was very much a man of his time, and his science is based in his not particularly logical faith that what was true for people of his time and place was in fact the eternal content of the human psyche. In particular, as Josephine Donovan says, "Freud was not a feminist" (91). In recent decades, there has been an extensive feminist critique of

Freud, focused on his biological determinism—the idea that the psychic makeup of women emerges directly as a consequence of their anatomy—and on the male bias of concepts like the castration complex and penis envy.

Meanwhile, however, other feminists have read Freud's theories as highly revealing of the means by which male culture has dominated women; and still others have revised Freud's and particularly Lacan's theories in ways that might liberate women from repressive cultural conventions. Nancy Chodorow has described how the dynamics of conventional family life work to produce the psychic makeup Freud described as typical of males and females, and has suggested that change can and will occur when men and women learn how to be different kinds of parents. French feminists like Julia Kristeva and Hélène Cixous turn Lacanian psychoanalysis on its head by focusing on how the place it defines for women, on the margins of the repressive structures of power, offers opportunities for subversion. According to Kristeva, "if women have a role to play . . . it is only in assuming a *negative* function: reject everything finite, definite, structured, loaded with meaning, in the existing state of society" (Donovan 114).

EXPLORATION: After reading a psychoanalytical commentary such as Bettelheim's *Uses of Enchantment,* explore your own position on these matters. To what degree is it relevant that you might not be conscious of the unconscious aspects of texts?

ARCHETYPAL THEORIES

Bettelheim's description of the Oedipal content of "Cinderella" relates the story to dream imagery and to many other stories and novels that Freudians would call different versions of the basic family drama of sibling rivalry and sexual jealousy, a drama that all families share but which nevertheless develops independently in each human being. The Swiss psychoanalyst Carl Jung broke with Freud when he decided that the contents of the unconscious transcend the individual experience of separate people. Instead, Jung posited a *collective unconscious,* shared by and present in all humans, and saw the images of the collective unconscious, as expressed both in dreams and in literature, as *archetypes:* whenever we express ourselves, then, our utterances can be seen to contain archetypal imagery and to express the universal meaning attached to those archetypal images. In this section, I explore approaches to the archetypes of literature suggested by Jung himself and by Northrop Frye.

Carl Jung and the Collective Unconscious

According to Jung, when we experience the presence of archetypes, "the voice of all mankind resounds in us" (320) and "that is the secret of great art, and of its effect upon us. The creative process . . . consists in the unconscious activation of an archetypal image, and in elaborating and shaping this image into the finished work" (321).

From a Jungian viewpoint, children's fiction can be explored for archetypal plots, such as the recurring story of "the hero with a thousand faces" that Joseph Campbell finds retold in myths from around the world. The basic story pattern of children's fiction, in which characters leave home to seek adventure and then are sufficiently transformed by their adventure to return home in triumph, is a version of this archetypal plot.

A key archetype is the *shadow,* which for Jung represents the dark aspects of the personality. In *Mere Creatures,* Elliott Gose sees the Wild Things in Sendak's *Where the Wild Things Are* as the child Max's antisocial tendencies—as his shadow. They are animal-like, for the shadow represents the more base aspects of our being that we tend to identify with animals; they are also tricksters, beings like those found in myths around the world that represent the power of anarchic impulse. For Gose, this makes Sendak's picture book into a retelling of a basic Jungian story about how one recognizes and absorbs one's shadow in the process of becoming an integrated, healthy person.

EXPLORATION: Read a Jungian interpretation of a children's text, such as those in Gose's *Mere Creatures*. Try (or invite children to try) to explore a literary text using a similar approach. What does your exploration reveal? Are there unique or individual aspects of the text that you have to neglect in focusing on archetypes? Does that matter?

Northrop Frye's Archetypes

While the complex theory of literary classification developed by the Canadian critic Northrop Frye relates closely to Jung's idea of archetypes, Frye focuses on literary archetypes: "I mean by an archetype a symbol which connects one poem with another, and thereby helps to unify and integrate our literary experience" (*Anatomy* 99). Frye sees literature as a whole as having built up its own internal archetypal images and patterns of organization over the centuries.

He also suggests that, due to the intense degree to which European culture was immersed for many centuries in the language and thought of Christianity, the archetypal images and structures of European and therefore, mainstream North American literature have emerged from the central images and narrative patterns of the Bible. In *The Great Code* and *Words with Power,* Frye isolates these structures and images. Many of them are still commonly found in texts written for children. The association of trees and water with paradise, which would have made great sense to the desert dwellers who produced the Old Testament, can still be found in books like *Where the Wild Things Are;* and many books describe gentle and innocent lambs and stupid donkeys. Because these images and narrative patterns still define our sense of what literature ought to be, even texts written by enthusiastic atheists and devout Muslims express values, ideas, and images that are originally Jewish or Christian.

EXPLORATIONS: (1) If Frye's theory has any validity, it might raise questions about the relationships between religion, literature, and education. Through their imagery and structures, do contemporary North American texts for children promote Judeo-Christian values even when they claim to be without religious content? If so, should teachers and children be aware of that?

(2) After reading *The Great Code,* and learning more about the Biblical origins of common images and story patterns, read some texts from a non-Christian culture. Do they use the same images and patterns in the same way, or not? To what degree do you distort these texts by imposing your expectations of common story patterns and the common meanings of images upon them?

In *The Anatomy of Criticism,* Frye developed a system for classifying literature by means of archetypal patterns that throws light on all kinds of literary texts—on comic books and Nancy Drew novels as well as on recognized classics. Frye's system places each work of literature at a particular place in an intersecting set of classifications—including differing forms of symbols; differing genres like drama, poetry, and fiction; and differing perspectives from which authors speak. For our purposes, I think, the most interesting of Frye's classifications is *mode:* the relationship between characters and their environments. There are four modes, and the chronological sequence in which they appeared, over time, reveals that each is a *displacement* of the one historically preceding it; that is, each succeeding mode tells the same story in a version less ideal and imaginary and more naturalistic than the mode before it.

The first and purest mode is *myth,* which tells of heroes superior in kind to other humans and to their environment: gods. The second mode, *romance,* tells of heroes superior in degree to other humans and to the environment: not gods, but idealized men and women. The two types of the third mode, *mimetic,* describe realistic fiction: *high mimetic,* which tells of heroes superior in degree to others but not to the environment; and *low mimetic,* which tells of heroes superior neither to others nor to their environment. The final, and most displaced, mode is the *ironic,* which tells of characters inferior to others in power or intelligence.

A certain kind of children's literature fits into each of these categories. Most obviously, there are many children's versions of traditional myths, and many stories about the fantastic exploits of great heroes. Frye himself identifies fairy tales like "Cinderella" and "Snow White" as romance. High fantasies like Ursula Le Guin's *A Wizard of Earthsea* would also qualify, and so would many nostalgic or pastoral texts for children that focus on the idealized innocence of child heroes and heroines; many children's poems fit this mode as well.

Charlotte's Web might be considered to be high mimetic: Charlotte is superior to others, but subject to the forces of nature that bring about her death. Indeed, most children's novels are to some degree high mimetic, because their main characters do finally triumph over the environment. Nevertheless, some might be considered low mimetic: certainly Laura Ingalls Wilder's *Little House* books describe ordinary people who rarely master their naturalistic environments and must often learn to accept defeat.

In light of the basic optimism of children's literature, we might expect the ironic mode to be the least well represented. But "The Princess and the Pea" and the poems by Belloc I discussed in chapter 8 describe characters less intelligent than their audience is supposed to be. Indeed, a surprising amount of children's literature is ironic, in that it gives us the pleasure of feeling superior to characters like Simple Simon or the Three Sillies.

EXPLORATION: Consider (or invite children to consider) which of the modes a particular text falls into. Does it increase your understanding and/or pleasure to think about these matters?

Just making these classifications isn't particularly interesting. But doing so might offer teachers a way to organize children's reading experiences. According to the critic Virginia Wolf, as they become more displaced, children's novels imply an increasingly sophisticated audience, and so confirm "Frye's theory that the cycle of literature from the mythic mode, through the romantic and mimetic modes to the ironic mode requires an increasingly sophisticated reader" (49). If we accept Wolf's conclusion, it provides a logical way of organizing the literary experience of children from least displaced to most displaced, so that previous reading provides a solid base for later reading. Furthermore, children who can recognize particular modes or other patterns can use their knowledge as schemata in approaching new texts.

But in terms of our response to individual texts, I believe Frye's classifications are revealing only when we use them as schemata and become conscious of what they leave out of consideration. Each of the works I named as representing a mode can also be seen to contain some characteristics of the other modes. Since there are moments in *Charlotte's Web* that ask us to laugh at Wilbur because we feel superior to him, the text is ironic as well as high mimetic. On the other hand, the very fact that people read "The Princess and the Pea" without consciousness of its irony suggests that it still offers some of the pleasure of the form it parodies: It is a romance as well as a displaced parody of a romance. Meanwhile, the most popular versions of fairy tales tend to be those that place the central romantic story in a displaced ironic context: Disney movies that focus on dwarfs or mice we can feel superior to as well as perfect princes and princesses we can look up to. Even children's versions of myths tend to mix modes: They often add realistic details in order to humanize the heroes and make them seem less distantly ideal. Our consciousness of a classificatory system like Frye's modes allows us not only to consider the significance of these uncharacteristic features but also to perceive what makes distinct works distinct.

STRUCTURAL PATTERNS

Frye's classifications focus on the plots of literary works as a whole. Other literary theorists have looked for inherent similarities in the parts that make up those wholes, in order to develop a grammar of stories: a description of the basic elements that are common to all stories but that relate to each other in particular stories in ways that give the stories their distinctiveness. In this section I'll consider the theories of Claude Lévi-Strauss, Vladimir Propp, and Roland Barthes.

Claude Lévi-Strauss and Structuralism

The French anthropologist Claude Lévi-Strauss approached his discipline as Lacan approached psychoanalysis: in terms of structural linguistics as put forth by Ferdinand de Saussure. Saussure focused on the ways in which language becomes meaningful in terms of how various *signs* (the sounds we use to name objects and activities), while inherently meaningless in themselves, develop meaning in terms of their relationships to each other. For instance, the inherently meaningless symbols R, E, and D put together to form the sound "red" can represent a particular color for us only through their relationship to a whole network of other such signs: letters of the alphabet, sounds, other signs for other colors, and so on.

Building on this focus on the structures that allow things to become meaningful, Lévi-Strauss postulated that all cultures are formed of the same basic elements, just as all sentences are formed of the same basic parts of speech. The elements of cultures are social groupings: families, clans, classes. The differences in cultures, like the differences in the meanings of sentences, come from the different ways in which these elements are related to each other: Individuals derive their sense of who they are and the meanings of their own behavior from the places they occupy within these structures. To explore cultures in this way is to perform a *structural analysis*. If we apply this principle to literature, we can determine the elements—the central ideas and images—and then explore particular texts in terms of how these elements relate to each other.

The most obvious way to do so would be to operate on the structuralist principle that, because what distinguishes cultures from each other is their unique way of structuring experience, every artifact produced by a culture manifests the same central structures—and that includes not just systems of kinship but also the ways in which the rooms in houses are laid out and the way literary texts are constructed. Lévi-Strauss himself asserts that myths represent significant transformations in the cultures that produced them—that myths are stories of the change from one orderly system of relationships to another. If we assume that all stories follow that model, then we can explore one story in order to see how it describes a shift of relationships. We can determine its essential elements, and then explore how the relationships between the elements shift between the state of equilibrium described at the beginning and the one described at the end.

In the fairy tale "Snow White," for instance, I might identify the characters with elements representing values: the stepmother with aggressiveness and Snow White with passivity. I can then see the story as moving from a state of affairs in which aggressiveness has authority to one in which passivity has authority. I might conclude that the story justifies a conservative attitude, for the independent-minded woman who tries to get her own way is defeated by the woman who accepts the way things are without question.

The structural analysis I've just done assumes, as all such analyses do, that stories comprise major ideas competing with each other in an intellectual debate. Seen in this way, the elements of literature are opposing ideas like good and evil, appearance and reality, aggression and passivity, hope and despair, and even more basic oppositions like softness and hardness, cold and warmth, growth and stagnation—binary opposites like those I described as characteristic of children's literature as a genre in chapter 8. Stories describe how these binary opposites conflict with and relate to each other in various ways. Thus "Snow White" is a story of good, identified with softness and passivity, triumphing over evil, identified with hardness and aggression. Because we might not expect weakness to triumph over strength, the story is also about the difference between appearance and reality. The images in the story relate to these ideas. The Queen's magic mirror, suggesting her self-involvement, is contrasted with the open window through which Snow White's mother first sees snow and wishes—not egotistically for beauty, but charitably for the growth of new life. These relationships shift into a new pattern when the Prince sees Snow White neither through a window nor in a mirror, but apparently dead inside a glass coffin.

This kind of focus on basic elements and their relationship to each other accomplishes two things: It points out the unity of stories by revealing how their parts relate to one another in the structure of the whole. And as I suggested in considering the binary oppositions of children's literature, it shows how a literary work relates to others by describing differing relationships between the same basic elements.

Vladimir Propp and Functions

Other structural theories focus less on patterns of binary opposites than on components of plots. According to the folklorist Vladimir Propp, the plots of all the Russian folktales he explored consist of thirty-one basic *functions,* which he listed and numbered. While not all the tales contain all the functions, the functions always appear in the same sequence. The functions are a grammar of actions—an underlying structure of relationships among events that gives coherence to the plots of these and presumably all stories. Consider how stories as diverse as "Cinderella," *Peter Rabbit,* and *Charlotte's Web* express some of this representative group of Propp's functions (the wording is mine):

2a. The hero is forbidden to do something.
 3. The hero violates the rule.
8a. One member of a family lacks something or desires to have something.
 9. Misfortune or lack is made known; the hero is approached with a request or a command and is allowed to go or is dispatched.
11. The hero leaves home.
12. The hero is tested, interrogated, attacked, etc.; the action prepares the way for the hero's receiving either a magical agent or helper.
20. The hero returns.
24. A false hero presents unfounded claims.
27. The true hero is recognized.

EXPLORATION: Consider (or invite children to consider) how one of the texts mentioned above or another text of your choice expresses these functions.

If we combine the binary opposites of structuralism with Propp's functions, we can see how each text represents two crosscutting structural patterns: the pattern of ideas and images that make up the binary opposites and the sequenced pattern of events in the plot. These two kinds of patterns are the ones I described in chapter 4 as interweaving in the discourse of a text.

Roland Barthes and Codes

Building on the idea that all of the activities and artifacts of a culture mirror its central structures, some theorists focus on the ways in which objects of all sorts act as *signs*—as, in Umberto Eco's words, "something [which] stands to somebody for something else in some respect or capacity" (Blonsky 176). To give an obvious example: the color red doesn't inherently mean danger, but drivers stop at a red light because "red light" is a sign and has a particular meaning for them, learned from previous experience of their culture.

To think of things in this way is to take a *semiotic* approach: As Marshall Blonsky says, "the semiotic 'head,' or eye, sees the world as an immense message, replete with signs that can and do deceive us about the world's condition . . . if the sign isn't the thing, we can use the sign to lie" (vii—viii). Clearly, then, semiotics is closely related to a concern with ideology. Roland Barthes wrote a series of fascinating books analyzing the sign systems of matters such as wrestling and fashion and the cultural information they convey; my discussion of toys in chapter 6 considers their possible meaning as signs.

If we approach literature from a semiotic point of view, we see that our ability to find meaning in stories and poems depends on our knowledge of numerous codes and signs: the dictionary meanings of words, the meanings indicated by the position of words in sentences, the connotations we attach both to words and to the objects they represent, our methods of consistency building, our understanding of story patterns, our expectations of genre, and so on. In *S/Z,* Barthes suggests that a given work of literature represents the combination and intersection of five basic kinds of signs or codes. The codes can be summarized as follows:

- The *proairetic* code, which evokes our knowledge of actions as implied by a text: For instance, what walking or sitting or gossiping is. Decoding a story requires our ability to perceive it as a series of separate but connected actions (the plot).
- The *hermeneutic* code, which defines our expectations of how stories raise questions, create suspense, and provide answers. "Hermeneutic" refers to interpretation—how we are invited to make sense of events in terms of our knowledge of how stories work.
- The code of *semes,* or connotations: the range of associated meanings that the words of a text bring with them beyond their primary, or dictionary, meaning. For instance, the word "girl" connotes femininity and youthfulness—and possibly, also, passivity and nurturing.
- The code of *symbols:* the meanings the words of a text have as representations of ideas separate from their primary meaning. For instance, in a particular context the word "path" might symbolize a person's course of action.
- The *cultural* code, which evokes our knowledge of the values and practices of specific cultures as expressed in a text.

Barthes shows how a text can be broken down into basic units, or *lexias,* each of which evokes a specific code. Using this method, I've developed the following analysis of the beginning of *Peter Rabbit:*

The Tale of Peter Rabbit[1]
Once upon a time[2] there were four little bunnies[3] who lived with their mother[4] in a sandy bank under a tree.[5]

[1] The title raises a question that will be answered later: what is Peter Rabbit? A human? An animal? A recipe for preparing rabbit meat? (hermeneutic)

[2] The phrase arouses our knowledge of and expectations for a certain kind of story—the fairy tale. (cultural)

[3] The word "bunnies" has connotations that are different from those of the word "rabbits." It evokes the softness and cuteness of humanized fantasy animals. (semic)

[4] "Mother" evokes our cultural understanding of the roles of mothers in the lives of children (cultural—knowledge of sociology and psychology). Another question is raised. Why just with mother? Where is father? (hermeneutic)

[5] As opposed to bunnies, who live in humanlike houses, real rabbits live in sandy banks, which usually are a good place for fir trees to grow. (Cultural—knowledge of zoology and horticulture.) This adds another question: How can these "bunnies" also be "rabbits"? (hermeneutic)

As this analysis suggests, even the barest beginning of the story suggests a culture's fascination with questions about children and their animality, and about the relationship of children and parents.

Semiotics and Picture Books. The semiotic analysis of *Peter Rabbit* I've just presented focuses exclusively on the text and ignores the pictures that accompany it. The pictures could easily become a part of an amplified analysis. As visual representations, pictures obviously stand for something else—what they depict. A picture is a classic example of a sign. Any given picture not only represents something, but communicates further information about the thing it depicts by the ways in which it depicts it. In my discussion of picture books in chapter 10, the approach I take is primarily semiotic; I focus on how pictures imply attitudes toward their subject through their composition, their style, and through details in their content. If what I've said in this section has sparked your interest, you can learn more about semiotic approaches in chapter 10.

UNITY AND DECONSTRUCTION

The various strategies and theories of reading literature I've considered so far in this book all operate on the same underlying premise. They assume that literary texts have unity or consistency—that is, that all their elements support each other, that they are coherent and complete, and that they express coherent visions of the world.

That's an assumption shared by many readers. We approach texts, as outlined in chapter 4, with the idea that, for example, the glass objects of "Snow White"—the mirrors, windows, coffins—connect meaningfully to each other. Or we try to understand how the many lists in *Charlotte's Web* relate to the story's central concern with "the glory of everything." And once we discover (or, perhaps, create) such relationships in a text, we praise it for its unity.

In recent years, literary theorists have questioned both the possibility and the desirability of unity. Something can be unified only if it is complete. How can a text be complete if its meanings depend on contexts outside itself: on the meanings of the words of which it is composed, on the codes and connotations it evokes, on its relationships to other works of literature? No text is truly closed off—no more than, as we saw again and again in Part II of this book, human individuals are unified or closed off from forces outside themselves.

According to the theorist Jacques Derrida, our sense of the meaning of a word depends on our ability to separate it from all the things it does *not* mean. Consequently, any given word evokes and depends on meanings unlike or opposite to its own; in fact, each word implies the idea of its opposite. If we explore a text carefully, we'll find passages in which that process becomes apparent—where we can perceive what we earlier called absences. We'll discover the cracks in its structure, places where it disguises illogicalities or hides gaps in order to seem complete, or even turns on its apparent meanings and says just the opposite.

Such a place is called an *aporia,* and this sort of reading is called *deconstruction*. It is not destruction, but an exploration of the constructions of literature to determine the extent of the artificiality, how they *are* constructed or manufactured, and how they work to disguise their own artifice. If we believe that literature represents the real world, we might find it disconcerting to realize how artificial and incomplete are the worlds it describes. But if we believe, with theorists like Barthes, Lacan, and Derrida, that "reality" is itself a series of fictions we create, a set of artificial constructs, then the process of "deconstructing" a text becomes an act of consciousness-raising, an insight into the relationships of imagination and logic, fiction and reality.

For instance, we might "deconstruct" *Peter Rabbit* by noticing how it moves against its apparent message. The plot seems to suggest that he who disobeys mother deserves punishment—that mother is always right. But mother, who knows her son well, nearly defies him to disobey her: It is almost as if she encourages his raid on the garden. Peter then has an exciting adventure, whereas his obedient sisters spend a boring day in the heat. Furthermore, Peter survives, despite his mother's warning about his father's death. Perhaps Peter proves his superiority to his father? Perhaps his mother is unconsciously offering him a test to see if he is fit to take charge of the family—a test that he passes? If the story can evoke these possibilities, then the apparent unity with which it supports a message of passive obedience is clearly just an illusion: It can make both that statement and its opposite.

All literature can be seen to make contradictory assertions—and reading with the ingenuity to discover how it does so can be highly enjoyable. This isn't to say that anyone can read any text and assume it means anything at all—for meaning depends on context, and in order to persuade others of the meanings we find in literature, we have to explain the contexts that allow us to read as we do. Not just any meaning will do, then. But any meaning we can justify and that we can take pleasure in explaining is worthy of consideration. From this point of view, the contexts within which a text might be understood are boundless—and so, therefore, are its meanings.

VALUE IN LITERATURE: THE CANON

The various theories of literature I've considered here raise questions about the idea that some literary works are better than others, that some texts are "trash" and others are classics or masterpieces. Frye's archetypes and Barthes's codes are present equally in Nancy Drew novels and *Charlotte's Web.* If they can be found in all sorts of literature, how do we determine what makes a literary text worthwhile? What is the difference, if there is any, between good literature and trash?

We tend to assume that good literature is serious—that, unlike trash, it expresses important truths about life. In fact, what is usually identified as trashy literature usually says obvious things in obvious ways—including, sometimes, some important truths about life. Paradoxically, furthermore, "good" literature seems to be far more open to interpretation than trash is. Its "truths" are elusive; scholars have been finding new ways of reading Shakespeare's *Hamlet*—and Potter's *Peter Rabbit* and White's *Charlotte's Web*—for a long time.

In fact, it's possible that what distinguishes the most important literature is its ability to engender new interpretations from its readers. Frank Kermode suggests that what makes literary texts classics is "an openness to accommodation which keeps them alive under endlessly varying dispositions" (44). What keeps them alive and causes us to consider them great is our ability to keep reading them in new ways, to be continually attentive to the as-yet-unconsidered possibilities of meaning within them.

An openness to interpretation does seem to be a quality of those texts of children's literature that I find myself particularly admiring, and that I know many children and many other adults particularly enjoy reading and thinking about: texts like Sendak's *Where the Wild Things Are* or Angela Johnson's *Toning the Sweep*. These texts are simple enough to be heard with enjoyment by very young and very unsophisticated children, yet complex enough to resonate inside more sophisticated minds in surprisingly subtle ways—and therefore, to engender an astonishing variety of interpretations from literary scholars. For instance, the articles by Eastman, Frey, Scott, MacDonald, and Nikola-Lisa listed at the end of this chapter all offer different readings of *Peter Rabbit,* a story much enjoyed by two-year-olds. Other texts—the ones I find myself admiring less—are either so simple as to make interpretation obvious, or so in need of interpretation that they lack the simplicity to be understood by unsophisticated readers.

Whether or not that combination of access and interpretability represents excellence in children's literature, the general question of literary value remains a contentious one. In the last few decades, even the concept that certain literary texts might have more inherent worth than others has been called into doubt. Feminists and members of minorities have pointed out the extent to which the texts usually considered worthy of study in schools and universities—the *literary canon*—represent the values and confirm the authority of males of a particular class and color. Much effort has been put into trying to broaden the canon, by rediscovering and revaluing forgotten texts written in the past by women and by members of minorities; and these efforts are having a profound influence on the way people think about literature. It's not as easy as it once was to take it for granted that Shakespeare's reputation—and Beatrix Potter's—depend on the inherent superiority of their work rather than on the insistence of powerful people and institutions that their work is superior.

Nevertheless, I believe that the concept of a canon continues to be useful, if only because it allows us to think about the implications of the idea that some books are inherently better than others. The process of thinking, of being human, is almost always a matter of valuing some things over others—of making decisions about what foods we prefer to eat and what clothes we want to wear, and even about what principles we choose to live by—on the basis of which ones we believe to be useful, pleasurable, or helpful. Knowing what we think is good—and, just as important, trying to understand why we think it's good—we can make thoughtful judgments about our new experiences.

We can, then, develop our own *personal* canons of value: and having done some thinking about these matters, we'll be able to resist both the idea that there is just *one* standard of taste, just *one* canon, and the attempts of others to impose their values and their canons upon us. In literature, for instance, we might choose to value texts that represent minority voices—or texts that subvert the traditional values of Shakespeare or Potter. We can develop our own versions of what the poet Matthew Arnold called *touchstones:* texts that have proven to be so satisfying or important to us that we can use them as schemata for evaluating other books. We can compare other books with them, and in doing so, understand both what makes the touchstones valuable to us and what the other books have to offer.

EXPLORATION: What texts would you name as your own touchstones for children's literature? Why?

Obviously, the canons we develop for ourselves are not the only ones that exist. Many people and institutions develop and maintain specific canons of literature, and not just through consciously choosing to do so. For instance, people who specialize in literary study may create a canon merely by choosing to focus their attention on the same texts that others have already interpreted and written about. It's interesting that many of the feminists who have attacked the male-centred values of canonical texts have done so by writing yet more about the same old texts by Shakespeare and Milton that literary scholars have always concentrated their efforts on. A quick glance through the programs for children's literature conferences or the pages of journals such as *The Children's Literature Association Quarterly, Children's Literature, Children's Literature in Education,* or *The Lion and the Unicorn* reveals that those of us who work in this scholarly field clearly consider these and a few other texts to be of special significance and therefore, presumably, value: *Peter Rabbit, Where the Wild Things Are, Treasure Island, Anne of Green Gables, The Wind in the Willows, Charlotte's Web, The Secret Garden, Little Women, The Little House* books, *Tom's Midnight Garden, M. C. Higgins, The Great.* These texts are, I believe, what can only be called a canon. People interested in children's literature ought to know them, even if only to understand what the intense interest in them implies about the way many adults think about children's literature. In other words: We need to know which texts experts include in their canons whether or not we believe those texts actually have special value; we need to understand how experts establish value even or especially if we want to question their judgments.

Purves, Rogers, and Soter offer one final reason why we ought to know texts that are canonical:

A group of texts . . . has been set aside by communities as forming a part of the communal experience. These communities have selected them to be read aesthetically. Each encounter with those texts helps to bring an individual reader deeper into a particular community of readers. . . . By virtue of this process, the texts and readers have developed a set of associations with each other. Writers subsequently acculturated into this tradition have produced texts that are highly allusive to the communal set of literature. (50)

Knowing canonical texts not only helps us understand other texts: It brings us together with other readers and enables us to enter into dialogue with them. It helps make us members of the intertextual community of readers. Children deserve to be members of that community also.

EXPLORATION: The literary theories I've considered in this chapter represent different opinions about what matters in literature and about which ways of reading are likely to be most stimulating. My earlier discussions of reading strategies and of the characteristics of children's literature as a genre also represent such opinions, and surely my discussions of these matters reveal my own biases. It might be useful for you to consider how my discussions of these matters reveal *my* biases. Which of the theories outlined here do I favor in the approaches I recommend, which ones do I seem to ignore or dislike? To what degree are you willing to share my assumptions and/or conclusions? Why or why not?

WORKS CITED

Arnold, Matthew. "The Study of Poetry." *Essays in Criticism: First and Second Series.* London: Everyman's Library-Dent, 1964.

Barthes, Roland. *S/Z.* Trans. Richard Miller. New York: Hill and Wang, 1974.

Bettelheim, Bruno. *The Uses of Enchantment: The Meaning and Importance of Fairy Tales.* New York: Knopf, 1976.

Blonsky, Marshall, ed. *On Signs.* Baltimore: Johns Hopkins UP, 1985.

Burnett, Frances Hodgson. *The Secret Garden.* 1911. New York: Dell Yearling, 1973.

Campbell, Joseph. *The Hero with a Thousand Faces.* New York: Pantheon, 1949.

Chodorow, Nancy. *The Reproduction of Mothering: Psychoanalysis and the Sociology of Gender.* Berkeley: U of California P, 1978.

Derrida, Jacques. *Of Grammatology.* Trans. Gayatri Chakravorty Spivak. Baltimore: Johns Hopkins UP, 1976.

Donovan, Josephine. *Feminist Theory: The Intellectual Traditions of American Feminism.* New York: Continuum, 1985.

Eastman, Jackie F. "Beatrix Potter's *The Tale of Peter Rabbit:* A Small Masterpiece." *Touchstones: Reflections on the Best in Children's Literature.* Ed. Perry Nodelman. Lafayette, IN: ChLA Publications, 1989. 100–107.

Eco, Umberto. "Producing Signs." Blonsky 176–183.

Frey, Charles. "Victors and Victims in the Tales of *Peter Rabbit* and *Squirrel Nutkin*." *Children's Literature in Education* 18,2 (1987): 105–112.

Frye, Northrop. *Anatomy of Criticism: Four Essays*. Princeton: Princeton UP, 1957.

——. *The Great Code: The Bible and Literature*. Toronto: Academic Press Canada, 1982.

——. *Words with Power: Being a Second Study of "The Bible and Literature."* San Diego: Harcourt Brace Jovanovich, 1990.

Gallop, Jane. *Reading Lacan*. Ithaca: Cornell UP, 1985.

Gose, Elliott. *Mere Creatures: A Study of Modern Fantasy Tales for Children*. Toronto: U of Toronto P, 1988.

Johnson, Angela. Toning the Sweep. New York: Orchard, 1993.

Jung, Carl G. *The Portable Jung*. Ed. Joseph Campbell. New York: Viking, 1971.

Kermode, Frank. *The Classic*. Cambridge: Harvard UP, 1983.

Lacan, Jacques. *Ecrits: A Selection*. Trans. Alan Sheridan. New York: Norton, 1977.

——. *The Four Fundamental Concepts of Psycho-analysis*. Trans. Alan Sheridan. New York: Norton, 1981.

Le Guin, Ursula K. *A Wizard of Earthsea*. New York: Parnassus, 1968.

Lévi-Strauss, Claude. "The Structural Study of Myth." *Structural Anthropology*. Trans. Claire Jacobson and Brooke Grundfest Schoepf. Garden City: Doubleday Anchor, 1967. 202–228.

MacDonald, Ruth K. "Why This Is Still 1893: *The Tale of Peter Rabbit* and Beatrix Potter's Manipulations of Time into Timelessness." *Children's Literature Association Quarterly* 10,4 (Winter 1986): 185–187.

Nikola-Lisa, W. "The Cult of Peter Rabbit: A Barthesian Analysis." *Lion and the Unicorn* 15,2 (1991): 61–66.

Propp, Vladimir. *Morphology of the Folktale*. Austin: U of Texas P, 1970.

Purves, Alan C., Theresa Rogers, and Anna A. Soter. *How Porcupines Make Love III: Readers, Texts, Cultures in the Response-Based Literature Classroom*. White Plains: Longman, 1995.

Scott, Carole. "Between Me and the World: Clothes as Mediator between Self and Society in the Work of Beatrix Potter." *Lion and the Unicorn* 16,2 (December 1992): 192–198.

Sendak, Maurice. *Where the Wild Things Are*. New York: Harper, 1963.

White, E. B. *Charlotte's Web*. 1952. New York: Trophy-Harper & Row, 1973.

Wilder, Laura Ingalls. *The Little House in the Big Woods*. 1932. New York: Trophy-Harper & Row, 1971.

Wolf, Virginia. "Paradise Lost? The Displacement of Myth in Children's Novels." *Studies in the Literary Imagination* 18.2 (Fall 1985): 47–64.

part IV

Kinds of Children's Literature

So far in this book, I've considered a repertoire of schemata that effect all kinds of children's literature, from nursery rhymes to young adult novels. In addition to these overall patterns and assumptions, many kinds of children's literature—including nursery rhymes and young adult novels—have their own special characteristics, provide distinct pleasures, and raise specific questions of their own.

If I had the space to do so, I could fill many pages discussing the intriguing differences among all the different subgenres of children's literature: What distinguishes children's science fiction novels from other kinds of fantasy; what's special about teen romances or historical fiction or adventure stories. Unfortunately, I don't have all that space. All I can do is recommend that you recognize that all these different types do exist, and encourage you to consider what their distinctive qualities are, and what specific problems and pleasures they offer young readers.

EXPLORATIONS: (1) Choose one specific kind of children's literature: nonsense poems, time fantasies, tall tales, baseball stories, doll stories, Choose-Your-Own-Adventure stories, and so on. Read (or invite children to read) some texts that seem to belong to this category. Can you develop a schema for this subgenre of children's literature? If you can, how might it help or hinder your appreciation of the individual texts you're exploring?

(2) Many people disagree with my contention above that young adult fiction is merely a subgenre of children's literature. I've been told that I ought not to have even mentioned young adult literature in this book about children's literature: As a kind of writing in-

tended for teenagers, a group of people quite different from younger children, young adult literature is a completely different kind of writing, with its own distinctive characteristics. Explore (or invite children or young adults to explore) this possibility by reading and comparing a few novels for young adults with a few novels about similar characters or situarions but intended for younger children. Do the young adult novels represent a variation on the characteristics of fiction for younger children, or are they so different that we need to develop a different sense of their generic qualities?

Meanwhile, the chapters in this section explore the characteristics, pleasures, and questions raised by three especially important kinds of children's literature—kinds that are distinct enough to raise some especially interesting problems of their own. I discuss them in the order that young children might first experience them: poetry, picture books, and fairy tales.

chapter **10**

Poetry

POETRY FOR CHILDREN?

What distinguishes children's poetry from other kinds of children's literature is simply that it *is* poetry. In fact, many of the poems published in books intended for children weren't written with the idea that their audience would consist specifically of children: They are poems originally intended for adults that editors of collections of poetry thought might interest young readers. Clearly, then, the distinction between children's poetry and adult poetry is much less firm and clear-cut than the distinction between children's fiction and adult fiction; and the strategies children need to make sense of and derive pleasure from their experiences of poetry are the same ones we adults need to make sense of and derive pleasure from our own experiences of poetry.

As a result, the discussion of the characteristics of children's poetry that follows is less an attempt to see what distinguishes children's poems from adult ones than it is to see what distinguishes poetry in general from non-poetic texts. While many of the examples I offer in this chapter are poems actually intended for an audience of children, most of what I say merely represents my ideas about poetry and the pleasures it offers readers in general. The chapter ends with a consideration of some issues that relate specifically to the poems actually written for children and the question of how we teach children to respond to poetry.

THE PLEASURES OF SOUND AND IMAGE

Many children first experience the pleasures of literature in the form of poems: rhyming songs or nursery rhymes like this one, recited to them long before they themselves can speak or even understand much language:

Humpty Dumpty sat on a wall,
Humpty Dumpty had a great fall.
   All the king's horses,
    And all the king's men,
Couldn't put Humpty together again.

These words are so familiar to many of us that we might not realize just how strange they actually are. What could they possibly mean? Why might we consider a story that appears to be about a violent death appropriate for youngsters?

I suspect most of us don't think about the violence, or about what these words might mean at all. I think they please many of us even though they don't seem to mean much of anything; in fact, we probably like them exactly because they *are* so weird.

As it happens, however, these strange words do have a meaning. The rhyme is a riddle, and it does make a sort of sense once we realize that Humpty Dumpty is an egg. And once we learn the answer to the riddle—that Humpty Dumpty's an egg—it's hard not to think about the poem differently than we did before we considered that possibility.

Nevertheless, we aren't likely to forget the specific words of "Humpty Dumpty" after we've understood their meaning—as, for instance, readers might forget the specific words of a textbook like this one once they've grasped the concepts being conveyed. The main purpose of the words in a textbook is to convey the concepts. Most of us tend to notice them only when they seem to be doing their job badly and getting in the way of our understanding. But once we've understood "Humpty Dumpty," I suspect many of us will want to go back and reread it, to enjoy (or perhaps to be annoyed by) the clever way in which these unnecessarily but delightfully complicated words express something so straightforward.

In other words, what matters about "Humpty Dumpty" is less what it means than *how it says what it means:* the sounds of the words and the pictures they evoke rather than the simple ideas about eggs or violent death that the words express. That's true of all nursery rhymes and of the popular songs we often sing to soothe infants. I believe it's true of all poetry.

This focus on *how* something is said is most obvious in poems in which the oddities of the specific words draw attention to themselves, as they do in "Humpty Dumpty" or in poems like this one by Carolyn Wells:

A tutor who tooted the flute
Tried to tutor two tooters to toot.
   Said the two to the tutor,
    "Is it harder to toot or
To tutor two tooters to toot?"

The poem would be much less interesting if it went,

A couple of flute students
wondered if their teacher
found it more difficult
to play the instrument or
to teach them to play it.

Without all those similar-sounding words, the meaning Wells expresses hardly seems worth communicating at all.

A little less obviously, the specific words are still an essential part of the pleasure in A. R. Ammons's "Small Song":

The reeds give
way to the

Wind and give
the wind away

This poem hinges on the different meanings of similar-sounding phrases about giving way to something and giving something away; it surely wouldn't be as likely to engage the attention of most readers if it said, "the reeds yield to the wind, and thus reveal it."

The specific words are just as significant a part of the experience of poems that are so insistent on the importance of their meaning that they state it clearly. We know what Langston Hughes wants to tell us in "Dreams" because he proclaims it loudly in the first line:

Hold fast to dreams
For if dreams die
Life is a broken-winged bird
That cannot fly.

Hold fast to dreams
For when dreams go
Life is a barren field
Frozen with snow.

What's being said here is straightforward, even obvious: don't stop aspiring, or your life will be bleak; without hope, you'll be hopeless. But Hughes makes that obvious statement interesting and important (and so, I believe, a poem) by expressing it in words that do more and say more than the prose version, and say it much more specifically.

One way Hughes's words do that is by creating patterns of sound: repeating rhythms and repeating rhymes that depend on these exact words being said in this exact order. These words also evoke pictures of a bird and a field that allow us to consider just what it might feel like to be without hope. Furthermore, since birds are meant to fly, Hughes's words say not just that we should aspire, but that humans are meant to aspire; that hopelessness is as uncharacteristic of humans as the inability to fly is of birds. Fields frozen with snow can melt and grow crops; thus, those who learn to aspire can move beyond despair.

Or we might read the poem quite differently. As in many poems, the apparently straightforward meaning may not be so straightforward after all. The "dreams" here might be, not aspirations, but imaginary happenings: daydreams or fantasies. If they are, then holding fast to them is less a matter of hope than of a necessary self-delusion. Hughes may be asking us to realize that life *is* really bleak and hopeless after all, and that we couldn't bear the bleakness if we got rid of our illusions: Perhaps the truth is that the bird will never fly again, and that life is as barren as that field of snow.

The possibility that we could read the poem in this way may be one of the things that make it a poem. The poem is ambiguous; despite first impressions, its meaning isn't straightforward. Rather than merely telling us what to think, the words seem to resonate beyond themselves, to encourage us to consider several possible meanings instead of focusing on the most obvious one. In discussing literary value in chapter 9, I suggested that some of the most interesting fictional texts for children share this quality of suggesting a variety of interpretations. Perhaps we offer children access to poetry of all sorts, including poems first written for adults, because we unconsciously recognize that even poetry intended for adults has much in common with the most interesting texts written especially for children.

EXPLORATION: In order to explore the degree to which a poem is ambiguous or resonant, choose (or invite children to choose) a poem and paraphrase it: that is, say what it means to you in your own words. Then reconsider the words of the poem. Do they imply anything more, or different? How are your words different from the words of the poem? Which are more interesting?

A Reading Strategy?

It may be that I'm just imagining that poems resonate in the way I describe above, and so I find meanings in them that I only imagine to be there. Perhaps poems are no different from any other use of language, and their special qualities depend purely on the fact that readers think about them differently from the way they think about ordinary conversations or textbooks or recipes.

I might, for instance, treat the dictionary definition of "egg" as if it were a poem. I could write it out like this:

the roundish reproductive body
produced
by the female
of animals,

consisting of
an embryo
and
its envelopes

Now it looks like a poem, and so it's pretty easy to think of it is as one, to dwell on the significance of the words in the particular way that people tend to think about words identified as poems.

EXPLORATION: Think (or invite children to think) about the dictionary definition of "egg" or about some other non-poetic use of language as if it were a poem. Does your attitude affect the experience of reading the words? How?

Reading the words as if they were a poem, you might conclude that they don't make a very good one—for they don't seem to have the significance or deep meaning many people expect of poetry. Or you might decide that they are an exceedingly difficult poem—because you can't figure out what their significance might be. Or you might in fact find something "poetic" about them. You might read them as a description of the planet earth. Or accepting that they do describe eggs, you might see something poetic in the use of the word "envelopes": It might remind you of mailing letters, and perhaps give you the idea that eggs are something like love letters, a blank exterior hiding a soft center of love.

Many poets have taken advantage of the special way of thinking many of us engage in when we decide that a text is a poem by doing just what I've done here—finding poems in other uses of language. "Found poems," as they are called, are often funny, since they remove words from their original contexts and thus encourage us to find additional meanings in them. For example, consider this poem that John Robert Colombo "found" in the *Concise Oxford Dictionary:*

FAMILY

Animals of different kinds
In one cage

Found poems can also be startlingly evocative. A scholar found this one in the journals of Dorothy Wordsworth, the sister of nineteenth-century British poet William Wordsworth:

The lake was covered all over
With bright silverwaves
That were each
The twinkling of an eye

EXPLORATION: Try (or invite children to try) to find a poem, in some words from a book or magazine or newspaper that weren't intended to be poetry. Explore what happens when, after reading the words you've borrowed, you think about them as if they were poetry.

EXPERIENCING POETRY

Found poems affirm the extent to which all poetry might become pleasurable if experienced in terms of one specific attitude: a playful delight in the ways in which words become interesting in and for themselves. In this section, I'll explore eight specific ways in which we can take that attitude and in doing so, I believe, enrich our response to poems.

Paying Attention to the Words Themselves

I comforted my children when they were babies by reciting to them not only nursery rhymes but also poems by W. B. Yeats, T. S. Eliot, and Shakespeare. Shakespeare may not seem to be expressing anything that would appeal to an infant when he says,

> The expense of spirit in a waste of shame
> Is lust in action; and till action, lust
> Is perjured, murderous, bloody, full of blame,
> Savage, extreme, rude, cruel, not to trust . . .

But to the children, the sounds were interesting enough to attract their attention and pleasing enough to soothe them—just as they were soothed by strange sounds like "humpty dumpty" and "hickety pickety" and "higglety pigglety" in nursery rhymes, and by my singularly unmusical renditions of rock songs and Broadway show tunes.

Not just sounds, but entire words can be interesting because they are peculiar. This anonymous poem takes advantage of peculiarities of spelling:

> OUGH
>
> As a farmer was going to plough,
>   He met a man driving a cough;
>   They had words which led to a rough,
> And the farmer was struck on his brough.

And this anonymous rhyme creates pleasure from the fact that the same words can have different meanings:

> Little Willie from his mirror
>   Sucked the mercury all off,

Thinking, in his childish error,
    It would cure his whooping cough.
At the funeral Willie's mother
    Smartly said to Mrs. Brown:
" 'Twas a chilly day for William
When the mercury went down."

Paying Attention to the Patterns Words Make

In the Shakespeare poem about "the expense of spirit," the repeated *s* sounds form a pattern and attract our attention. The repetition of consonants is called *alliteration*. The repetition of vowels such as the *a*'s in "*a waste of shame*" is called *assonance*. Repeating sounds is an obvious part of the pleasure of Carolyn Wells's poems about the flute tutor—and so are repeating words, rhythms, and rhymes. Repetitions of words and rhymes offer a different kind of pleasure in this poem by Gwendolyn Brooks:

WE REAL COOL
    THE POOL PLAYERS.
    SEVEN AT THE GOLDEN SHOVEL.

We real cool. We
Left school. We

Lurk late. We
Strike straight. We

Sing sin. We
Thin gin. We

Jazz June. We
Die soon.

The lines of this poem are so short that the repetitiveness of their sounds is very noticeable; and that repetitiveness is amplified by all the alliterations and assonances. But here, I think, the purpose is not to evoke laughter. The strong repetitions come to seem inevitable and thus make the sad story the poem tells seem inevitable. The repeated "We" not only reinforces the beat but sets up the significance of its absence in the last line: After "We/Die soon," there is no more "We."

Rhyme. Part of the effect of "We Real Cool" depends on its forceful, obvious rhymes. Rhyme has been a feature of English poetry for centuries, and it's only in the past hundred years or so that a lot of poetry hasn't rhymed. As I suggested earlier while discussing developmental theories (in chapter 5), it's easy to assume that history represents evolution, and that individual lives replicate history. As a re-

sult, many people believe that nonrhyming poetry, because it came later historically, must be more sophisticated and that therefore it's not appropriate for young
children.

As a source of repetitive pattern, rhyme is certainly appealing, perhaps in a
more obvious and more accessible way than some other patterns. Like the poems
I've considered so far, most of the poems written for children, and most of the poems in anthologies of poems selected for children, do rhyme.

Poems don't have to rhyme, however. In my experience, babies will respond
to the blank verse of T. S. Eliot's *The Waste Land* just as they respond to the rhymes
in Shakespeare's "Expense of spirit." Dennis Lee's "The Muddy Puddle" creates
strong, interesting patterns with almost no rhyme:

I am sitting
In the middle
Of a rather Muddy
Puddle,
With my bottom
Full of bubbles
And my rubbers
Full of Mud,
While my jacket
And my sweater
Go on slowly
Getting wetter
As I very
Slowly settle
To the Bottom
Of the Mud.
And I find that
What a person
With a puddle
Round his middle
Thinks of mostly
In the muddle
Is the Muddi-
Ness of Mud.

Shape.   As well as containing repeated *s* and *m* sounds, and similar words, like
"middle" and "muddle," Lee's poem has another pattern: its shape on the page. The
short lines break up the sentences as we would normally speak them, slow us
down, and force our attention to the repetition of the sounds.

The shape a poem takes on the page can become its central focus, as in Colleen Thibaudeau's "Balloon":

```
            as
       big      as
     ball    as   round
   as sun   . . .  I tug
   and  pull  you  when
   you  run  and when
         wind blows I
          say polite
              ly
               H
                  O
                    L
                       D
                          M
                             E
                                T
                                  I
                                     G
                                        H
                                     T
                                       L
                                          Y.
```

Conventional Verse Forms.   Another sort of pleasure in pattern develops when we become conscious of the history of poems. Carolyn Wells's poem about the flute tutor has the pattern of a standard verse form: the *limerick,* a form made popular in the nineteenth century by Edward Lear. In a limerick, the first and second line rhyme with the fifth line, and the shorter third and fourth lines rhyme with each other. In Lear's limericks, the last line is often a repetition of the first. Once we're aware of this conventional pattern, we can find enjoyment in the pattern itself, and in our ability to recognize it in other poems, such as this one by Lear:

> There was an Old Man in a tree
> Who was horribly bored by a Bee;
> When they said, "Does it buzz?"
> He replied, "Yes, it does!
> It's a regular brute of a bee."

Our knowledge of the form can also operate as a schema that teases us when our expectations of it are aroused but then not quite met, as in this poem by W. S. Gilbert:

> There was an Old Man of St. Bees
> Who was stung in the arm by a wasp,

> When asked, "Does it hurt?"
> He replied, "No, it doesn't,
> But I thought all the while 'twas a hornet."

Other conventional forms include the *sonnet,* a fourteen-line poem with a specific rhyme scheme (the lines from Shakespeare's "Expense of spirit" are the first four lines of a sonnet); and the *haiku,* a short, three-line poem in which the first line and last line each have five syllables and the middle line has seven syllables, and the last line sums up the essence of the experience expressed in the poem. This is a famous haiku by the master of the form, the seventeenth-century Japanese poet Basho:

> Furuike ya
> Kawazu tobikomu
> Mizu no oto

Or in English, in my own not particularly accurate version,

> A quiet old pond;
> A frog disrupts the surface
> And the splash resounds.

Paying Attention to the Pictures Words Make

If we can visualize or otherwise concretize the situations that carefully chosen words describe, then the words will help us create imaginary pictures that afford us two kinds of pleasure: having the pictures evoked for us, and perceiving how the words evoke them. Both sources of pleasure are available in Ruth Whitman's "Listening to Grownups Quarrelling":

> standing in the hall against the
> wall with my little brother, blown
> like leaves against the wall by their
> voices, my head like a pingpong ball
> between the paddles of their anger:
> I knew what it meant
> to tremble like a leaf.
> Cold with their wrath, I heard
> the claws of the rain
> pounce. Floods
> Poured through the city,
> skies clapped over me,
> and I was shaken, shaken,
> Like a mouse
> between their jaws.

There are two kinds of pictures in this poem. The first, the main picture of a child listening to grown-ups quarreling, evokes the child's painful feelings with a clarity that for me, paradoxically, makes the evocation enjoyable. The second is a series of subsidiary pictures that offer visual equivalents for the child's feelings and help us understand them. These subsidiary pictures, often called *images,* include blowing leaves, a game of Ping-Pong, and a thunderstorm. The image of the thunderstorm, which suggests the sounds of the quarrel, is itself evoked in yet another picture, that of a cat, as we hear of "the claws of the rain" pouncing, and guess that the sky that "clapped over me" represents not just a thunderclap but also the action of being struck quickly, as when a cat claps its paws over a mouse. These pictures offer visual parallels for the feelings the poem expresses. As we imagine the pictures, we can recognize their appropriateness as descriptions of a particular situation.

Paying Attention to the Patterns of Pictures Words Make

The pictures in "Listening to Grownups Quarrelling" do something else. They create patterns of repetition and variation. The image of leaves blown against a wall is echoed by the image of the head tossed by the Ping-Pong paddles, and then by the "claws of the rain." The different images are different versions of the same action: hitting or being hit by something hard and dangerous. We can dwell, not just on the pictures themselves, but also on their interesting similarity to and difference from each other.

Paying Attention to the Voices Words Create

Like all words, poems imply the voices that speak them—and also, sometimes, the people who might hear those voices. When we read or hear poems, we can think about who might be speaking them, and who their speakers might be speaking to. Walter de la Mare's "The Dunce" sums up not just a situation but the personality of the character who tells us about it:

> Why does he still keep ticking?
>   Why does his round white face
> Stare at me over the books and ink,
>   And mock at my disgrace?
> Why does the thrush call, "Dunce, dunce, dunce!"?
>   Why does the bluebottle buzz?
> Why does the sun so silent shine?—
>   And what do I care if it does?

The poem as a whole gives us enough insight into the character of the person speaking to understand that the strident dismissal of the last line is just bravado—not genuine at all. Many poems give similar insight into characters and their situations by creating distinctive voices, voices like that of the sadly comic speaker in John Cunliffe's "The Mutinous Jack-in-the-Box":

> Why should I always jump up
> When they press that stupid button
> always at their call?
> Next time . . . *next* time . . .
> I'll stick my tongue out at them!
> I'll spit!
> I'll shout rude words!
> I'll pull horrid faces!
> I'll make their baby cry
> and turn the milk sour;
> I will!
> Just you wait and see!
> They can't fool me;
> not for ever a slave;
> next time I'll be brave.
> B o o o o o o o o o o i i i i i i i i n n n n n n n g g g !
> Oh dear, I jumped up again,
> Grinning as though I had no brain.
> But . . . just you wait and see,
> Next time I'll do it;
> I will . . . I will . . .

Other poems evoke voices as diverse as the threatened child of "Listening to Grownups Quarrelling" and the annoyed child of "The Muddy Puddle."

The Voices of Children. It's not accidental that these two poems and de la Mare's "Dunce" sound as if they were spoken by children. Many poems written for children, and many other poems selected for inclusion in anthologies of poetry intended for children, imply speakers who are children. Some, like these three, convincingly create childlike moods that are meant to be taken seriously, and that even mature adults can empathize with.

But a number of poems theoretically intended for children seem to adopt a childish voice so that we can see through and feel superior to the speaker's innocence. While this technique might appear to be condescending or patronizing, poets often have an honorable reason for using it: They've adopted some of the assumptions about childhood I discussed in chapter 5, and they want to capture an attitude that they believe to be so exclusively childlike that adults are no longer capable of sharing it; adults, they believe, have learned too much to be so joyfully innocent and have no choice but to admire innocence from a distance. That was probably Robert Louis Stevenson's purpose in writing "My Shadow":

> I have a little shadow that goes in and out with me,
> And what can be the use of him is more than I can see.

He is very, very like me from the heels up to the head;
And I see him jump before me, when I jump into my bed.
The funniest thing about him is the way he likes to grow—
Not at all like proper children, which is always very slow;
For he sometimes shoots up taller like an india-rubber ball,
And he sometimes gets so little that there's none of him at all. . . .

But despite its honorable purpose, I think the poem is still a little condescending. Appreciating it seems to depend on knowing more than the speaker—understanding shadows well enough to realize how wrong and how cute the speaker's ideas are. In other words, it seems to be asking us to take pleasure in the child's ignorance. We might wonder what children who share the speaker's ignorance about shadows make of such a poem. Does it merely confirm their ignorance? We might also wonder about the effect on inexperienced children of modern poems that revel in similarly immature attitudes, such as Dennis Lee's "Special Person," in which a child innocently describes the future he imagines with his favorite day-care worker:

I guess I'm going to marry Lynn
    When I get three or four
And Lynn can have my Crib, or else
    She'll maybe sleep next door.

The main source of pleasure this poem offers is the humor in the speaker's ignorance of the limitations of his own perceptions—a humor other innocents couldn't perceive.

EXPLORATION: Find some poems spoken in the voices of children. Do they allow you to empathize, or does your pleasure derive from the limited understanding of the speaker? If the latter, how might inexperienced children respond to them? Test your own response by sharing the poems with young children.

Paying Attention to the Stories Words Tell

As well as evoking the voice of a specific character, "The Mutinous Jack-in-the-Box" describes a series of events that have a beginning, a middle, and end. The Jack works himself up to rebellion in a suspense-building set of intensifying statements, after which his jump up is a humorous climax: An event that is surprising in the context of the poem, but also inevitable. In other words, the poem offers the satisfactions of a story.

Many other poems, however, don't so much describe stories as imply them. In responding to "Listening to Grownups Quarrelling" or "The Muddy Puddle" or "We Real Cool," we can imagine the situations that led up to or that are likely to result from the specific events being described. These poems thus present small scenes in ways that suggest larger and more complicated stories.

Paying Attention to the Meanings Words Express

The pleasure in many poems stems from the thoughts they arouse. Words aren't just sounds, but sounds that have meaning. Many people treasure particular poems that state truths they hold dear, such as, "Hold fast to dreams." And in classrooms in schools and universities, discussions of poems often center on the way we respond to what we're able to summarize of their meaning, so that children read Hughes's "Dreams" in order to learn the importance of aspirations and college students read T. S. Eliot to consider his philosophy of life.

This approach to poems has the same limitations as any reading of literature that focuses on its themes: the limitations I discussed in chapter 4. When we focus our attention on the meanings of poems, we shouldn't forget that it's primarily their *way* of expressing meanings that is likely to be what makes them most interesting. In my experience, poems rarely say all that much that's unique or deeply meaningful when considered as philosophy—and almost nothing clear and unambiguous enough to be considered philosophical at all. It's our perception of the rightness of the specific words and images that leads us to treasure poems that express significant truths to us.

Furthermore, as we saw earlier, the words of poems like "Dreams" express general truths in ways that provide other, more detailed and more ambiguous meanings. Exploring such meanings can be a significant source of the pleasure we take in poetry.

EXPLORATION: Consider (or invite children to consider) whether poems you like are important for their ideas or for their language. Choose a poem that expresses an idea that's important to you. Is the language in which it expresses the idea a significant part of your appreciation of the poem? Why or why not?

Not all poems make the sort of serious statement about life that a poem like "Dreams" does, but all poems do have meanings and encourage us to think. "Humpty Dumpty" and many other "nonsense" poems can't give us advice about how to live, but we can pleasurably think about all the different ways in which such poems might possibly be meaningful: Are they about eggs or violent accidents?

While "Dreams" is organized to encourage us to agree with the ideas it expresses, Hilaire Belloc's "The Frog" offers the opposite pleasure. As I pay careful attention to it, I begin to realize the horrifying but delightful fact that I've been manipulated into thinking the very thoughts and enjoying the very words the poem itself pretends to be telling me not to enjoy:

> Be kind and tender to the Frog,
>   And do not call him names,
> As "Slimy skin," or "Polly-wog,"
>   Or likewise "Ugly James,"

Or "Gap-a-grin," or "Toad-gone-wrong,"
    Or "Billy Bandy-knees":
The Frog is justly sensitive
    To epithets like these.
No animal will more repay
    A treatment kind and fair;
At least so lonely people say
    Who keep a frog (and, by the way,
They are extremely rare).

"Listening to Grownups Quarrelling" is more serious. But while it encourages serious thought, it doesn't offer the sort of general statement about life that "Dreams" does. This poem is not about quarreling in general or about parents in general: It's an evocation of a specific feeling in specific circumstances. As we read it, we may think about the significance of the feeling as it's evoked in the poem. We may wonder whether the feeling speaks to us of our own lives or gives us insight into the lives of others or even into life in general. But we shouldn't confuse those thoughts with the poem itself. A poem is *not* the memories it evokes for us, nor the thoughts it makes us ponder: It *is* what evokes those memories and thoughts.

Paying Attention to the Patterns of Meanings Words Make

As well as thinking about the meanings of poems, we can also enjoy the patterns those meanings create—the structure of the poem. For instance, we can examine the ways in which the pictures in "Listening to Grownups Quarrelling" create a shifting pattern of ideas about being battered. Or we can explore the way in which the pattern of sounds and images in Randall Jarrell's "The Bird of Night" not only describes how small creatures like mice and bats might respond to the call of an owl that could kill them, but also, creates a fascinating pattern of ideas. This poem encourages us to think about the relationships of sound waves and waves of water; about the possibility of drowning and the possibility of death; about the word "trying" as meaning "attempting" and as meaning "difficult"; about the stillness of death and the act of keeping still in order to prevent death.

A shadow is floating through the moonlight.
Its wings don't make a sound.
Its claws are long, its beak is bright.
Its eyes try all the corners of the night.
It calls and calls: all the air swells and heaves
And washes up and down like water.
The ear that listens to the owl believes
In death. The bat beneath the eaves,
The mouse beside the stone are still as death—
The owl's air washes them like water.

The owl goes back and forth inside the night,
And the night holds its breath.

In this poem, everything—the sounds, the rhythms, the rhymes, the line breaks, the images, the ideas—all comes together, to create an intense and, for me, intensely pleasurable experience.

EXPLORATION: Carefully reread "The Bird of Night," any of the other poems discussed above, or read any poem of your choice. Explore (or invite children to explore) its text in detail, in terms of all eight of the aspects of poetic response I've suggested. What happens to your perception of the poem when you think about all of them at the same time?

CHILDREN'S POETRY: THE MAKING OF ANTHOLOGIES

As I suggested at the beginning of this chapter, the distinctions between children's literature and adult literature get blurry when it comes to poetry: Children's poems have as much or more in common with other poems as they do with other texts of children's literature, and so I've talked both about poems by Dennis Lee, John Cunliffe, and Robert Louis Stevenson that were expressly written for children, and about poems by Shakespeare, Langston Hughes, and Ruth Whitman that were originally written for adults. In this way, my selection of poems is like almost all *anthologies* of selections of poems intended for children.

Editors of collections mix up adult and children's poetry in the belief that poems adults enjoy can also offer pleasure to children—at least to those children who know how to become the implied readers of poems, and who have learned (or perhaps not yet unlearned?) the playful attitudes that allow people of any age to respond positively to poetry. I share that belief and encourage others to share it also. Those who know how to enjoy the patterns in poetry have the potential to enjoy any group of words on any subject and of any level of subtlety that deserves to be called a poem, even if they aren't interested in its subject or don't understand the meanings of all of the words.

I suspect that none of us would want to assert that all adult poems are equally suitable for children. But that raises an interesting question: Which ones are? The specific poems each of us thinks suitable for children not only reveal much about our attitudes toward children—how tolerant we think they are of new experiences, what subjects they're interested in or ought to be interested in, what they're capable of understanding—these choices also reveal something of our ideas about what poetry is.

EXPLORATION: Consider (or invite children to consider) poems by a number of different authors included in any collection of poems intended for children. What kinds of poems are included, and what kinds left out?

What do these choices reveal about the anthologizer's attitudes toward children? Toward poetry?

Furthermore, and more significantly, these choices provide children with *their* ideas about what poetry is. The nature of poetry will be defined for them by the qualities of the poems we offer them. Some years ago, Kenneth Koch said:

> The usual criteria for choosing poems to teach children are mistaken, if one wants poetry to be more than a singsong sort of Muzak in the background of their elementary education. . . . These criteria are total understandability, which stunts children's poetic education by giving them nothing to understand they have not already understood; "childlikeness" of theme and treatment, which condescends to their feelings and to their intelligence; and "familiarity," which obliges them to go on reading the same inappropriate poems their parents and grandparents read. (12)

Many people still use these inadequate criteria, even though they interpret them a little differently. We tend to believe that childhood now is so different from what it was in the past that contemporary children wouldn't find the sweet, gentle poems their parents read either familiar or childlike. What they would be familiar with, and find understandable—and, therefore, what we think of as being most child-like—are poems meant to be funny and focusing on acts of violence. Or so we believe.

Myra Cohn Livingston describes such poems, the work of poets like Jack Prelutsky, Dennis Lee, Roald Dahl, and many others, as a "glorification of the unconscious . . . a sort of 'garbage delight' that assaults literature itself" (157–158; *Garbage Delight* is the title of one of Lee's books of poems). Referring to a poem by Lois Duncan about a girl who teases a dog so unmercifully that it gets mad and eats her up, Livingston writes: "There are some who will say all of this is simply in fun, and children themselves know it is nonsense. . . . But there are others, like myself, who believe that the irresponsible images of the unconscious may be understood by adults, but have no place in the child's world unless there is some helpmeet, some guide, something on which the child may fall back" (159).

EXPLORATION: In the following paragraphs, I express my disagreement with what Livingston says here. Read (or invite children to read) some poems by Lee, Prelutsky, Dahl, or Duncan. Then consider both Livingston's position and mine, and try to determine where you stand on this issue.

If such poems are dangerous, I don't believe that it's because of the irresponsibility of their images. Livingston seems to assume such images will be new to youngsters. But they merely parallel images and ideas that most young North American children will have experienced already, on TV or in the playground—and usually find funny, if only because TV and other children on the playground encourage them to do so.

Furthermore, the source of the poems' humor is in their anarchy: They dwell dangerously on matters adults work hard to persuade children are vulgar or impolite. In other words, they break rules, and therefore allow children the freedom to test rules and to imagine defiance of them. Indulgence in anarchy is a common form of pleasure in many texts for children, from Mother Goose nonsense which breaks the rules of language through stories that celebrate fools or sillies. I wonder if adults actually object to poems of this sort because they object to the imaginary escape from the repressions of adult authority that the poems imply—and the pleasurable empowerment they therefore offer children.

If there's a danger in these poems, I think, it's in the fact that in recent years we've tended to provide children with a steady diet of similar poems, and nothing else. Explore anthologies of poetry published in the last decade or so, or browse through the children's poetry section in a library; you'll have to conclude that almost *all* the poems many children read nowadays are this same sort of funny, anarchic doggerel. While many children do enjoy these poems, some of them may come to believe that all poems must rhyme, must have jaunty, obvious rhythms and rhyme schemes, and must focus on the comedy of anarchy and violence. And this belief might well deprive them of the pleasures of other kinds of poems, such as the thoughtfulness of "Dreams," the evocative painfulness of "Listening to Grownups Quarrelling," the music and terror of "The Bird of Night."

If we wish to help children respond fully to what poetry can offer, then I believe we need to expose them to as many different kinds of poems as possible. As parents and educators, we can each develop our own anthologies of poems we enjoy, and that we would like children to be able to enjoy. I would hope that these anthologies would represent a range of possibilities—that we ourselves can enjoy and are willing to share our pleasure in different kinds of poetry.

EXPLORATION: Read (or invite children to read) a number of poems, and select some—five or six—that are particularly enjoyable, or that you think others ought to experience. Explore why you chose each poem, and what attitudes toward poetry your choices might suggest.

WHY MANY PEOPLE DON'T LIKE POETRY— AND WHAT TO DO ABOUT IT

Not everybody likes to ski or to do needlepoint; not everybody likes to read poetry. Nor should they, any more than everybody should have to like needlepoint. It's possible to be a happy and complete human being without ever reading a poem. Nevertheless, fewer people enjoy reading poems than might. Linda Hall reports a survey conducted among children in Great Britain that revealed the startling fact that, "Where 47 per cent of pupils indicated they read no poetry out of school, as many of 36 per cent professed to be utterly hostile to it" (5). I'd be surprised if the percentage wasn't at least as high in North America.

I suspect that so many people dislike poetry simply because they've never learned *how* to like it. In elementary school classrooms, teachers often ask children to sit back and enjoy having poems read to them, without providing them with any understanding of what poems are, or any way of perceiving the technical complexities that make even simple poems work. Even more often, teachers, with what I believe to be a misguided faith in the innate creativity of all children, ask their students to write their own poems, often without even providing them with a repertoire of poems by others that will help them develop schemata for what poetry is or might be.

Furthermore, many people—both teachers and people who write about poetry—believe that it's dangerous for adults to talk with children about their responses to poetry. They claim that our responses to poems are always personal, that all responses to any given poem are equally valid, and that our attempts to discuss children's responses with them is a destructive act of meddling. Such people would agree with Agnes Repplier, who said, many years ago, "When poetry is in question, it is better to feel than to think" (263).

But with no thought—no discussion of poems, no help in knowing how to make sense of them and enjoy doing so, and thus no sense of the complex craft of poems—children often remain ignorant of the skills that make responding to poetry enjoyable. Unless we're prepared to believe that poetry has the strange and magical ability to communicate automatically—and I don't—we need to teach those skills.

Meanwhile, in many high school and university classrooms, the enjoyment of poems is taken for granted, and the focus is on determining poetry's significance. The implication is that, when it comes to poetry, it's better to think than to feel. There's so much discussion of what poems mean that many people come to believe that poetry is purposely obscure—that for no clear reason, poets like to frustrate others by never saying exactly what they mean. According to this common assumption, all poems have "hidden meanings": secret messages that are fairly simple but that poets have concealed under layers of complicated symbols and images. When we read poetry, then, our job isn't to explore or enjoy the meaning of the language of the poem, but, instead, to find the hidden meaning—the one thing the poem does not actually state. The words of poems are just husks—we unwrap them to find the nutritious kernel inside, and then we throw the husks away.

This is frustrating: If the point is the "hidden meaning," then why bother hiding it? Why not just state it and get it over with? Poetry ends up seeming like a self-defeating attempt *not* to communicate what it's trying to communicate. This way of thinking about poems prevents many people from getting any enjoyment from them.

Clearly, then, some ways of thinking about poetry make it as unlikable as not knowing how to think about poetry at all. If we want children to enjoy poetry, we need to provide them with knowledge of the possibilities of poetry and of helpful attitudes toward the experience of it, and with techniques and strategies for deriving both understanding and pleasure from that experience.

Most of the strategies I outlined in chapter 3 about teaching literary strategies to children apply to poetry as well as prose. A particularly significant one is making sure that children have adults who like poetry read it to them as often as possible. Not only will this increase the children's repertoire of poems and their sense of the possibilities of poetry; it also allows children to experience one of the central pleasures of poetry: the carefully crafted orchestration of sounds that becomes apparent when any interesting poem is read aloud. Knowing how to read a poem expressively, and being willing to do so without fear of embarrassment are skills that give great pleasure both to the adults and children who learn them and to their listeners.

EXPLORATION: Each of the suggestions I make about responding to poetry in this chapter—paying attention to the words themselves, to the patterns and pictures they make, to the voices they create, to the stories they tell, to their meanings and to their patterns of meaning—represents a strategy that might well be shared with children. Choose one of these approaches and devise a way of helping children to make use of it in their response to poetry.

WORKS CITED

Ammons, A. R. "Small Song." *The Selected Poems 1951–1977*. New York: Norton, 1977.

Anonymous. "Ough." *A Whimsey Anthology*. Ed. Carolyn Wells. 1906. New York: Dover, 1963.

———. "Little Willie . . ." *The Golden Treasury of Poetry*. Ed. Louis Untermeyer. New York: Golden Press, 1959.

Basho. *The Narrow Road to the Deep North and Other Travel Sketches*. Trans. Noboyuki Yuasa. Harmondsworth, Middlesex: Penguin, 1966.

Belloc, Hilaire. "The Frog." *Selected Cautionary Verses*. Harmondsworth, Middlesex: Penguin, 1964.

Brooks, Gwendolyn. "We Real Cool." *Blacks*. Chicago: David, 1987.

Colombo, John Robert. "Family." *Translations from the English: Found Poems*. Toronto: Peter Martin, 1974.

Cunliffe, John. "The Mutinous Jack-in-the-Box." *A Second Poetry Book*. Ed. John Foster. Oxford: Oxford UP, 1980.

Dahl, Roald. *Revolting Rhymes*. New York: Knopf, 1983.

de la Mare, Walter. "The Dunce." *Collected Rhymes and Verses*. 2nd ed. London: Faber & Faber, 1970.

Eliot, T. S. *The Waste Land*. London: Faber & Faber, 1922.

Gilbert, W. S. "There was an old man." *A Whimsey Anthology*. Ed. Carolyn Wells. 1906. New York: Dover, 1963.

Hall, Linda. *Poetry for Life: A Practical Guide to Teaching Poetry in the Primary School*. London: Cassell, 1989.

Hughes, Langston. "Dreams." *The Dream Keeper and Other Poems*. New York: Knopf, 1932.

Jarrell, Randall. "The Bird of Night." *The Bat Poet*. New York: Macmillan, 1963.

Koch, Kenneth. *Rose, Where Did You Get That Red? Teaching Great Poetry to Children*. New York: Random House, 1973.

Lear, Edward. "There was an old man." *The Complete Nonsense of Edward Lear*. Ed. Holbrook Jackson. New York: Dover, 1951.

Lee, Dennis. "The Muddy Puddle." *Garbage Delight*. Toronto: Macmillan, 1977.

———. "The Special Person." *Alligator Pie*. Toronto: Macmillan, 1974.

Livingston, Myra Cohn. "David McCord's Poems: Something Behind the Door." *Touchstones: Reflections on the Best in Children's Literature*. Ed. Perry Nodelman. Vol. 2. West Lafayette: Children's Literature Association Publications, 1987. 157–172.

Prelutsky, Jack. *The Sheriff of Rottenshot*. New York: Greenwillow, 1982.

Repplier, Agnes. "The Children's Poets." *Children and Literature: Views and Reviews*. Ed. Virginia Haviland. Glenview: Scott, Foresman, 1973. 263–268.

Shakespeare, William. "Sonnet 129." *The Complete Works of Shakespeare*. Ed. Hardin Craig. Chicago: Scott, Foresman, 1961.

Stevenson, Robert Louis. "My Shadow." *A Child's Garden of Verses*. 1885. Harmondsworth, Middlesex: Penguin, 1952.

Thibaudeau, Colleen. "Balloon." *The New Wind Has Wings: Poems from Canada*. Ed. Mary-Alice Downie and Barbara Robertson. Toronto: Oxford UP, 1984.

Wells, Carolyn. "A tutor . . ." *A Whimsey Anthology*. Ed. Wells, 1906. New York: Dover, 1963.

Whitman, Ruth. "Listening to Grownups Quarrelling." *The Marriage Wig and Other Poems*. New York: Harcourt, 1968.

Wordsworth, Dorothy. *The Poetry of Dorothy Wordsworth: Edited from the Journals*. Ed. Hyman Eigerman. Westport: Greenwood, 1970.

chapter **11**

Picture Books

**THE VISUAL IMAGINATION
AND PICTORIAL COMPREHENSION**

In my experience, when most people think of books for children, they think first of *picture books:* short books that tell stories with relatively few words, but with large, usually colorful pictures on every page. They're right to do so. Not only is the picture-book story the most common form of children's literature, but it's a form of storytelling almost exclusively reserved for children. While there are both children's novels and adult novels, children's poems and adult poems, they aren't many fictional texts intended for adults that communicate their tales by means of few words and many pictures. It's worth considering why we tend to reserve this particular form of storytelling for children, and why it has become so predominant in children's literature.

When I ask people about these matters, most of them seem to give me one of two explanations

1. Children *like* pictures.
2. Children *need* pictures.

Let's consider these explanations further.

Many children do like pictures—for children are human beings, and a lot of human beings of all ages like pictures. On first picking up a book, people of any age tend to look at the pictures before reading the words. In fact, most of us automatically look at *any* picture we happen to see. As historian E. H. Gombrich says, "The visual image is supreme in its capacity for arousal" ("The Visual Image" 82). The fact that pictures attract our attention and excite our interest accounts for the

215

presence of pictures in print advertising as well as in many children's books. But there's no special reason to assume that children especially like pictures, or like them more than adults do.

Children presumably need pictures in books because they find them easier to understand than words, and need pictorial information to guide their response to verbal information. This theory depends on two assumptions; one about children and one about pictures. The assumption about children is that their imagination is "visual" in a way that gives them an intuitive ability to understand pictorial information. The assumption about pictures is that they are automatically understandable. Neither of these assumptions is true.

The idea that the imagination of children is qualitatively different from that of adults is no more valid than any other generalization about children. The specific suggestion that children are more visually oriented than adults relates to Piaget's theory that younger children think in more concrete terms: We assume that visual images are more concrete than verbal ones, and that therefore children have a better chance of understanding them. In doing so, we forget that babies respond to voices before they do to pictures, and learn to speak before they learn to draw. I suspect many young children, new to picture books, have a better understanding of a verbal text read to them by an adult than they have of the pictures accompanying that text.

I suspect that because I believe pictures are no more "concrete" and no less abstract than words are. They are representations—signs whose meaning depends on a repertoire of learned strategies. It's true that, simply because they are attempts to communicate visual information, many pictures more obviously resemble the objects they represent than do spoken or written words. Even so, the resemblance is not necessarily apparent to all viewers—a visual depiction understandable to one human being can seem meaningless to another.

In earlier times before Euro-American culture became so pervasive, many anthropologists and explorers showed people from other cultures in Africa or South America realistic drawings and even photographs. These people, unacquainted with Euro-American culture, were often unable to recognize what the pictures depicted. Because such depictions didn't exist in their cultures, they had no strategies for making sense of them.

The pictures that did exist had purposes different from our pictures and showed the world in a different way. Jan Deregowski reports a study in which some African villagers preferred a split-type drawing of an elephant (showing it from above as if it had been split open, so that all four feet could be seen), while Europeans preferred a top view that didn't show the feet. Deregowski says that the different responses come from a different understanding of what pictures are for: "Split-representation drawings develop in cultures where the products of art serve as labels or marks of identification. In the cultures where drawings are intended to convey *what an object actually looks like,* this style is muted and the 'perspective' style is adopted" (187–188).

Even that comment reveals a cultural bias: Deregowski believes he knows "what an object actually looks like." But the assumption he's making—that realistic pictures depict objects as seen from a distance from one specific point of view—is a relatively new idea, having developed only in Europe and only in the last four hundred or so years. To say that the perspective style represents reality more accurately than other styles and that therefore it is readily or even automatically understandable by children may merely reveal our own ideological prejudices.

Like words, in fact, pictures don't convey much meaning until we know the language in which they are expressed. Like words, then, they are "abstract," even when they are not the kind of modern art we call "abstract." Even representational pictures—the ones we call realistic—exist within systems of learned codes, and thus make little sense to anyone without a previous knowledge of those systems. Because pictures are permeated by the ideological assumptions of their culture, children won't understand pictures until they develop some understanding of the culture.

And that's not all. Children also have to understand the systems of codes and signifiers that are specific to pictures. In *Art and Illusion*, E. H. Gombrich persuasively shows how artists can make visual depictions of objects only in terms of their previous knowledge of earlier visual images—of a repertoire of schemata they've learned from their knowledge of previous art. "Everything points to the conclusion that the phrase the 'language of art' is more than a loose metaphor, that even to describe the visible world in images we need a developed system of schemata" (87).

And once we've accomplished that basic task, there's still more. We also need knowledge of a wide variety of different kinds of art in order to make sense of any individual visual depiction, which inevitably emerges from and makes best sense in the context of its maker's knowledge of art and art history. As Arthur Danto asserts, "To see something as art requires something the eye cannot descry—an atmosphere of artistic theory, a knowledge of the history of art: an artworld" (431). In order to understand pictures, we must share their visual repertoire—and that includes everything from the most apparently concrete, representational images to the ones that require an even greater knowledge of the "artworld" and that many people tend to actually identify as "abstract."

The fact that so many children *can* interpret a wide range of different kinds of pictures at an early age doesn't mean that understanding pictures is easy. Instead, I believe, it's a result of their great flexibility and as great an accomplishment as learning to use spoken language, a skill that children also miraculously teach themselves.

If pictures aren't particularly easy for inexperienced minds to make sense of, then why *are* there picture books? There may be no answer to that question but convention. The fact is, picture books do exist in our culture. People do believe that children like and need pictures, and so publishers can make a profit by providing books to fulfill that perceived need.

Furthermore, because we do provide so many children with the experience of so many pictures—not just in picture books, but also on television and in video games—the children do often become amazingly sophisticated interpreters of the language of pictures, long before they're able to decode the visual signs that represent words. As a result, many children do make use of the information they gather from pictures as they embark on the process of learning to read words—sometimes counterproductively, because they read the pictures instead of the words. According to Evelyn Goldsmith, research into these matters suggests that pictures can hinder the development of reading skills as much as they help it.

But that doesn't mean that picture books aren't a worthwhile form of literature. Pictures *can* help us all to understand words. When it comes to describing how things look—how to recognize the difference between, say, a bay window and a bow window—a picture is more communicative than any number of words, even the proverbial thousand. But more important, some of the most pleasurable experiences offered by children's literature are in picture books. If children may be said to like and need picture books, I believe it's mainly because they need and ought to have the many pleasures these books can provide.

THE PLEASURE OF PICTURE BOOKS

Because they contain illustrations, picture books offer a form of pleasure different from other types of storytelling. Likewise, because they contain words, the pleasure they offer is different from other forms of visual art.

Pictures are inherently different from words, and communicate different sorts of information in different ways. Pictures, which occupy space rather than time, lack an easy means of expressing the temporal relationships of cause and effect, dominance and subordination, and possibility and actuality that the grammar of language so readily expresses because it occupies time rather than space. A picture on its own can't convey that what it depicts happened long ago, or represents someone's dream or conjecture. Meanwhile, as I suggested earlier, words can't easily communicate the information about the appearance of physical objects that pictures so readily convey. Even a complete verbal description of a face or a setting is more focused on the implications of specific details than is a simple caricature, which readily conveys a sense of a visual whole.

The unique pleasure picture books offer is our perception of how illustrators make use of these differences between words and pictures. Consider the following examples:

- The text of Margot Zemach's *Jake and Honeybunch Go to Heaven* says, "there were angels everywhere." It doesn't tell us what the pictures do: that the angels are all African Americans dressed in glitzy costumes of the 1930s, and that heaven itself is a nightclub full of exuberant jazz musicians. These images distinguish "heaven" from conventional ideas of it enough to change the meaning of the story significantly.

- The text of Annalena McAfee and Anthony Browne's *The Visitors Who Came to Stay* says, "'Dad, do you see what I see?' asked Katy." The picture changes the significance of her apparently casual remark by showing us what she sees: a wildly improbable beach scene that includes a gorilla in a muscleman pose, a woman's foot shaped like a high-heeled shoe, a boy with a fish swimming inside his diving mask.

- The text of one page of *Brian Wildsmith's ABC* says merely "DOG." The word could refer to a wide variety of animals of different shapes and sizes, but the pictures show just one, a jowly bassethound. The image changes the vague potential of the original text into a specific, limited image that invites our attention to its specifying details.

HOW PICTURES PROVIDE INFORMATION ABOUT STORIES

In order to notice the distinctions between words and pictures, we need strategies for picture books that are different from our strategies for understanding stories told only in words, and that are also different from the ways we often view other pictures. When we look at the pictures in art galleries, we're supposed to absorb and delight in visual impressions. But when we look at the pictures in picture books, we're meant not just to do that but also to think about how they relate to the accompanying words and also to the pictures preceding and following them. In other words, we must consider not only their beauty but also how they contribute to our unfolding knowledge of the story.

In fact, *everything* in such pictures is less important a source of aesthetic delight than a source of information about a story. Their shape, their style, their composition are means of conveying information about how we're to respond to the story.

In the following sections, I look at some ways in which the pictures in picture books offer information about the stories they help to tell. So that you can consider the validity of my opinions, I've reproduced a few of the pictures I talk about. But only a few of them: Picture-book illustrations are property, and under copyright. Not only did I need permission to reproduce the ones you'll see here, but I had to pay for that permission. There are as many illustrations in this chapter as Longman and I could afford without having to greatly increase the amount you had to pay for this book. I apologize for not being able to include more pictures, and I encourage you to seek out the other books I refer to in libraries and bookstores.

EXPLORATION: As you work your way through this section, explore (or invite children to explore) how other picture books of your choice make use of the various ways in which pictures provide story information.

Format and First Impressions

Once we have experience in books and reading, visual information directs our response to the story in a picture book before we even open the book. Particular expectations arise from each of the physical qualities of a book: its size and its shape, even the kind of paper it's printed on.

We tend to associate the largest and smallest picture books with the youngest children. In the case of small ones, like Beatrix Potter's *Peter Rabbit,* that may be because smaller objects seem better suited to the small hands of young readers. In the case of the large ones, like Richard Scarry's *Best Word Book Ever,* it may be that we assume children lack the dexterity to manipulate smaller objects. Such books seem to be large for the same reason that the print in books for the least experienced of readers is large. What's interesting about these assumptions is how directly they contradict each other. That suggests how very much our understanding of these books depends on conventional assumptions, and how conventional and illogical those assumptions are.

Sometimes, though, the effect of a book's physical format on its meaning goes beyond convention: Particular physical qualities create real restraints. For instance, even narrow picture books, once they're opened, provide illustrators with a wide space to fill. But the human body is relatively tall and narrow, so illustrators are left with a lot of empty space after they draw their characters. They often fill the space by placing the characters in detailed settings. Arthur Yorinks and Richard Egielski's *Bravo, Minski* is almost twenty-two inches wide when opened. When Minski gives a demonstration of his singing, he appears in a panoramic scene containing him and more than twenty other people and a dog, each of whom seems to be about the same distance away from us and therefore to be about the same size. (See Figure 11.1.)

Because we see Minski as a member of a social group, we consider his effect on the group rather than understand him in terms of his own feelings or point of view. Because of their physical form, picture books tend to show characters in wide scenes seen from a distance, and they tend to demand less involvement with their characters than stories without pictures.

Covers.   As we glance at a book before reading it, the cover is the most significant source of our expectations for it. The picture on a cover or dust-jacket often evokes the essential quality of the story. For instance, Satomi Ichikawa's cover illustration for Patricia Lee Gauch's *Dance, Tanya* shows a young girl in a spotlight against an empty background, both her feet off the floor as she exuberantly swings a piece of cloth through the air: Everything is free, open, moving. In contrast, the cover of another book about dancing, Catherine Brighton's *Nijinsky,* consists of a series of constraining boxes, one of which contains a picture of the young Nijinsky manipulating a toy figure of a dancer, just as he himself is made to seem manipulated and constrained in the pictures throughout the book.

Inside a Book.   Once we get past a book's cover, other aspects of its design affect our understanding of it. We respond differently to books whose pictures have borders than we do to those that don't, to different sizes and kinds of type, to different placements and relationships of pictures and of words.

EXPLORATION: Consider (or invite children to consider) the effect of aspects of a book's design by imagining how the book would look with a

FIGURE 11.1 Illustration from *Bravo, Minski* by Arthur Yorinks, illustrated by Richard Egielski.

different design. How would you respond to, say, *Dance, Tanya* if the text were in 𝕺𝖑𝖉 𝕰𝖓𝖌𝖑𝖎𝖘𝖍 𝖙𝖞𝖕𝖊, or to *Where the Wild Things Are* if the words were printed over the surface of the pictures rather than in a white space underneath or beside them?

Borders are a particularly interesting example of the effect of design. Events seen through strictly defined boundaries imply detachment and objectivity, a fact that many illustrators of fantasy worlds use to advantage. The white borders in books like Chris Van Allsburg's *The Polar Express,* Dennis Nolan's *Dinosaur Dream,* or Mary Pope Osborne's *Moonhorse* add a quality of documentary truth to the fantastic events they depict. As in *Nijinsky,* illustrators also use the constraining quality of borders to suggest the tensions of intense activity.

Variations in borders suggest shifts in meaning. As Max gets into trouble in *Where the Wild Things Are,* we see his frenzy depicted in small pictures surrounded by a constraining border of white space; but as his imaginative freedom grows, the pictures get larger and the borders smaller. Steve Johnson's illustrations for Ann Mazer's *The Salamander Room* offer an even more complex set of variations, as borders form around various objects that stick out past the otherwise square blocks of pictures, thus visually replicating the gradual transformation of a square-angled bedroom into a free-form natural forest.

Mood and Atmosphere

If the words "I fall down the stairs" are said in anguish, the effect is painful, but if they're said with a giggle, we might laugh at them. The specific meaning depends not on the words themselves but on the tone of voice in which they are spoken. The mood of a picture is like the tone of a text. It's an overall quality that affects the meaning and the attitude we take toward it. Illustrators convey mood in a number of ways: through predominating hues, shades, and saturations of colors; through different predominating shapes; and through their choices of media.

Color.   *Hues* are classifications of colors, like "red" or "blue," that refer to different parts of the spectrum. Books in which specific hues predominate create different moods for two reasons. The first is that certain hues evoke real objects or settings in which the hues predominate. We see pictures in which greens predominate—in *The Salamander Room,* for instance—as restful because we associate green with peaceful forests. The second is that certain hues have conventionally come to signify certain emotions that have no actual relationship to them. Because of its traditional association with the Virgin Mary, for instance, pale blue suggests serenity. For those who know this association, a book like Marjorie Flack's and Kurt Wiese's *The Story About Ping,* in which blues predominate, evokes a serene mood. But someone who didn't know the association with Mary but was familiar with the kind of music called "the blues" might see the same pictures as sad.

Shades are degrees of brightness and darkness—for instance, light or dark red. We tend to identify darker shades with gloomier subjects, lighter ones with happier subjects. A dark book like *Nijinsky* is somber in mood, while the pastel tones of *Dance, Tanya* seem cheerful.

Saturation is the relative intensity of colors—the degree to which they have been mixed with white. More saturated colors seem more vibrant, less saturated ones more gentle. The vibrant colors of Marcia Brown's *Shadow* are highly assertive, while the less intense tones of her *Cinderella* are quietly elegant; the difference implies her understanding of the mood of two different stories.

Illustrators can also convey meaning by *avoiding* predominating effects. Books that use patches of unrelated colors in shocking combinations share a quality of energy and excitement, whereas more subtle blends of related hues or shades express calm. An illustrator can change the mood within a book by moving from one effect to the other. When we first see Max in his bedroom in *Where the Wild Things Are,* his upset is conveyed by the discordant patches of purple bed and pink bedspread. When he returns to the bedroom at the end of the book, the bed has become a shade of pink, and the more harmonious colors reflect Max's peaceful feeling.

Black and White.   Perhaps because of our experience of newspaper photographs and documentary films, pictures in black and white tend to imply seriousness and authenticity. Illustrators often use this quality to underpin the reality of fantasy situations, as in Van Allsburg's black and white depiction of wallpaper coming to life in *The Mysteries of Harris Burdick.* (See Figure 11.2.)

Shape and Line.   We associate rounded shapes with softness and yielding, angular ones with rigidity and orderliness; and we tend to see uncompleted lines as unstable and energetic, while lines that enclose space seem more stable and restful. When one of these possibilities predominates in a book, there's a strong effect on its mood. The story of urban blight told in Virginia Lee Burton's *The Little House* never seems particularly sad because nothing in the book, not even the angular apartment buildings, is actually straight-edged—every line in this comforting book is slightly rounded. On the other hand, the incomplete lines in Charles Keeping's spiky drawings make them seem filled with nervous energy. Even when Keeping depicts a corpse, in his version of Alfred Noyes's *The Highwayman,* the explosive lines make the picture disturbingly energetic. (See Figure 11.3.)

Media.   As Gombrich says in "Standards of Truth," "The image cannot give us more information than the medium can carry" (248). Consequently, illustrators' choices of medium affect the meanings of the stories they help to tell. For instance, black lines on white paper can't convey the moods of color. Block prints can reveal texture only with difficulty. Collage inhibits the creation of depth. Watercolor in its translucency creates the impression of light more readily than tempera does. Fur-

FIGURE 11.2 "Third Floor Bedroom," illustration from *The Mysteries of Harris Burdick* by Chris Van Allsburg.

thermore, many media are associated with specific ideas or emotions: We tend to see woodcuts as simple and folk-like, oil paintings as richly elegant. The more we know about media and the conventional uses of them, the richer will be our experience of picture books.

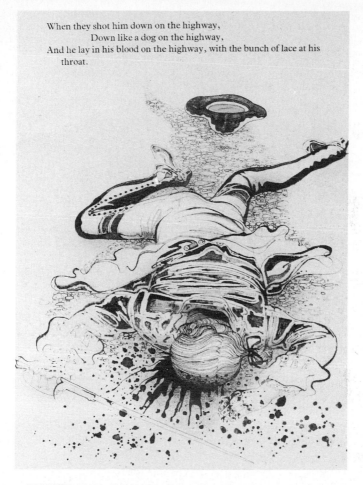

When they shot him down on the highway,
    Down like a dog on the highway,
And he lay in his blood on the highway, with the bunch of lace at his
    throat.

FIGURE 11.3 Illustration from *The Highwayman* by Alfred
Noyes and Charles Keeping.

SOURCE: Copyright © Oxford University Press. Reprinted by permission of
Oxford University Press.

EXPLORATION: Choose (or invite children to choose) a picture book and
determine what mood its pictures convey. What qualities of these pictures
help to convey that mood and how?

Style

Unlike hue or media, *style* isn't a separable quality. It's the effect of all the aspects
of a work considered together, the way in which an illustration or text seems distinct or even unique. Style develops from the various choices an artist makes, about
both subject and means of presentation. Beatrix Potter's style, for instance, depends

They set out toward the prince's castle with the glass coffin on their shoulders. But they had not gone far when they stumbled and dropped it.

FIGURE 11.4   Illustration from *The Happy-Ever-After Book* by Jack Kent.

SOURCE: Copyright © 1976 by Jack Kent. Reprinted by permission of Random House, Inc.

not just on her use of gently unsaturated watercolors but also on the fact that she depicts small animals in human situations. A book in soft watercolors about a talking elephant or rutabaga would seem as unlike Potter as would a book about a talking rabbit done in saturated reds and oranges.

The styles of picture books can communicate meanings by drawing upon stylistic conventions that already have connotations. For instance, even children with little literary experience have learned to expect pictures in the style of *cartooning*—exaggerated *caricatures*—to be funny. So we expect humor in Jack Kent's cartoon depictions of fairy tales like "Snow White" and "Cinderella" in his *Happy-Ever-After Book* even before we look closely enough at the pictures to find the humorous details; and we expect anything but humor from the more representational pictures for the same tales by illustrators like Trina Schart Hyman or Marcia Brown. (See Figure 11.4.)

Reminders of existing styles of art also provide connotations. The theoretically dangerous tale of how a fox stalks a chicken in Pat Hutchins's *Rosie's Walk* becomes humorous because the style of the book evokes the charm of folk art, while the precise black-and-white drawings in Van Allsburg's *Garden of Abdul Gasazi* make an essentially comic tale seem broodingly serious by evoking the style of documentary photographs.

In the sections that follow, I consider several types of artistic styles that illustrators use.

Surrealism. Browne's pictures for Annalena McAfee's *The Visitors Who Came to Stay* are in the surrealistic style of artists like Salvador Dali and René Magritte. They depict unrealistic situations in a highly representational way that makes the impossible seem strangely possible. The book is filled with surrealistic visual puns. As Katy greets her father's visitors, an image of a train in a picture on the wall puffs real smoke that reaches beyond its frame; a bottle and a carrot stand on a shelf beside a half-bottle/half-carrot; and other shelves contain versions of the paintings of Magritte, come to life. (See Figure 11.5.) These visual puns not only relate to the theme of practical jokes running through the text but also create an eerie atmosphere that, ironically, undermines Katy's insistence that everything is and must remain ordinary.

Impressionism. Whereas surrealism evokes strangeness, *impressionism* tends to be dreamy and romantic. As a result, Sendak's depictions of lush green landscapes in *Mr. Rabbit and the Lovely Present*, reminiscent of the paintings of the impressionist Claude Monet, alter the effect of Charlotte Zolotow's jaunty, staccato text about a little girl seeking help from a giant rabbit in choosing a gift for her mother. In this case, the visual style clearly operates in ironic counterpoint to a text rather than in support of it.

National Styles. Many of the stories in picture books are versions of tales from countries around the world. Illustrators often convey the special atmosphere of these tales by working in styles that are evocative of their places of origin. Barbara Cooney's characters in her version of a Greek legend, *Demeter and Persephone*, look like those painted on ancient Greek vases. Gail Haley's pictures in her version of an English legend, *The Green Man*, look like the painting on signboards for English inns. Blair Lent's pictures for the Chinese story *Tikki Tikki Tembo*, by Arlene Mosel, are reminiscent of old Chinese watercolors; and Ed Young's pictures for his version of the Chinese "Red Riding Hood" story *Lon Po Po* make use of the brushstroke and bordering techniques of ancient Chinese panel art. Gerald McDermott borrows the style of the wall paintings found in the kivas, or sacred places, of the Pueblos for his retelling of a Pueblo story in *Arrow to the Sun*, and Elizabeth Cleaver's pictures for William Toye's *The Mountain Goats of Temlaham* include ceremonial objects in the visual style of the Tsimshian people who originally told this story.

Styles of Individual Artists. Illustrators sometimes even borrow the styles of particular artists. In his various books of magical illusion, Mitsumasa Anno uses techniques of the graphic artist M. C. Escher; in *Stevie*, John Steptoe uses the bright colors and heavy black lines of the French painter Georges Rouault, as does David Diaz in his illustrations for Eve Bunting's *Smoky Night;* and in his versions of fairy tales like Perrault's "Cinderella," Errol Le Cain evokes the elegantly decadent style of the British illustrator Aubrey Beardsley.

FIGURE 11.5   Illustration from *The Visitors Who Came to Stay* by Annalena McAfee and Anthony Browne.

EXPLORATION: Find pictures of works in the original styles or by the original artist that any of the books mentioned in this section refer to. Compare (or invite children compare) the original with the illustrations in the picture book, and explore the significance of similarities and differences.

The Meanings of Borrowed Styles. When styles are borrowed, they rarely mean to the borrower what they meant to those who created them. Because we see the various styles of art through the filter of history, we interpret them in terms of our own understanding of their times and their makers. For Monet and other impressionists, for instance, the style implied a concern with transient appearances, with the way things momentarily look in particular circumstances of light and shade. But for many people nowadays, impressionist works evoke a more specific meaning: they suggest Monet and his time. They show a preindustrial world of peaceful rural settings that we tend to feel nostalgic about. Thus, when Sendak uses the impressionist style in Zolotow's *Mr. Rabbit and the Lovely Present,* it conveys pastoral calm as much as it does a concern for light and shadow.

The Meanings of Visual Objects

While overall qualities like design and style help convey the mood and meaning of a story, most of the information that pictures provide comes from the specific objects they depict. These objects become meaningful through the contexts they evoke, which allow us to relate them to our knowledge and experience of life, literature, and visual art. It's our contextual knowledge that allows us to look at a picture, recognize part of it as a representation of something familiar, and say, "This is a chair," or "This is a Chippendale chair," or even "This is the kind of chair van Gogh shows in his picture of his room at Arles." Our familiarity with a context leads us to focus on specific details—to give them more *weight* in our interpretation of a picture. There are two important ways in which visual objects in pictures develop weight: through symbolism and through codes.

Symbols. Visual symbolism is the use of physical objects to represent abstract ideas. When a shadow of a cross appears on the forehead of a boy in Charles Keeping's *Through the Window,* for example, those familiar with Christian imagery will understand the boy's situation differently than those who aren't acquainted with such images.

EXPLORATION: The versions of the Grimms' tale "Snow White" illustrated by Nancy Ekholm Burkert and Trina Schart Hyman depict many traditional symbols. Look up (or invite children to look up) the traditional meanings of various objects these books depict: apples, black cats, holly, spiders, bats, dragons, mistletoe, the tarot card for the number thirteen. Consider what meanings they add to the story.

Freudian Symbols. As I suggest in chapter 9, both Freudian and Jungian psychoanalysts invest specific visual images with a deeper unconscious content. Presumably, all products of the human mind can be read for their unconscious content, so

FIGURE 11.6   Illustration from *George Shrinks* by William Joyce.

SOURCE: Copyright © 1985 by William Joyce. Reprinted by permission of HarperCollins Publishers.

it's not difficult to find dark Jungian shadows or pointed Freudian phallic objects in picture books. In William Joyce's *George Shrinks,* for instance, George shoots off a toy cannon strategically placed in front of his lower torso. (See Figure 11.6.)

Not all Freudian imagery is so obvious, but the surprise of finding these subtle implications in apparently innocent pictures can be a source of pleasure (or discomfort) for many sophisticated and unsophisticated readers. S. H. Saelig's moody illustrations for Osborne's *Moonhorse* or Ian Wallace's mysterious ones for Tim Wynne-Jones's *Architect of the Moon* become far more interesting for those who have read Freud's *The Interpretation of Dreams.*

Codes and Gestures.   Some of the more obvious narrative implications of pictures depend not on specific symbols but on basic cultural *codes*—signs that we tend to take for granted. Because we identify dark with evil and light with goodness, many picture books show evil characters in the shadows and good ones in the sunlight. Similarly, we associate peace and joy with green spaces, and relatively empty, boxlike spaces like Max's bedroom in *Where the Wild Things Are* or Brian's in *The Salamander Room* with sterility. Cultural assumptions also enable us to derive information from the gestures and postures of characters. We understand that upturned heads mean happiness, slumped heads despair, and so on. We also have ideas about the connections between physical appearance and emotions. We know we should dislike the two brothers in Hyman's illustrations in Barbara Rogasky's *The Water of Life* because one of them has the sort of narrow, moustached face we associate with devilishness, and the other the thick-necked stolidity we associate with stupidity. Picture books both depend on and teach such conventional assumptions: They provide young viewers with ideas and attitudes about matters such as beauty and ugliness, cleanliness and filth, vice and virtue.

Pictorial Dynamics

While the meaning of the objects in pictures depends in part on the external contexts through which we perceive them, much of their significance comes from within a picture itself, particularly from the ways in which the objects relate to one another—the *pictorial dynamics*. There are two possible forms of relationships: those between objects on the two-dimensional plane of the picture's surface, and those between objects in the three-dimensional space the picture implies.

Two-Dimensional Effects.

Shapes.   Square shapes are rigid, round ones accommodating. So characters placed inside constricting boxes seem oppressed, and the rounded shape of Peter Rabbit's body escapes constriction as he moves past a severe rectangular picket on his way into Mr. McGregor's garden.

Certain shapes can also make us pay attention to other shapes. Throughout McDermott's *Arrow to the Sun,* the hero's stylized, pointerlike hand points toward the focus of the action throughout the book.

Size.   Larger figures tend to have more weight than smaller ones. We realize how threatened Katy feels by the fake monster's hand that Sean wears in *The Visitors Who Came to Stay* because the perspective of the picture puts the hand in the foreground and her in the background, making the hand appear much larger than she is. But other qualities can give smaller objects more importance: We pay attention to Sendak's little Max among the big Wild Things because there's only one of him and many of them.

The size of characters in relation to their background may imply relationships between character and environment. Characters depicted as small shapes surrounded by forests or large empty rooms seem threatened or lost. If we enlarged the figure of a character so that it filled the space, the same figure would seem much less bleak.

Location and Composition.   The location of an object on the picture plane can give it more or less emphasis. A figure at the center of a picture, like the little house throughout Burton's book, tends to have more weight than those on the sides. This often becomes a problem for illustrators, who wish to attract our attention to figures other than those in the center; they must do so by making use of one or more of the other techniques outlined here.

Honeybunch went rampaging all over Heaven. She was so excited that she rolled in the clouds, kicking and carrying on, scattering angels in every direction.

"That sure is one jumpy mule," God said. Some of his angels tried to catch Honeybunch, but they couldn't even get near her. So God said to St. Peter: "All right, go get Jake. Tell him to come and catch his crazy mule."

FIGURE 11.7   Illustration from *Jake and Honeybunch Go to Heaven* by Margot Zemach.

SOURCE: Copyright © 1982 by Margot Zemach. Reprinted by permission of Farrar, Straus & Giroux, Inc.

EXPLORATION: Consider (or invite children to consider) why our attention is attracted to a certain object and not another. For instance, why might we focus on the figure of God at the edge of the picture of the mule that causes havoc in *Jake and Honeybunch Go to Heaven* (Figure 11.7) rather than to the woman in the center of the picture? Why might our attention be directed to Minski in the picture of him singing in Milan in *Bravo, Minski* (Figure 11.1), rather than to the woman near the center?

The layout of the objects in a picture in relation to one another implies invisible shapes: circles, rectangles, squares, or triangles that form the picture's composition. Since these patterns create order and balance, a disruption of them implies disorder. Because the pictures represent the tension in stories, they rarely have balanced compositions: Consider the many lines and shapes moving discordantly in different directions in the pictures of the mule causing disruption in *Jake and Honeybunch Go to Heaven*. The main exception is often the final picture in a book, depicting the order of a happy ending.

Figure and Ground.   Objects in a field of other objects stand out less than isolated ones, and figures sharply isolated from their background stand out more than those that blend in. This is why the important characters in illustrations, unlike the less important ones, are often outlined in black. The dog at the center of the picture of

Mama in the arbor in Sendak's *Outside Over There* lacks outlines, for instance, while Mama has them. We also pay more attention in *Dance, Tanya* to Tanya posed alone against a ground of blue carpet than we do to the other members of her family all in a group together. As happens in *Dance, Tanya,* illustrators often show characters against blank grounds when they wish us to focus on the emotional meaning of the figures' gestures and expressions, and against fuller grounds when what's important is the effect of their environment on them.

Left to Right and Top to Bottom. Probably because we expect heavier objects to sink, the bottom of a picture usually suggests more weight than the top. Thus, we become uncomfortable when heavier figures appear in the top half of a picture, a fact that allows many illustrators to convey the sensation of characters, like Jake and Honeybunch, flying. Meanwhile, pictures whose bottom halves are less busy than their top halves often express distress.

We tend to read pictures from left to right, as we who use English have learned to read print. Mercedes Gaffron suggests that pictures contain a *glance curve*—that we look at the figures on the lower left first, and then move our eye in a curve to the upper right. Because we often identify with the first figure we see, the main characters in many picture-book stories appear in illustrations on the lower left, and the characters they struggle with on the upper right. A typical example is the picture of Katy meeting her visitors for the first time in *The Visitors Who Came to Stay* (Figure 11.5); Katy's father in the upper right greets the visitors as Katy watches from the lower left. In *The Salamander Room,* it's often not Brian who appears at the lower left, but the salamander: Perhaps the pictures imply a different version of the story than the text tells, this one from the salamander's point of view.

Color. As with the overall effects of predominating colors, the colors of specific objects provide information about those objects. The mere fact that objects are in colors that stand out gives them weight. We focus on one red object in a field of green, or on bright objects like the children in lighted nightclothes in the dark bedroom depicted in Brighton's *Nijinsky.*

Illustrators can also imply relationships between objects of the same or similar colors. In Hyman's illustrations for *The Water of Life,* a dwarf's red hat and green garments reflect the red and green worn by two evil brothers and imply a mysterious connection those brothers themselves ignore. Sendak implies a connection between the moon and Max's wild dance in *Where the Wild Things Are* by making the moon and Max the only white objects in the pictures.

Three-Dimensional Effects. Most picture-book illustrations are in some form of representational perspective that implies an imaginary three-dimensional space existing on the other side of the surface of the paper. Thus, as well as being shapes that form patterns on the surface of a picture, the figures that illustrators depict have relationships within this imaginary space. These relationships also contribute to the meaning of a picture.

FIGURE 11.8 Illustration from *Nijinsky* by Catherine Brighton.

SOURCE: Copyright © 1989 by Catherine Brighton. Used by permission of Doubleday, a division of Bantam Doubleday Dell Publishing Group, Inc.

Perspective. The diagonal lines that create the sense of depth in perspective drawing act like arrows focusing our attention on the objects they lead toward. By using these lines, illustrators can give greater visual weight to small figures. For instance, in *The Visitors Who Came to Stay,* Anthony Browne uses the perspective lines created by railway tracks to draw attention to the small patch of blue sky seen through a tunnel on an otherwise cloudy day as Katy waits for the train.

Point of View. We understand events differently when we see them from different points of view. Characters who are seen from below look large and isolated from their backgrounds—we see them against empty skies or ceilings—and seem to be alone and in control of their situations, as is the figure of God throughout *Jake and Honeybunch Go to Heaven.* But when the young dancer falls from a chair in *Nijinsky,* we look down on him from above, falling past a mirror and over a visibly hard, bare floor; and that increases the sense of disorder in the picture—the dancer seems trapped by the background. (See Figure 11.8.) Earlier in the book, however, a picture of the three Nijinsky children seen from above as they sleep on the grass seems comfortingly secure: The background envelops rather than constricts them.

Focus. As in movies, variation in focus also affects the way we respond to a scene. *Long shots,* which show characters surrounded by environment, like most of the pictures in *The Little House,* emphasize the figures' relationship with places and other people, their social situation. *Close-ups* of characters' faces tend to make us focus on private feelings. But as I suggested earlier in exploring the shape of picture books, most of the illustrations in picture books are *middle-distance shots,* showing the characters' entire bodies but within settings, much as we see actors onstage in the theater; the effect is a balance between intimacy and distance.

Overlap. In perspective drawings, the spaces that depictions of objects occupy on the page interfere with or overlap each other. Artists can use overlapping to suggest the relationships of the objects they depict. For instance, Katy's feeling of isolation from her visitors as they eat breakfast is amplified by the fact that her face is overlapped and confined by cereal boxes and condiment bottles. Earlier, however, her attachment to her father is revealed by the way her figure overlaps his as they wait for the train.

Light Sources and Shadows. The light implied by pictures may come from sources both inside and outside the pictures. Like the bright lamps often seen in *Nijinsky,* an actual light source depicted in a picture draws attention both to itself and to what it casts light on. For example, each of the lamps in the scene of a theoretically happy family evening nevertheless lights only one of the Nijinsky children, and so implies their isolation from one another. The light that the shines onto Brian's face from an unseen but implied sun as he peers through a window in *The Salamander Room* emphasizes the way in which the window itself, its borders jutting out from the rest of the picture like a jet taking off, offers an opening into the bright and free world outside. An implied light from the rear of a picture places characters in front of it in shadow, and Hyman takes advantage of this to place the evil brothers in shadow throughout *The Water of Life* (Figure 11.9); but when the good brother first meets the dwarf, the light comes from the front and illuminates his face (Figure 11.10).

We expect light to fall from above, and therefore variations from this convention, like those Van Allsburg uses throughout *The Polar Express,* create an atmosphere of strange mystery.

Blocking. The characters in a picture book often form what directors call "stage pictures": They are "blocked"—that is, given positions in relation to each other that imply their social or emotional relationships. In fact, the illustrations in picture books are often much like stage pictures: The characters leave the side of a table closest to us empty so we can see their faces, the central character is often at the apex of a triangle in relation to less-important characters, and the characters overlap each other when the overlapping is meaningful. One of the reasons that picture books seem so capable of telling stories is our usually unconscious assumption that all their characters' positions and gestures do in fact convey information about the events they are taking part in—just as good staging does in the theater.

FIGURE 11.9 Illustration from *The Water of Life.*

SOURCE: Copyright © 1986 by Trina Schart Hyman. Reprinted from *The Water of Life* by permission of Holiday House.

Movement and Time in Pictures

Since stories are about movements and changes, they necessarily take place in time. But a picture is fixed, and can show only one moment separated from the flow of time. How then can illustrations imply the passage of time necessary to depict actions and tell stories? Several conventions allow illustrators to suggest movement.

FIGURE 11.10   Illustration from *The Water of Life*.

Incomplete Actions.   An illustrator can suggest activity by choosing to depict a moment when an action isn't complete, thus forcing viewers to imagine its completion. For instance, walking involves moments when the feet are on the floor and moments when they are off it; but since feet on the floor seem to be at rest, an illustrator wishing to depict a character walking would have to show one foot off the ground.

FIGURE 11.11 Illustration from *The Tale of Peter Rabbit* by Beatrix Potter.

SOURCE: Copyright © Frederick Warne & Co., 1902, 1987. Reproduced by permission of Frederick Warne & Co.

Linear Continuance. We tend to complete the lines in pictures by imagining them to extend beyond their depicted length. So when Minski invents the rocket in *Bravo, Minski,* we mentally complete the lines that depict the rocket's flight and so imagine it moving upward. The "action lines" used by cartoonists create a similar effect—by echoing the line of an arm or a foot three or four times, these lines invite us to fill the space in between and imagine a continuous movement. Likewise, many lines radiating out from a central point imply explosive activity.

Distortion. Certain forms of distortion suggest movement. When Peter Rabbit runs from Mr. McGregor, he leans forward at an impossible angle with his head shaped like a bullet; the distorted shape implies his speed. (See Figure 11.11.)

Left-to-Right Movement. I said earlier that people tend to look at pictures from left to right. As a result, we assume that time passes from left to right—that what happens on the left of a picture happens *before* what happens on the right. When Minski tests his rocket, he stands at the left still holding a lighted match even though the rocket in the middle has already taken off; directly beneath it Minski's father still holds his ears, but by the time our eyes move to the right of the picture the noise of the explosion is over and a group of figures with uncovered ears watches the rocket rise.

Because we assume that time passes from left to right, we assume that characters (and objects like Minski's rocket) are in motion when they point toward the

FIGURE 11.12   Illustration from *Dance, Tanya* by Patricia Lee Gauch.

right. And because we tend to feel uncomfortable when characters in motion face toward the left, we assume that they're moving with difficulty. As a result, Jake and Honeybunch always move toward the right; the few times we see Honeybunch pointed to the left, the text tells us she's at rest.

Continuous Narrative.   Picture books often use what Joseph Schwarcz calls *continuous narrative;* they show the same character in a number of different poses within the same picture. We are to assume that each of the poses represents one moment out of a series of connected actions, moving in time from left to right. For instance, Satomi Ichikawa uses continuous narrative to show Tanya dancing. (See Figure 11.12.)

Context.   The most obvious way in which illustrators can convey the passage of time is simply by counting on our knowledge that a picture is meant to show part of a story. When we understand that, we tend to explore the picture for information about what it *doesn't* actually show: We ask what happened to lead up to the situation and what might be the result of it. While any picture provides details that demand explanation, those in picture books are deliberately designed to imply the passage of time by making us ask questions about causes and effects.

The Context of Other Pictures.   I've described how one picture conveys movement. But picture books contain a sequence of pictures, and as we move from one to the next, we have to imagine what might have happened to account for the change we see between one picture and the next one. Of course, the words of a text often give us the details about what happens between pictures; but once we've developed the strategy of looking for these connections, we can make them even when there are no words. It's this skill that illustrators depend on when they produce *wordless* picture books—ones that imply stories just by providing a sequence of connected pictures.

EXPLORATION: Consider (or have children consider) the extent to which a wordless book depends on your possession of this skill. Take a wordless book such as Claude Ponti's *Adele's Album,* Raymond Briggs's *The Snowman,* or Pat Hutchins's *Changes, Changes* and consider the difference between what you actually see and what you guess happens in between the pictures.

STORYTELLING IN WORDS AND PICTURES

The most obvious context that makes the illustrations in picture books meaningful is the words that accompany them. We can totally change the meaning of a picture simply by putting it in the context of different words. For instance, the picture of Nijinsky falling from a chair (Figure 11.8) would be different if the text said, "Suddenly everything in the room began to float upward, including the boy," and different again if the text said, "The boy fled in terror as his reflection in the mirror suddenly exploded through the glass and materialized in the room." As these examples reveal, words draw our attention to specific details of pictures and cause us to interpret them in specific ways.

At the same time, as I've suggested throughout this chapter, the pictures focus our attention on specific aspects of the words and cause us to interpret them in specific ways. As a result, a picture book contains at least three stories: the one told by the words, the one implied by the pictures, and the one that results from the combination of the other two.

EXPLORATION: Explore the extent to which this statement is true by separating the words in a picture book from the pictures, or vice versa. Respond (or invite children to respond) to a text without seeing the pictures; then reread it *with* the pictures and comment on the difference. Or respond to the pictures in a book without reading the words; then look at the pictures while reading the words and comment on the difference. How was the story different without either the words or the pictures?

What do these differences tell you about the specific contributions that words and pictures make to picture-book storytelling?

In some of the most interesting picture books, the third story, the one told by the words and pictures together, emerges from the contradictions between the other two stories. Such books take advantage of the essential doubleness of the form by using it for ironic purposes.

For instance, Nigel Gray's text for *A Country Far Away* is the words of a child describing an ordinary day in his life, but Philippe Dupasquier's pictures provide an ironic counterpoint by revealing that the words are actually being spoken by two different boys at the same time, each unconscious of the other. There are two different sets of illustrations, one above the text and one below. While both accurately illustrate the text, one set depicts a suburban child surrounded by the objects of affluence, the other an African in a tribal village. The result is an ironic confrontation of different life-styles. More subtly, the text of *Nijinsky* never suggests what the pictures constantly show us—that even in moments of triumph the young dancer remains sad, that even the flowers and toys thrown at him by happy audiences look like and must seem to him like heavy weapons.

EXPLORATION: Choose (or invite children to choose) any picture book, and explore whether the difference between the information provided by the words and the information provided by the pictures has ironic implications.

As we shift our attention between the pictures and the text, we must shift between different ways of thinking. The words of a good story are suspenseful; they force us to ask, "And then what happened?" But a good picture is attractive; it forces us to stop and look and absorb its details. As a result, the developing action of the plot is regularly interrupted by our perusals of the pictures.

Furthermore, I suspect that as we first experience a new picture book, many of us look at each of the pictures more than once. Because pictures are attractive, we probably at least glance at the picture on each double-page spread first, before we read the text it illustrates. Then, during or after reading the text, we're likely to look at it again, perhaps more closely, to confirm the presence of details the text has invited us to focus on. Our attention then moves constantly between pictures and words, and each distracts us from the other.

In some picture books, it's clear that little thought has been given to these matters: Our stopping to examine the pictures makes the text seem choppy. But in more carefully constructed books, this back-and-forth movement becomes a strength rather than a liability. The text is divided in such a way that the pauses in the story caused by the presence of illustrations adds to the suspense. We desperately want to turn the page and find out what happens next, but we also want to stop where we are and pay close attention to a picture. The characteristic rhythm of picture books consists of a pattern of such delays counterpointing and contributing to the suspense of the plot.

EXPLORATION: Consider (or have children consider) whether the way the text is divided in a picture book adds to or interferes with the suspense.

While the mere presence of pictures changes the shape of a story by breaking it up in the way I've just described, the pictures always depict something—and that changes the story even more. What the pictures depict takes place in only one instant; and even the simplest actions occur over many instants. As a result, an illustrator must choose which moment to show out of the many possible ones described in even the briefest text: a picture accompanying the words "John took a step" could show us an infinite number of different instants in which a foot rises from the ground and then sinks again. As I've suggested, the moments chosen imply what happens before and after them; but the specific moment depicted takes on particular significance, and strongly influences the way we understand a story. For instance, we would see the story as less gloomy if Brighton had chosen to depict Nijinsky perched on top of the pile of chairs, an action also included in the text accompanying the picture of him falling.

EXPLORATION: Choose one picture from any picture book. Consider (or invite children to consider) the way in which the specific moment chosen influences your response to the story. Does it create a particular emphasis?

PICTURE BOOKS AS PUZZLES

Throughout this chapter, I've assumed that picture books offer the pleasure of stories. But some don't tell stories, and don't even seem to be designed primarily to give pleasure: In theory, at least, the purpose of alphabet books and number books is to convey information. But I wonder if that theory is accurate: Is that their purpose, and if so, do they do what they promise?

EXPLORATION: What information do alphabet or number books convey, and how do they do so?

People usually assume that the purpose of alphabet books is to teach children the letters of the alphabet. Presumably, they see the picture of an apple, name it, and thus learn that the accompanying symbol "A" represents the sound that begins the word "apple." The trouble with this theory is its assumption that visual symbols relate directly to specific words. Unfortunately, they don't. One child might look at the apple and accurately name it "fruit," and another child might accurately label the same picture "Golden Delicious." In fact, rather than using the visual information to help us understand the verbal, most of us treat alphabet books in the opposite way: We use our previous knowledge of the letter as a way of identifying the right word to describe the object. If the apple appears on the A page, then it's an apple; if it appears on the F page, it's a fruit.

The implication of this is that alphabet books are not especially educational: We have to know what they're supposed to be teaching before we can make use of them. Instead, they are a form of puzzle, and pleasurable (and even instructive) for that reason. The same is true of number books. If we already know our numbers, we can have fun counting up the objects in the picture to see if they match that number.

Many illustrators know that such books are enjoyable puzzles, and they create pictures that encourage readers to indulge in this sort of pleasure. For instance, in addition to the main animal depicted on each page of Graeme Base's *Animalia,* there are many other objects that begin with the same letter; we can play the game of finding their names.

The fact that even these most practical kinds of picture books offers the pleasure of puzzle solving is revealing. In an important sense, all picture books are puzzles. The details of pictures invite our attention to their implications. The unmoving pictures require us to solve the puzzle of what actions and motions they represent. The pictures in wordless books require us to solve the puzzle of what story they imply. In books with text, the words and pictures together tell different stories that require us to solve the puzzle of how to connect them. The pleasure of picture books is not just in the stories they tell but in the game of figuring out what those stories are.

WORKS CITED

Anno, Mitsumasa. *Topsy-Turvies: Pictures to Stretch the Imagination.* New York: Weatherhill, 1970.

Base, Graeme. *Animalia.* Toronto: Irwin, 1987.

Briggs, Raymond. *The Snowman.* London: Hamish Hamilton, 1978.

Brighton, Catherine. *Nijinsky.* New York: Doubleday, 1989.

Brown, Marcia. *Cinderella.* New York: Scribner's, 1954.

———. *Shadow.* New York: Macmillan, 1982.

Bunting, Eve. *Smoky Night.* Illus. David Diaz. San Diego, New York, and London: Harcourt Brace, 1994.

Burton, Virginia Lee. *The Little House.* Boston: Houghton Mifflin, 1942.

Cooney, Barbara. *Demeter and Persephone.* New York: Doubleday, 1972.

Danto, Arthur. "The Artworld." *The Philosophy of the Visual Arts.* Ed. P. Alperson. New York and Oxford: Oxford University Press, 1992. 426–433.

Deregowski, Jan B. "Illusion and Culture." *Illusion in Nature and Art.* Ed. R. L. Gregory and E. H. Gombrich. London: Duckworth, 1973. 161–189.

Flack, Marjorie. *The Story About Ping.* Illus. Kurt Wiese. New York: Viking, 1933.

Freud, Sigmund. *The Interpretation of Dreams.* Trans. James Strachey. London: Penguin, 1976.

Gaffron, Mercedes. "Right and Left in Pictures." *Art Quarterly* 13 (1950): 312–331.

Gauch, Patricia Lee. *Dance, Tanya.* Illus. Satomi Ichikawa. New York: Philomel, 1989.

Goldsmith, Evelyn. *Research into Illustration: An Approach and a Review.* Cambridge: Cambridge UP, 1984.

Gombrich, E. H. *Art and Illusion: A Study in the Psychology of Pictorial Representation.* New York: Pantheon, 1961.

———. "Standards of Truth: The Arrested Image and the Moving Eye." *Critical Inquiry* 11 (Winter 1980): 237–273.

———. "The Visual Image." *Scientific American* 227 (September 1972): 82–94.

Gray, Nigel. *A Country Far Away*. Illus. Philippe Dupasquier. New York: Orchard, 1989.

Grimm, Jacob and Wilhelm. *Snow White and the Seven Dwarfs*. Illus. Nancy Ekholm Burkert. New York: Farrar, Straus & Giroux, 1972.

———. *Snow White*. Illus. Trina Schart Hyman. Boston: Atlantic-Little, Brown, 1974.

Haley, Gail E. *The Green Man*. New York: Scribner's, 1979.

Hutchins, Pat. *Changes, Changes*. New York: Macmillan, 1971.

———. *Rosie's Walk*. New York: Macmillan, 1968.

Joyce, William. *George Shrinks*. New York: Harper & Row, 1985.

Keeping, Charles. *Through the Window*. London: Oxford UP, 1970.

Kent, Jack. *Happy-Ever-After Book*. New York: Random House, 1976.

Mazer, Anne. *The Salamander Room*. Illus. Steve Johnson. New York: Knopf, 1991.

McAfee, Annalena. *The Visitors Who Came to Stay*. Illus. Anthony Browne. London: Hamish Hamilton, 1984.

McDermott, Gerald. *Arrow to the Sun*. New York: Viking, 1974.

Mosel, Arlene. *Tikki Tikki Tembo*. Illus. Blair Lent. New York: Dutton, 1977.

Nolan, Dennis. *Dinosaur Dream*. New York: Macmillan, 1990.

Noyes, Alfred. *The Highwayman*. Illus. Charles Keeping. Oxford: Oxford UP, 1981.

Osborne, Mary Pope. *Moonhorse*. Illus. S. M. Saelig. New York: Knopf, 1991.

Perrault, Charles. *Cinderella*. Illus. Errol Le Cain. London: Faber and Faber, 1972.

Ponti, Claude. *Adele's Album*. New York: Dutton, 1988.

Potter, Beatrix. *The Tale of Peter Rabbit*. London: Frederick Warne, 1902.

Rogasky, Barbara. *The Water of Life*. Illus. Trina Schart Hyman. New York: Holiday House, 1986.

Scarry, Richard. *Best Word Book Ever*. Rev. ed. New York: Golden, 1980.

Schwarcz, Joseph H. *Ways of the Illustrator: Visual Communication in Children's Literature*. Chicago: American Library Association, 1982.

Sendak, Maurice. *Outside Over There*. New York: Harper & Row, 1981.

———. *Where the Wild Things Are*. New York: Harper & Row, 1963.

Steptoe, John. *Stevie*. New York: Harper & Row, 1969.

Toye, William. *The Mountain Goats of Temlaham*. Illus. Elizabeth Cleaver. Toronto: Oxford UP, 1969.

Van Allsburg, Chris. *The Garden of Abdul Gasazi*. Boston: Houghton Mifflin, 1979.

——— . *The Mysteries of Harris Burdick*. Boston: Houghton Mifflin, 1984.

——— . *The Polar Express*. Boston: Houghton Mifflin, 1985.

Wildsmith, Brian. *Brian Wildsmith's ABC*. London: Oxford UP, 1962.

Wynne-Jones, Tim. *Architect of the Moon*. Illus. Ian Wallace. Toronto: Groundwood, 1988.

Yorinks, Arthur. *Bravo, Minski*. Illus. Richard Egielski. New York: Farrar, Straus & Giroux, 1988.

Young, Ed. *Lon Po Po*. New York: Philomel, 1989.

Zemach, Margot. *Jake and Honeybunch Go to Heaven*. New York: Farrar, Straus & Giroux, 1982.

Zolotow, Charlotte. *Mr. Rabbit and the Lovely Present*. Illus. Maurice Sendak. New York: Harper & Row, 1962.

chapter **12**

Fairy Tales and Myths

UNIVERSALLY KNOWN TALES

For almost two decades, I've started my courses in children's literature by asking the students to tell me which fairy tales they know so well that they could tell them to a child without consulting a book. While individual suggestions vary, the students always end up agreeing on the same eight stories:

"Little Red Riding Hood"
"The Three Little Pigs"
"Goldilocks and the Three Bears"
"Hansel and Gretel"
"Jack and the Beanstalk"
"Snow White and the Seven Dwarfs"
"Sleeping Beauty"
"Cinderella"

Many of us know these same few fairy tales so well that we don't know *how* we know them—where we first heard them. We just seem to have always known them. People who produce cartoons and commercials assume that even the youngest children will have these stories in their repertoire, and will understand allusions to girls in red hoods or giants who say "Fee fie fo fum." A consideration of the history of these eight tales reveals much about their distinctive features and the unique place of fairy tales in children's literature.

EXPLORATION: What is your personal repertoire of fairy tales? List the fairy tales you recall well enough to tell from memory, without consulting a book. Is your list different from my students'? What might account for the similarities and differences?

THE HISTORY OF FAIRY TALES

Oral Stories, or Folktales

Versions of the eight tales listed above—indeed all the stories we call *fairy tales*—are now found in books intended primarily for children, but these stories were originally what folklorists call *folktales*. Some centuries ago, the stories circulated orally. People who couldn't read remembered them and told them to other people who remembered them and told them again. The fact that these tales had to be remembered without the aid of a written text meant that they had to have memorable features—features that, as I'll show later, survive in printed versions.

But other features also survive—features that disturb many adults, like the frightening violence with which wolves threaten Red Riding Hood and the three pigs, or the stereotyping of stepmothers and wolves as evil. Not only do the tales express the conventional assumptions of earlier times, but as I suggested in chapter 5, children in those earlier times weren't singled out as needing a different kind of story than adults; the original audience for oral tales would have included both children and adults, and so the tales defy current ideas of what is appropriately childlike.

EXPLORATION: Assuming that fairy tales preserve the outmoded values of an earlier time, are they suitable literature for children today? Consider (or invite children to consider) the degree to which fairy tales you know might be communicating attitudes we no longer consider appropriate. Is it appropriate for children to read them?

We're not sure where or how any of the folktales originated. Stories similar to "Cinderella" can be found in historical records from as far back as the seventh century, and from a variety of places around the world. It may be that initially just one inventive person created each of these stories; but the tales changed as they passed from one teller to another, so that the versions we know today have been influenced by many different people over a long period of time. It's still a quality of the fairy tales we tell today that they can be told in different ways and yet remain essentially the same story. While the Walt Disney movie version of "Cinderella" differs from the story as told by Charles Perrault, it's still recognizably the same story, and *Snow White in New York* is still "Snow White" even when Fiona French moves the events to another time and place and turns the seven dwarfs into seven jazz musicians.

Folktales are so prone to being told differently that folklorists identify them not as individual stories but as *types*—as similar plots that can be told in different ways.

A system of classification, developed by Antti Aarne and revised by Stith Thompson, divides the stories from oral sources around the world into 2,499 distinct types. For example, "Cinderella" is 510A, a subtype of type 510: the story of a girl mistreated by members of her family who receives magical help to get out of trouble and gain the attention of a marriageable male. Tales identifiable as belonging to type 510 include versions from North America and Japan as well as the European story many of us know. The girl can be abused by her mother or her stepmother, and she can be covered in ashes or disguised under animal skins. Her helper can be a fairy or a magical tree or a cow. She can reveal herself to her intended through a glass slipper or a magic ring.

EXPLORATION: Read (or have children read) some of the versions of type 510 included in *Cinderella: A Casebook,* edited by Alan Dundes. Why might they be identified as the same type of story? What do they have in common with one another?

From Oral Tale to Written Story

The tales came to be recorded in printed collections only when people in general stopped telling them orally. Before that, there was no reason to write them down, for the people who wanted to hear them already had access to them orally; and in any case, most of them couldn't read. Note how that continues to be true for young children—today's main audience for oral storytelling by parents and others. It seems that the ability to read tends to make people less likely to want to hear stories orally, and that includes both children learning to read now and those segments of the populace, both children and adults, who became literate back in the seventeenth century.

Why, then, did people who could read and write start recording these stories in print? To begin with, at least, it certainly wasn't a desire to provide reading experiences appropriate to children in particular. The first written records of the tales make it clear they weren't originally intended specifically for children—at least not children with the tastes and interests we usually assume modern children have. In a version of "Sleeping Beauty" recorded in Giambattista Basile's *Pentameron* in 1634, the prince so likes the looks of the sleeping princess that he climbs into bed with her and enjoys "the first fruits of love" (374). Then he deserts her, pregnant, but still sleeping. She doesn't wake up until one of the twins she has given birth to in her sleep gets hungry enough to suck from her finger the enchanted piece of flax that kept her sleeping.

The First Familiar Tales: Perrault's Versions

Recognizable versions of some of the tales we know first appeared in print in 1697, when Charles Perrault, a man of letters associated with the French court, published a book called *Histoires ou Contes du Temps Passé:* stories of past times. It contained eight tales, including versions of three named by my students: "Little Red Riding

Hood," "Cinderella," and a "Sleeping Beauty" in which the pregnancy occurs *after* the awakening.

EXPLORATION: Perrault's versions are recognizable but still different from most current versions of fairy tales. Read (or invite children to read) accurate translations of Perrault's tales such as those by Angela Carter, and consider what aspects of Perrault's versions surprise you.

When Perrault tells us that the Prince and Sleeping Beauty were married immediately after he awakens her, he then adds that they didn't sleep much that night because, for some reason or other, "the princess didn't seem to feel much like sleeping" (translation mine). For readers nowadays, ironic details like this suggest that Perrault is telling these stories not just for innocent children but also for knowing adults. But there were different ideas about the nature of childhood current in his time, and it seems more likely that he believed that children were, or ought to be, exactly this knowing. Perrault allows Little Red Riding Hood to go off into the woods without any warning of potential danger—not because her mother thinks there is none, but because she seems to take it for granted that a child capable of surviving in a dangerous world *should already know* about such things. So Little Red, who "didn't realize how dangerous it is to pay attention to wolves," and who later ingenuously accepts the wolf's invitation to take off her clothing and climb into bed with him, is justly rewarded for her ignorance. This is the way the story ends:

> "What big teeth you have, granny!"
> "They're to eat you with!" said the wolf.
> And he threw himself on Little Red Riding Hood and ate her up. (Translation mine)

And that's it. No being saved either in the nick of time or afterward; the girl is dead and remains so.

But Perrault does add a moral that emphasizes the dangers of ignorance: Those girls who are innocent enough to talk to strangers are the ones likely to be devoured by wolves. Furthermore, there are "some very mannerly and apparently tame wolves who follow young girls down the streets and even into their homes; and as everybody knows, alas, these sweet-talking, apparently harmless wolves are actually the most dangerous ones" (translation mine). This implies that young girls who *don't* know that lesson deserve to suffer from their ignorance. It seems likely that Perrault expected the youngsters in his audience to be just as conscious of the irony in his stories as the adults would be.

The Grimm Versions

The first edition of the next important collection of folktales, by the brothers Jacob and Wilhelm Grimm, appeared in Germany in 1812, and eventually included over two hundred tales. To begin with, it seems, Jacob and Wilhelm Grimm weren't interested in an audience of children. What later in the nineteenth century became Germany was then a number of duchies and princedoms, and the Grimms collected folktales with the political purpose of supporting unification by finding evidence of the basic linguistic and cultural oneness of the German people.

Unlike Perrault, then, whose interest in the tales was in their entertainment value, the Grimm brothers were scholars and pioneering folklorists. But while they made great claims for the authenticity of their tales, their methods wouldn't satisfy the more stringent demands of modern folklorists, who insist on recording stories exactly as told by oral informants. The Grimms accepted as authentic "folk" tales ones that they heard from literate middle-class sources, who claimed in turn to have heard them from less-literate peasants. As John Ellis shows, for instance, there's evidence that the version of "Little Red Riding Hood" the Grimms identified as authentically German came from a relative whose French background would have provided her with access to a printed text of Perrault's version.

Furthermore, while modern folklorists believe that tales should be recorded exactly as told by one informant, the Grimms thought they could uncover the most authentic version of a tale by combining the supposed best features of the various versions they heard. But in the process of adding to and deleting from the tales they heard, the Grimms gave preference to events and characterizations that suited their own middle-class, Christian values. For instance, the stepmothers in stories like "Hansel and Gretel" and "Snow White" as the Grimms originally recorded them were birth-mothers, an idea that seems to have disturbed the Grimms enough to disguise it. I find it still distresses students I tell about it today.

Despite their original scholarly intentions, the Grimms soon discovered that children could be a significant audience for these stories. The changes they made to the tales from edition to edition imply an attempt to meet the moral needs of children; and in 1825, they published a shorter edition of the tales clearly directed at a popular audience, particularly children. Included in that edition are versions of five of the eight tales my students know best: versions of "Little Red Riding Hood," "Sleeping Beauty," and "Cinderella" different from the ones Perrault told; and two stories first printed by the Grimms, "Snow White" and "Hansel and Gretel."

The Grimms' "Little Red Cap" shows that they or their informants had very different ideas about children than Perrault did. Before the little girl leaves for grandmother's house, her mother gives her many warnings: "Walk properly like a good little girl, and don't leave the path or you'll fall down and break the bottle [of wine that Red Cap is to take to grandmother] and there won't be anything for grandmother. And when you get to her house, don't forget to say good morning, and don't go looking in all the corners" (Manheim 99). Unlike Perrault's mother, this mother believes her daughter is too innocent to look after herself. And she's right: The child ignores the warnings and is eaten by the wolf.

But since the problem was her disobedience rather than her lack of knowledge, she is allowed a second chance. A hunter comes along and rescues her, and she herself makes the significance of her adventure clear to young readers: "She said to herself, 'Never again will I leave the path and run off into the wood when my mother tells me not to'" (Manheim 101). For Perrault, children should know enough about evil to protect themselves from it. For the Grimms, children need only know how much they *don't* know, so that they can see the wisdom of accepting the wise advice of their parents—and of cautionary fables like this one, which the Grimms made out of a not necessarily cautionary oral tale.

EXPLORATION: Few of the over two hundred Grimm tales are widely known. In a complete text like Manheim's, read (or invite children to read) some of the less familiar tales: stories such as "Clever Hans" (no. 32), "The Robber Bridegroom" (no. 40), "The Two Brothers" (no. 60), "The Glass Coffin" (no. 163), "The Goose Girl at the Spring" (no. 179). In what way do they vary from your expectations of fairy tales? Why might they not have become as popular as the better-known tales?

Fairy Tales after Grimm

The Grimm brothers' collection wasn't widely read until Edward Taylor translated some of the stories into English in 1823. Taylor's *German Popular Stories* was specifically advertised as being for "young minds" (Opie 25) and included comical illustrations by George Cruikshank. It seems to have been the success of this English edition that gave the Grimms the idea of producing the 1825 abridged edition that made the stories popular with German children.

Later in the nineteenth century, when admirers of the Grimm tales in many parts of Europe collected and published tales from their own countries, they took the connection between the tales and children for granted. Fairy tales had achieved the status they still have as children's literature.

The most famous gathering of fairy tales from England, compiled by Joseph Jacobs from a variety of early written sources that claimed oral roots, clearly implies an audience of children. It focuses on the entertainment value of mysteries and adventures, ghosts and giantkillers, and offers the pleasure of an energetic writing style. Of the eight best-known tales I listed earlier, three are of English origin and appear in Jacobs: "The Three Little Pigs," "Goldilocks and the Three Bears," and "Jack and the Beanstalk."

EXPLORATION: Read (or invite children to read) a selection of tales from another tradition, such as the Russian tales first collected by Aleksandr Afanas'ev, the Norwegian tales first collected by Peter Asbjørnsen and Jørgen Moe, or the Italian tales collected by Italo Calvino. What do these tales have in common with the other fairy tales you know? How do they vary?

Tales from Around the World. In this century, as we've developed knowledge of the similarity in folktales told in widely different parts of the world, it has become common to think of the tales as a painless way of encouraging cultural and racial tolerance in children. On the jacket of a typical contemporary collection, Jane

Yolen's *Favorite Folktales from Around the World,* Isaac Asimov is quoted as saying, "A book like this is worth a thousand homilies on the brotherhood of humanity. This collection of tales bubbling up from the thoughts and imaginations of ordinary people everywhere in all cultures shows amply the common reservoirs of hopes, fears, love, and rascality that we all share."

I have no doubt that the immense variety of stories from many cultures can be richly satisfying; I personally derive great pleasure from some of the Haitian stories collected by Diane Wolkstein in *The Magic Orange Tree* or the Native American stories selected by Richard Erdoes and Alfonso Ortiz, both of which have tremendous energy and humour. I recommend them to you.

Not surprisingly, however, my students never mention any stories from other cultures as ones they already know and remember, and they often tell me that they find such stories boring. For those with European backgrounds, stories from Asia or South America can seem disturbingly alien—even though they often represent tale types we're familiar with. My own pleasure in the Haitian tales derives in no small part from their strangeness, and particularly from their exotic use of onomatopoeic language: words like "HEE-huh" to represent the sound a donkey makes, or "Fsst," the sound of hairs being pulled out, or "Whee-AIIII," the sound of a man with hot peppers in his mouth.

Ironically, furthermore, students from non-European backgrounds often find the versions of stories from their own cultures that are included in anthologies intended for children equally boring or distressing. The stories have been distorted to suit conventional Euro-American values.

For instance, a student of Chinese background once told me that the version of a folktale, which he had first heard as a child and which was included in Joanna Cole's *Bestloved Folktales of the World,* was a lot like the story as told him by his grandmother in his childhood. But, he added, the title given in the anthology distorted it. The story is about a woman's conviction that she is meant to marry one specific man, who asks for her hand too late and dies of remorse. On the day of her wedding to another man, she stops the wedding procession, falls on the grave of her true love, and says, "If we were really intended to be man and wife, open your grave three feet wide" (533). The grave opens and the woman leaps into it. Finally, she and her true intended become rainbows. According to my student, to call this tale "Faithful Even in Death" distorts it to make it fit non-Asian cultural assumptions. That title implies that a woman's faithfulness is a matter of choice on her part and, therefore, a virtue that is being rewarded, whereas the story itself makes it clear that the woman had no choice but to love him whom she was meant to love, and that the situation has nothing to do with virtue or reward. Despite Cole's claim that stories of different cultures "deal with universal human dilemmas that span differences of age, culture, and geography" (xvii), this story expresses a distinctly non-European conception of fate.

EXPLORATION: Read (or invite children to read) some tales from non-European sources in picture books or in collections of fairy tales from different cultures. Do you find them interesting? Why or why not? To what degree do they vary from traditional European tales? Try to find versions of the same tales in scholarly sources. To what degree have the children's versions been changed to suit current conventional values and assumptions?

In recent years, a Disney movie version has made many people aware of a tale of another culture that might seem to contradict my theory that stories from other cultures reflect other values, and not universal human ones. In both Disney's *Aladdin* and the story it's based on, an apparently powerless young man wins a rich princess with the aid of a magical helper. Not only does this sound much like a version of the conventional European Cinderella story, but the tale as told on screen and in most written texts expresses values similar to the ones found in popular versions of "Cinderella": Aladdin is a kindhearted person who tries to help others and so deserves his reward. If this story is indeed one of the traditional Arabian tales collected under the title *The Thousand and One Nights* (or, as in Husain Haddawy's edition, *The Arabian Nights*), we might conclude that values like the Christian Golden Rule can indeed be found in non-Christian traditions like those of the Islamic tradition from which these tales emerged.

But the tale of Aladdin is probably not Arabic in origin. While the other tales in *The Arabian Nights* can be found in Arabic manuscripts dating back to the fourteenth century, the story of Aladdin first appeared in Arabic in the late eighteenth century, *after* it had appeared in what claimed to be a French translation by Antoine Galland. Husain Haddawy concludes that the Arab text is a forgery, produced "by translating Galland back into Arabic" (xiii). While Galland claimed to have been told the tale by an Arabian, we have to conclude that the tale seems to express European values simply because the person who actually wrote it down, and who may even have made it up, was European.

ORAL TALES FROM WRITTEN VERSIONS: VARIANT VERSIONS AND CULTURAL VALUES

The way most of us remember fairy tales has little to do with the versions recorded in the pioneering editions. Intriguingly, fairy tales seem to retain the oral characteristic of memorability even for those who first experience them through reading. Once they've appeared in print, people who read them tend to remember them and then retell them, either orally or in other books. Not surprisingly, the retellings differ from the originals, transformed just as were Perrault's and the Grimm brothers' versions by the specific values and attitudes of those who tell them.

EXPLORATION: Write down (or invite children to write down) one of the eight popular tales as you already know it yourself. Then look up the version of the tale by Perrault, the Grimms, or Jacobs, and consider the implications of any differences between your version and the one in the text.

The tendency of tales to be modified as they are retold explains why the tales as most people know them now differ from the versions recorded in traditional sources. Nowadays, for instance, we're so fearful of frightening children with the depiction of violence that in many printed versions of the tale, Little Red Riding Hood isn't eaten at all. She runs away just in the nick of time, or sometimes, even, beats up the wolf and saves herself. And few contemporary versions record the details of "Ashputtel," the Grimms' version of "Cinderella," in which the wicked stepsisters cut off their toes and heels in order to fit the shoe, and finally have their eyes pecked out by birds.

This habit of making fairy tales fit patterns we feel comfortable with also explains the peculiarity of "The Three Bears." Who are we supposed to sympathize with, the nice family whose home is invaded or the nice little girl who has to deal with scary bears? The central character in early versions of this story was a nasty old woman, a vagrant who clearly was at fault for breaking into someone else's house. But probably because we expect the main characters in fairy tales to be young innocents, the old woman became a girl in later tellings. That change made the tale as ambiguous as it now is, particularly when other tales like "Little Red Riding Hood" and "Three Little Pigs" assert the essential villainy of all hairy beasts, presumably including law-abiding bears. These changes and choices clearly reveal the extent to which our versions of fairy tales express the ideological values of mainstream North American culture: our consciously or unconsciously held attitudes about goodness and justice.

They also reveal the extent to which the mass media have created our images of fairy tales. My friend Jill May, who teaches children's literature at Purdue University, has pointed out to me that each of the eight tales I listed above has been made into a movie by the Disney studio. That might account for the fact that they are the most widely known of all fairy tales. More than one of my students has expressed discontent with picture-book versions of these tales that are closer to Grimm or Perrault but look and sound different from the Disney films; these students tell me they always believed that Walt Disney actually created these stories, and so they resent those who dare to change them.

In recent years, in fact, since Disney has produced film versions of "Aladdin" and "Beauty and the Beast," people in my classes have begun to suggest that they could tell these tales too without a text. These tales were never mentioned before the Disney versions appeared.

In any case, most people I've asked to tell me the story of Snow White give each of the dwarfs a name and insist that it's "love's first kiss" that awakens Snow White, and not the jarring of her glass coffin as reported in Grimm. These are inventions of the Disney movie, the most widely known version of the story in the fifty years since it first appeared. When we criticize fairy tales for being outmoded, we need to consider the possibility that the archaic sexist or ageist values they express may be those of the United States in the 1930s and 1940s, not necessarily those of an ancient oral tradition or even those imposed on the tales by writers like Perrault and the Grimms.

EXPLORATION: Compare (or invite children to compare) a number of current or recent versions of a popular fairy tale with an earlier version by the Grimms, Perrault, or Jacobs. To what degree do the differences represent different cultural assumptions?

WHICH VERSIONS SHOULD CHILDREN READ?

As I suggested in chapter 9, the psychoanalyst Bruno Bettelheim believes that fairy tales in their original versions speak directly to the unconscious concerns of children. Because the tales emerge from an anonymous oral tradition that allows them to express something beyond the limited perceptions of any individual writer, Bettelheim feels they deal with "universal human problems" (6). Bettelheim's position is seriously undermined by his incorrect assumption that the Grimm versions accurately represent the oral tradition; I've already reported the evidence suggesting that they don't. But there may well be a case for arguing that fairy tales as told by writers like the Grimms and Jacobs *should* be read by children, exactly because their expression of outmoded nineteenth-century values distinguishes them from the literature currently being written for children.

In chapter 5, I explored the common assumption that children are vulnerable. Because we wish to protect them, the literature we write for them—and the fairy tales we rewrite for them—tend to leave out unsettling ideas and events. Such censoring deprives children of a basic pleasure of literature, the chance to experience painful circumstances without actually suffering from them, and therefore, to rehearse difficult situations and emotions before having to deal with them in real life.

Older versions of fairy tales, which weren't specifically written with the needs of children in mind, offer that opportunity. Furthermore, they do so in terms of richly evocative situations and language that is subtle and often beautiful: Fairy tales can be a richly satisfying form of literary pleasure. Not only will children exposed to a wide variety of new and old stories have access to a variety of enjoyable experiences, but also, I believe, they aren't likely to be indoctrinated into the values of any one of them. They will have a large menu from which to choose and thus determine their own values.

Fairy tales are particularly useful in this way, simply because the existence in print of so many different versions of the same tale allows them to act as schemata for one another. The sameness of the shared plot puts the variations, most of which imply different values and assumptions, into sharp relief.

EXPLORATION: There are hundreds of picture-book versions of stories like "Cinderella" and "Little Red Riding Hood," from cheap reprints for sale in supermarkets to sumptuously ornate and exceedingly tasteful books by leading illustrators. Each offers different ideas about what these character look like or what their actions mean. Read (or invite children to read) several different versions of one fairy tale. In what ways do the differences in these versions express different values and ideological assumptions?

CHARACTERISTICS OF FAIRY TALES

Despite their ability to be told in different ways and to convey different values, fairy tales still share many characteristics. In this section, I explore several of them, again focusing on the eight tales my students know best.

Setting

EXPLORATION: Before reading what follows, explore your answers to the questions I'm considering here. When is "once upon a time"? What did the people wear in fairy tales? What kinds of buildings did they inhabit?

Where and when do fairy tales take place? The phrase, "Once upon a time," evokes a combination of real time and fantasy. Magical things happen: Pumpkins turn into coaches, people sleep for a hundred years, pigs and wolves talk. But the settings of fairy tales aren't places in which anything at all can happen—the talking pigs don't turn into pumpkins. The magic seems restricted to one or two elements in each story. Otherwise, things are as they once were in what we assume was the real past of our own real world. Unlike science fiction, which uses fantasy to describe complex future times, fairy tales express nostalgia for a simpler past time.

But "once upon a time" doesn't refer to any specific time, not Germany in the fifteenth century or Wales in the seventeenth. When I ask people to explore their mental images of fairy tale settings, they usually describe a vaguely medieval Europe, a place free of the uglier aspects of modern technology. People ride around on horses and hang their clothes on lines outside.

In the imaginary time and place of fairy tales, the castles are sumptuous. But frighteningly dense woods, where people live in huts, begin just outside the castle walls. There are few "middles," few ordinary houses between the sumptuousness of the castles and the harshness of the huts. The people are usually either incredibly rich or incredibly poor, and the women usually wear either ornately bejeweled gowns or rags.

While the lack of middles makes the fairy tale world seem harsh, it is actually utopian. With none of the confusion caused by reality's complex mixtures of good and bad, problems are easily understood, choices obvious. Adversity is the result of the specific actions of individuals rather than of uncontrollable forces like social inequity or war. People are free to focus on their own problems and even control their own destinies.

Characters

In the clear-cut world of fairy tales, it's easy to figure out whom we should admire and whom we should hate. The distinctions between those who are admirable and those who are hateful are clear from the beginning. Anyone familiar with the pattern of fairy tales expects that as soon as a story begins with a description of someone in trouble that person will end up happily. In fairy tales, in fact, goodness is defined by situation rather than by action: A character who begins in the position of being abused is automatically defined as good.

Some characters do little to deserve their identification as good. While Perrault tells us that Cinderella is kind, the events of the story show her being acted upon by others rather than acting herself; she performs no act that confirms her goodness. Snow White does even less, and Sleeping Beauty does nothing but sleep. On the basis of these characters, we might conclude that goodness in fairy tales consists of passivity, even stupidity. Magical assistance comes to those whose lack of ability puts them most in need of help.

EXPLORATION: Is that statement true? Consider (or invite children to consider) the goodness of good characters in these or other tales.

Once characters' situations define them as good, furthermore, we tend to continue to consider them good no matter what they do; no bad act seems able to change our judgment of them. Because Jack is in the role of abused victim, we don't seem to care that his exploits in the giant's house are acts of thievery (although some modern versions try to justify his thefts by adding that the giant first stole these objects from Jack's father). And even though the violence directed against characters like Snow White and the three pigs first defines them as good, we don't change our minds about their goodness when they perform acts of violence against their enemies.

In order to fill the role of good hero or heroine, a fairy tale character must seem powerless in relation to someone more powerful: someone recognizably evil because he or she has power and misuses it by directing it against someone weaker. The villains of fairy tales have high social status (the queens in "Cinderella" and "Snow White"), or great size and strength (the giant in "Jack and the Beanstalk," the wolves in "Little Red Riding Hood" and "Three Pigs"), or great knowledge (the witches of "Hansel and Gretel" and "Sleeping Beauty"). The heroes and heroines are children, poor people, or foolish people like Jack, who sells a cow for a few beans.

Events: A Basic Story Pattern

The movement from the beginning of typical fairy tales to the end is one of the most basic story patterns, one found in numerous other children's stories: The events allow the powerless underdog to exchange places with the character who first had power over him. Usually through some form of magical assistance, the underdog comes to a position of great wealth or social influence, and the previously

powerful character dies or becomes an outsider, an underdog. If there were a sequel to "Cinderella" that fulfilled our expectations of fairy tales, Cinderella herself
would probably have to be the villain; her marriage has given her the sort of status
and power we expect to be a source of evil.

In the real world, underdogs don't often win, for the simple reason that those
who are powerful use their power to control things. But the magical elements in
fairy tales allow events to take place that couldn't easily happen in real life. As I
said earlier, the magic in fairy tales isn't capricious; in fact, the laws of physics or
logic are suspended only to get the "good" characters into trouble or to help them
get out of trouble, or both. Pumpkins become coaches only when underdogs like
Cinderella are in enough trouble to *need* a suspension of reality; the magic allows
her to triumph, and then it stops.

Wish-Fulfillment Fantasy.   The most significant truth about fairy tales is that
they represent things not as they really are, but as we imagine they ought to be. Because the plots of the tales offer the satisfaction of an imaginary fulfillment of the
wish for power, they are *wish-fulfillment fantasies* for people who perceive or who
enjoy pretending to perceive themselves as underdogs. As such, they are emotionally useful stories. Nevertheless, the pleasure fairy tales offer depends on the degree to which we understand that they do represent a wish fulfilled—a distortion of
actual reality. Those who question the value of fairy tales for children usually do so
because they assume that children can't distinguish between fantasy and reality and
read wish-fulfillment fantasy as a description of the way things actually are.

EXPLORATION: Consider (or invite children to consider) whether fairy
tales are good for children. Can the distortions that allow the tales to act
as wish fulfillments—the extremely good heroes and extremely bad villains, the triumph of the weak over the strong—be seen as realistic? Is it
bad if they are?

Meaning

Despite the obvious tendencies of fairy tales toward wish fulfillment, most interpreters of fairy tales suggest that they do in fact represent the "truth," that the fantasy of the tales is a symbolic depiction of the way things actually are. As I suggested earlier, Bettelheim called the tales symbolic representations of the truths of
the unconscious. From a more mystical perspective, Joyce Thomas identifies the
truth of the tales as *the* truth hidden within reality itself, "the unfamiliar asleep
within the familiar, the magical housed within the shell of the mundane. . . . This is
the world, the tales say, and it is truly marvellous, mysterious, wonder-full" (115).
In awakening our sense of wonder, fairy tales teach us to appreciate the mystery of
the real world.

Critics like Bettelheim and Thomas find basic "truths" in fairy tales because
they wrongly believe that the tales accurately represent an anonymous oral tradi-

tion that transcends the distortions of individual retellings. But even critics who understand the degree to which the meanings of tales depend upon the values of a specific teller maintain that the tales contain deeper truths. James M. McGlathery, who acknowledges that tellers like the Grimms changed the meanings of the tales, nevertheless insists that the tales still represent "popular wisdom" (196) and insists that the attitudes toward erotic desire he sees them as expressing "surely belonged as well to the popular as to the literary culture" (197). In *Fairy Tales and the Art of Subversion,* similarly, Jack Zipes says that "the fairy tales we have come to revere as classical are not ageless, universal, and beautiful in and of themselves. . . . They are historical prescriptions, internalized, potent, explosive, and we acknowledge the power they hold over our lives by mystifying them" (11). But Zipes "mystifies" them himself when he insists that the "historical prescriptions" of bourgeois writers like Perrault and the Grimms are distortions of a saner—that is, truer—folk tradition that represents the more radical political values he himself shares. In *Breaking the Magic Spell,* he speaks of "the imaginative motifs and symbolical elements of class conflict and rebellion in the pre-capitalist folk tales" (24). Again similarly, Ruth Bottigheimer focuses on the repressive nineteenth-century attitudes imposed on the tales by the Grimm brothers, but discovers a "latent content" hidden within the Grimm versions, which she sees as the truth inside the tales and which mirrors her own late-twentieth-century feminist values.

I find it hard not to suspect that the truths these critics find in the tales represent fulfillments of their personal wishes. McGlathery more or less admits the personal basis of his interpretations when he asserts that his study is "essentially ahistorical" (11) and that he has made no attempt "to discover the Grimms' intentions in telling the stories the way they did. . . . We will restrict ourselves to what these stories, taken collectively, may suggest to us regarding underlying patterns and meanings" (9). What they suggest to him often sounds more like contemporary pop psychology than like the attitudes of earlier times.

Even when I find myself agreeing with scholars' conclusions, I can't help noticing that Zipes, a Marxist, finds the truths of Marxism in the tales, and Bottigheimer, a feminist, finds the truths of feminism, and the psychoanalyst Bettelheim finds messages for the unconscious. Thus, even for interpreters, the tales seem to be wish-fulfillment fantasies.

EXPLORATION: After quoting the last two sentences in a review of the first edition of *Pleasures of Children's Literature,* Ian Wojcik-Andrews makes this comment: "Presumably, by the same specious logic, the reader-response theories used but never acknowledged by Nodelman to structure his book are wish-fulfillment fantasies" (160). Do you think they are? Consider that possibility as you respond to my theory about the meaning of fairy tales as outlined in the next few paragraphs. Am I merely fulfilling my own wishes? Will you be fulfilling your own if you find yourself agreeing with me?

Despite their connections with individual values, the differing interpretations of different commentators have something in common. In finding an underlying truth, they all imply that in fairy tales, things are not what they seem.

That general idea may actually be the meaning of the tales that gives us most pleasure. Seen from a different point of view, the passivity and stupidity of fairy tale heroes and heroines may be a wise ability to accept that which transcends the limitations of ordinary reason and logic. Cinderella is passive and stupid enough—or wise enough?—to accept the help of her fairy godmother without question. European fairy tales express the paradoxes central to the Christian culture they emerged from: The fool in his folly is wise, and the meek do inherit the earth.

On the other hand, Wojcik-Andrews may be right, and what I've just said may merely be another retelling: my own version of stories whose basic quality is that they are capable of taking on so many different meanings.

Structure

If we look at a number of versions of a single fairy tale, it's not hard for us to distinguish between what varies and what remains the same. What changes are the details that establish an individual storyteller's sense of the meaning of the tale and its function for an audience. What's left after we eliminate the details is a sequence of events that recurs in version after version—the sequence of events that defines the tale's type.

This sequence isn't itself the authentic or original story. It's merely a basic structural pattern to which details can be added in order to create one of many possible stories. For instance, this central sequence of events underlies most versions of "Little Red Riding Hood":

1. Mother gives Little Red instructions and sends her to grandmother.
2. Little Red converses with the wolf.
3. The wolf goes to grandmother (and in most versions, eats her), and then disguises himself as grandmother.
4. Little Red arrives, and the wolf invites her in.
5. Little Red and the wolf discuss his appearance, a conversation culminating in the wolf's threat to eat her.

Beyond this basic structure, various events may occur.

What's significant here is that most of us probably wouldn't consider a story to be a version of "Little Red Riding Hood" if it didn't contain the listed events in the listed order. But most people probably would agree that any story that contains these events *is* "Little Red Riding Hood," even if other details are included—for instance, if Little Red meanders through the woods picking flowers or talking to chipmunks between episodes 2 and 3—and no matter what specific instructions Little Red's mother gives her or whether Little Red escapes death at the end.

Many of the best-loved versions of the tales, like those by the Grimms, describe only the central moments in detail and quickly pass over or summarize what happens between them. Rather than the gradually developing plots we conventionally expect of fiction, these versions offer a series of intense moments separated from each other by less intense and more broadly summarized connecting passages.

These central moments tend to have interesting relationships with each other. In "Snow White" the picture of a woman looking at herself in a reflecting glass and wishing to be beautiful counterpoints the picture in the previous central moment of another queen looking through clear glass and wishing that someone else would be beautiful. The other central moments in the tale also involve looking, often through glass: The huntsman refuses to kill Snow White because he looks at her and finds her beautiful; Snow White looks at the dwarfs' house; the dwarfs look at Snow White asleep; the Queen entices Snow White by talking with her through a window; and the Prince falls in love with Snow White when he sees her through her glass coffin.

Versions that include more details lose the revealing counterpoints that a focus on central moments offers. On the other hand, versions with little detail can't provide the suspenseful plot and evocation of setting and character that are often the basis of our pleasure in other kinds of fiction.

EXPLORATION: Read (or invite children to read) several different versions of the same tale. Identify the central moments and their relationships with one another. Then compare the degree to which the different versions focus on these central moments. Consider which version satisfies you most, and why.

LITERARY FAIRY TALES

Once fairy tales were collected and retold for children, they became models for writers like Hans Christian Andersen, George MacDonald, and Oscar Wilde, who created similar stories of their own. These stories, based on traditional fairy tales but often substantially different from them, are called *literary fairy tales*.

One such story is Andersen's "Princess and the Pea." This story is modeled on all the traditional fairy tales about princesses finding their princes. But as I suggest in chapter 8, it has a sophisticated irony quite unlike the traditional tales. Similarly, Andersen's "Little Match Girl" starts out like a typical fairy tale, but then Andersen replaces the traditional happy ending in which an underdog achieves worldly power with something more complex. This time the underdog dies an underdog, from cold and hunger. But for those who have eyes to see, the misery is false—she has entered the glory of heaven. Andersen's story of "The Little Mermaid" ends in a similar way; the prince for whom the mermaid gave up the sea chooses to marry a human princess, but the mermaid herself gets the greater award of entering heaven. It's interesting that in their cartoon version, the Disney studio reverted to a more traditional and less ambiguously happy ending in which the mermaid gets the prince.

Liberated Fairy Tales

In recent years, in response to the presumed danger of the violence and sexism of traditional fairy tales, a whole body of literature has developed that presents variations of fairy-tale situations with more acceptable values, particularly in terms of the way women are portrayed. In Robert Munsch's *The Paperbag Princess,* for instance, the determined princess Elizabeth reverses our expectations by using her wits to rescue Ronald, the prince she plans to marry, from a dragon, only to discover that he's too conceited to be worthy of her. In the end, she decides to remain single.

Such stories often strike adult readers as both enjoyable and useful: They are funny, and they present worthwhile role models. What we forget to consider, I think, is the degree to which our own pleasure in these stories depends on our knowledge of all those other stories in which the princes rescue the princesses. Without the outmoded, sexist schema of those stories to compare it with, *The Paperbag Princess* loses much of its humor and almost all of its point. If we assume that such stories are good for children, then we must believe one of the following:

- We must first teach children the outmoded, traditional role models in order to unteach them.
- Children *already* know these role models:
  1. It is natural for children to assume that women are weak and men strong;
  2. or else they learn the notion so early in their life that it's firmly established by the time they're old enough to hear simple stories like *The Paperbag Princess.*

In fact, this last possibility seems to be the truth. In interviews with children about *The Paperbag Princess,* Bronwyn Davies discovered that they interpreted—we adults might say, misinterpreted—the story in order to make it fit into their already established ideas about appropriate behavior for males and females. When Ronald thanks Elizabeth for rescuing him from the dragon by telling her she looks awful and that she should go away and come back only when she looks more like a princess, these children were convinced that he's only doing what needs to be done. Elizabeth needs to be warned about the danger of behaving in such an unfeminine manner, because her actions are a threat both to her and to Ronald.

According to Davies, these children understood Ronald's cruel words as what she calls *category maintenance work:* behavior "aimed at maintaining the category as a meaningful category in the face of individual deviation which is threatening the category" (326). In this case, the category is gender roles, and the children Davies interviewed knew and believed traditional ideas about them thoroughly enough to reinvent the meaning of Munsch's story—and they had serious trouble making sense of Elizabeth's apparent happiness at the end of it. Davies concludes, "Certainly the idea that children learn through stories what the world is about or that they use the characters in stories as 'role models' is not only too simplistic but it entirely misses the interactive dimension between the real and the imaginary" (331).

In any case, all stories reflect the ideologies of their tellers. If we aren't yet as liberated as we might wish we were, then the stories we tell, despite their good intentions, won't be any more liberated. In "Cinderelma," from *Dr. Gardner's Fairy Tales for Today's Children* by Richard A. Gardner, M.D., a liberated woman still achieves happiness by marrying the man of her dreams. Indeed, marriage is the happy ending of a surprising number of supposedly liberated fairy tales. We only superficially change our perception of what a woman's worth consists of if we still identify the real significance of that worth, whatever it is, as its ability to attract a potential husband.

In his "Introduction for Adults," Dr. Gardner objects to the happy endings of traditional tales because they misrepresent real possibilities in a way that "contributes to our general dissatisfaction and low frustration tolerance" (5). So after his mistreated Cinderelma realizes there's no such thing as a fairy godmother, makes her own dress and walks to the ball, she rejects the rich prince because she feels she has nothing in common with him—he is too enmeshed in the interests of his class. But the story replaces one wish-fulfillment fantasy with another—one that Dr. Gardner so takes for granted as an American that he seems to assume it couldn't possibly cause dissatisfaction or frustration. Cinderelma falls in love with a man who, like herself, is poor but hardworking, and the two live out the American dream, becoming wealthy through entrepreneurship and diligence.

EXPLORATION: Read (or invite children to read) some liberated fairy tales, such as those collected in Zipes's *Don't Bet on the Prince.* Consider the degree to which they escape repressive, outmoded, or dissatisfying values.

Variations

"Cinderelma" isn't quite the story of "Cinderella"; it's different enough not to represent the basic tale type. But it's still enough like "Cinderella" to remind readers who know "Cinderella" of it; and a main pleasure it offers is a perception of how the events it describes vary from the equivalent ones in the original tale. In recent years, variations of well-known fairy tales have become something of a fad in publishing for children.

For instance, French's *Snow White in New York* describes how a poor orphan, mistreated by a wicked stepmother, finds herself alone on the dark, wild streets of the urban jungle, until she's taken in by seven kindly jazzmen and then rescued by a handsome reporter for the *Daily Mirror.* In Michael Emberley's *Ruby,* also set in a modern city, a young mouse in a red cape sets out for her grandmother's house, only to be confronted on the street by a loudmouth bully of a lizard; while this street-smart mouse gives the bully as good as she gets, calling him "barf-breath" and "creepo," she finally does need to be rescued—by a suspiciously sweet-talking cat, who then rushes off in a cab to Ruby's grandmother's house, where he intends to have grandmother as a snack before the main course of Ruby herself. Fortunately, Ruby, no ingenuous Little Red, has a trick of her own up her sleeve, and at the end, it's the cat who seems to have been eaten.

Both these stories allow readers the double pleasure of using schemata. We can recognize a pattern we're familiar with. Then, because we can do so, we can perceive and understand the significance of divergences from it. In *Snow White in New York* and *Ruby,* we can enjoy the clever commentary on modern life implied by the fact that the mirror and the wild forest of tradition have been replaced by a newspaper and a typical modern city street; and we can note the implications of the fact that the street-smart Ruby, decidedly unlike Little Red, manages to perceive and solve her own problem.

A number of different variations on "Three Little Pigs" reveal the scope for ingenuity and subtle meaning this kind of story offers. Mary Rayner's *Mr. and Mrs. Pig's Evening Out* offers a modernized version of the old encounter between some pig siblings and an evil wolf. When Mrs. Wolf, who was hired as a babysitter by a pair of dangerously inattentive parents, decides to have a snack, she turns on the oven in the kitchen and then heads upstairs for a pig to roast in it. It takes all nine of the pig's siblings to save the day. The pleasure here emerges from the way in which the story plays the dangerous but tantalizing game of bringing the horrific events of the original much closer to home: In the context of contemporary life, these events become a kind of Stephen King story for young children.

Rather than bringing the story up to date, Jon Sciezska's *The True Story of the 3 Little Pigs by A. Wolf* offers a new interpretation of the familiar old events; the wolf claims he was only trying to borrow a cup of sugar, that the pigs' houses were blown down by accidental sneezes, and that it would have been wasteful for him not to eat the nutritious ham dinners that resulted from those accidents. This version asks us to see through the lies of a patently unreliable narrator, but many readers seem to end up sympathizing with the wolf more than human justice might suggest they should.

Yet another variation offers a totally different sort of reversal: In Eugene Trivizas's *The Three Little Wolves and the Big Bad Pig,* it's the wolves who are soft and cuddly, and the pig proves he's bad by knocking down their brick house with a sledge hammer, their concrete house with a pneumatic drill, and their armor-plated house with dynamite. But the smell of the flowers out of which they build their last house transforms the pig into a good and happy member of the family. On the face of it, this is wildly sentimental—so much so that it's hard not to find some irony here. This story not only acts as an ironic reversal of the original, I suspect it makes fun of anyone impractical enough to pretend to believe that flowers might be stronger than armor-plate.

MYTHS

Folklorists once posited the theory that fairy tales are distorted remnants of ancient myths about nature; for instance, the wolf's devouring of Red Riding Hood was supposed to represent the dark of night devouring the sunset. Such theories have been discredited. As far as we know, the tales were always intended to be entertaining stories, even when they were in the oral tradition. But while fairy tales are not myths, many people think that myths can become fairy tales.

Myths as Stories

Myths are stories with a special status. For those who believe in them, they are true—not symbolically true or allegorically true, but absolutely true; a factual accounting of the nature of the world as it is. If we accept their truth, furthermore, myths tell us how to live: what to believe and how to behave. In other words, "myth" is the name we give to stories that express religious truth, when we happen not to believe they are true. For the ancient Greeks, what we call the Greek myths were accurate accounts of real events that not only explained the nature of the world but also defined proper conduct. Similarly, for people who aren't Christians, the biblical stories of the creation of the world and the resurrection of Christ are myths.

Nowadays, nobody believes in the literal existence, for example, of Persephone; the particular religious truths in the story of the young woman abducted by Hades have indeed become myths. But the story of Persephone is still a story, even if it's no longer a true one; so it might well be told to those who don't believe its truth for the same reason that we tell fairy tales—for the pleasure of it.

Anthologies of children's literature contain many stories of this sort—not just Greek and Norse myths, but also stories about supernatural beings from the traditional cultures of Native Americans and other societies around the world. Sometimes these stories are treated as if they were no different from folktales. Both Cole's *Bestloved Folktales of the World* and Yolen's *Favorite Folktales from Around the World* contain not only genuine folktales—stories that started out as entertaining fictional tales—but also a few stories based on godlike beings, such as the Algonquian Glooscap and the Ojibwa Nanabozho, who have the status of myth.

The custom of using myths as entertaining stories raises some provocative questions:

- Can these stories, as some adherents of Carl Jung's teachings believe, convey essential and enduring archetypal truths even to those who don't share the culture they emerged from?
- Separated from their original religious or mythic purposes, are they still good stories?
- For those of European background to treat stories of Glooscap or Nanabozho as entertaining literature is exactly like a publisher in Iran producing a book about the magical exploits of the fictional hero Christ for the entertainment of an audience of Muslim children. Even if they're good stories, I believe we need to think about the moral implications of reading what is or once was true and sacred to someone else as just a fiction, as a source not of spiritual truth but of imaginative pleasure.

EXPLORATIONS: (1) After reading an earlier version of this section, my colleague Mavis Reimer responded this way:

> The logical consequence of the view that we ought *not* to read as a fiction that which is true to someone else is that we finally can read nothing that doesn't confirm our own system of beliefs, a view that is egocentric in the extreme, and a view that you yourself have been urging readers of this book to move past, by unmasking the many different ways we refuse to acknowledge differences in our culture. As a Christian, I have no objection to Iranian children hearing of Christ as a magic hero; I suspect the only Christians who would are extreme fundamentalists. Does the passion with which someone holds a view qualify it as "off-limits" to other readers and writers? That would certainly tend to support the ban on a book such as Salman Rushdie's *The Satanic Verses*. All ideas, ideologies and belief systems must be open to inquiry in a free society—and as you've been suggesting in this book, just such an inquiry is one of the pleasures of reading fiction. Using the texts of people from other cultures in an attempt to access their meanings without having to encounter them as human beings is a deplorable and immoral procedure, and one that we can and should expose; but that's an issue separate from the one you raise here.

Consider (or invite children to consider) these views. Read Padraic Colum's or Garfield's and Blishen's versions of Greek myths or Dorothy Reid's versions of stories about the Ojibwa Nanabozho, and consider their value as fiction. Does the fact that people have believed these stories to represent absolute truth interfere with your pleasure in them? Should it?

(2) In response to my comment above about the absolute truth of myths for those who believe in them, Virginia Wolf, who teaches children's literature at the University of Wisconsin–Stout, writes:

> This may be how a fundamentalist views his religion; it may be how some people prior to the twentieth century viewed their religion. But an educated believer today is more likely to acknowledge the metaphorical nature of models of god, creation, the human relationship with god and creation, and so forth. There is a full awareness in much theology today of the inadequacy of words and other efforts to do more than point to something outside the human context. Post-modern, post-structuralist theologians know full well that we are each trapped in our individual hermeneutic circle.

Consider your response to these comments. How might the position Wolf presents here influence your understanding of myths and other religious narratives as stories for children?

Myths and Cultural Education

It's possible to suggest reasons other than just entertainment for children to read myths. As I suggested above, Jung and his followers, and some religious thinkers also, believe that myths of all ages and cultures express archetypal knowledge and therefore convey important truths even to those who aren't members of the culture that produced them. These thinkers would share such stories with children to enable them to experience the archetypal knowledge. Even those who don't accept the existence of archetypes sometimes argue that the roots of Western society can be found in the values of ancient Athens, so that reading the Greek myths teaches children something important about the roots of European culture. And others say that the Greek myths are still a significant part of the Western cultural repertoire, so that children should learn them as quickly as they can. About stories from non-European cultures like the legends of Nanabozho, people sometimes say that widespread knowledge of these texts can only increase our tolerance and understanding.

Such arguments depend on the assumption that these stories *accurately* represent cultures different from our own—that they are authentic. Unfortunately, as I suggested in regard to folktales, the versions of myths and legends found in books intended for children have almost always been reworked to suit current ideas about what children might enjoy or ought to hear. They represent a form of the "claw back" I discussed earlier in regard to TV, a version of the alien that makes it more familiar and less frightening.

In a collection not intended for children, such as Erdoes's and Ortiz's *American Indian Myths and Legends,* it's not surprising to discover that trickster figures like Glooscap or the Sioux Coyote had humorous sexual adventures of the sort that never appear in the stories about them intended for contemporary children. Even the stories that do appear in children's texts have been watered down. In Reid's version, Nanabozho flies with geese, then falls into a swamp of oozing mud; in more trustworthily authentic versions of this tale, he falls into an enemy camp, where he is tied to a stake and his enemies relieve themselves on him until only his head remains uncovered. It's not mud that he has to wash off.

EXPLORATION: Nevertheless, it might be argued that "children's versions" that distort the original tales might have other redeeming educational value for child readers. Explore your own opinion about that.

Furthermore, retelling the stories for children causes differences in style and structure that further distort their meanings. When Christie Harris retells the story "Mouse Woman and Porcupine Hunter," a legend of the Tsimshian people of the North American Northwest coast, she begins the story with the word "once," causing us to expect a fairy tale rather than a description of the sacred activities of divine beings. She also changes the Chief Porcupine. He is no longer the divine being in the impressive shape of a human chief who is described in a more-authentic version collected by Franz Boaz; instead he is a figure of fun, "near-sighted, solitary, pigeon-toed, bowlegged, slow, and peaceful" (8).

Even stranger, she turns Porcupine Hunter, who is the villain of the original story because he kills too many porcupines, into another figure of fun—a hen-pecked husband at the mercy of an acquisitive wife. This wife, barely mentioned by Boaz but a central character in Harris's story, is the traditional comic shrew of European tales like the Grimm brothers' "The Fisherman and His Wife." Without knowledge of the original legend, we would have to believe, inaccurately, that the Tsimshian were as sexist as traditional European culture. In retelling the story in the style of a comic European tale, Harris totally misrepresents its tone and its meaning.

EXPLORATION: Jungian thinkers would probably argue that we gain more by focusing on the archetypal content remaining in new versions of old myths than on the distortions of the rewriting, as I've done here. Explore your response to that possibility by thinking of two different, rewritten versions of a myth in terms of how they vary and what they share. Which is more important in your response, the similarities or the differences?

Ironically, perhaps, even when the stories of non-European myths have been watered down or reshaped to fit our conventional expectations, they still express a view of the world different enough to seem alien to many members of the domi-nant culture. After reading a story about Nanabozho, one of my students described him as "egocentric, cocky, and conceited. I find his character very weak, and I don't have any particular respect for him." This student's European assumption that good is separate from evil and God morally superior to humans prevented her from understanding a godlike figure capable of being both human and divine, helpful and hurtful, good and bad. As Erdoes and Ortiz say, "To those used to the patterns of European fairy tales and folk tales, Indian legends often seem chaotic, inconsis-tent, or incomplete. Plots seem to travel at their own speed, defying convention or at times doing away completely with recognizable beginnings and endings. [The trickster] Coyote is a powerful creature one moment, a snivelling coward the next. . . . To try to apply conventional (Western) logic is not only impossible but unnec-essary" (xii).

It may well be that children can benefit from access to myths and legends of different peoples. But as the issues I've raised here suggest, we can't simply assume they will do so without first providing them with some sense of the distinct qualities of this special kind of story.

EXPLORATION: As I suggested while discussing multiculturalism in chap-ter 7, some Native Americans and members of other minority groups com-plain about those in the dominant culture "appropriating" or stealing their stories, retelling them in ways that change their meaning. Is retelling the story of a culture different from one's own an act of theft? In exploring your response to this question, you might consider the arguments about "the right to represent individuals or topics belonging to a minority culture" (188) reported in Barbara Godard's "The Politics of Representation: Some Native Canadian Women Writers."

WORKS CITED

Afanas'ev, Aleksandr. *Russian Fairy Tales*. Trans. Norbert Guterman. New York: Pantheon, 1945.

Andersen, Hans Christian. *Hans Andersen's Fairy Tales: A Selection*. Trans. L. W. Kingsland. Oxford: Oxford UP, 1984.

Asbjørnsen, Peter Christian, and Jørgen Moe. *Norwegian Folk Tales*. New York: Pantheon, 1982.

Basile, Giambattista. *The Pentameron*. Trans. Richard Burton. London: Spring, n.d.

Bettelheim, Bruno. *The Uses of Enchantment: The Meaning and Importance of Fairy Tales*. New York: Knopf, 1976.

Boaz, Franz. *Tsimshian Mythology*. Based on texts recorded by Henry W. Tate. 1916. New York: Johnson Reprint Co., 1970.

Bottigheimer, Ruth. *Grimms' Bad Girls and Bold Boys: The Moral and Social Vision of the Tales*. New Haven: Yale UP, 1987.

Calvino, Italo. *Italian Folktales*. Trans. George Martin. New York: Pantheon, 1980.

Cole, Joanna. *Bestloved Folktales of the World*. Garden City: Doubleday, 1982.

Colum, Padraic. *The Children's Homer*. New York: Collier, 1982.

———. *The Golden Fleece and the Heroes Who Lived Before Achilles*. New York: Collier, 1983.

Davies, Bronwyn. "Lived and Imaginary Narratives and Their Place in Taking Oneself Up as a Gendered Being." *Australian Psychologist* 25, 3 (November 1990): 318–332.

Dundes, Alan, ed. *Cinderella: A Casebook*. Madison: The U of Wisconsin P, 1982.

Ellis, John. *One Fairy Story Too Many: The Brothers Grimm and Their Tales*. Chicago: U of Chicago P, 1983.

Emberley, Michael. *Ruby*. Boston: Little, Brown, 1990.

Erdoes, Richard, and Alfonso Ortiz. *American Indian Myths and Legends*. New York: Pantheon, 1984.

French, Fiona. *Snow White in New York*. Oxford: Oxford UP, 1986.

Gardner, Richard A. *Dr. Gardner's Fairy Tales for Today's Children*. Englewood Cliffs: Prentice Hall, 1974.

Garfield, Leon, and Edward Blishen. *The God Beneath the Sea*. London: Longman, 1970.

———. *The Golden Shadow*. London: Longman, 1973.

Godard, Barbara. "The Politics of Representation: Some Native Canadian Women Writers." *Canadian Literature* 124–125 (Spring-Summer 1990): 183–225.

Grimm, Jacob and Wilhelm. *Grimms' Fairy Tales*. Trans. Edward Taylor. Harmondsworth, Middlesex: Penguin Puffin, 1971.

———. *Grimms' Tales for Young and Old*. Trans. Ralph Manheim. Garden City: Doubleday, 1977.

Haddawy, Husain. "Introduction." *The Arabian Nights*. Trans. Haddawy. New York and London: Norton, 1990.

Harris, Christie. *Mouse Woman and the Mischief Makers*. Toronto: McClelland and Stewart, 1977.

Jacobs, Joseph. *English Fairy Tales*. London: Bodley Head, 1968.

MacDonald, George. *The Light Princess*. New York: Farrar, Strauss & Giroux, 1969.

McGlathery, James M. *Fairy Tale Romance: The Grimms, Basile, and Perrault*. Urbana and Chicago: U of Illinois P, 1991.

Munsch, Robert. *The Paperbag Princess*. Toronto: Annick, 1980.

Opie, Iona and Peter. *The Classic Fairy Tales*. London: Oxford UP, 1974.

Perrault, Charles. *The Fairy Tales*. Trans. Angela Carter. New York: Bard Avon, 1977.

Rayner, Mary. *Mr. and Mrs. Pig's Evening Out*. London: Macmillan, 1976.

Reid, Dorothy. *Tales of Nanabozho*. Toronto: Oxford UP, 1963.

Scieszka, Jon. *The True Story of the 3 Little Pigs by A. Wolf*. Illus. Lane Smith. New York: Viking, 1989.

Thomas, Joyce. "The Tales of the Brothers Grimm: In the Black Forest." *Touchstones: Reflections on the Best in Children's Literature*. Ed. Perry Nodelman. Vol 2. West Lafayette: Children's Literature Association Publications, 1987. 104–117.

Thompson, Stith. *The Types of the Folktale: A Classification and Bibliography*. 2nd rev. ed. Helsinki: Folk Lore Fellows Communications, 1961.

Trivizas, Eugene. *The Three Little Wolves and the Big Bad Pig*. New York: Margaret K. McElderry-Maxwell Macmillan, 1993.

Wilde, Oscar. *The Happy Prince*. Englewood Cliffs, NJ: Prentice Hall, 1965.

Wojcik-Andrews, Ian. "An Ambivalent Revolution." *Children's Literature* 21 (1993): 155–161.

Wolkstein, Diane. *The Magic Orange Tree*. New York: Knopf, 1978.

Yolen, Jane. *Favorite Folktales from Around the World*. New York: Pantheon, 1986.

Zipes, Jack. *Breaking the Magic Spell: Radical Theories of Folk and Fairy Tales*. Austin: U of Texas P, 1979.

——. *Fairy Tales and the Art of Subversion: The Classical Genre for Children and the Process of Civilization*. London: Heinemann, 1982.

——, ed. *Don't Bet on the Prince: Contemporary Feminist Fairy Tales in North America and England*. New York: Methuen, 1986.

Finding Out More about Children's Literature

CONTINUING THE DIALOGUE

Throughout this book I've tried to encourage readers to enter into a dialogue with my ideas about children's literature, and to arrive at their own conclusions about the issues I discuss. I've done so because I find this sort of dialogue one of the most pleasurable aspects of my own encounters with literature. It's always intriguing to learn how differently different readers respond to the same texts; and for me and for many of the adults and children I know, it's always fun to discuss the implications and relative merits of the different responses.

While I enjoy actual conversations about books with other readers, a major part of the dialogue occurs in my reading of books and articles that describe the responses of readers I've never met. In response to an earlier draft of this appendix, Linnea Hendrickson, who teaches at the University of New Mexico, told me of her own interesting history as a reader of these kinds of responses:

> As I read this section, I thought about how I came to children's books in large part through reading the criticism about them first. I didn't know most of the authors in the children's literature canon when I started working in this field, but certain ones stimulated such interesting criticism that I had to read them. I found myself going along the shelves at the public library and having names pop out at me begging to be read. Joan Aiken, Natalie Babbitt, Leon Garfield, Alan Garner, Ivan Southall, Patricia Wright-son. . . . Reading criticism is another version of what happens in the classroom when one student tells another about a book, or discusses a book with the class.

This, it seems to me, is the real significance of criticism: It encourages and enriches our reponse to literature.

Nevertheless, when it comes to critical analysis, I'm a distrustful reader. I explore the opinions of others in terms of my own repertoire of experiences and responses, and so I rarely find myself in total agreement with those other readers' conclusions about a text as they report them in critical articles or books. But I almost always find myself stimulated by their ideas into thinking new thoughts of my own. Reading critical discussions helps me continue my dialogue with texts and with literature in general.

I'd like to encourage other readers to continue their own dialogues with literature in this way. In order for you to do so, you need to find the materials to enter into dialogue with. This appendix is a mere beginning: a brief introduction to ways of finding printed discussions of children's literature and the other matters discussed throughout this book.

I have to emphasize that this is a *very* limited guide to children's literature. While it offers a few hints about ways of finding new and interesting children's books to read yourself and to share with children, it focuses on something else: finding discussions that deal with either interpretations of specific texts or else questions of literary criticism, literary theory, and literary pedagogy. It therefore ignores the vast amount of materials that deals with other aspects of children's literature, such as teaching basic reading skills, using literature in teaching information or values or as part of a social studies or science curriculum, selecting books and developing children's book collections. These aren't matters I know all that much about; for help on finding information about them, you'll have to consult other books by experts in those fields.

Finding Children's Books

Reference rooms are filled with guides to children's literature. Some list new books; some list all the books written by one author; some list books according to topics or subjects or in terms of their relevance to specific seasons and holidays. Still others list books in terms of the specific physical handicaps or psychological disorders suffered by their main characters, so that the books can be recommended as therapeutic reading for children with the same problems. If you're looking for books to use with children in specific circumstances, all these guides can be helpful. But I'm not going to name any of those guides here, because I don't believe they're the best way to find interesting children's books if you're reading for pleasure—in search of any of the pleasures the title of this book refers to.

A good way to do that is to seek advice from other readers. People who love to read are always happy to tell you about particularly pleasurable or stimulating or infuriating reading experiences. And if you read what they recommend, you know you'll have someone who'd love to talk about it with you. Another way to find interesting books is the one Hendrickson suggests—browse through critical articles on children's books, and read the ones that the critics make sound interesting.

But I think the best way to do it is randomly, even by accident—by browsing through collections of children's books, dipping into ones that look like they might be interesting, and then, reading as many as you have time for. Therefore, my main advice to both children and adults about finding children's books worth reading is this: Visit children's bookstores and the children's sections of libraries. Rummage through the collections of children's books owned by children you know. Browse. Browse imaginatively, with an openness to new and different possibilities that will expand your repertoire of reading experiences. Try new things out. Read widely, think deeply. Talk about it.

If you're looking for more books than can be found in a library or a bookstore, there are other good places to browse. One is *Children's Books in Print,* an annual guide found in many library reference rooms. This three-volume reference tool, published by R. R. Bowker, lists the titles of close to 100,000 books; two volumes provide brief annotations of many of them, and a third volume offers a subject guide to the titles listed in the other two.

It's also helpful to browse through reviews of new children's books, in newspapers, in standard reviewing resources such as *Publishers Weekly* or *Booklist* (available in the periodical sections of most good libraries), or in journals specifically devoted to children's literature, such as *Horn Book* (described below). But don't be too willing to trust a reviewer's judgment about a book. Remember that we all read differently, and that reviewers are only human, with human prejudices and flaws. Therefore, it's helpful in reading a review to think about the basic assumptions about books and children implied by the reviewer's opinions. Then you can use those opinions as a basis for making your own decision about whether or not a particular book might interest you. Sometimes, for instance, you can figure out enough about a reviewer's prejudices to realize that everything the reviewer likes you won't, and vice versa—and that makes that reviewer's work as useful to you as someone's whose opinions you tend to agree with.

Finding Criticism: Basic Resources

Let's assume you're intrigued by a particular children's novel or picture book, or fascinated by a number of novels by the same author; and you'd like to know how other people respond to these texts, or what sense others have made out of them. The best place to begin a search for critical discussions of specific authors of children's books is the reference room of any good library. There you'll find a number of guides to books and articles that contain discussions of specific texts or the work of specific writers.

A good place to start is *The Dictionary of Literary Biography (DLB),* published by Gale Research. This is a many-volumed series. There are currently over 150 volumes, and the series is still growing. Each volume deals with writers of a specific kind—playwrights or writers of crime fiction—or writers from a specific place or time in history. The volumes that deal with writers of children's literature are: *American Writers for Children 1900–1960,* v. 22; *American Writers for Children Before 1900,* v. 42; *American Writers for Children Since 1960: Fiction,* v. 52; *Ameri-*

can Writers for Children Since 1960: Poets, Illustrators, and Nonfiction Authors, v. 61; and *British Children's Writers 1880–1914,* v. 141. In addition, discussions of writers for children who were also known for other kinds of writing can be found scattered throughout the other volumes.

But how can you find them? Fortunately, each volume contains a cumulative index for the entire series so far; so if you want to find the entry on a particular writer, just look the name up in the index in the volume with the highest number you can find, and it'll tell you in which of the earlier volumes to look.

The entries on specific writers in *DLB* offer critical commentary on their work in the context of the events of their lives. The entries are of varying length and quality, but all of them offer a place to begin thinking further about a writer's work. Each *DLB* entry also includes a bibliography of other critical discussions of the author's work, and these bibliographies are worth consulting. Not only will they lead you to critical articles about the author, but the "Lists of Works Cited" in those articles might well contain the names of still other articles you can find and read. In this way, you can enter into an intertextual chain of dialogues and discussions with a variety of differing opinions about the same texts. (I also recommend the same use of the lists of "Work Cited" for each chapter of *Pleasures.*)

Another particularly useful resource you'll find in the reference room is *Children's Literature Review,* also published by Gale. This too is a series that's growing: as I write this, there are 34 volumes in my university's reference room. Each volume provides entries on fifteen or twenty writers for children, and each entry offers excerpts from a number of different critical discussions of specific works that were previously published elsewhere. Some of the excerpts are from book reviews, some from articles published in newspapers or popular magazines or in scholarly journals. Some excerpts are only a paragraph or two. Some are many pages, and reprint most of the contents of an entire article. The contents of each volume is quite random: commentary on a diverse group of children's writers. But each volume contains cumulative indexes to both authors and titles of books, so that you can find the entry on a specific writer or text by consulting the indexes in the volume with the highest number.

This series can be useful in two ways. First, reading through the excerpts can give you a good general sense of the central concerns readers most often have in response to specific texts. It becomes clear as you read through excerpts from a number of different sources how often they come back to the same central issues and express differing opinions and conclusions about them. Second, you can determine which of the pieces excerpted interest you most—and then, go find them and read the entire article or book these excepts come from.

In addition to these tools, there are a few bibliographic guides devoted specifically to listing literary discussions of children's literature that you might find in a good reference room. The most useful one is Linnea Hendrickson's own book: *Children's Literature: A Guide to the Criticism* (Boston: Hall, 1986). It's comprehensive, but out of date: It doesn't cover work done in recent years. I am told a new edition may soon appear, either as a book or online; watch for it. The 1986 version *is* now online through the NMSU Gopher; see below, under "On the Internet."

In order to find guides to criticism published more recently, you'll have to leave the reference room and look at some journals.

Children's Literature Abstracts. This is a quarterly guide to books and periodical articles about children's literature and allied topics. It is international in scope, and covers articles and books published around the world in many languages. It provides brief critical descriptions of the articles and books, and organizes them in terms of which authors they are about and also, in terms of a variety of subjects, such as "Fantasy and Science Fiction" and "Canon, Censorship, and Stereotyping." *Children's Literature Abstracts* is an excellent guide for browsing, especially since the brief abstracts give a pretty clear idea of what the articles and books are about. It's a little bit less useful if you're looking for something on a particular text or topic, since there's no cumulative annual gatherings of the contents of the separate issues (there is, however, an annual index). If your library doesn't have *Children's Literature Abstracts,* it can by obtained by writing:

Gillian Adams, Editor
Children's Literature Abstracts
5906 Fairlane Drive
Austin, TX 78757

Children's Literature Association Quarterly (ChLAQ). This is a journal devoted to critical investigations of children's literature, and I'll say more about the articles it prints later. In addition to those articles, the *ChLAQ* provides detailed annual guides to research in children's literature—and particularly to critical discussions of specific texts. You'll find these guides in *ChLAQ* 14.2 (Summer 1989); 15.2 (Summer 1990); 16.3 (Fall 1991); 17.2 (Summer 1992); 18.2 (Summer 1993); and 20.2 (Summer 1994); they are extensive listings, and fill almost all of each of these issues. The current policy appears to be to print this guide annually in the summer issue of the *ChLAQ;* so look for it there first in succeeding years.

This guide not only lists selections about specific authors and illustrators, but also about a number of other subjects: censorship, critics and critical approaches, illustration, and so on. This means you can look for opinions about specific topics as well as discussions about specific authors or texts. Each entry offers a brief description of what the selection is about. This is currently the most useful guide available for finding further discussions of the topics covered in *Pleasures.*

Unfortunately, the *ChLAQ* isn't as widely available in libraries as it ought to be. If you can't find it, you might encourage your librarian to order it; there's information about subscribing below.

Other Guides. Meanwhile, though, you'll have to look elsewhere. The contents of many journals that run articles related to children's literature are indexed in standard annual bibliographies, available in most research reference rooms, that cover wider areas of research. For instance, *Current Index to Journals in Education*

(Oryx Press) and *The Education Index* (Wilson), both of which cover work done in all aspects of education research, includes listings of the contents of some journals that discuss children's literature in the context of education. They are good places to look for discussions about teaching children literary skills and strategies. Both *The Humanities Index* (Wilson) and *The British Humanities Index* (Library Association) include listings of articles about children's literature in a range of journals devoted to subjects like anthropology or art where you might not expect to find them. And you might find some useful articles about topics like censorship and book selection by consulting the appropriate heading in *Reader's Guide to Periodical Literature* (Wilson), which lists articles in popular journals like *Time* and *The New Yorker.*

In terms of the kinds of questions about children's literature that *Pleasures* deals with, the most helpful general guide is the annual *MLA [Modern Language Association] International Bibliography*. Some reference rooms have the *MLA Bibliography* available on CD Rom. It's the most extensive listing of scholarly writing about all aspects of literature and literary theory, from deconstruction to Shakespeare to children's literature. It can be accessed by looking up specifics authors or specific topics, such as, say, censorship, or animals as characters. But as with all bibliographic tools, you have to approach this one with some caution. It doesn't necessarily index all the different periodicals that might have published materials of potential interest. And it doesn't always represent the complete contents of the journals it does index; for instance, it seems to leave out all articles in the children's literature journals it indexes that deal with illustration or picture books—because the compilers foolishly think these matters have nothing to do with literature?

Journals

So far, I've suggested ways of finding materials about specific authors or specific topics that you've already chosen. But what if you haven't chosen any? What if you'd just like to get an idea of the kinds of things people say in print about children's literature? Or what if you haven't yet chosen a specific author or text to think further about, and would like some ideas about ones that might be interesting? Once more, browsing is a good idea; you can look through current or back issues of journals devoted to considering aspects of children's literature.

As I suggested earlier, children's literature can be approached and discussed in the context of a large variety of concerns. There are journals that focus on each of these concerns: journals for reading specialists that are devoted to the teaching of reading; journals for teachers that are about the use of literature across the curriculum; journals for librarians devoted to questions about book selection. All of these can offer interesting insights, and are useful to browse in; you might want to look at journals such as *Language Arts, The Reading Teacher, Book Links,* or *School Library Journal.* But in the paragraphs that follow, I describe the journals most likely to contain articles that use or consider the kinds of literary approaches and literary issues *Pleasures* centers on.

Horn Book. The most traditional and the most widely available children's literature journal, *Horn Book* focuses on authors more than it does on texts. It often prints articles by authors about their work and how they came to write it; as I write this, the current issue contains pieces of this sort by the novelist Vera B. Williams and the picture book writer and illustrator Allan Say. *Horn Book* tends to approach children's literature primarily in the ways I outline in chapter 1 as "the old certainties." It devotes a lot of attention to making evaluative judgments about books in terms of a traditional set of standards about what makes for quality writing: originality of style, depth of characterization, and so on. *Horn Book* writers tend to place an especially high value on texts that express traditional humane, liberal values such as tolerance for and celebration of nonconformity. Horn Book pays little attention to the actual reading interests of children, to the cultural context in which children read, or to current trends in literary theory. Nevertheless, the journal offers useful information about how authors view their own books; and it reviews a large number of the more unusual and therefore, more likely to be interesting, children's book published each month.

For subscription information to *Horn Book,* write:

Horn Book
Circulation Department
11 Beacon Street
Suite 1000
Boston, MA 02108

Children's Literature. This is an annual journal: There's only one book-length number each year. This means it may not be kept with the other periodicals in a library, so you'll have to look in the catalog or ask a librarian where you can find it. *Children's Literature* has a prestigious publisher: Yale University Press. Not surprisingly, then, it represents high standards of scholarship. The focus is firmly and completely literary: The authors of the articles approach texts of children's literature in the same ways that other literary scholars approach Shakespeare or Virginia Woolf, and little is said about issues of literature in children's education or book selection. The articles have the strengths and failings of most contemporary scholarly discussion of literature: While they sometimes make excessive and over-complex use of the jargon of literary theory, they almost always represent interesting new ideas and interpretations. Their main failing is that they often sound like each other: The articles don't often convey much sense of authors' distinct voices or personalities. Even so, *Children's Literature* is probably the most consistently groundbreaking and interesting of the journals I discuss here.

The articles in *Children's Literature* cover everything from the narrative structures of picture books to the ideology of *Charlotte's Web*. A fairly high proportion of them are about children's literature of the past, by writers such as Maria Edgeworth or Lewis Carroll. Many others are about well-known classics of more recent years; articles about texts by Maurice Sendak, Ursula LeGuin and E. B. White appear frequently. *Children's Literature* often publishes "special issues" consisting of groups of articles on the same topic. For instance, volume 20, published in 1992, contains eight articles dealing with various aspects of the work of Rudyard Kipling.

Each issue also includes a number of reviews of books about children's literature: These are extensive discussions, longer and more detailed than most book reviews. As examples of scholars responding to each other, they offer fascinating insights into the nature of our dialogues about literature.

If you're interested in subscribing to *Children's Literature,* the best way to do so is to become a member of the Children's Literature Association. See the end of the next section for more information.

Children Literature Association Quarterly.   This is one of two journals made available to members of the Children's Literature Association; the other is *Children's Literature,* which I've just described. The Association consists of professors, librarians, educators, and others interested in the whole range of literary approaches to children's literature—not just in interpretation of texts and literary theory, but also in questions about how children respond to books and in ways of teaching children literary skills and strategies. The *Quarterly* reflects this wide range of interests. The articles offer interpretations of specific books, discussions of texts in terms of ideological and narrative theory, descriptions of ways of teaching children literary strategies. In addition, columns appear on an occasional basis on subjects such as children's drama, children's literature and literary theory, and cultural pluralism. As I reported above, one number of the *Quarterly* each year is devoted to an extensive bibliography of criticism and discussion of children's literature. There are also reviews of books about children's literature, many of them quite lengthy and interestingly involved in detailed dialogues with the books in question.

Perhaps because of the wide range of its interests, the *Quarterly* is the most eclectic of the journals I discuss here. The articles vary widely in complexity, from simple descriptive summaries of a selection of books dealing with a particular subject to complex theoretical discussions of metafictional narrative or feminist ideology. The *Quarterly* often runs groups of articles related to a specific topic; for instance, the Winter 1993–94 issue (18,4) contains five articles about depictions of mothers and daughters in children's literature. The *Quarterly* is less consistently toughminded and groundbreaking than *Children's Literature* but often much more interesting to read; there's more sense of a variety of different voices finding expression in it.

Anyone interested in the topics and approaches discussed in *Pleasures* might well consider joining the Children's Literature Association. A membership means you'd get your own copies of both the journals it publishes: *Children's Literature* and the *Children's Literature Association Quarterly.* You'd also get information about the annual conference of the association, and information about a number of other activities it engages in, from publishing books of criticism to awarding scholarship for research in children's literature. Membership information is available from:

Children's Literature Association
P.O. Box 138
Battle Creek, MI 49016

The Lion and the Unicorn. While the articles in this journal discuss everything from abridged versions of classics to depictions of musicians, most of them tend to approach texts of children's literature in terms of political, social, and cultural concerns. That makes the journal less eclectic than *Children's Literature* or the *Quarterly*. But the articles do cover a range of issues, from the politics of gender and socialization to the ideological content of texts. *The Lion and the Unicorn* is also the only children's literature journal that often pays attention to movies, TV, and popular culture for children, and attempts to look at literary texts in terms of these important contexts. The articles are varied in length and complexity: from fairly short, simple pieces and interviews with authors of children's books to some of the most densely complex of ideological theorizing.

There are two issues of *Lion and the Unicorn* each year. Most issues have a special topic; for instance, all the articles in the December 1993 issue (17,2) deal with theories of class in children's literature, and the June 1994 issue (18,1) contains a number of articles about the Nancy Drew series.

To subscribe to *Lion and the Unicorn,* write:

The Johns Hopkins University Press
Journals Division
2715 North Charles Street
Baltimore, MD 21218–4319

Children's Literature in Education. As its title suggests, this journal focuses on questions about teaching children literary skills and strategies. But it does that in the faith that good teaching emerges from engaged responses to and involvement with texts. As a result, the articles tend to be knowledgeable about both literary and pedagogical theory, and often offer rich and subtle interpretations of texts. *Children's Literature in Education* therefore represents the meeting of literary criticism and theory and literary pedagogy for children. It's a journal anyone interested in the literary education of children should know about.

Children's Literature in Education publishes articles on a variety of topics. Recent issues contain pieces about the usefulness of structural analysis in teaching children literature and about ways of reading postmodern picture books as well as interpretations of texts by Maurice Sendak and Lewis Carroll.

Children's Literature in Education has an interesting editorial policy. It has two different sets of editors, one in the United States and one in Great Britain. Each set of editors is responsible for half the contents of each issue. The journal therefore always represents a dialogue between the viewpoints of people in different countries and continents.

Subscription information can be obtained from:

Children's Literature in Education
Subscription Department
Human Sciences Press, Inc.
233 Spring Street
New York, NY 10013–1578

The New Advocate.   This journal also focuses on children's experience of literature in the classroom, and often offers descriptions of specific classroom projects that involve teaching children strategies for making sense of literature. Recent issues have contained discussions of children's responses to texts about children in other lands and on political correctness in writing for young people.
Subscription information can be obtained from:

The New Advocate
Christopher Gordon Publishers, Inc.
480 Washington Street
Norwood, MA 02062

Journal of Children's Literature.   A publication of the Children's Literature Assembly of the National Council of Teachers of English, this journal used to be called the *Children's Literature Assembly Bulletin*. Under its new name, it still focuses on issues involving literature in education but now promises to present more in-depth critical discussion than in the past. A recent special issue focused on the topic of children's literature and basal readers. You can obtain subscription information through the editor:

Dan Hade, Editor
Journal of Children's Literature
255 Chambers Building
The Pennsylvania State University
University Park, PA 16802

Signal.   This British children's literature journal is something of a cross between *Horn Book* and *Children's Literature:* It publishes everything from interviews with authors to descriptive reviews of all the new poetry books published in a given year to discussion of feminist theory. Recent issues include a look at the intertextuality of Maurice Sendak's *Down in the Dumps with Jack and Guy* and a discussion of parent observations of children's reading. It's a delightfully quirky journal; the authors write in a wide variety of styles, often personal, often intriguingly innovative. As a result, the articles are neither consistently interesting nor consistently useful; but when they are good, they are very good indeed.
Signal comes out three times a year. For a subscription, write:

The Thimble Press
Lockwood
Station Road
South Woodchester
Stroud UK GL5 5EQ

Bookbird. *Bookbird* is the journal of the International Board on Books for Young People (IBBY), and its contributors include a worldwide network of associate editors communicating information about children's literature in their own countries. *Bookbird* is a useful resource for anyone interested in multicultural issues or just in knowing more about how books for children differ in different places. To subscribe, write:

Bookbird Subscriptions
P.O. Box 3156
West Lafayette, IN 47906

Canadian Children's Literature. My national pride requires me to mention this journal: Not only does it consistently publish criticism of high quality, but most of it is about children's literature written by Canadians and published in Canada. This makes *Canadian Children's Literature* essential for Canadians interested in children's literature; but the theoretical depth and value of the criticism it publishes makes it relevant for readers in other countries also. Furthermore, Canada has produced a surprising amount of entertaining and often unusual children's literature in the past decade or so, and this journal provides an excellent guide to it, not only in its critical discussions but in the many reviews it publishes of children's books.

Canadian Children's Literature publishes articles on all aspects of Canadian picture books, poetry, and children's fiction; it also contains interviews with Canadian authors. The issues often have special topics. Recent ones have focused on depictions of masculinity, recycled fairy tales, and the children's literature produced in the province of British Columbia.

For subscription information, write:

Canadian Children's Literature
Department of English
University of Guelph
Guelph Ontario N1G 2W1
Canada

On the Internet

As I write this, I'm the owner of a brand new computer and I have my first connection to the Internet. I'm just beginning to explore it, but I already know that there's a lot of information out there, including much about children's literature. And I've already discovered places where I can indulge my desire to engage with others in dialogue about children's books.

What I've discovered so far has been mainly by random browsing—and I'm sure that you can find more if you do your own browsing. Just enter information retrieval systems like Gopher or the World Wide Web and start looking. What follows is a bare beginning of places to look.

First of all, you can access the catalogs of many libraries for information about their holdings. For instance, you can reach the Library of Congress by going online to the Internet and then typing this:

telnet locis.loc.gov

Another useful resource to know about is Uncover, a commercial service that will send you copies of articles from a vast range of journals; they claim to be adding thousands of new citations every day. The service provides a list of articles containing the key words you identify in their titles. You don't have to actually order any copies to enter this database, so it's an excellent way of finding articles about specific topics or writers, which you can then either order or else look for in your own library. To reach this service, go online to the Internet and then type:

telnet database.carl.org

For information about children's literature in particular, an excellent resource is the children's literature Gopher service at New Mexico State University. Enter Gopher and then type this:

telnet library.nmsu.edu

Then, once connected, ask for "resources," then "education," then "children's literature" from the lists of selections that come up on your screen. You'll get a variety of information, including a handy guide to reference materials relating to children's literature and some actual texts of books for children online. Also, don't forget you can use the various subject guides available in Gopher, such as Veronica, to find further information.

If you have an interface that connects you to the World Wide Web (WWW), such as Mosaic, Netscape, or Lynx, you can access information through it. If you don't, you can still gain access to the WWW by typing this:

telnet telnet.w3.org

The subject directory you'll find here can point you toward information about children's literature. One resource I found is a discussion group at:

rec.arts.books.childrens

Here people are trading ideas about questions such as what's the worst children's book ever written.

On WWW there are also a number of "home pages" providing information that relate to children's literature, for instance,

http://mindvox.phantom.com/~fairrosa

or

http://www.armory.com/~web/web.html

But the most complete one seems to be the Children's Literature Web page maintained by David K. Brown of the University of Calgary. It includes all sorts of useful (and not so useful but fascinating) information, as well as links to most of the other sites I've mentioned so far. The address is:

http://www.ucalgary.ca/~dkbrown/index.html

If you're particularly interested in taking part in discussion of children's literature then I recommend joining an E-mail list. Once you do, you can read all the messages people send to it and if you wish, take part in the discussion yourself. There are a number of such lists.

One called KIDLIT involves teachers, librarians, students, and others interested in the field. To subscribe, send E-mail to:

LISTSERV@BINGVMB.CC.BINGHAMTON.EDU

Your message should contain the following line:

subscribe KIDLIT-L [your first name] [your last name]

To send a message to the membership of the list, send E-mail to:

kidlit-l@bingvmb.cc.binghamton.edu

PUBYAC is a list for children's and young adult librarians in public libraries. To subscribe, send E-mail to:

LISTSERVER@NYSERNET.ORG

Your message should contain the following line:

subscribe PUBYAC [your first name] [your last name]

To send a message to the membership of the list, send E-mail to:

pubyac@nysernet.org

But the list that most interests me is CHILDLIT. Here the discussion focuses on children's literature and literary theory, and I sometimes take part in it myself. You can join CHILDLIT by sending E-mail to:

LISTSERV@RUTVM1.BITNET

or

LISTSERV@RUTVM1.RUTGERS.EDU

Your message should contain the following line:

subscribe CHILDLIT [your first name] [your last name]

Finally, there's me. If you have comments about *The Pleasures of Children's Literature* or want to share your response to something in it, I'd be glad to hear from you. You can contact me by E-mail at:

nodelman@io.UWinnipeg.ca

Glossary

This section gathers together definitions of words and concepts that appear throughout the book. The terms come from a variety of scholarly disciplines: literary criticism and theory, ideological theory, cognitive and developmental psychology, psychoanalysis and others.

Absences. The ideas or assumptions—often about class or gender or race—that a literary text takes for granted and therefore does not actually assert. We "read against a text" when we focus on absences and try to surface them, that is, determine what they are.

Accommodation. In developmental theory, the process by which we adapt our systems of meaning-making in the light of new information.

Agnosis. James Moffett's term to describe the motivation of many would-be censors of books: It means "not-wanting-to-know." For those suffering from *agnosis,* knowledge is seen as threatening to their values. To know is to see beyond what one has always believed, to be unable to take it for granted any longer.

Alliteration. Repeated consonants that produce a pattern of the same or similar sounds, particularly in poetry—such as the *p* and *s* sounds in this sentence.

Ambivalence. Uncertainty about something: inability to choose between a variety of different and contradictory interpretations of it. Many of the most interesting literary texts seem to be ambivalent about the meaning of the actions they describe, and leave readers either to choose one of a group of possibilities or else to share the uncertainty.

Anthology. A collection of literary texts by different authors, gathered together in the same book.

Aporia. According to the theory of *deconstruction,* a point in a literary text at which its apparent meaning turns on itself and seems to imply the opposite, and the text's apparent wholeness or unity crumbles and disintegrates. The sentence you are now reading, in which I claim that there is no such thing as an aporia, contains an aporia.

Appropriation. The act of making a claim on someone else's culture or group by telling a story depicting members of that culture or group. Those who object to this practice believe that the ways in which stories represent people are always distorted by the conscious and unconscious attitudes of their authors. Since readers come to accept fictional representations as the truth, stories by writers of racial or cultural backgrounds different from their characters will always be dangerously misleading—a claiming or appropriation of the right to say what it means or feels like to belong to a particular group.

Archetypes. The basic symbols and meanings which, according to the psychoanalytical theorist Carl Jung, make up the collective unconscious of the human race. Similar symbols or story patterns that appear in the myths and religions of cultures around the world are different expressions of the same archetypes. Whenever we express ourselves, our utterances can be seen to contain archetypal imagery and to express the universal meaning attached to those archetypal images. For Northrop Frye, archetypes are not necessarily aspects of the unconscious; they are symbols and patterns found frequently in literary texts, perhaps because new writers think of older texts as they write. Frye sees literature as a whole as having built up its own archetypal images and patterns of organization over the centuries.

Assimilation. In developmental theory, the process by which we integrate new information into our previously established systems of meaning.

Assonance. Repeated vowels that produce a pattern of the same or similar sounds, especially in poetry: for instance, "*a bad man with a tan cat lacks a mammoth lamb.*"

Assumption. Any idea or opinion we take for granted, sometimes without even being aware of it. When we explore assumptions, we consider their validity. We try to determine if they are logical or if there is evidence to support or to question them.

Back-story. In toy merchandising, a narrative that establishes the personality and history of a character toy or set of toys. Back-stories are provided by packaging and in TV cartoons and commercials.

Binary opposite. In structural theory as discussed in chapter 9, opposing ideas such as hard and soft, good and evil, pleasure and pain, which conflict with and relate to each other in various ways in order to create the structure of cultures, artifacts, and literary texts. In chapter 8, I suggest that certain combinations of binary opposites are characteristic of children's literature.

Cartoon and caricature. Styles of visual art in which people and objects are represented in terms of a few lines that emphasize and exaggerate their most obvious features, often for humorous effect.

Castration complex. In Freudian psychology, the fear that one's genital organ may be (or has been) removed as punishment for Oedipal feelings. See *Oedipus complex*.

Category maintenance work. The psychologist Bronwyn Davies's term to describe the actions of children who tease or taunt others whose behavior defies their conceptions of gender. The purpose is to bring others into line in order to feel more secure about one's own assumptions.

Character and character development. Characters are the people evoked by the words of a literary text. When we focus on characters and characterization as we read literary texts, we assume the consistency of the text will emerge from what it says about motivation and personality, and we look for information about the personalities of the people the text describes. Characters are understood to *develop*—change and grow—both when they are described as changing and when readers come to understand more about them as a story progresses. See also *Flat characters; Round characters*.

Character toys. Toys that represent human or imaginary characters, such as G. I. Joe or My Little Pony, who occupy a particular imaginary setting in an implied narrative or *back-story*. Such toys often come in collectible sets.

Claw back. A process by which cultures conform the validity of their ideologies. On TV and in written texts, members of other species and other cultures are depicted in terms of their resemblances to ourselves, so that we find in their behavior metaphoric equivalences with our own culture's way of organizing its affairs.

Climax. The highest or most intense point in the development of a story.

Codes. See *Signs*.

Collective unconscious. The psychoanalyst Jung's theory that the unconscious does not, as Freud postulated, develop separately and differently in different people. Instead, it is shared by and always present in all humans, underlying and influencing our conscious thoughts. The contents of the collective unconscious are *archetypes:* symbols and patterns shared by all human beings, and expressed in different but surprisingly similar ways by different religions and cultures.

Colonization. Literally, what a country does in taking charge of another country and controlling its economy and its politics, on the theory that those colonized are not capable of handling their own affairs. In order to be successfully colonized, people must accept their own inability to run things for themselves. In relation to children, *colonization* is the act of teaching them to see themselves as we would like to imagine them, so that we can feel justified in our exercise of power over them.

Concrete operational stage. In Piagetian theory, the stage occupied by children from age six to eleven. They are beginning to understand some of the basic concepts that underlie our ability to think about the world, but only in terms of concrete examples.

Concretization. The process of forming mental pictures—imagining what is being described as exactly as the words of the text allow us to. Concretization includes not just *visualization*—imagining what things look like—but also mental evocations of smells and sounds and other senses.

Consistency and consistency-building. We imagine texts have consistency when we assume that everything they say or do fits together to make a meaningful whole: that all the words and patterns fit together. Once we assume that consistency exists, we work as readers to perceive what the whole is. We use the schemata developed from our previous experience of literature to unfold the consistency. Reader-response theory calls this activity *consistency-building* on the assumption that the consistency exists more as a result of a reader's mental activity than it does as something actually existing in a text. Texts give us the information we need in order to build the consistency for ourselves as we read them.

Constructivism. The theory that knowledge is an active construction built up by individuals who act within social contexts. These contexts shape and constrain but don't absolutely determine what we come to understand about ourselves and others. Constructivism focuses on the balance between the freedom of individual response and the constraint of communal participation.

Context. The set of circumstances surrounding a particular object or event that might help to account for its qualities and characteristics. For instance, events in the life of a writer might be a context for understanding the texts the writer produced. In terms of language and literature, meaning always depends on context, and the same utterance can shift its meaning in a different context. "Watch out" can mean "Get out of the way" in the context of a safe falling from a second-story window, or "Look at the door marked OUT" in the context of hoping to see a celebrity emerge from an office building. In picture books, words and pictures act as contexts for each other.

Continuous narrative. Joseph Schwarcz's terms for pictures that show the same character in a number of different poses, implying a series of consecutive actions.

Cultural studies. As applied to literature, this term refers to approaches to literary texts that attempt to place them in the context of culture at large. Attention is paid to social and ideological concerns as expressed in and influenced by literature, and to the relationships between literature, popular culture, and mass media. Cultural studies approaches assume that values and ideas circulate in a culture: Texts are influenced by and expressive of preexisting cultural forces, and in turn themselves influence their culture's view of itself.

Deconstruction. A poststructural theory of language suggesting that, because any given use of language is meaningful only through its relationships with other uses of language, no discrete text is ever complete or unified or cut off from other texts. Deconstruction explores texts to discover the subtle inconsistencies or *aporia* in their apparently unified meanings—the ways in which their central assumptions are at war with each other. A deconstructive reading is not an act of destruction, but an exploration of the constructions of literature to determine the extent of the artificiality, how they *are* constructed or manufactured, and how they work to disguise their own artifice.

Developmental stages. According to Piaget and many other developmental psychologists, a series of discrete and definable phases or periods that children pass through as they mature: *preoperational, concrete operational,* and *formal operational.* Each stage can be defined in terms of the kinds of thinking that can occur within it; each succeeding stage allows more sophisticated thought than the one before it. Children pass from one stage to the next through a process of encountering experience and teaching themselves how to make sense of it.

Dialogue. The intersection of different voices expressing different points of view that derive from different backgrounds, characters, and experiences. Writers of texts enter into dialogue with earlier texts, and with the world around them: and this means that texts themselves can be viewed as "dialogic," as multi-faceted conversations amongst different voices and ideas. Reading is an act of dialogue with a text; and it allows us to enter into further dialogue with other readers.

Didactic. Literature that has the primary purpose of teaching its readers, particularly moral lessons, is called *didactic*.

Discourse. The way in which the events of a story are told. It is in the discourse that flashbacks occur: As we move forward in the discourse, we are told of events that took place earlier in the sequence that makes up the story. The sequence of a discourse also includes descriptions of places and people. It is in the discourse that some of the events being told about are described in great detail, others merely skimmed over.

Displacement. Northrop Frye's term for the process by which mythic structures and story patterns become hidden within surface details, images, and symbols of apparently realistic fiction. The more displaced a myth becomes, the more irony there is in its presentation: Jon Scieszka's *The True Story of the 3 Little Pigs by A. Wolf* is a displaced version of the original fairy tale, which, some might argue, is itself a displaced version of an ancient religious myth about natural forces contending with each other.

Embed. To place someone or something in a position in relation to other people or objects. In terms of ideology, to become embedded is to have one's positions and power defined in relation to one's social role as defined by others: to be defined and required to act as a man or woman or taxpayer—or as a child.

Escape. Many people believe that one of the central pleasures of literature is the opportunities it gives us to "escape"—to immerse ourselves in a different person or world, to imagine we are someone or somewhere else and thus escape for a time from being ourselves. Much popular literature is specifically designed as escape literature; much escape literature is *wish fulfillment fantasy*.

Essentializing. Assuming that all members of a culturally or nationally defined group—people of African or Asian background, French-speaking people, Native Americans—all share the same essential characteristics by virtue of the membership in the group, and that all members of the group will always express and cannot escape the essential ethnic or racial soul that is theirs by genetic inheritance. Essentializing ignores the fact that both racial and national groups emerge due to historical circumstances that define the situations and therefore the generalizable characteristics of their members. Changes in history and culture will inevitably create changes in groups: Even considered as a group, American Jews have different assumptions and values than their European counterparts. Furthermore, the mere experience of different ways of life in different times and places will cause changes in individual members of groups.

Expectations. The assumptions we make or general understanding we develop from previous experience and apply to new experience. Response theory suggests that we start reading a literary text in terms of expectations built up by our previous reading of literature. Then, as we proceed through the text, new information causes old expectations to be confirmed or changed, and new ones to develop. Reading through an interesting text is a matter of constant shifts between expectation and surprise.

Exploration. The process of investigating an opinion, an idea, or a response to a text, in order to develop a greater understanding of it. Like explorers of new countries, we explore with the desire and expectation of knowing more but with no clear sense of exactly what we might end up discovering.

Fable. A story that isn't really about the characters in it, but about its readers. The characters described represent general human behavior in order to teach readers specific truths that can govern their own future actions. The fables included in the New Testament are called *parables*.

Fairy tale. A story that was once an oral *folktale,* but that has at some point in its history been written down and printed as a published text.

Feminist. One of a variety of approaches to reading literature that focuses on the significance of gender. Feminist approaches include both an interest in the depictions of female characters in books by men and women, and also, an exploration of the history, nature, and characteristics of writing by women.

First-person narrator. A first-person narrator or storyteller reports from his or her own subjective point of view events that he or she has personally experienced. Such a person speaks in the grammatical first person, as "I."

Flat characters. Those with a few easily distinguished traits which don't change or develop as a story progresses.

Flow. See *Fragmentation and flow.*

Focalization. In discussing narrative, this term is used to identify the position of the person who sees and understands the events being described, as opposed to the position of the person who tells about them. A *third-person narrative* may be focalized from one particular character's point of view.

Focalizers. The characters or narrators through whom texts are focalized. See *focalization.*

Focus. The position of a viewed object in relation to the viewer. See *Shots.*

Folktale. A story that circulates orally without having been written down. The folktales from cultures around the world have been organized by scholars in relation to tale *types:* basic plot lines shared by a variety of different versions. Fairy tales are written versions of folktales.

Formal operational stage. In Piagetian theory, the stage at which children can begin to handle abstract concepts. It is believed to occur from age twelve to fifteen.

Formula. A conventional kind of storytelling. Romance or horror stories are formula fiction: They offer their readers pleasure by following a common pattern of events and by always focusing on the same kinds of characters, events, and interests.

Fragmentation and flow. The characteristic way in which TV constructs experience. TV emits signals and information in an endless flow, with no beginning or end. But the flow consists of individual bits of information or parts of stories separated from each other: the many different shots that make up one commercial, the parts of a program interrupted by commercials, and so on. Viewers must make their own connection among the fragments.

Functions. According to the folklorist Vladimir Propp, the plots of all the Russian folk tales he explored consist of thirty-one basic units or *functions,* which he listed and numbered. While not all the tales contain all the functions, the functions always appear in the same sequence. The functions are a grammar of actions—an underlying structure of relationships between events that gives coherence to the plots of these and according to some later theorists, all other stories.

Gap. Something that a text does not actually tell us, but which we need to understand in order to make sense of it. Gaps are like holes in texts: We fill them up, and make the texts meaningful, with knowledge that we as readers provide ourselves—information from our own *repertoire,* or guesses about what words or actions imply derived from our previous experience of literature. Furthermore, narratives possess gaps in terms of encouraging readers to ask questions about what has not yet happened, or about why things happens as they do. If we read about a little girl meeting a wolf, we wonder if she will survive the encounter and how—and continue reading in order to fill those gaps. As something not there, a "gap" doesn't actually exist: Different readers perceive different gaps, and fill them in different ways. See chapter 4.

Gender. Ideas about what constitute maleness or femaleness, or what activities are masculine or feminine, as defined by cultural forces. Gender is different from sex: the biological state of having organs specific to males or females. Both gender and sex are different from sexuality, as in heterosexuality or homosexuality: the nature of one's desire in relation to the kinds of people that excite it. These terms are useful simply because so many differing combination of gender, sex and sexuality exist.

Genre. A category of literary texts defined by their shared characteristics. Poetry, drama and fiction are genres; so are romance fiction, horror fiction, and fiction for children. Within children's literature, there are many subgenres: nonsense poetry, time fantasies, tall tales, and so on.

Glance curve. According to Mercedes Gaffron, the usual manner in which people look at visual images: from the lower left in a curve toward the upper right.

Haiku. A short, three-line poem form originating in Japan. The first line and last line each have five syllables and the middle line has seven syllables. The last line sums up the essence of the experience expressed in the poem:

> A definition
> Of haiku poems provided—
> And so now you know.

Hailing. See *Interpellation.*

Hidden curriculum. A view of the world that many teachers, parents, and TV producers foster without realizing they are doing so, and which children can absorb without even realizing they are doing so. Many school curricula and many educational materials on TV and in written texts contain hidden curricula of ideological assumptions and cultural values.

Home/away/home story. One of the most basic story patterns of children's literature. A young child or childlike animal leaves the boring security of home in order to have exciting but dangerous adventures. Having learned the truth about the big world, the child or creature returns to the security it at first found burdensome, concluding that, despite its constraints, home is best. In many home/away/home stories, "away" is a place the child imagines.

Homosocial desire. The theorist Eve Kosofsky Sedgwick's term for what she sees as the major force that has traditionally driven heterosexual men: their desire for approbation from or mastery over other males. Sedgwick suggests that men's dealings with women are seen to have most significance in numerous literary texts as the medium by which men develop their bonds and establish their hierarchies of power with each other in their pursuit of homosocial desire. In order to be expressed safely, homosocial desire must distinguish itself from homosexual desire, and therefore, it leads to homophobia: the fear and repression of homosexuality.

Hues. Classifications of colors, like "red" or "blue," that refer to different parts of the spectrum.

Hybridization. The process by which the values and attitudes of members of minority groups are influenced and changed by their dealings with a dominant mainstream culture. A focus on hybridization lessens the dangers of *essentializing*.

Identification. The process by which readers come to see connections between characters in literature and themselves. To identify with a character is to empathize, to see a relationship between the character and oneself, and perhaps to imagine oneself in terms of what happens to the character.

Identification/Manipulation. The process by which readers who identify with characters are persuaded into believing that what happens to the characters is in fact a message about themselves and how they ought to behave.

Ideology. The body of ideas and beliefs common in a society or culture that controls (or at least, tries to control) how we as participants in the society or culture view the world and understand our place within it. Ideological beliefs may be expressed and acted upon consciously and unconsciously. As usually understood, their most significant effect is to define our power in relation to others: who has power over whom, and why they must have it or keep it.

Idyll, idyllic. See *Pastoral*.

Image. The contents of a visual picture or illustration. For instance, an illustrated version of Snow White contains images of dwarfs. Also, a mental picture evoked by the words of a verbal text. Texts contain various levels of imagery. A poem about a tree might create an image or picture of the tree, but also ask us to see it as a woman raising her arms in prayer; both the tree and the woman might be identified as images.

Implied reader. The imaginary reader a text suggests that it expects. Thinking about a text's implied reader is a way of developing an understanding of the kinds of interest it engages and the skills and strategies required to make something like the intended sense of it.

Implied speaker. The character of the storyteller implied by the words of a text. In some stories, the speaker or teller is someone telling about things that happened to himself or herself. In others, the storyteller isn't a character in the story, but nevertheless reveals specific character traits by the choice of words and the way in which the story is told.

Impressionism. A style of visual art first used in the nineteenth century, which uses short brushstrokes of many different colors in an attempt to capture the effect of how light falls on objects. Famous impressionist painters include Paul Cézanne, Jean Renoir, and Claude Monet.

Interpellation. The ideological theorist Louis Althusser's term for the process by which we are "hailed" by our culture as certain kinds of individuals or *subjects*. We come to see ourselves in the way our culture wants us to see ourselves in the process of acknowledging that it is indeed we who are being hailed. TV commercials often act as clear attempts at interpellation. They say, for instance, "Hey, you, the person out there who worries about your body odor, our deodorant will help you." If you agree that you need the deodorant—see yourself as a person who smells and worries about it—then you have been successfully hailed.

Intertextuality. The network of words and texts that ties all language and literature and all experience of language and literature together. To consider a text's intertextuality is to explore the ways in which it relates to and depends on the existence of other texts and other uses of language. A dictionary reveals the intertextuality of language by defining all words in terms of other words. See *Text*.

Irony. Irony exists when the apparent literal meaning of a statement or a text is different from and usually opposite to the intended meaning. It would be ironic to say, "Nice day, isn't it?" in the middle of a blizzard. In Northrop Frye's archetypal theory, the *ironic mode* tells of characters inferior to others in power or intelligence; stories in the ironic mode represent the most *displaced* form of myth.

Isomorph. An object which has the same form or appearance as another, but which has come into existence by different means. In ideological terms, an isomorph is a representation of ourselves or our world invented by other people but which we believe to be an accurate vision of actual reality.

Lexia. One of the basic units into which Roland Barthes breaks a literary text, in order to show how the lexias engage our knowledge of codes. A lexia can consist of a word, a few words, a sentence—any piece of a text that can be separated from the whole and considered in itself. By extension, a *lexia* is any discrete fragment of a text as broken down by a reader or interpreter.

Limerick. A humorous poem consisting of five lines. The first and second rhyme with the fifth, and the shorter third rhymes with the shorter fourth. In the limericks by the popularizer of the form, Edward Lear, the last line is often a repetition of the first.

Literary canon. The body of literary texts considered to be most worthy of study. Canonical texts are the ones every educated person is expected to know, either because they are the most beautiful or because they express the greatest and most universally applicable ideas. From another point of view, the canon consists of texts written and designed to protect the interests of those in power. The traditional canon of English literature therefore consists almost exclusively of texts by and in defense of the power of white European males.

Literary fairy tale. A story modeled on the characteristics of traditional fairy tales but made up by one specific writer and therefore available in only one version.

Lived narratives. Bronwyn Davies's term for "the storylines that make up one's life." *Lived narratives* are the means by which we act out the *subject positions* we choose to occupy: we live out the story line the subject position implies.

Medium. The type of material out of which a visual depiction is made. Media include pencil, watercolor, oil paint, wood block printing, and so on.

Metaphor. A word or phrase that describes something as being something else, thus implying a similarity between the two: for instance, "children are the icing on the cake of life." If the comparison includes the words "like" or "as," then it's a particular kind of metaphor called a *simile:* "children are like icing."

Mimetic. Imitative of reality: Realistic fiction is mimetic of the world as we usually perceive it. For Northrop Frye, the *high mimetic* mode includes tales tells of heroes superior in degree to others but not to the environment, and the *low mimetic* mode includes tales of heroes superior neither to others nor to their environment.

Mirror stage. In Lacan's psychoanalytical theory, that period in early childhood when one develops a sense of self. This is an act of limitation: To be conscious of one's existence as a separate entity is to see oneself as just a small separate part of a larger whole—something like imagining oneself to be as limited as the part of oneself that oneself and others see in a mirror. Thus, to be a self is also, paradoxically, to be conscious of all that one is not and therefore lacks.

Mode. The literary theorist Northrop Frye's term for classifications of literary texts in terms of the relationship between characters and their environments. There are four modes: myth, romance, mimetic, ironic. Each is a *displacement* of the one preceding it; that is, each succeeding mode tells the same story in a version less ideal and imaginary and more naturalistic than the mode before it.

Multiculturalism. An approach to literature and literary education that focuses on the diversity of texts written by and representing people of a variety of racial, ethnic, and cultural backgrounds.

Myth. Myths are stories with a special status. For those who believe in them, they are true—not symbolically true or allegorically true, but absolutely true, a factual accounting of the nature of the world as it is. If we accept their truth, furthermore, myths tell us how to live: what to believe and how to behave. In other words, "myth" is the name we give to stories that express religious truth, when we happen not to believe they are true. According to the structural anthropologist Claude Lévi-Strauss, myths represent significant transformations in the cultures that produced them. They are stories of the change from one orderly system of societal relationships to another. For Northrop Frye, the *mode* of myth tells tales of heroes superior in kind to other humans and to their environment: gods.

Narrator. A person in the act of telling or narrating a story. See *Implied Speaker, First-person narrator,* and *Third-person narrator.*

Nonfiction. Informational writing that purports to describe real people, events, and objects as they actually are.

Obviousness. The ideological theorist Louis Althusser's term for an assumption, idea, or belief we simply take for granted, without even being aware that we are doing so. It goes without saying that, upon investigation, obviousnesses may turn out not to be true. In fact, it's obvious.

Oedipus complex. In psychoanalysis, the desire of children to eliminate the parent of their own sex and thus pave the way for the relationship they unconsciously desire with the parent of the other sex.

Omniscient narrator. A storyteller who knows the thoughts of some or all of the characters.

Orgastic pattern. The literary theorist Robert Scholes's term for describing the most common fictional plot: a series of actions that create a gradually increasing suspense until they reach a culminating point at which our interest is at its most intense—a *climax*—and then quickly come to an end. Scholes sees this sequence as equivalent to the sequential pattern common in human sexual activity.

Other. According to a number of deconstructive and ideological theorists, we tend to see groups over whom we have power as something *other* than ourselves: as our direct and exact opposite. If we white men are wise, then women or blacks or children are ignorant; if we are civilized, then members of those other (or, theorists sometimes say, *othered*) groups are savage. To perceive members of a group as "the other" is to marginalize them, to deny their sharing in our humanity as a way of justifying the power we have relative to them.

Parable. See *Fable*.

Paradox. A paradox consists of two ideas which appear to be contradictory, but both of which are true at the same time.

Pastoral idyll. A traditional form of poem that celebrates the joys of the unsophisticated rural life, close to nature and in the company of friends. Some commentators see children's literature, in its nostalgia for the unsophisticated world of childhood and in its focus on animals and on the healing nature of gardens and woods and fresh air, as a form of pastoral idyll. See *Utopia*.

Penis envy. Freud's theory that young girls feel deprived by their lack of a penis, and envy males.

Perspective. In visual art, a technique of depicting the depth and relative distance of three-dimensional object on a two-dimensional plane. Perspective drawing shows the relative size of objects at various distances as seen from one particular point of view.

Phallus. A symbolic representation of a penis. In Lacan's psychoanalytical theory, the phallus is a symbolic representation of the power of the father, an important part of the language of the unconscious: "the phallus is a signifier."

Pictorial dynamics. The ways in which the various objects depicted in a visual image are related to each other. The dynamics of a picture both create interesting and involving visual patterns for viewers and communicate information about the narrative significance of the objects' relationships to each other.

Picture book. As used in this book, this term refers to short fictional or nonfictional books for children that contain a large picture on each double-paged spread, usually accompanied by a short verbal text.

Pleasure. In this book, I use this word to refer to the state of feeling or being pleased, and with the understanding that many different kinds of activities have the potential to please us, including the gratifications of thought and the satisfaction of having power.

Plot. The sequence of events that make up a story. Successful plots get us so interested in finding out what happens next that they create suspense and encourage us to keep on reading.

Point of view. The perspective from which a story is told. Considering point of view is a matter of asking from whose perspective the events are being described: Is it a detached narrator, or a specific one of the characters? See also *Focalization*.

Preoperational stage. In Piagetian theory, the stage of development at which children, while beginning to use symbols, lack the ability to think about what they are doing. Preoperational children are egocentric, that is, unable to understand any point of view but their own. The stage is believed to span from age two to seven.

Presentist. An attitude to past events that distorts them by viewing them in term of our own modern values.

Protagonist. The main character in a story.

Psychoanalysis. Theories of the human mind including the original ones developed by Sigmund Freud and variations on it by a number of followers, involving the relationship of conscious and unconscious processes. Psychoanalytical theory gives rise to a number of strategies for interpreting literary texts.

Reader-response theory. An approach to literature that focuses on the processes we follow in reading and responding to texts. The assumption is that what happens to readers as they read is more significant than what authors intended to say, both in the production of meaning and in our understanding of what reading is for: Why we do it. As developed by theorists like Louise Rosenblatt and Wolfgang Iser, reader-response theory offers descriptions of reading activities and strategies that can help us to enrich our experience of texts.

Repertoire. A body of knowledge of literature and life that texts assume and allude to, or that readers know and can make use of in understanding texts. Both readers and writers possess repertoires, but the two don't always match.

Representation. A rendering of a person, object, or event in language, signs, or symbols. Literary texts and illustrations, movies and TV shows are forms of representation. A representation often purports to be the likeness or equivalent of what it represents, or is understood by some readers as if it were a likeness or equivalent. But all representations are selective, and based in the understanding, assumptions and values of those who make them. Therefore, all representations can be viewed as being in some way distorted. That's particularly important to remember about representations that claim to be realistic or factual.

Resolution. That point in a plot where the various matters we have been made to wonder about or feel suspense about come to an end, and we know what has been withheld from us so far.

Response. As used in this book, *response* refers to the whole range of activities that follow upon our experience of a literary text: not just immediate emotional reactions, but what and how we think about it, the ways in which we integrate it into our understanding of ourselves and our world, and the physical or mental actions that follow upon that.

Romance. For Northrop Frye, the mode of romance includes tales of heroes superior in degree to other humans and to the environment: not gods, but idealized men and women. In contemporary literature *romance* refers to stories in which female protagonists meet and fall in love with a man they will decide to marry at the end.

Round characters. Ones whose motivations are subtle and complex enough to seem realistic. Round characters tend to develop further depth and complexity as a story progresses.

Saturation. The relative intensity of colors, as determined by the amount of white mixed in with them. More saturated colors—those with a smaller proportion of white mixed in—seem more vibrant and assertive.

Schema (singular), schemata (plural). In cognitive psychology, a schema is a pre-existing mental structure built up in response to experience, which directs perceptual activity and is modified as it occurs. Looking at one specific cat for the first time, we view it in terms of our general schema for cats, and thus notice ways in which it diverges from the general idea and becomes distinct. The distinct qualities of this particular cat then contribute to and modify the schema.

Semiotics. The study of *signs*.

Series. A group of connected literary texts about the same characters in similar situations.

Sex and sexuality. See *Gender*.

Shades. Degrees of brightness and darkness of color—for instance, light and dark red are different shades of red.

Shadow. In Jungian psychoanalysis, the dark aspects of the human personality. It is represented in myth and literature by archetypal shadow figures.

Shot. In movies and TV, a unit of action photographed without interruption and consisting of a single camera view. *Long shots* show characters surrounded by environment and emphasize the figures' relationship with places and other people, their social situation. *Close-ups* usually show characters' faces and tend to make us focus on private feelings. *Middle-distance shots* show the characters' entire bodies but within settings, much as we see actors onstage in the theater; the effect is a balance between intimacy and distance. Examples of the different kinds of shots can be found in picture-book illustrations.

Signs. Sounds, words, images, gesture, and objects that stand for other things. Signs are sometimes called *codes*. Signs are conventional. That is, there is no inherent resemblance between a sign and what it means, so that an understanding of the meanings of signs is culture-specific and must be developed through experience: We must learn the conventions that tell us that a stylized stick figure on a door means that we will find a toilet inside, or that a red light means we should not drive a car into an intersection, or that a waving hand means hello. *Metaphors, symbols,* and *similes* are specific kinds of signs.

Simile. See *Metaphor.*

Sonnet. A form of poem having fourteen lines. A traditional Italian sonnet is divided into the octave (the first eight lines) and the sestet (the last six lines); in English, sonnets often consist of three quatrains or four-line verses with the same verse pattern (often an a-b-b-a pattern: the first line rhymes with the fourth, the second with the third), followed by a couplet (two lines that rhyme with each other).

Story. A series of events that join together sequentially to make a whole: the contents of a narration. In relation to *discourse,* story refers to the sequence of events themselves, as opposed to the way in which the narrator presents them to us. See *Discourse.*

Story pattern. A sequence of events common to many different stories. Story patterns are conventional, formulaic plots, recognizable to readers as such and enjoyable exactly because of their replication of a familiar pattern. Some basic story patterns include: the underdog story; the *home/away/home* story; the horror pattern, in which an apparently normal place is invaded by something monstrous; the therapeutic fable, in which a child or teenager deals with an emotional problem or physical handicap by meeting a wiser adult who teaches self-acceptance.

Strategy. As used in this book, a strategy is a mental procedure, a specific method of thinking used in the process of making sense of a literary text. Our understanding of texts depends on the strategies with which we approach them.

Structural linguistics. A study of the nature of language that focuses on the ways in which its parts are related to each other: thus the focus is on the *structure* of the language. Theories of structural linguistics originally developed by Ferdinand de Saussure led to structural approaches to literature, and were the basis of Jacques Lacan's reinvention of Freudian psychoanalytic theory.

Structure. The way that the various parts of a literary text relate to each other and form patterns; or the ways in which many texts relate to each other. Structure depends to a great extent on repetition and variation of the same or similar elements. Literary theory that focuses on structures, particularly the structural relationships of large bodies of literary texts, is called "structuralism." To approach texts in this way is to perform a *structural analysis.*

Style. The distinguishing overall quality of a text or picture. Style is the effect of all the aspects of a work considered together, the way in which an illustration or text seems distinct or even unique. Style develops from the various choices an artist makes, about both subject and means of presentation.

Subject. In ideological theory, to be a subject is to be subjective—that is, capable of individual, personal thought, of being a self. But it is also to be subjected—to be dominated as a monarch dominates his subjects. In other words, to be a subject is to imagine oneself a separate, free individual in terms that put one under the control of ideology.

Subject positions. Conventional ways of being human the adoption of which can make us understandable to ourselves and others. For instance, young girls might choose to occupy the subject position of traditional femininity—that is, they would come to see themselves as being feminine in the.traditional way. They would then become *embedded* in that subject position.

Surface. To bring into awareness. We surface our own unspoken assumptions about ourselves and others when we try to become conscious of them. We surface *absences* in texts when we try to become conscious of the cultural and political assumptions being taken for granted in them.

Surrealism. A style of art which depicts improbable fantasy situations in a highly representational way, using perspective and precise details. Some important surrealistic artists are Salvador Dali and René Magritte.

Suspense. The paradoxically pleasing tension evoked when the events of a plot are left incomplete enough to cause readers to wonder how they will be completed. Suspense is created through a carefully orchestrated interplay of questions raised, answers given, and answers not given yet.

Symbol. A word or visual object that stands for something else, usually for an abstract idea or body of ideas. The cross is a symbol of Christianity. Unlike *signs,* symbols are part of what they represent and have an inherent value separable from what they represent. The cross is not just a sign of Christianity with no inherent connection to it: An actual cross plays a part in the story of Christ, and crosses in general have their own value and significance in Christian worship. Symbols are much harder to separate from what they signify than are signs.

Tale type. One of 2,499 basic plot-lines for folk tales from oral cultures around the world, as identified and organized by folklore scholars. The types are categorized and numbered: "Cinderella" is an example of type 510a.

Text. A collection of words or other signs or symbols joined together with the purpose of forming a meaningful whole. The word "text" has its roots in words referring to weaving (as do, for instance, "texture" and "textile"); it still evokes connotations of things being netted together to form something larger. I refer to literary texts rather than to literary works throughout this book to emphasize connections. *Works* are the products of individual authors, so we assume their content is controlled by those who made them and is separate from outside forces. But simply because they use words that are shared by more than one person, *texts* are connected to all the contexts of language outside themselves. They are part of the network of *intertextuality*.

Theme. The central idea of a text; the core of meaning that ties it together.

Third-person narrator. A narrator or storyteller who is separate from the events being described. Such a narrator talks about characters as "he" or "she."

Touchstones. According to the Victorian poet and critic Matthew Arnold, texts or parts of texts that have proven to be so satisfying or important to us that we can use them as schemata for evaluating other texts.

Trajectory. According to the children's novelist Jill Paton Walsh, "the route chosen by the author through his material. It is the action of a book, considered not as the movement of paraphrasable events in that book but as the movement of the author's exposition and the reader's experience of it." See *Discourse*.

Trash. What people who mistrust popular taste call those formulaic literary texts or TV shows most popular with most readers.

Unconscious. In psychoanalytical theory, those aspects of our being that are buried in parts of our mind about which we have no conscious knowledge. According to Freud, the unconscious develops in early childhood, as we begin to have feelings and desires we understand to be unacceptable and then repress them. Many of these feelings, relating to sexual desire for the parent of the opposite sex and a consequent hatred for the parent of the same sex, are associated with what Freud called the *Oedipus complex*. According to Lacan, the unconscious consists of something like grammatical rules. It is a set of codes or conditions hidden from us which allow us to speak as and perceive ourselves as individuals.

Underdog story. One in which an apparently powerless person faced with apparently powerful enemies defeats the enemies and comes out on top at the end.

Unity. A literary text possess unity if consistency can be built from it: if all of its various parts or elements support each other, if it is coherent and complete, and if it expresses a coherent vision of the world. Traditionally, unity is a sign of excellence in a literary text. According to the theory of deconstruction, however, a literary text cannot possibly possess unity.

Utopia. A perfect society imagined and depicted in a literary text is a utopia. Many literary texts for children can be considered utopian in their depiction of a paradise-like vision of childhood. *Pastoral idylls* describe one particular kind of utopia; science fiction often describes different kinds.

Validity. An opinion is valid if it can be supported by a logical argument or by factual evidence. The fact that we are all entitled to an opinion does not mean that all of our opinions are equally valid: It is their relative validity that we discuss when we enter into dialogue with each other.

Variation. A different form of the same basic pattern. In literature, a variation is a text (or part of a text) that clearly resembles another text, but is also clearly different from it. Many children's books can be read as variations of each other: They are similar in formula or story pattern, but they tell the same story in a quite different way.

Verbal text. As opposed to a *visual text*.

Visual image, visual text. The word *text* refers primarily to a collection of words put together to represent a thought or story by means of signs which don't actually resemble the thing they stand for. The word *image* refers primarily to a picture which offers an actual visual resemblance to the object it represents. But since words can evoke pictures, they can create images; and since pictures can contain layers of meaning beyond the visual resemblance, they can be considered as a form of text. Therefore, we can talk of visual texts when we focus on the meaningful content of pictures, and verbal images when we talk of the pictorial implications of words.

Visualization. See *Concretization.*

Visual pun. A pun is a humorous use of words that emphasizes different meanings: a play on words, like suggesting that a gardener who insists on growing vegetables in straight rows likes to mind her peas in queues. A visual pun is the visual equivalent, such as Anthony Browne's depiction of a smoker's pipe emerging from a chimney and boots hanging from a rubber tree in *The Visitors Who Came to Stay.*

Visual weight. See *Weight.*

Weight, or **visual weight.** The degree to which a particular object depicted in a picture attracts the attention of viewers. More attractive objects have more weight.

Wish-fulfillment fantasy. A story that allows readers the pleasure of identifying with a character who has the kinds of experience we might like to imagine ourselves having. As we read such stories, we experience an imaginary fulfillment of our wishes for ourselves.

Wordless picture books. Ones that imply stories just by providing a sequence of connected pictures. *Wordless* books are not absolutely wordless: They usually do have titles, for instance.

Work. See *Text.*

Index